We Have Never Been Private

Ioanna Piniara

Based on her Ph.D research undertaken at the Architectural Association School of Architecture

The Housing Project in Neoliberal Europe

Contents

I would like to express my deepest gratitude and appreciation to the most dedicated and inspiring PhD supervisors I could ever wish for, Pier Vittorio Aureli and Maria Sheherazade Giudici, whose attentive guidance and rigorous commitment was foundational throughout the development of this thesis at the Architectural Association School of Architecture. I am thankful to them for sharing their intellectual wealth and providing me with a platform to communicate my research with colleagues and peers. On a personal note, Maria and Pier Vittorio have influenced me with their radical perspective and honored me with their trust, solidarity, and endorsement in my pursuits during this four-year journey and ever since.

I owe a special debt of gratitude to some people who have had a considerable influence to my trajectory; to Elia Zenghelis, my dear mentor, for his generosity, for seeing in my young self the potential to make a contribution to the theory and design of domestic space and for planting in me the seeds of such an aspiration; to the late Mark Cousins and to Mark Morris, for offering me my teaching engagements at the AA and sharing their valuable experience throughout the years; finally, to Stavros Stavrides, for sharing his expertise in the field of housing-as-commons and for our teaching collaboration at the National Technical University of Athens School of Architecture. Together these collaborations have given me the opportunity to discuss my research, field work and architecture in general with students, academics and practitioners from across the globe.

There are also a number of people to whom I am indebted for their contribution to my archival research and field work: the late Aristides Romanos for sharing his personal archive of studies and proposals for Kessariani; Christos Voskopoulos, the then Mayor of Kessariani, and the municipality's Technical Department for their generous help; and, not least, the residents of the Trigono block settlement, especially the wonderful ladies Eirene Kladi, Mimoza Chalilaj, Vasiliki and Despoina Tsourapa, Elpida and Georgia Moutafe, for welcoming me into their homes and lives over the years of my field work.

For the visual material featured in this publication, I would like to thank the photographers Luis Young, Sue Barr, Anton Rodriguez, Yiorgis Yerolymbos and Babis Louizidis, the photographic archives of the Benaki Museum Athens and the C. A. Doxiadis archives, Polly Powell and the heirs of Geoffry Powell, the Aldo Rossi Foundation, the Ungers Archive for Architectural Studies, the Department of Public Health and Social Welfare for the Region of Attica, the Office for Metropolitan Architecture, the architects Yannis Aesopos, Sofia Tsiraki, K-Lab Architects, and Sodia Properties. This edition would not have been possible without the support of the Onassis Foundation.

My most heartfelt thanks go to my family for their unconditional love and support. This publication is dedicated to them, along with my gratitude for being the cornerstones of my life.

Foreword

Learning from Neoliberalism by Pier Vittorio Aureli

Since the early 2000s, the term "neoliberalism" has entered mainstream discourse —most of the time with very negative connotations. Especially after the onset of the current recession in 2008, not even the most committed capitalist can use the term with confidence (with the notable exception of theorist Patrik Schumacher). Within architecture, responses to the topic range from the "leftist rant" (which usually take place in short and assertive columns shared on social media), the critique of the usual suspects, the "starchitects" of the roaring 1990s and early 2000s (Rem Koolhaas, Zaha Hadid, you name it) or the analysis of economic conditions and policies that have produced what now we can finally call "the neoliberal city." While the first and second responses focus on the more superficial attributes of neoliberalism, the last one is certainly the most productive, but it often misses a clear explanation on how policies are translated into specific architectural projects. Ioanna Piniara's book offers a welcome and radical alternative to these responses, focusing on the relationship between policy making and architectural typology in the production of housing in neoliberal Europe.

Born in the late 1930s, as a school of thought, neoliberalism's main concern was the possibility of an encompassing social and economic policy based on market competition. The group of people behind this idea —Ludwig von Mises, Friedrich von Hayek, Alexander Rüstow among others— were seeking a radical response to the lethal crisis of classical liberalism which at that time was crushed simultaneously by Fascism, Socialism and the unprecedented state initiative within liberal democracy represented by Franklin Delano Roosevelt's New Deal. Since their early meetings, the protagonists of the neoliberal school were in disagreement about to what extent the state had to be in charge of the system. The dilemma was as follows: if the state withdraws, the system develops towards some sort of neo-feudalism, in which hierarchical relationships proliferate without control; if the state is involved —a position supported by Rüstow and the so-called "ordo-liberal school"— the market would betray its own liberal premises and become de facto a state-driven system.

As argued by Massimo De Carolis, it was precisely this conundrum that plagued the very essence of the neoliberal project from its inception, because it posited the central contradiction between the supposed spontaneity of the market and the fact that the latter can work only if it is properly designed by an all-encompassing institution.[1] This contradiction became evident when neoliberalism was put in practice in the economic restructuring advanced by conservative (but highly innovative) political leaders such as Ronald Regan and Margaret Thatcher. In the 1980s, the triumph of the market was de facto a state project whose ostensible and paradoxical goal was to undermine itself. Within this contradiction lies another one, even more crucial: the private sector as the main subject of neoliberal economy can only thrive with favorable legislation. This contradiction has its origins within the very concept of private property, whose bundle of rights can only exist if supported by an institution that can enforce it, like the state.

If the market system requires the privatization of everything that exists in order to make it susceptible to be appropriated and exchanged as commodity, only state policy can initiate and manage such a process. This is exactly the starting point of Ioanna Piniara's book. Her argument is that the core of the neoliberal project was a contradictory idea of the private. Behind its ostensible ideology of empowering individualism and competition, the private is a totalizing managerial framework through which many aspects of life, including housing, are transformed into commodities. The main merit of Piniara's work is to emphasize the role of public stakeholders in initiating policies whose goal was to support privatization as the cornerstone of social reproduction.

Piniara supports her innovative perspective by offering a close-reading of housing projects that are certainly not the "usual suspects" within the story of neoliberalism. The Barbican Estate in London and the IBA housing program in Berlin have been celebrated as milestones in the history of European housing. These projects estab-

1 Massimo De Carolis, *Il rovescio della libertà. Tramonto del Neoliberismo e disagio della civilità* (Macerata: Quodlibet, 2017), 55–67.

lished high standards in terms of architectural innovation and typological invention that are still celebrated to this day. Yet, as Piniara argues, such initiatives were formidable precursors of the neoliberal turn by conceiving housing as a matter no longer of quantity but of quality. With its assorted array of housing types, a strong architectural image that evoked a sci-fi medieval castle, and its plethora of social and cultural spaces, the Barbican is portrayed by Piniara as the prototype of the neoliberal housing project in which image, experience, and social interaction were deemed fundamental attributes for innovative residential architecture. Here the austere aesthetic of brutalism —which emerged from the countless council housing estates built in England during the 1950s— was upgraded in order to engineer an attractive product to be consumable by middle- and upper-class homeowners. The Barbican is thus the project that best embodied the liberal idea of a democracy as a society made no longer by tenants but by homeowners, whose social security consists of their own house as an asset.

In Berlin, the strategy of recovering the image of the traditional city made of housing blocks anticipated the contemporary forms of urban renewal in which the valorization of the city depends on branding a dynamic yet reassuring image. The project of transforming housing into an economic asset is even more explicit in another case study presented by Piniara: "One Athens," a luxury housing complex that reused the headquarter of Doxiadis Associates. Analyzing this example, Piniara offers a rigorous architectural close reading of how the hypercommodification of domestic space is made possible by a combination of financial mechanisms coupled with a carefully customized image of the "private" in which traditional domestic tropes are exaggerated so that living is no longer a necessity but an experience. One Athens shows at its best the current trend of resuscitating modern architecture —very well exemplified by Constantinos Doxiadis's technocratic style— into a slick mansion consumable by a metropolitan elite.

Ioanna Piniara's approach to housing in the neoliberal era can be compared with Manfredo Tafuri's critique of architectural ideology.[2] Following Marx, Tafuri under-

2 Manfredo Tafuri, "Per una Critica dell'ideologia architettonica," *Contropiano 1* (1969), 31–79; translated by Stephen Sartarelli as, "Towards a Critique of Architectural Ideology," in K. Michael Hays, ed. *Architecture Theory since 1968* (Cambridge, MA.: The MIT Press), 6–35.

stands ideology as the complex of those institutions, professional roles and cultural movements that arise as consequence of the way society is organized in order to produce and reproduce itself.[3] Every mode of production produces its own ideology. In the case of neoliberalism, one of the leading modes of production is the rentier economy, the real estate complex whose proprietary logic is at the core of urban development. The ideology is housing itself, its architecture and the subjectivity it produces. But for Marx (and Tafuri) ideology is not just a thin veil that covers something deeper, it is also a force that has the power to influence and even structure the way in which society works. This is why Tafuri's interpretation of architecture as ideology was deeply rooted in a careful close-reading of the discipline. For Tafuri, architectural form was a process of sublimation, a way to introject the problems of the city by transforming them into operative "values." Piniara's close-reading of housing projects reveals how this process of sublimation relies both on architecture as image and as typology.

In terms of image, the idea of *being private* is supported by an inclusive architectural language in which the anonymity of modernism is countered by an architecture that seeks a strong stylistic identity. This tendency went so far that Colin Rowe called IBA Berlin "an architectural zoo"[4] because in order to reinforce the pluralistic ideology of the housing program every building was commissioned to a different architect, a strategy that proved exemplary for urban projects in the following decades. However, the main site of Piniara's critique is typology. As the eighteenth century French theorist Antoine Chrysostome Quatremère de Quincy argued, type is not a model to be copied, but the underlying order of how things are structured.[5] Any architecture, no matter how bizarre or unprecedented, is always the realization of a type. In this way typology is a deep analysis of architecture in which form is understood as a structural principle. In his book, *Theories and History of Architecture*, Tafuri spoke of a "typological critique of architecture."[6] For Tafuri, architectural typology had the potential to become a fertile ground for historical critique as long as typological analysis acknowledged the historicity of types. Tafuri warned against the study of typology as a mere disciplinary datum of architecture which would make the historian blind towards the questioning of the ideological roots of architecture itself as a discipline.[7]

3 Karl Marx, Friedrich Engels, *Collected Works*, 1845–47, vol. 5 (New York: International Publisher, 1976), 36–37.
4 Colin Rowe, "IBA. Rowe reflects," *The Architectural review*, no. 1051 (1984): 93.
5 Antoine Chrysostome Quatremère de Quincy, "Type," in *Dictionaire Historique de l'Architecture*, vol.2 (Paris: Libraire D'Adriene Le Clere, 1832), 88.
6 Manfredo Tafuri, *Theories and History of Architecture*, translated by Giorgio Verrecchia (London: Granada, 1980), 158–163.
7 Ibid., 162–63.

Following Tafuri, it is possible to argue that there is nothing timeless or technical about architectural types: their structural formation is always contingent to power relationships. By reading architecture typologically, Piniara foregrounds the way in which, over the last seventy years, the discipline of architecture has reclaimed a traditional idea of domesticity in order to reinforce the liberal idea of a home-owning society. Endless variation of types, the resurgence of archetypes like the urban block, the monumentalization of traditional domestic tropes like the balcony, and the reinforcement of the family apartment as the only typological format for housing. Types are thus choreographies of space that translate economic conditions and political mentalities into specific spatial templates. It is precisely this aspect of typological critique that is, in turn, instrumentalized by Piniara in order to formulate a counterproject to neoliberal housing.

The last part of the book is perhaps the most controversial, but it is also the most innovative. With the existing literature on architecture and liberalism we have become accustomed to the format of the critique in which the alternative to what is being criticized is left to the imagination of the readers. Piniara, instead, turns the tools of typological critique towards the formulation of an alternative housing scheme: the Trigono community in the Kessariani district of Athens. The project consists of retrofitting an existing social housing estate developed between the 1930s and 1960s. The goal of the project is to improve the existing housing stock by preventing its commodification (which is what normally happens when social housing is being upgraded) and reinforcing the tenancy of the existing community by federating them into a non-commercial association. In this project, which combines policy making and typological invention, Piniara reclaims the idea of privacy against the idea of the private. Here lies the crux of the whole book: how can architecture reclaim the idea of privacy —which represents the use value of domestic space, its biological, existential and affective dimension— away from the idea of the private, which represents the managerial character of private property?

Piniara answers this question not through an utopian scheme, but by offering plenty of technical knowledge in order to support the residents' right to privacy as a collective —not an individual— project. Here it is important to emphasize how her design contribution takes the form of a manual through which the architect does not act as demiurge but as technical expert. What emerges in this project is a different role for the architect who does not impose a vision on behalf of the client (public or private), but offers a clear framework, both rigorous in terms of architecture, but also legible in terms of the residents' use. There is something Brechtian in the way Piniara presents her design project. In his epic theater Bertolt Brecht wanted the audience to be activated by sharping their critical faculties. This goal was pursued by estranging every element of the theatrical drama, such as gestures, speech etc. Piniara does the same with architecture, by estranging every component of the project: the policy, the catalogue of tools, the logistics of transformation, everything is tabulated in order to make construction, transformation and maintenance accessible to the residents. Like in Brecht's theater, in Pinara's project there is nothing romantic: like architecture itself, the commoning of domestic space can only be conceived as a carefully devised plan that goes from discussing forms of onwership to consultation on construction details.

While, in the projects critiqued by Piniara, the most important architectural datum besides typology is the architectural image, in her proposal Piniara reclaims a fundamental aspect of the modern project, that is its being a systematic reform of what exists. Yet this systematic reform is not imagined as a managerial utopia, but as a specific intervention that can work with a specific community. With the retrofitting of the Trigono housing project, Piniara offers a powerful critique of housing in neoliberal Europe in which architecture becomes a site for contestation of the idea of the private implicit in the commodity form of contemporary housing. This conclusion highlights the fact that the critique of neoliberal housing advanced in this book is first and foremost a critique from *within* architecture, its history and its disciplinary knowledge. And yet, as in Tafuri's case, such critique understands the discipline of architecture not *in vacuo*, but as the product of power relationships of which architecture continues to be one of the most important ideological forms.

Introduction

Context and Research Question

This book outlines the historical transformation of the *private* as a concept for the management of domestic space within the socio-economic regime of neoliberalism. In doing so the central argument aims to subvert the established idea of the term's institutional and spatial autonomy. Since antiquity, we have been domesticated to accept the idea of the house as the private sphere and thus independent from the public realm, which is the sphere of state governance. This dualism intensified in modernity, when the distinction of the "private" and the "public" transformed each into powerful administrative categories. Within neoliberalism —or free market capitalism— during the second half of the twentieth century, the private reached its apotheosis as an independent mechanism of housing provision. By claiming the neoliberal idea of a social order generated by the market,[1] it has evolved into an institutional process of subsuming social and spatial relations under its own governance[2]: *privatization*. At the same time, this process has been identified as being at the core of the neoliberal reforms that led to the 2008 global mortgage crisis, making it impossible to address the issue of housing or the housing crisis without interrogating this concept. The conceptualization of the private as the counterpart of the public fails to acknowledge that the template of this opposition has always been the state. Further, the neoliberal promotion of the market as a self-regulating provider of private goods, such as housing, fails to acknowledge that the risks of this process remain the responsibility of the state, which provides the regulatory framework. The research objective is to demonstrate how the private, as a concept for the control of domesticity, has been at the service of the orderly function of the state, and therefore, has hardly existed *as such* in the neoliberal era.

1 Friedrich A. von Hayek, *Law, Legislation and Liberty* (Chicago, IL: University of Chicago Press, 1973–1979).

2 On the neoliberal idea of Governance without (State) Government, see James N. Rosenau and Ernst-Otto Czempiel, *Governance without Government: Order and Change in World Politics* (Cambridge: Cambridge University Press, 1992).

What is at stake with privatization as the key process of neoliberalism is a carefully designed pedagogy of domestic privacy that administers social relations and sets urban housing at the epicenter of social and economic antagonism. The foundation of this dissertation is an attempt to disentangle privacy, as a physical experience, from the social, economic and spatial construct of the private realm. The book begins by diving deeper into the phenomenology of the private as a fundamental concept for delineating both an institutional and spatial boundary between the home and the city. Since antiquity, the private has been spatially determined by the domestic realm, governed by private property and administered by the family, while the public has been identified with the urban realm and the political governance administered by the state.[3] In ancient thought, the private was defined as the deprivation of any public —political or military—status.[4] However, Arendt, in her reading of Aristotle, positions privacy among the various biological needs that are to be satisfied in the private realm in order for political freedom to be acquired in the public realm. Arendt portrays the private as a prerequisite for sound citizenship based on Aristotle's idea of the household community as the primary unit constituting the broader community of the city.[5] Engels further elucidates the instrumentality of private property in the division of labor that served the administration of the state since its origin.[6] Household administration in the Middle Ages is classified within "late antiquity"[7] based on the two main characteristics —one social and one economic— that differentiate it from the modern conception of the "home." The notion of greatness permeating the late-medieval royal household —which still required a degree of public spectacle in order to ritualize the expression of hierarchies within the extended family[8]— was far from the "intimate sphere" established in the modern conjugal (or nuclear) family.[9] Additionally, the medieval household remained the primary place of production, a quality lost during the early modern capitalist revolution, which increasingly separated the workplace from the "private" household.[10] However, this period became the incubator for a social class that would "create a new urban civilization" through a novel idea of citizenship and freedom linked to domestic comfort: the bourgeois.[11]

3 Aristotelis, *Politica [Politics]*, trans. V. Moskovis (Athens: Law Library, 1989), 1252b5–1253b20.

4 The ancient Greek word for private is "idíos-a-on" (adj.): personal, one's own, "idiotikōs" (adj.): personal property, "idiōtēs" (n.): a "private person" of no political rights (non-subject). See Werner Jaeger, *Paideia: The Ideals of Greek Culture*, trans. Gilbert Highet (Oxford: Oxford University Press, 1945), III. The Latin counterpart derives from "privo": to cause to be parted from, deprive or rob of, "privatus-a-um" (adj.): personal property, "privatus" (n.): a "private person" of no civil office / military position. See Isidore, *Origines*, 9. 4.30, in Richard Maltby, *A Lexicon of Ancient Latin Etymologies*, ARCA 25 (Oxford: Francis Cairns Publications, 1991), 496. This lexicon documents every Latin and Greek etymology attested in antiquity from the time of Varro to Isidore of Seville.

5 Aristotelis, *Politica*, 1263a10 and Hannah Arendt, "The Public and the Private Realm," in *The Human Condition* (Chicago, IL: University of Chicago Press, 1958), 22–78.

6 Friedrich Engels, *The Origin of the Family, Private Property and the State*, trans. Alick West (London: Lawrence and Wishart, 1972 [1884]).

7 The Middle Ages is generally regarded as the period in European history from the collapse of the Roman Empire in the fifth century to the period of the Renaissance, variously beginning in the thirteenth, fourteenth and fifteenth centuries, depending on the region of Europe. *Encyclopaedia Britannica*, s.v. "Middle Ages," https://www.britannica.com.

8 According to McKeon, this idea of family in the medieval household was not insitutionalized, but rather still bore an analogy to the state (referring to the power of feudal lords and the clergy, as there was still no idea of national citizenship). The ritualization of hierarchies was nowhere more evident than in the ceremony of eating and banquettes. The "public" feasts were inseparable from the magnificence of the lord and co-extensive with the servants that produced them. See "From State as Family to Family as State", in Michael McKeon, *The Secret History of Domesticity: Public, Private and the Division of Knowledge* (Baltimore: Johns Hopkins University Press, 2006), 110–161.

9 Jürgen Habermas, *The Structural Transformation of the Public Sphere: An Inquiry into a Category of Bourgeois Society*, trans. Thomas Burger and Frederick Lawrence (Cambridge, MA: MIT Press, 1989), 28–31.

10 Ibid.

11 Witold Rybczynski, *Home: A Short History of an Idea* (London: Penguin Books, 1987), 24–5.

The formulation of the private as a distinct category marked a defining shift in the transition from antiquity to modernity.[12] The abstraction involved in the modern separation of the private from the public established the rhetorical alienation of their respective spheres: domesticity and state governance. The signification of the private "as such" became subject to the values of the Enlightenment and modern capitalism, meaning "belonging to oneself (not to the state), not shared, individual."[13] This created a new cultural and social role for privacy as the desire and the privilege to isolate, to withdraw from the fuss of the city.[14] The nature of this transformation is a subject of explicit enquiry within the epistemological framework of the liberal philosophy, consolidated between the seventeenth and nineteenth centuries, advocating for the restraint of governmental intervention in the economic regulation of social life. According to Arendt and Habermas, the establishment of the liberal regime triggered a radical reconceptualization of freedom, removing it from the public, as the place of participation in state governance, and instead locating in the private, as an independent sphere.[15] By the nineteenth century, the demarcation of private space was bound to the idea of the domestic interior,[16] which reinforced the role of the outer shell of the house as as a mediator between two clashing realms. It also encouraged the rise of the urban apartment type, an even further subdivision into interiors for isolation.[17] Liberalism equated individual autonomy —the right to privacy— with economic freedom —the right to property,— attributed to the social status of the bourgeois subject as the "private" individual. What is not acknowledged, however, is that the reduction of the private into an economic and social title encouraging individualism and property was part of the "rationalization" process, which lay at the core of the organization of the liberal state.[18]

The economic usage of the private was amplified under the neoliberal mantra, which allowed the entire body of social relations to be completely regulated by market imperatives. What marks neoliberalism as a phenomenon beyond liberalism in the second half of the twentieth century, is the professionalism surrounding the commodification of all aspects of life in the market economy, a process

12 According to McKeon, the division of knowledge and the constitutive differentiation of conceptual categories in the seventeenth century is what separates "modernity" from "antiquity." This definition of a "starting point" is a formal consequence of a method to situate the transition from relations of distinction to those of separation between the public and the private. While acknowledging the development of bourgeois dwelling structures from the fifteenth through the eighteenth centuries, this method dwells on the socio-economic and spatial rediscovery of the private realm between the seventeenth and nineteenth centuries. McKeon, "The Age of Separations," in *The Secret History of Domesticity*, 3–312.

13 The adjective "private" (from Old French privé "friendly, intimate," and Latin privatus "private, personal") with this meaning emerged in the late fourteenth century. However, it only grew popular in the seventeenth century against the category of the public, bearing connotations about the exclusive use of space. *Encyclopaedia Britannica*, s.v. "Private," https://www.britannica.com.

14 Privacy (from Old French "privauté"), on the other hand, as "secret deed, solitude, seclusion", emerged in the late sixteenth century and acquired the meaning "state of freedom from intrusion" no earlier than 1814. *Encyclopaedia Britannica*, s.v. "Privacy."

15 Arendt, *The Human Condition* and Habermas, *The Structural Transformation of the Public Sphere.*

16 Charles Rice, *The Emergence of the Interior: Architecture, Modernity, Domesticity* (London: Routledge, 2007).

17 McKeon, "Subdividing Inside Spaces," in *The Secret History of Domesticity*, 212–268.

18 Tony Waters and Dagmar Waters, eds., *Weber's Rationalism and Modern Society: New Translations on Politics, Bureaucracy, and Social Stratification*, trans. Tony Waters and Dagmar Waters (New York: Palgrave Books, 2015). This version is the latest translation of Weber's original work entitled "Politics as Vocation" written in 1909.

which instrumentalized the private in order to build a new ideal of domesticity. Neoliberalism demonstrated a unique capacity for marketing a narrative of the private as the luxury of a middle class, which was constituted and addressed as the main consumer force to resuscitate post-war urban economies.[19] The promotion of personal freedom in the ability to acquire privacy, as exclusive access to urban space, exemplified the exchange value over the use value of housing (and the city). In the field of urban planning, this dictated an enclosure of urban land that signified the private as an exclusive luxurious interior and the public as a shared undesirable exterior. In the field of housing design, the distancing from central (state) planning, which suppressed individual identity, was reflected in the neoliberal principles of "differentiation" and "freedom of choice."[20] The façade became not only a reflection of the different qualities and organizations of private space, but also an invitation to a process of social upgrade. As the symbolic capital of the private and the city grew inextricably linked, processes of alienation, gentrification and displacement accelerated, eventually leading to the inaccessibility of urban housing for a growing part of society. Thus, neoliberalism created a paradox that political philosopher Massimo de Carolis identified as "the flipside of freedom."[21] De Carolis argued that this new governmental mechanism was strengthened to the detriment of personal empowerment, since power relations enhanced by the "freedom of choice" were based on preventive control over people's choices.[22] In promoting the private as a commodity, the types of proposed living arrangements were explicitly designed to reproduce the social and economic hierarchies that bound people to state control. Despite the alleged withdrawal of the state during the neoliberal era, this book will show that instead it has constantly partnered with the market, evidenced by policies that enabled and encouraged the aspirational mandate behind the neoliberal housing project; *being private in the heart of the city*.

Therefore, I believe the most critical duty of contemporary architecture is to problematize the neoliberal housing crisis that affects European capital cities as an institutional and spatial issue rather than merely an economic one. In the 1970s, a period

19 Massimo De Angelis defines "middle-classness" as "constituted through an idea of betterment and order achieved within the boundaries of capitalist system." Massimo De Angelis, *Omnia Sunt Communia: On the Commons and the Transformation to Postcapitalism* (London: Zed Books, 2017), 280.

20 Friedrich A. Hayek, *The Road to Serfdom*, (Chicago, IL.: University of Chicago Press, 1944). Friedrich Hayek is among the key theorists of neoliberalism and its principles of planning.

21 Massimo de Carolis, *Il rovescio della libertà: Tramonto del neoliberalismo e disagio della civiltà* [*The Flipside of Freedom: The decline of neoliberalism and the crisis of civilization*] (Macerata: Quodlibet, 2017).

22 For an excerpt of de Carolis's neoliberal critique in English, see Massimo de Carolis, "The neoliberal (counter) revolution: its parabola and decline," *Phainomena* 26, no. 102/103 (2017): 141–52.

identified with the wide introduction of neoliberal governmental policies, Marxist academic Raymond Williams highlighted *the private* as being among the keywords of everyday life, offering an insightful critique of the ideological shift of society.[23] Considering that the idea of the private as being synonymous with a certain configuration of domesticity has been prevalent for centuries, limited work within the architectural discipline has been dedicated to interrogating how the conceptual category operates once it is translated into living culture. Even scarcer are attempts to unveil and question the ideological structures behind the formation of conceptual categories through architectural tools and methods. Such an undertaking will not only elucidate the instrumentalization of the private, but will also provide a conceptual and design interpretation to dismantle this systemic division of knowledge as a framework of intentionally eliminated alternatives. It is not by chance that the economic vector of the private is asymmetrically developed over any other principle of housing administration under the neoliberal mantra of "no alternative." Neither that Williams exemplifies the semantic development of the private in a moment when neoliberal housing policies come to be forcefully implemented, denoting the cultural embeddedness of the term "as such" in everyday life. To challenge the premises of this discourse vis-à-vis the failure of the neoliberal ideology is to argue that we have never been private.[24]

RESEARCH FRAMEWORK AND METHODOLOGY

A socio-spatial interpretation of the private in the neoliberal era is sought on two levels: the ideological, which shapes the social values and institutional forms of governance (philosophical research), and the typological, which reveals the organization through which this ideology is materialized and embodied by the subjects of domesticity (design research). This requires, first, clarification of the operational framework of neoliberalism as an ideology and not a specific political program. Neoliberalism has been traditionally identified with the policies of economic restructuring during the 1970s, as introduced by Ronald Reagan and Margaret Thatcher in the United States and Britain respectively. However, my approach views

23 The seminal text by Raymond Williams, *Keywords: A Vocabulary of Culture and Society* (London: Croom Helm, 1976). Hints are taken here from a revised edition, see Tony Bennett, Lawrence Grossberg and Meaghan Morris, *New Keywords: A Revised Vocabulary of Culture and Society* (London: Blackwell Publishing, 2005), 280–2.

24 The structure of this argument takes inspiration in Bruno Latour's observation that, despite the careful distinction between nature and culture, the construction of modern systems still mix politics, science, technology, and nature, which leads him to his suggestion that we should rethink the definition and constitution of modernity itself. Bruno Latour, *We Have Never Been Modern*, trans. Catherine Porter (Cambridge, MA: Harvard University Press, 1993).

these as technocratic amendments in the broader policy of appropriation of housing as an "enabling framework," whose revision was forced by the crisis of modern state planning. According to de Carolis, the latter was the by-product of the crisis of modern civilization that, after Nietzsche, had become the dominant theme of European culture.[25] Neoliberalism was then theorized in the 1930s and introduced in the early 1940s as a response to the consequences of the Great Depression and the rise of totalitarian states in Europe.[26] Despite the post-war welfare state consensus in Western Europe, the social and economic crisis in cities necessitated a new civil order paradigm. Urban sociologist Neil Brenner identifies the rise of urban governance in Western European cities as a key mechanism of processes of state restructuring, not state withdrawal, already at work in the late 1950s.[27] The promise of the neoliberal order, which permeated social processes and collective life, lay in moving away from harsh reality towards attractive possibilities —from austerity to growth. Within this philosophy, which became the "new global order" in the 1980s, the private narrative did not address the housing project as what it should be, but as what it *could* be. Therefore, the thesis understands neoliberalism as a broader cultural project to change the ethos, culture and organization of domesticity, rooted in post-war planning for the socio-economic resuscitation of urbanity in Europe.

This framework invites a reading of neoliberalism both as a socio-economic philosophy and a form of planning. Neoliberal critique in the field of urban planning and architecture has notably focused either on the production of policies or on the language of formal production, failing to address these two as inseparable and methodologically linked. In their study of the neoliberal spatial order, Marcuse and Van Kempen, while acknowledging the involvement of the state in the perpetuation of the socio-spatial divisions produced by the market, address these as patterns on the metropolitan scale without scaling down to architectural production.[28] After the 2008 crisis, more attention has been given to housing, as an essential pillar of the neoliberal political economy. A comprehensive study of the crisis by Madden and Marcuse addresses housing as an administrative category but is, however, limited to the

25 De Carolis, "The neoliberal (counter) revolution," 143.

26 A group of 25 liberal intellectuals, including Friedrich Hayek, Ludwig von Mises, Walter Lippmann and Alexander Rüstow, who coined the term neoliberalism, organized the Walter Lippmann Colloquium in 1938 in order to restore the damaged ideology of classical liberalism. In these early stages there was much controversy: Rüstow and Lippmann advocated for strong state supervision of the economy, while von Mises and Hayek insisted that the only legitimate role for the state was to facilitate the market and considered socialist states as totalitarian.The colloquium was overshadowed by the outburst of World War II, but served as the precursor of the Mont Pelerin Society, which pioneered the neoliberal movement after the war.

27 Neil Brenner, "Urban Governance and the Production of New State Spaces in Western Europe, 1960–2000," *Review of International Political Economy* 11, no. 3 (Aug. 2004): 449–462. See also Neil Brenner and Nik Theodore, *Spaces of Neoliberalism: Urban Restructuring in North America and Western Europe*, (London: Blackwell Publishers Ltd, 2002).

28 Peter Marcuse and Ronald Van Kempen, *Globalizing Cities: A New Spatial Order?* (London: Wiley Blackwell, 1999).

political and economic premises of a radical policy shift.[29] On the other hand, a part of the critique has sought to identify the language of neoliberal architecture. Douglas Spencer describes "a self-styled parametric and post-critical" glossary in projects in the fields of education, consumption and labor by influential figures (such as Zaha Hadid, Patrik Schumacher, Rem Koolhaas and Greg Lynn).[30] Although, he identifies the intrumentalization of notions of liberty by mechanisms of control and the compliance of human subjects, the projects are presented as independent examples and are not placed within the context of certain policy objectives. By focusing on only one of the two aspects —policy or design— one runs the risk of either overlooking the neoliberal spatial (trans)formations, which enable the socio-economic divisions and inequalities, or identifying them with a particular style.

Therefore, the subject of this study is the complex interplay between socio-economic philosophy, urban housing policies and housing architecture, since the organization of everyday life is viewed as the most intimate level of social relations that neoliberalism has exploited. To demystify the neoliberal rationale, the methodology first identifies the theoretical aspirations and principles of the new socio-spatial order and then investigates how they were applied as policy guidelines and design methods. To draw the link between theory and the built environment is quintessential as this study, unlike early philosophical accounts of neoliberalism such as the one by Michel Foucault,[31] cannot afford now to misjudge the promise of a social order for the reality of it. While acknowledging the prolific Leftist critique, the theoretical survey focuses on a primary examination of neoliberalism as put forward by some of its key theorists. It dwells primarily on the work of two analysts of the market-based societies in modern Europe; Friedrich Hayek, advocating for the freedom in the economic restructuring of societies,[32] and Karl Polanyi, identifying also the weaknesses and shortcomings of this model.[33] This reading brings together the neoliberal signification of the private as an institutional issue, linked with property, and a spatial issue, linked with individuation and differentiation. At the same time, the analysis of the private employs the historical materialist perspective that the

29 David Madden and Peter Marcuse, *In Defense of Housing: The Politics of Crisis* (London: Verso Books, 2016).

30 Douglas Spencer, *The Architecture of Neoliberalism: How Contemporary Architecture Became an Instrument of Control and Compliance* (London: Bloomsbury Academic, 2016).

31 Michel Foucault, *Security, Territory, Population: Lectures at the College de France, 1977–78*, ed. Arnold I. Davidson, trans. Graham Burchell (Basingstoke: Palgrave MacMillan UK, 2009). On a critique of Foucault's distancing from the concept of social resistance in favor of the possibilities of individual autonomy offered by neoliberalism, see Daniel Zamora and Michael C. Behrent, *Foucault and Neoliberalism* (New York: Wiley, 2015).

32 Hayek, *The Road to Serfdom*.

33 Karl Polanyi, *The Great Transformation: The Political and Economic Origins of Our Time* (Boston: Beacon Press, 1957 [1944]).

abstraction, to which capital submits social relations, can only be uncovered at the level of the history of ideas. Thus, the neoliberal housing project is posited within a constitutive historicization of the private that suggests a major conceptual shift from the ancient to the liberal regime, accentuated in neoliberalism. The common thread among the specific notions of the private is the latent role of the state administration and, thus, its neoliberal notion emerges as a way of construing questions about the role of the market-state.

To trace how the neoliberal ideals were extrapolated into the configuration of urban and domestic space across Europe, the methodology focuses on a review of housing policies and typologies in specific realized case studies. Policy documents describe the intended urban and social vision, or model, and frame it through stan-dards and specifications. However, usually their language is intentionally enigmatic and open to interpretation. To respond to this, the typological study illuminates how the requirements and intentions for a certain lifestyle are translated and enacted. Architectural historian Anthony Vidler describes the instrumentality of typology as a system of study: "only an internal understanding of the constructive laws of types, and the dynamic transformations of these laws under the threat of external change or internal demands, could open the way to a comprehension of a kind of evolution in architecture."[34] Aldo Rossi further stresses both the "ideal" and the "ideological" character of type by building on Quatremere de Quincy's argument that the logical principle or idea is prior to the form that constitutes it:[35] "the word 'type' represents not as much the image of a thing to be copied or perfectly imitated as the idea of an element that must itself serve as a rule for the model."[36] This understanding of type reinforces the idea that design research into *actually existing neoliberalism*[37] is not to dwell in a style, but rather in the contextually specific interactions between market-oriented restructuring principles (which are universal) and inherited landscapes.[38] However, this does not reduce the importance of image-making, which has been the cornerstone of the market logic and the neoliberal project. Architectural theorist Colquhoun adds to the definition of type as form derived from

34 Vidler provides "Types of private houses" already established by the end of the eighteenth century. Anthony Vidler, "The Idea of Type: The Transformation of the Academic Ideal, 1750–1830," *Oppositions* no. 8 (Spring 1977): 109.

35 Quatremere de Quincy as quoted in Aldo Rossi, *The Architecture of the City* (New York: Opposition Books, MIT Press, 1988).

36 Ibid., 40.

37 Neil Brenner and Nik Theodore, "Cities and the Geographies of 'Actually Existing Neoliberalism,'" *Antipode* 34, no. 3 (December 2002): 351–5.

38 On the ideological character of types and the possibility of alternative forms of commons emerging from the transformation of their constructive laws, see Ioanna Piniara, "(Re)drawing the housing commons: A Typological Reading," *Stoà Journal* no. 2 (2021): 106–19.

"aesthetic ideologies"[39] and, as such, is susceptible to temporally and geographically dominant movements and established codes. Therefore, this study of typology includes the tropes that were adopted to communicate values and ideas morphologically and symbolically. By traversing from macro-political scenarios to housing policy documents, from the philosophical appropriation of the concept of the private to living typologies, the methodology aims to reveal why and how this narrative of domesticity became so powerful and was largely adopted without dispute.

STRUCTURE AND CASE STUDIES

Based on this methodology, the thesis has a tripartite structure. The first part consists of the first chapter (Chapter I) and offers a genealogy of the private, as a concept pertaining to the organization of domestic space that has always been at the service of the orderly function of the state. The emergence of the concept is explained through the economic theory of state emergence and the genealogy is structured around the separation between the ancient and the liberal regime, concluding with the final neoliberal acceleration. This separation is based on the categorical distinction of the private in the seventeenth century, which McKeon identifies as the critical instance in the history of modern domesticity.[40] A study of the socio-spatial organization of the private sphere in ancient Greek and Roman states reveals its understanding as distinct but subordinate to the public sphere, idealizing or replicating the administration of the state. The modern conception of the private "as such" exemplified the independence of the private sphere. Scholars, historically, have taken this independence for granted without interrogating the corresponding reconfiguration of the institutional process of society itself, namely the state structure. Thus, the modern history of privacy is viewed here as one of abstraction and shows how the assignment of a new status to the private was meant to serve the new structure of the liberal state. To address the translation of abstraction into domesticity at large, the private is investigated first as an institutional issue, where the liberal construction of class subjectivity is identified with private property as the

39 Alan Colquhoun, "Typology and Design Method," in *Essays in Architectural Criticism: Modern Architecture and Historical Change* (Cambridge, MA: Oppositions Books, MIT Press, 1981), 46.
40 McKeon, *The Secret History of Domesticity,* XVII-XXVII.

foundation of urban development.[41] Then, it is investigated as a typological issue, where the abstraction in exchange[42] —the most vital activity in capitalism— is served by the private apartment type that encapsulates both the value of property and the social status. The ultimate institutionalization of the private as an independent process was meant to serve the neoliberal market-state to inflate the exchange value of housing and urban land. The study analyzes the neoliberal principles (or the market mantra) that transformed the idea of being private into an aspiration and housing from a provision of social welfare into a project of social antagonism and exclusion.

Chapter II provides a review of three selected housing schemes in neoliberal Europe: the Barbican Estate in London (1959); the International Building Exhibition in Berlin (1987); and the "One Athens" conversion scheme in Athens (2007). The selection of these case studies allows, both chronologically and geographically, a comprehensive overview of the neoliberal course in European cities from anticipation to culmination and, finally, to severe crisis. At the same time, they comprise celebrated and emblematic housing models that were strategically devised in critical moments for the future of the respective cities. The Barbican incarnated a utopian ideal of urban growth as a way to escape post-war austerity and inspired a generation of housing projects in Britain in the decades that followed. The International Building Exhibition was an architectural experiment, which due to its international radiance and bold vocabulary was influential in putting Berlin on the global map not as a divided city but as a desirable place to live. One Athens was the swansong of the effort to spectacularize urban living by appropriating the symbolic capacity of an iconic architectural type and to maintain a metropolitan image of Athens amidst a galloping housing crisis. Either working their way into urban society bottom-up, springing from the social housing tradition, or top-down, as admittedly luxurious projects, all of them represent the attempt to exemplify the private as a capitalist idea of social betterment that elevates housing to a unique living experience. In each of these critical moments, when the cities were called upon the duty to radicalize the premises of living, the neoliberal project, supported by state policies, has restored the most conservative ideals

41 John Locke, *Second Treatise on Government*, ed. Crawford B. McPherson (Indianapolis and Cambridge: Hackett Publishing Company, 1980 [1690]) and Max Weber, *Economy and Society: An Interpretive Sociology*, eds. Guenther Roth and Claus Wittich, (Berkley: University of California Press, 1978 [1921]).

42 Alfred Sohn-Rethel, *Intellectual and Manual Labour: A Critique of Epistemology* (London: Macmillan, 1979).

of domesticity and urbanity. These examples are deployed as a means of reading the neoliberal city beyond the complicity of architecture with the market, revealing, instead, the more subtle relationship between spatial organization and social (re)production. Therefore, this chapter addresses in each case study the link between the political motives and state interference behind the project, its spatial (and typological) manifestation and the construction of the private subjectivity.

Chapter III includes a response to the premises of the thesis. The first part of the chapter proposes a conceptual shift from the economy towards *an ecology of the private*, offering a philosophical account of Logos as the rationality of the commons. As an operational principle, ecology suggests the simultaneous and reciprocal fashioning of the private with the commons subjectivity and conceptualizes domestic privacy as personal autonomy achieved through a practice of *commoning*. As a protocol for urban housing commons, it tries to disconnect the private from the governance of individualism and property and points at a form of self-administration of collective living operating outside market rules.[43] This concept emerges within the twenty-first century commons discourse framed as a radical political struggle against "the new enclosures" by George Caffentzis, Silvia Federici,[44] and Peter Linebough,[45] and as a praxis by Massimo De Angelis[46] and Pierre Dardot and Christian Laval.[47] The second part of the chapter offers the design response in the form of a manual for a step-by-step self-build adaptation of the historical Trigono community settlement in the area of Kessariani in central Athens. This is developed on three levels: a juridical framework, an urban strategy, and an architectural project. As a model it aims to reintroduce "the right to privacy" in the city by shifting the administrative struggle from the state-market partnership to an empowered community in collaboration with the local (municipal) government. As a typological exercise, it aims to establish egalitarian access to and participation in the configuration of private space as a precondition for the possibility of collective living. The institutionalization of communal spaces inside and outside the buildings, liberates privacy from socio-economic hierarchies and burdens and reinstates it as true freedom.

43 In the *The Gay Science* Nietzsche writes that "it is part of my good fortune not to be a home-owner!" Friedrich Nietzsche, *The Gay Science: With a Prelude in Rhymes and an Appendix of Songs by Friedrich Nietzsche*, trans. Walter Kaufmann (London: Penguin Books, 1974 [1882]), 240.

44 George Caffentzis and Silvia Federici are political philosophers from the autonomist Marxist tradition and founding members of the Midnight Notes Collective, a group whose work over the last 30 years has established a scholarship on anti-capitalism, "primitive accumulation" and the commons, feminism, reproductive labor and Marx's value theory. See George Caffentzis, "Two Themes of Midnight Notes: Work/Refusal of Work and Enclosure/Commons", in Craig Hughes, *Towards the Last Jubilee! Midnight Notes at Thirty Years* (New York: Autonomedia, 2010), 24–30, and Silvia Federici, *Revolution at Point Zero: Housework, Reproduction, and Feminist Struggle* (Oakland: PM Press, 2012). For their joint contribution, see Camille Barbagallo, Nicholas Beuret, and David Harvie, *Commoning with George Caffentzis and Silvia Federici* (London: Pluto Press, 2019).

45 Peter Linebough, *The Magna Carta Manifesto: Liberties and Commons for All* (Berkeley, CA: University of California Press, 2008).

46 De Angelis, *Omnia Sunt Communia*.

47 Pierre Dardot and Christian Laval, *Common: On Revolution in the 21st Century* (London: Bloomsbury, 2019).

The format of the manual underlines the intention for realistic scenarios, which were pursued through intensive fieldwork, careful socio-spatial documentation of the existing settlement, incisive study of the Greek legislative framework for possibilities, and close collaboration with the local residents and the municipal authority of Kessariani.

By creating links between architecture and economic philosophy, political theory, sociology and anthropology, the thesis aims to construct an operative tool for architects, policymakers and local authorities to address the fundamental issue of housing in European city centers. Through a radical rethinking of the architectural agency and the role of communities in urban governance, the thesis seeks to unsettle the existing urban domestic landscape, which is devised to cater for the market, and to further provide an alternative beyond the ideological structures that conceptualize it. The thesis is ultimately about the existential struggle to devise an architecture for privacy that signifies both the physical experience and social relations that are produced upon its organization and the abstract quality it represents, which needs to assure the holder that the idea of its value will have a continuous objectivity in the world.

I. The Private as a State Project

A Genealogy from Antiquity to Neoliberalism

The Private and the Emergence of the State

Understanding the relationship between the private and the state requires first revealing the socio-economic substructure of the latter, making the conceptualization of the former possible and relevant. In other words, I first seek to provide an analytical framework, starting from the economic theory of state emergence, that justifies how the private is unlikely to have been developed as a meaningful concept in pre-state or non-state societies. Anthropological data suggest a pattern of sharp population growth and concentration in geographic areas where states have developed,[1] supporting an economic theory of state emergence that acknowledges the role of transactions and, thus, the increasing demand for an order, as a means to eliminate threats. In the European continent, Hammond relates the rapid urban growth in Archaic Greece, taking place circa 800 BC, with the subsequent emergence of "city-states" in the mid-seventh-century BC.[2] This is considered to be part of a significant phenomenon of urbanization associated with trade which gave rise to a global market in which various governments (or empires) would compete.[3] These studies suggest an inversely proportional relationship between society and market: while the increased population density and lower transportation (and transaction) costs in the city benefited the function of the market, the larger size of society and the finer division of labor increased the relative isolation of the individual from that society. Therefore, Auster and Silver conclude that a society reaches a size at which the demand for collective protection and regulation of space is large enough to support a continuously functioning institution specializing in their production —the state.[4] When the role of the society is drawn as "the market for the provision of protection," the state or, "the government of the society," emerges as the instrument for the management of internal and external struggles, and for the regulation of a social order to sustain trade functions.[5]

1 The archaeologists Sanders and Price suggest minimum population figures (at least tens of thousands) that justify the existence of institutions of diverse sorts based on comparative data from Mesopotamia, the first Sumerian "city-states" at the end of the Bronze Age (3000 BC), and the tribal societies of Mesoamerica (1600 BC). William T. Sanders and Barbara J. Price, *Mesoamerica: The Evolution of a Civilization* (New York: Random House, 1968), 74–75.

2 Mason Hammond, *City-State and World State in Greek and Roman Political Theory until Augustus* (Cambridge, MA: Harvard University Press, 1951), 163–4.

3 Sanders and Price call this phenomenon of urbanization in the Teotiahuacan Valley in Mesoamerica around 300 BC "a single, huge sprawling [toward].... the center..." which resulted in the desertion of villages. Sanders and Price, *Mesoamerica*, 140–41.

4 Richard D. Auster and Morris Silver, "Theories of the Emergence of States," in *The State as a Firm: Economic Forces in Political Development*, ed. Randall G. Holcombe, Studies in Public Choice, Vol. 3 (Boston: Martinus Nijhoff Publishing, 1979), 15–26.

5 Ibid., 16.

Engels elucidates the role of private property in the emergence of the state by asserting that in pre-state societies, where life was organized in close affinity groups (gens) and property was held communally, the demand for vigilant "professional" protection was low.[6] However, the emergence of trade on a wide geographical scale, as a result of surplus production, and the concentration of property led to an increased inequality of wealth. Naturally, therefore, the proliferation of threats outside the protective physical realm of the gens, which later evolved into the hetero-normative monogamous family, fuelled owners' desire for security through a collective mechanism, that is the state. The anthropologist Morton Fried attests to this theory concerning the creation of "pristine" states as emerging from ancient civilizations in order to maintain social stratification.[7] The greater the stratification, the stronger the population's collective belief that the distribution of wealth is neither legitimate nor consensual and thus an increase in a society's demand for state services. Therefore, the state, as the controlling power by which a civil stratified society is kept together, is the product of two important spatial-economic forces: first, the growth and concentration of the population in cities and second, the success and dominance of markets. Although emerging as the arbiter of conflicts and allocator of resources, the state becomes an alienated power that, by claiming legitimacy as a normative protocol, rises as a monopolizing force.[8]

Kelsen, in his legal theory of the state, sketches the manner in which a state's constitution as a normative protocol establishes a certain socio-spatial order, and thus the social categories meant to maintain it.

"To be a state, the legal order must have the character of an organization in the manner and specific sense of this word, that is, it must establish organs which, in the manner of division of labor, create and apply the norms that constitute the legal order, it must display a certain degree of centralization. [...] Its "elements," territory and people, are the territorial and personal spheres of validity of that legal order."[9]

Engels's work is also based on the anthropological study *Ancient Society* by Lewis H. Morgan (1877). Friedrich Engels, *The Origin of the Family, Private Property and the State*, trans. Alick West (London: Lawrence and Wishart, 1972 [1884]), 54–59.

Fried defines a stratified society as "one in which members of the same sex and equivalent age status do not have equal access to basic resources that sustain life" and observes that "stratified societies lacking political institutions of state level are almost impossible to find." See Morton H. Fried, *On the Evolution of Social Stratification and the State* (Indianapolis: Bobbs-Merrill, 1960), 185–6.

It is instrumental for the argument of the thesis that the philosophers of the early liberal tradition, like Weber, who advocate for non-state intervention in economic affairs, emphasize the consent aspect of state emergence through the concept of legitimation, while those of the early socialist tradition, like Marx and Engels, dwell on the conquest component, which is the preponderance of coercive force. Both views, however, conclude on the monopolistic nature of state power, from which no aspect of society is excluded. See Tony Waters and Dagmar Waters eds., *Weber's Rationalism and Modern Society: New Translations on Politics, Bureaucracy, and Social Stratification*, trans. Tony Waters and Dagmar Waters (New York: Palgrave Books, 2015). On the state as the organ of class rule, see Engels, *The Origin of the Family, Private Property and the State*, 177–8.

9 Hans Kelsen, "Forms of Government: Democracy and Autocracy," and "Forms of Organization: Centralization and Decentralization," in *General Theory of Law and State*, trans. Anders Wedberg (Cambridge, MA: Harvard University Press, 1945), 286–303.

The growing division of labor in "pristine" market societies calls for, and is perpetuated by, the emergence of the state. The main question that arises for Kelsen is the subject of regulation or, "the material sphere of validity," of this legal order related to its basic elements: subjects and territory.[10] Following a division of labor, subjects are transformed into "organs" and the territory into "spheres," which validate the legal order. As a juridical entity, the state makes it possible to regulate human behavior by defining the norms of private law as those that protect the interests of subjects ("private persons") while using the norms of public law to safeguard its own interests. Thus, the emergence of the state inherently constructs and regulates both a "private" familial sphere and a "public" sphere of protective services.[11]

Conversely, the main economic factors leading to the emergence of the state —the urban concentration of populations and the proliferation of the market— suggest that the private, as a normative organization of a protected "close affinity" sphere, is unlikely to have been pursued in pre-state societies. Studies indicate that the demand for protection and punishment is lower in nomadic and pastoral (non-urban) communities because of the nature of their inhabitation, which is periodical and dispersed, and in less economically developed communities.[12] Spatially, the private emerges as a necessity to regulate dense co-habitation within urban contexts and the concentration of wealth which the possessing classes need to protect. In pre-state societies the lack of a collective order to express a transcendental force, which in state societies represents, the "general will," the "divine will," the "nation," or the "ruling class," proves that its demand is lower than the individual effort to provide an order.[13] Thus, it abrogates the possibility of an organized private sphere that would, otherwise, need to be subjugated to, and eventually validate, the existence of a state. The private as an organization can only be institutionalized by the state, "the monopolistic legitimate force within a given territory."[14] The emergence of the state, as a response to the need for collective regulation of the economic and social co-existence and reproduction, imposes an order constituting of "organs" and "spheres"; the private subject as an organ within the sphere of private property and the familial subject as an organ within the sphere of domesticity.

10 Ibid., 242.
11 On the state as the regulator of not only public law, but also of private and family law, and by extension of the public and private spheres, see Kelsen, "Private and Public Law," in *General Theory of Law and State*, 201–6.
12 Philip Carl Salzman, "Pastoral Nomads: Some General Observations Based on Research in Iran," *Journal of Anthropological Research* 58, no. 2 (Summer 2002), 245–264.
13 Auster and Silver, *The State as a Firm*, 21. On the state as the personification of the national legal order and the resulting community as the social body constituted by common will or interest, see also Kelsen, *General Theory of Law and State*, 181–4.
14 Waters and Waters, *Weber's Rationalism and Modern Society*, 136.

To clarify the existence of the private in antiquity, McKeon conceptualizes its differential relationship from the public as, "a distinction that does not admit of separation."[15] This axiomatic distinction rests not only on a complementary, interdependent relationship of the two, but, based on Kelsen's theorization of private and public law, also implies a distinction of superiority and inferiority.[16] Indeed, the ancient Greek city-state, which Aristotle defines as the all-encompassing social and political community, validates the nobility of its aims and objectives compared to any other organized community through the hierarchical structuring of human life. [17] By founding the principles of a political organization of the urban community,[18] it constitutes two spheres of life and types of human subjects. The private, the sphere concerning the household and family, is where simple nature as mere survival is maintained, while the public sphere, the "commons," is where human nature acquires true existence and becomes materialized through its participation therein. The distinguishing feature of the human capacity, which elevates human nature to the sphere of the commons, Aristotle argues, is argumentative speech or reason (λόγος)[19] as a form of persuasion instead of the uncontested, despotic rule of the head of the household community (οἰκία) over home and family life.[20] Although the organization of the state is different in the ancient Greek and Roman worlds, both the Greek and the Latin etymology of the private bear the same inferior connotation in comparison to the public[21]; when employed to describe a personal status ("idiōtēs" or "privatus"), it meant literally to be deprived of any public —political or military— position.

Despite this deliberate downplaying, a socio-economic analysis of the household organization in both worlds reveals that the private sphere is as instrumental to the functioning of state governance as is the public, or, in a manner of speaking, equally "political." Arendt, in her reading of Aristotle, distinguishes in the ancient Greek city-state the private as the realm of biological life and the public as the realm of political life.[22] It is considered as a precondition of political freedom that all matters of biological necessity are taken care of in the sphere of the household (οἶκος). The nomos, the legal order of the political community, defines citizenship through

15 Michael McKeon, *The Secret History of Domesticity: Public, Private and the Division of Knowledge* (Baltimore: Johns Hopkins University Press, 2006), xix.

16 Kelsen, *General Theory of Law and State*, 203.

17 Aristotelis, *Politica* [*Politics*], trans. V. Moskovis (Athens: Law Library, 1989), 1252a5. "But, if all communities aim at some good, the state or political community, which is the highest of all, and which embraces all the rest, aims at good in a greater degree than any other, and at the highest good." For this translation see Aristotle, *Politics*, trans. Benjamin Jowett (Kitschener: Batoche Books,1999), 3.

18 The word "political" derives from the word polis (city) and denotes that the very nature of the organization of the state is linked with an urban formation.

19 Aristotelis, *Politica*, 1253a5–25 and Aristotelis, *Ethica Nicomachea* [*Nicomachean Ethics*], trans. V. Moskovis (Athens: Law Library, 1993), 1252a5.

20 Hannah Arendt, "The Public and the Private Realm," in *The Human Condition* (Chicago: University of Chicago Press, 1958), 27.

21 Thucydides, in Pericles's funeral oration, writes "[We Athenians regard] him who takes no part in the civic duties, not as unambitious, but as useless." For this translation, see Thucydides, *The History of the Peloponnesian War*, trans. Richard Crawley (New York: DigiReads, 2009), 63. Isidore of Seville writes "This man, who was once such a triumphant general, now is a private citizen." See Isidore, *Origines*, 9. 4.30, in Maltby, *A Lexicon*, 496.

22 Arendt, *The Human Condition*, 22–37.

the subjectivity of a free male home-owner among equals within the physical and symbolic walls of the city and defines the public as the realm where these subjects distinguish themselves through speech (λόγος) and cooperative action (πρᾶξις).[23] Thus, the nomos excludes foreigners and confines slaves and women, as subjects without the right of speech (ἄνευ λόγου), to the private realm. There the economy, the nomos of the oikos,[24] reflects and justifies the household structure and private property requirements[25], that are, in fact, characteristic of the private realm, as the only means to master biological necessity and acquire freedom.

In this light, privacy is considered a material condition of co-habitation rather than an exclusive trait and certainly not a privilege; on the contrary, it is a sign of a person's inability to engage in public exchange even within the realm of the household. The architectural organization of a typical house in Olynthus, as documented by archaeological excavations[26], is consistent with the range of activities mentioned in literary sources: grinding grain, cooking, eating, weaving, performing ceremonies of a religious cult, storage, entertainment, socializing and sleeping. **(Fig. 1)** At first glance the rooms appear to be evenly distributed around the more public space of the open courtyard, however their roles are determined by specific architectural qualities, such as location, orientation and brightness, which, as Xenophon points out, make them suitable or inviting of a certain use.[27] Although there is a degree of variability in rooms sharing more than one function (washing and worship in the gallery, weaving and domestic storage in the gallery room(s), cooking and food preparation in the "flue" and kitchen), the spatial organization reveals a hierarchical order among the members. There is a public room exclusively for men's gatherings (ἄντρον), whose access through an antechamber made it one of the few exceptions to the general principle that rooms are only accessible from either the gallery or the courtyard. Its placement adjacent to an outside wall signaled, besides the ability to be lit through more windows, its separated position often at the corner of the house close to the entrance which directly welcomed guests without passing through the rest of the house. Again, this forms an exception to the idea of privacy through an inward-

23 Aristotelis, *Politica*, 1252b5.

24 The word "economy" derives from the ancient Greek oikos, denoting a condition of domesticity and domestic relationships, and nómos>némein: a) to distribute, to dispense, to pay one due respect, to manage b) to pasture. In antiquity, economy was theorized by Aristotle and Xenophon as a concept for the spatial arrangement, hierarchical distribution and financial management of tasks for the governance and self-sufficiency of the household. See also Xenophon, *Oikonomikos [Oeconomicus]*, trans. E. Moros (Athens: Zacharopoulos, 1939).

25 Aristotle defines "possessing as part of the economy (ἡ κτητικὴ μέρος τῆς οἰκονομίας)," Aristotelis, *Politica*, 1253b5–20.

26 Olynthus is an archaic city of Chalcidice, built under a provincially urban plan in a fertile plain at the head of the Gulf of Torone, which was brought to light by Professor Robinson in 1928. See M. Robinson, *Excavations at Olynthus: Architecture and sculpture, houses and other buildings*, pt. II (Baltimore: Johns Hopkins University Press, 1930), 118–21.

27 Such speculation is quite safely based on material artefacts suggesting use like mortar floors, clay objects or ashes. Xenophon, *Oikonomikos*, 9.2–9.4 and Xenophon, *Apomnemonevmata [Memorabilia]*, trans. E. G. Pantelakes (Athens: Zacharopoulos, 1937), 3.8.9–10.

Schematic plan
of house based on
type A VII 4, Olynthus,
ca. 400 B.C.

1 Courtyard
2 Gallery (παστάς)
3 North room
4 Flue
5 Loo
6 Kitchen complex
7 Gallery room
8 Men's dining room (ἄντρον)
9 Antechamber
10 Shop

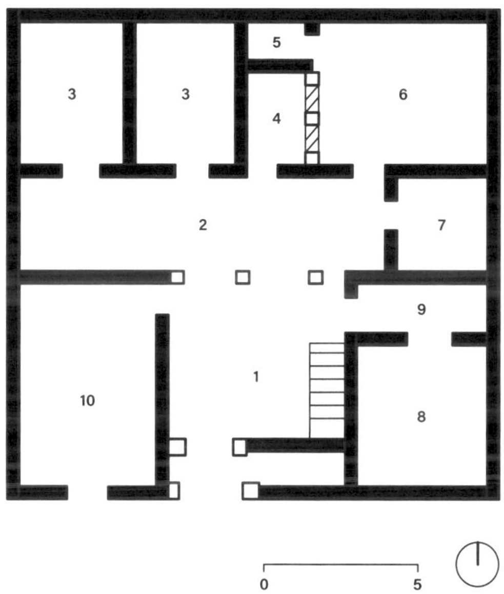

facing organization and emphasizes the public character of these rooms. The rooms for the women are usually separated from men's rooms, probably situated on the upper floor that the columns of the gallery support, so that reproduction, particularly of the slaves, is controlled.[28] Despotic supervision (πειρᾶσθαι δεσποτικῶς) of women's performance of household tasks, such as preparing food, weaving, tidying up and accounting, is considered as care (ἐπιμέλεια) of the household.[29] What prevents the nomos of the polis from annihilating the nomos of the oikos and enshrines its boundaries, is not a respect for private property. Rather, it is the fact that without home ownership a man could not claim a location of his own in the city within which to subordinate the social unit, the family, to the tasks of subsistence. Cahill, examining an enormous variety of patterns and differences in the design of houses in Olynthus, concludes that every domestic arrangement is responsible in its own way for the articulations between the household and the urban economy.[30] The private is administered as the spatial apparatus for the production and reproduction of all the hierarchical relationships —despotic, paternal, marriage and property relationships— that are necessary to support the idea of citizenship and the functions of the city-state.

In republican Rome, the relationship between the household and the state is more emphasized. Even before Caesar's death, Cicero explicitly argues in the *De Re Publica*, that sometimes even "a private citizen" can, or must, "bear the burden of the whole state," by serving a public function.[31] The point is that all private citizens, and by extension the private realm as a whole, are also primarily responsible for the functioning of the state, which is something of an unobjectionable republican sentiment. This is evident in the Roman house (domus) **(Fig. 2)**, the type occupied by the upper classes during the republican and imperial eras[32], which was built as a public space to incarnate a similar type of central rule. As Rome became more and more prosperous from trade and conquests, the homes of the wealthy increased in both size and luxury[33] with expanded central gathering areas and a proliferation of programs and rooms, emulating a microcosmic reduction of the state. The spatial configuration in this bipartite organization reflects the social status of the "father

28 Xenophon, *Oikonomikos*, 9.5.

29 Ibid., 10.10.

30 Nicholas Cahill, *Household and City Organization at Olynthus* (New Haven: Yale University Press, 2002).

31 Marcus Tullius Cicero, *De Re publica* [*Treatise on the Commonwealth*], vol. I, trans. Francis Barham (London: Edmund Spettigue, 1841–42), 2. This work on Roman constitutional theory, written in imitation of Plato's *Republic*, records a shift brought about by Caesar in the type of constitution that had been established in Rome by the kings, and explores the increasing role of "the private domain" in the new governmentality.

32 The domus represents the type of house of the richest families in ancient Rome, while most of them owned a separate country house outside the walled and fortified city, the villa. Thus, the modern English word "domesticity" derives from the Latin domesticus>domus to describe primarily a condition of *urban habitation*. Alfred Frazer, *The Roman Villa* (Philadelphia: University of Pennsylvania Press, 1998), 64. For a thorough etymological analysis of the relationship between the Roman "domus" and the Greek "domos" (another word for household and household training), see "Domus," in William Smith, LLD, William Wayte, G. E. Marindin, *A Dictionary of Greek and Roman Antiquities* (London: John Murray, 1890), 423–432.

33 Norbert Schoenauer, *6,000 Years of Housing*, third revisited expanded edition (New York: W. W. Norton & Company, 1981), 136.

2
Schematic plan of house based on Casa di Trebius Valens, Pompeii, ca. 200 B.C.

1 Courtyard (atrium)
2 Pool
3 Room
4 Men's room
5 Father's office (tablinum)
6 Study
7 Garden (peristylium)
8 Kitchen
9 Dining room
10 Shop

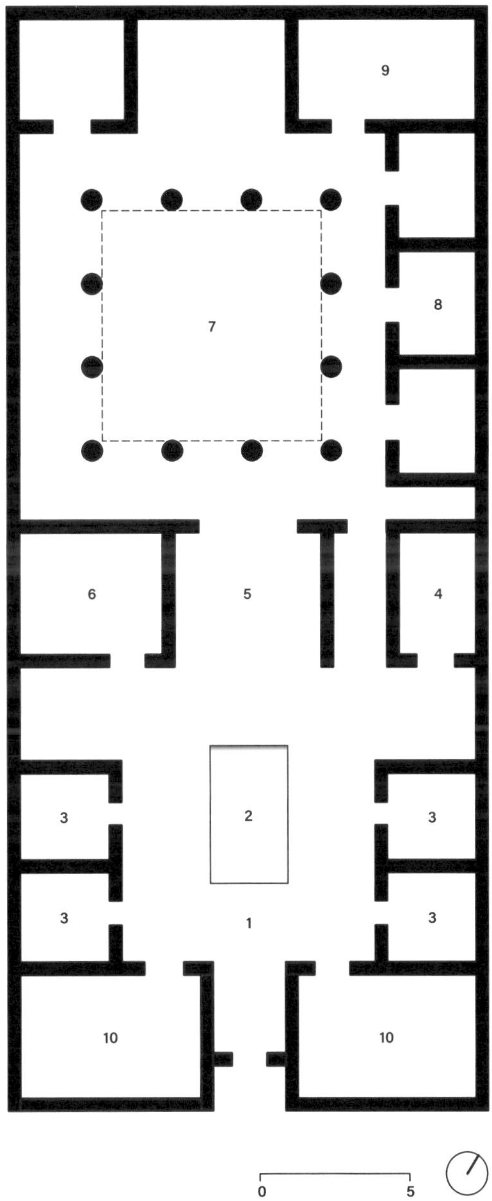

of the family" (pater familias) running the household analogous to an emperor ruling the state. Between the courtyard (atrium) and the garden (peristylium) is the *tablinum*, an office of sorts for the lord of the household (dominus), to address the household community in his morning salutation or from which he received his guests.[34] Principally, the central location of this room, which was accentuated by a podium for the father of the family to stand on in order to be seen, reflects the hierarchical organization of the house according to a state structure.

The age of Augustus marks the passage from the late republican state to the imperial state through a conscious shift in *governmentality*[35] with the depoliticized nature of the private being instrumentalized and transformed into the place of state intervention and political propaganda par excellence.[36] Octavian Augustus was Caesar's young successor who had funded a private army to overthrow the aristocratic oligarchy and avenge the assassination of his adoptive father. In exchange for building the temple of Apollo in his dedicated area on the Palatine hill, he was granted by the Senate a much larger area around the temple for his private residence (Domus Augusti).[37] **(Fig. 3)** The house was adjacent to the west side of the temple, next to the Caci staircase (Scalae Caci). Augustus reserved 2,100 square meters —half that of his predecessors and even smaller than some civilian's houses in Rome— constituting the remaining surface as a public house. Considered as a whole, Augustus therefore was able to take advantage of a much larger area measuring 22,000 square meters.[38] The private house is characterized by small and "thrifty" rooms which, "hardly belong to a private elegance,"[39] whereas the rooms hosting public functions boast better qualities of space and luxury. Political and social categories were particularly instrumental to Augustus's new governmentality, an order which he sought to endow with a more civilian rather than monarchical outlook. Therefore, the precedent for acquiring public consent was set by way of his private residence not as the monarch but as the First Citizen of the country.

34 From the elegant paintings and election graffiti referring to "Valens" and "dominus" in the tablinum (father's office), archaeologist Matteo della Corte participating at the excavation of Pompeii, was able to identify the owner of Casa di Trebius Valens and presume that the house would have been important for "l'instrumentum domesticum." Matteo della Corte, *Case ed abitanti a Pompei* [*Houses and inhabitants of Pompeii*], second edition (Rome: L'Erma di Bretschneider, 1954 [1914]), 425.

35 The term was coined by Michel Foucault to express the apparatus that constructs an idea of the physical, psychological and economic prosperity of its people, over which it exercises control and governs. As a concept, I would claim, it is as old as the emergence of state government itself. See Michel Foucault, *Security, Territory, Population: Lectures at the College de France, 1977–78*, ed. Arnold I. Davidson, trans. Graham Burchell (Basingstoke: Palgrave MacMillan UK, 2009).

36 Augustus (63BC–14AD) consolidated an enduring legacy as one of the most effective Roman emperors, whose reign from 27 BC until his death in AD 14 is considered the longest and most peaceful in the history of the Empire (Pax Romana). The Roman world was largely free from large-scale conflict for more than two centuries, despite continuous wars of imperial expansion on the Empire's frontiers in Africa, Asia and Europe. By law, Augustus was granted supreme military, judicial and administrative powers for life by the Senate, which he struggled to transform from a monarchical to a more civil framework of governance —a republican state led under his sole rule as First Citizen (Princeps Civitatis).

37 Velleius reports that Augustus purchased the land and house of Quintus Hortensius on the Palatine for his residence, but after it was burnt down by a fire that consumed a large part of Rome's houses, Augustus declared this to be public property and dedicated a temple to Apollo Palatinus. The senate regarded this as a "pious act" and decreed that the property around this area be conceded to Augustus from public funds. Velleius Paterculus, *The Roman History II*, trans. F. W. Shipley (Cambridge, MA: Harvard University Press, 1924), 81–3.

38 Ibid.

39 Suetonius Tranquillus, "The Life of Augustus," in *The Lives of the Twelve Caesars*, Loeb Classical Library, trans. J. C. Rolfe (London: Heinemann, 1913), 73.

3
Schematic plan
of the house of Augustus,
Palatine hill, Rome,
ca. 50 B.C.

1 Caci staircase
2 House of Augustus
3 Private house
4 Public house
5 Temple of Apollo
6 Portico of Danaids
7 Second portico
8 Arch of Octavia
9 Peristyle 1
10 Peristyle 2
11 Libraries

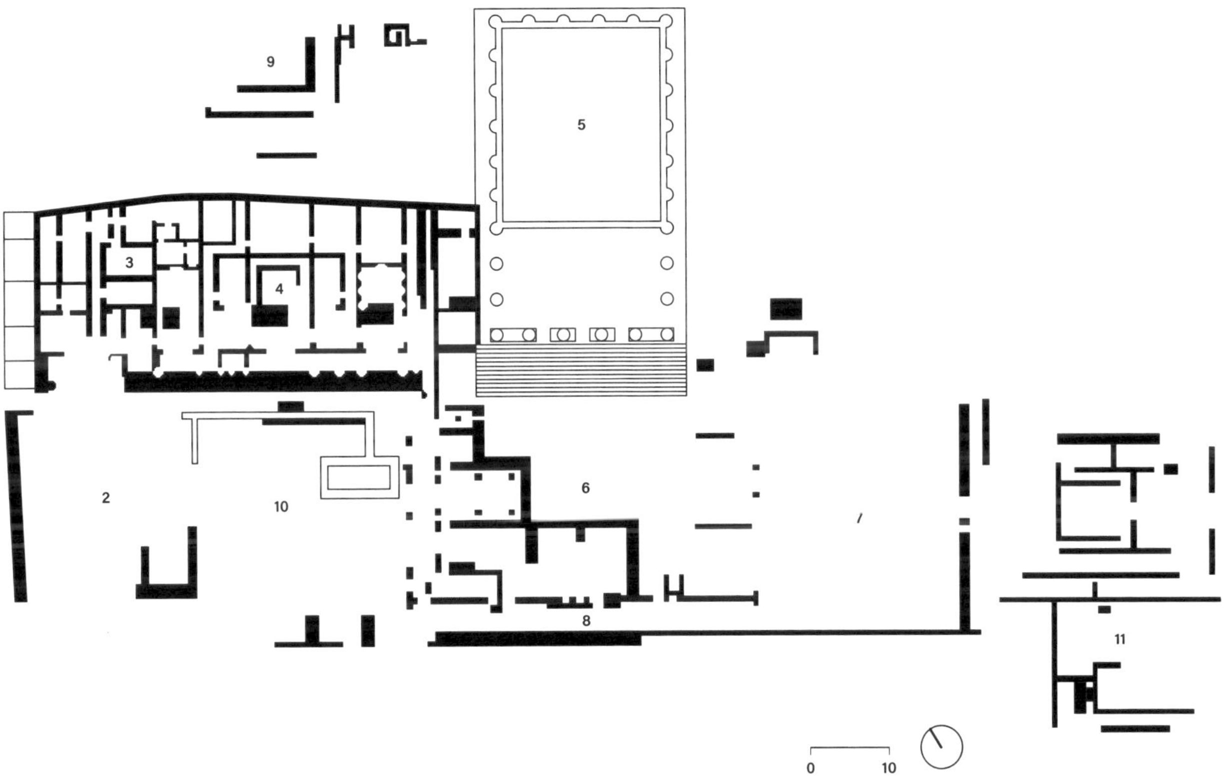

Augustus perpetuated this policy, which had earned him significant popularity among the Roman people. He organized a posthumous architectural project of a series of temples to be built in the most remote regions of the empire carrying inscriptions of the Res Gestae, a catalogue of his life's achievements.[40] The temple is a representation of the house of Divine Augustus with an inscription of his title as, "father of the country" (pater patriae). Taking into consideration the title of the master of the house as, "father of the family," the temple therefore draws a direct analogy between the state and the family.[41] The temples were to be included within a precinct surrounded by a *portico* (gallery) according to the principles of his public forum in Rome. The forum included a temple honoring Mars, for his victory in the battle of Philippi, as well as statues of all the Roman triumphatores, positioned in each of the portico's semi-circular niches. In doing so it linked the ancestry of Augustus to these men and the old Republic, an era he deliberately tried to invoke during his reign. While adopting this influential public typology, the temple is dedicated to himself as a symbol of a private residence with a protective father at the ends of the empire. **(Fig. 4.1-4.2)** What is more, above the entrance to the precinct was to be inscribed the beginning passage from Res Gestae remembering his major achievement as a *private individual* to liberate the Roman state by *private means*. This act of infusing the state agenda into the private, while transmitting the opposite idea, that the private is inscribed within the public precinct, is considered the most successful and peaceful propaganda of imperial ideology in the history of the empire, or, in liberal terms, a privatization of the state.

THE PRIVATE IN LIBERAL STATES

According to McKeon, the critical instance in the consolidation of modernity and modern domesticity is the categorical distinction of the private during the seventeenth century. The process is characterized by the transition from the ancient to the feudal states when the enclosures of common land and holdings were run by feudal lords as private realms.[42] However, McKeon, pursuing Marx's line of thought on the

40 It was an ambitious and quite successful project for stabilizing and culturally integrating imperial possessions and, thus, consolidating imperial power in the years following his death. Inscriptions have played a key role in the interpretation of Roman history not just as textual documents but also as cultural products contributing to the formation of narratives. The Res Gestae inscription coupled with a certain architectural typology is an extraordinary example of the creation of an imperial image.

41 Suna Güven, "Displaying the Res Gestae of Augustus: A Monument of Imperial Image for All," *Journal of the Society of Architectural Historians* 57, no. 1 (1998): 30–45.

42 For an insightful analysis of the maintenance of commons in the thirteenth-century English countryside, see Peter Linebough, *The Magna Carta Manifesto: Liberties and Commons for All* (Berkeley, CA: University of California Press, 2008). For the enclosure of these commons in the seventeenth-century English countryside, see Karl Marx, *Capital Volume I*, pt. VII, trans. Edward Aveling and Samuel Moore (London: Electric Book Co, 2001 [1887]), 812–829.

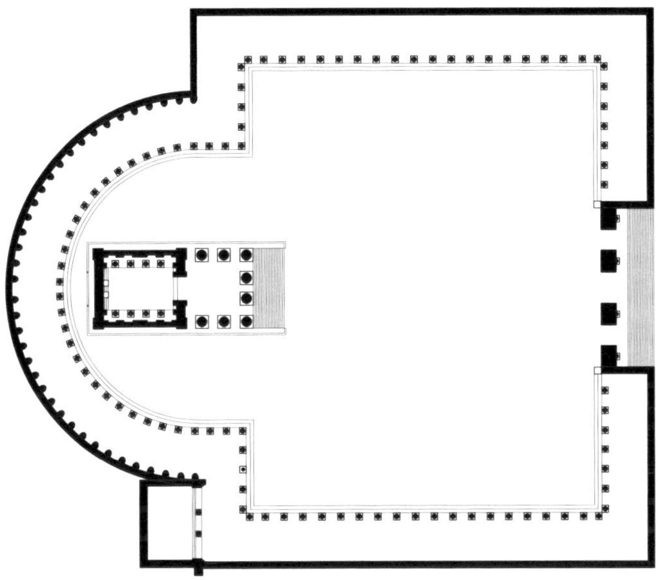

4.1
Plan of the Temple of Augustus in Antioch, Pisidia

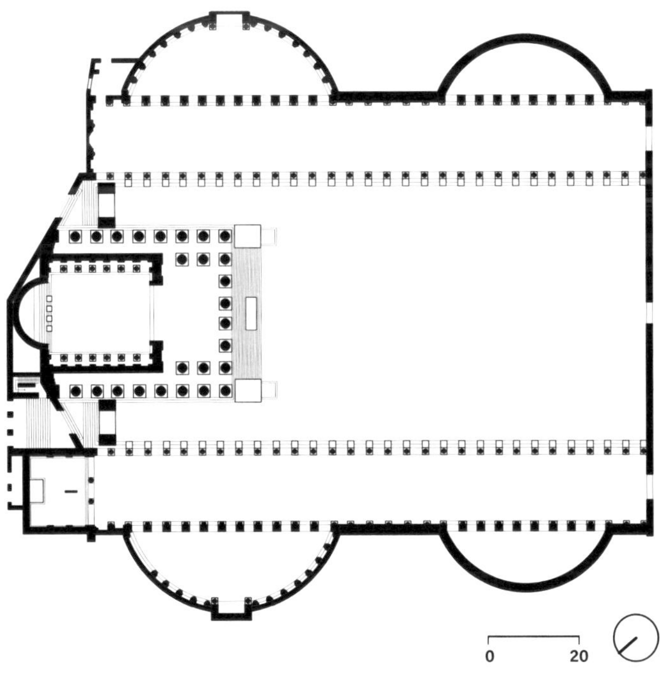

4.2
Plan of the Forum of Augustus hosting the Temple of Mars Ultor

category of "labor," argues that it is the moment of the conceptualization of the private "as such," when it is applied with the necessary abstraction which makes it an inclusive and influential category.[43] Similar to labor, which exemplifies the historical dialectic between material and conceptual development, the private, although also "immeasurably old" as a concept, when "economically conceived in this simplicity, is as modern a category as are the relations which create this simple abstraction."[44] So, first, the recognition of the private "as such" becomes predominant through: the inherent limitation of the term to specific individuals, the deliberate construction of a subjectivity and the spatial interpretation of specific forms. The multiplicity of experiences, conditions and behaviors related to these subjects and spaces (privacy) as well as the institutions and mechanisms that assign this character to them (privatization), are conceived as parts of a greater whole and induce further abstraction —a retrospective impression of the whole as having preceded the multiplication of its parts. The modern abstraction of the private complicates the example of labor through its reflexive objectification against the public as separate, independent and antagonistic categories (individually driven versus state driven).

The theoretical models developed principally by Arendt and Habermas, attest to the concept of the private, as it is currently understood in Europe, as being the product of a process directly related to the rise of market societies in the eighteenth and nineteenth centuries.[45] In modernity, Arendt observes the rise of the social realm, a realm concerned with providing for biological needs at the level of the state. She views itthe social as a threat to both the private and the public realm as it hijacks the former and gradually eliminates the latter: in order to provide for the needs of everyone it invades the private sphere, and because it makes biological needs a public matter, there is no longer a realm free from necessity.[46] Privacy, thus, takes on its modern meaning as intimacy and seclusion, the desire to withdraw from social exchange, and at the same time implies the luxury to do so, which is identified with the bourgeois social status.[47] The bourgeois figure embodies "the private individual," which Benjamin claims "makes his entry into history" at the turn of the nineteenth

43 McKeon argues that, ever since, the history of the private has been one of abstraction that is coextensive with the abstraction of labor and of knowledge itself. McKeon, *The Secret History of Domesticity*, xviii.

44 Karl Marx, *Grundrisse: Foundations of the Critique of Political Economy*, trans. Martin Nicolaus (London: Penguin Books, 1973), 103–5.

45 Hannah Arendt, *The Human Condition* (Chicago: University of Chicago Press, 1958) and Jürgen Habermas, *The Structural Transformation of the Public Sphere: An Inquiry into a Category of Bourgeois Society*, trans. Thomas Burger and Frederick Lawrence (Cambridge, MA: MIT Press, 1989).

46 Arendt, *The Human Condition*, 38–49 and Habermas, *The Structural Transformation of the Public Sphere*, 27–51.

47 "The Bourgeois Family and the Institutionalization of a Privateness Oriented to an Audience," in Habermas, *The Structural Transformation of the Public Sphere*, 43–50.

century.[48] At the same time, the concept of privacy as a privilege linked to social status evolves with the idea of the domestic interior.[49] The bourgeois fetishized material possessions (decorations, furnishings, clothing), giving an individual character to the interior and stressing the idea of ownership in the demarcation of private space.

To understand what this means for domesticity at large also means tackling the private's legal status which is meant to serve the new structure of the contractual state. The schematization that conveys the nature of this transformation more accurately than the antiquity-modernity dichotomy is the transition from the ancient to the liberal regime, which provides the context for the development of modern states and capitalism between the seventeenth and nineteenth centuries in Europe.[50] Liberal theory provides an argument on political economy which accommodates the transition from an absolutist/sovereign state to a contractual/civilian state. It sets the determination of value as the main criterion for the aforementioned division of knowledge, which marks a radical reconceptualization of freedom and the transformation of society.[51] In particular, it marks the conceptualization of *the right to privacy* not as a political but rather an economic freedom within a market society. The transformation of the private vis-à-vis the new state involves the process of its abstraction into a status that is contextualized here in terms of liberal philosophy. Locke's theory of property and Weber's theory of the rational-legal state examine the relationship between the cultural value of the private and the new structure of society determined by a market economy. At the same time, a historical materialist view is provided through Sohn-Rethel's theory of the abstraction of exchange as a critique of the practices of class societies that lead to the alienation of the physical experience (material labor) from the abstract notion.[52]

Locke's key contribution to this context is the establishment of reciprocity between subjectivity and (private) property within the emergent global capitalism of late-seventeenth-century Britain.[53] His argument sets off from a claim on personhood as, "a property in his [one's] own person," and in the products of one's labor,

48 Walter Benjamin, *Paris, Capital of the Nineteenth Century* (New Jersey: Princeton University Press, 1939), 19.

49 Charles Rice, *The Emergence of the Interior: Architecture, Modernity, Domesticity* (London: Routledge, 2007).

50 L'Ancien Régime (literally "old rule") in French sociology refers to the political and social system of the Kingdom of France from the Late Middle Ages (circa the fifteenth century) until the French Revolution of 1789, which led to the abolition (1792) of hereditary monarchy and of the feudal system of the aristocratic dynasties. The term is occasionally used to refer to similar feudal systems of the time elsewhere in Europe, but here expands to describe a long sequence of absolute monarchist states and administrative centralization since the fall of the Roman empire.

51 Both divisions distinguish the five fundamental dimensions of change: *individualism*, the advent of the individual as the hub of society; *differentiation*, the multiplication of choices in lifestyles; *rationalization* of processes of administration; *economism*, the domination of social life by economic activities; and *expansion*, the tendency of modern societies towards development and growth, especially in terms of space (i.e. "globalization"). The difference between the modernization and the liberal theory is that the former addresses these points from the cultural point of view, while the latter addresses the shift in governmentality that institutionalizes the cultural shift. See Olivier Galland and Yannick Lemel, "Tradition vs. Modernity: The Continuing Dichotomy of Values in European Society," *Revue française de sociologie*, no. 49 (May 2008): 153–186.

52 That is within the Marxist critique of abstraction in capitalist processes with a focus on the category of labor.

53 John Locke, *Second Treatise on Government*, ed. Crawford B. McPherson (Indianapolis and Cambridge: Hackett Publishing Company, 1980 [1690]). On a formulation of the affinity of philosophy to the categories of capitalist society based on a study of Locke, see George Caffentzis, *Clipped Coins, Abused Words, and Civil Government: John Locke's Philosophy of Money* (New York: Autonomedia, 1989) and George Caffentzis, *John Locke: Philosopher of Primitive Accumulation* (Bristol: Bristol Radical History Group, 2008).

as an egalitarian philosophy of consciousness which is supported by his proposal for a universal monetary policy.[54] The notion of self-ownership —or more precisely self-appropriation as a conception of identity— is the democratic notion described by Locke in the transition from an absolute to a civil government. This allows one to inscribe property in the natural commons while labor (cultivation, construction), and the appropriation it engenders, justify the end; the "improvement" of land "for the benefit of life," which would otherwise rightly be called "waste."[55] On the one hand, Locke's account struggles to differentiate itself from Hobbes's relentless acquisition in a totalitarian state by implying moral limits to appropriation.[56] On the other hand, it redefines private property away from local use-rights of the commons to discrete units of abstract value that become necessary to exit the insecurity of the state of nature to form a civil contract.[57] When it comes to the private realm, property is a reward for domestic labor and a stable measure of the value of domesticity with the aim of stimulating broad participation in contracts and transactions in a burgeoning world market. Property stands for a universal consent conferred upon the value of the freedom and security of *privateness* and a product of labor that the individual is free to sell, as they would sell their labor for a wage.[58] In addressing, "life, liberty and estate," as rights in terms of property, Locke's theory engages in questions of policy that bring us back to the question of how the state is structured. Resting with the premise that the capacity of property to store value generates the social contract in the first place,[59] Locke's account of the state acknowledges that "the chief end of men's [...] putting themselves under governments, is the preservation of their property."[60] Thus, the liberal state does not advocate for the restraint of governmental intervention in the economic regulation of social life. On the contrary, such a government as Locke describes is the reflection and maintenance of the contending interests more than any common interest in a society grounded in individual labor and private property as modes of participation.

Weber, in asserting a social transformation that understands collectivities only as a result of the actions of individuals,[61] describes a process of *rationalization* of society.

54 Locke, *Second Treatise on Government*, Section 27. On the underlying equivocation between identity and property, "being" and "having," the "self" and the "own" in the Lockean account of subjectivity, see also Étiene Balibar, *Identity and Difference: John Locke and the Invention of Consciousness* (London: Verso, 2013).

55 Ibid., Sections 32, 42. On the relationship between accumulation and "waste" in Locke, see also Onur Ulas Ince, "Enclosing in God's Name, Accumulating for Mankind: Money, Morality, and Accumulation in John Locke's Theory of Property," *The Review of Politics* 73, no. 1 (Winter 2011): 29–54. On improvement as a discourse on land in seventeenth-century England, see Gary Fields, "From land reimagined to landscapes remade: The discourse of improvement and enclosing the common fields," in *Enclosure: Palestinian Landscapes in a Historical Mirror* (Oakland, CA: University of California Press, 2017), 45–91.

56 See Crawford B. McPherson, *The Political Theory of Possessive Individualism: Hobbes to Locke* (Oxford: Oxford University Press, 2011).

57 Modern knowledge is predicated upon all sorts of conceptual dichotomies besides the private-public, such as nature-culture, freedom-tyranny etc. Particularly here, Locke points at private property and his proposed universal monetary system as freedom from state tyranny and improvement from the wilderness of nature.

58 Caffentzis argues that the labor theory of property "projects the privateness of the person into the ontological transformation of the earth," which sets property and freedom at the same ontological order. Caffentzis, (1989), *op.cit.*, 50. Marx intensely critiques the philosophy of the right to property in this framework where free will survives only as the predicate of private property. See Karl Marx, "A Contribution to the Critique of Hegel's 'Philosophy of Right': Introduction," in *Karl Marx: Early Writings*, trans. Rodney Livingstone and Gregor Benton (London: Penguin, 1975 [1843–4]), 243–257.

59 Caffentzis, *Clipped Coins*, 71.

60 Locke, *Second Treatise on Government*, Section 124.

61 A description of methodological individualism is found in the first chapter of Max Weber, *Economy and Society: An Interpretive Sociology*, eds. Guenther Roth and Claus Wittich (Berkley: University of California Press, 1978 [1921]).

This pervades the economic level, the intensification and standardization of production, to the political level, a professional public administration, and the cultural level, the victory of the bourgeois values of individualism, thriftiness and efficiency.[62] In his portrayal of the bureaucratic state apparatus as the most efficient administration for calculation, planning and organization of human activities, he admits the establishment of legal norms to codify social relations that are not restricted to a given area of life but embrace life as a whole. This, I argue, severely compromises the organization of private life which becomes an issue of class and status, despite Weber's effort to dissociate social status from economic qualities. Insofar as one's status has consequences in terms of life chances and opportunities to *improve* one's life,[63] the private sphere acquires an economic relationship to the market and to social stratification. Habermas, in his critique of modernity, also challenges the potential of modern privateness, freed from all forms of external authority (including nature and tradition), for democratization.[64] What Weber fails to acknowledge is that the idea of "individual freedom" dissolves in the face of the principle of the modern world wherein "the subject wills only those laws that recognizes as rational." [65] What is more, since the state is the monopolist force of legitimation,[66] it is by definition the legal instrument used to codify norms of spatial organization. Modern privacy, therefore, is the submission to institutions, ideas and principles that form the basis of "traditional" behavior. The state, once again, regulates the private sphere, only this time the main objective of the configuration of domesticity is addressed through the state's bureaucratic nature. Policy documents are responsible for defining in detail the main aspects of the rationalization of domestic space; a clear form of a spatial unit to facilitate private property, a clear spatial hierarchization of a social unit, which is the family, and a clear formal differentiation to reflect social status. To the degree that everyday life was affected by this rationalization, the society created in this process embraced the private in the abstraction of its status as the "object of rational will." Thus, it became less and less welcoming of the individual's autonomy to create his or her own life conditions.

62 Waters and Waters, *Weber's Rationalism and Modern Society*, 129–198.

63 This echoes Locke's concept of *improvement* linked to accumulation of wealth. Reinhard Bendix, *Max Weber: An Intellectual Portrait* (Orlando, FL: University of California Press, 1977), 85–87.

64 Habermas, *The Structural Transformation of the Public Sphere*.

65 Jürgen Habermas, "Modernity's Consciousness of Time and its Need for Self-Reassurance," in *The Philosophical Discourse of Modernity: Twelve Lectures*, trans. Frederick Lawrence (Cambridge, MA: The MIT Press, 1990), 17.

66 Waters and Waters, *Weber's Rationalism*, 129–198.

Architecturally, the domestic type becomes the ultimate abstract form with the capacity to store value and the potential to stimulate and regulate behavior: that is, basically, to identify privacy with domesticity and with property. Vidler's historicization of *type*, as emerging in the Enlightenment philosophy and bleeding into the Modernist ideology and the Neo-rationalist perspective, is revealing of the belief in rational science's task: to confirm that the mission of architecture is to master type as the agent of progress.[67] In his critique, he further argues that the type, "having the connotations of a law," becomes particularly instrumental during these three crucial passages of modern society by addressing the classification and fragmentation of the capitalist city.[68] Thus, the rise of the urban private apartment type is linked to the rise of a social class, which is the bourgeoisie, but is meant to endure and permeate society as the machine of reproduction. The bourgeois private apartment emerges from the tradition of city palaces and is adjusted to urban, multi-story residential buildings. **(Fig. 5.1)** It introduces the rational organization of two mirrored apartments per floor, as a clear-cut boundary of property —marked by the middle perpendicular wall— and a sequential subdivision of rooms, exuding the feeling that privacy is the privilege of those occupying the farthest corners. It is, indeed, as these are the rooms of the husband, in the front façade, and the wife, in the rear, while the bedrooms of the children and servants overlook the inner courtyard. The courtyard is gradually completely interiorized and identified as the living room. The rationalization is exemplified in the type for the working classes, where all the main services for a nuclear family structure are individualized and squeezed within the minimum standards. **(Fig. 5.2)** Communicating the message that this class is the foundation of the industrial capitalist society that needs to be reproduced, it aims at also stimulating people of modest means to become owners. The rise of the middle class, as the engine of social aspiration that sustains stratification, is synchronous to my framing of the rise of neoliberalism in the second half of the twentieth century. Frampton's critique on Krier's designs captured the essence of the twentieth-century housing project for the middle classes **(Fig. 5.3)**; the plan is "determined by shapes and sequences according to nineteenth-century bourgeois standards of deportment but realized through the minimum standards of social housing."[69]

67 Anthony Vidler, "The Third Typology," *Oppositions* no. 7 (Winter, 1977): 1–4.

68 Anthony Vidler, "The Idea of Type: The Transformation of the Academic Ideal, 1750-1830," *Oppositions* no. 8 (Spring 1977): 94–115. For the feminist perspective, see Maria S. Giudici, "Counter-planning from the Kitchen: For a Feminist Critique of Type," *The Journal of Architecture* 23, no. 7–8 (2018): 1203–29. On the instrumentality of type at the service of the contemporary city in the neorationalist approach, see Aldo Rossi, *The Architecture of the City* (Cambridge, MA: MIT Press, 1982 [1966]) and Robert Krier, *Urban Space* (New York: Rizzoli, 1979).

69 Kenneth Frampton's critique as discussed in Katharina Borsi, Nicole Porter and Megan Nottingham, "The Typology of the Berlin Block: History, Continuity and Spatial Performance," *Athens Journal of Architecture* 2, no.1 (January 2016): 54.

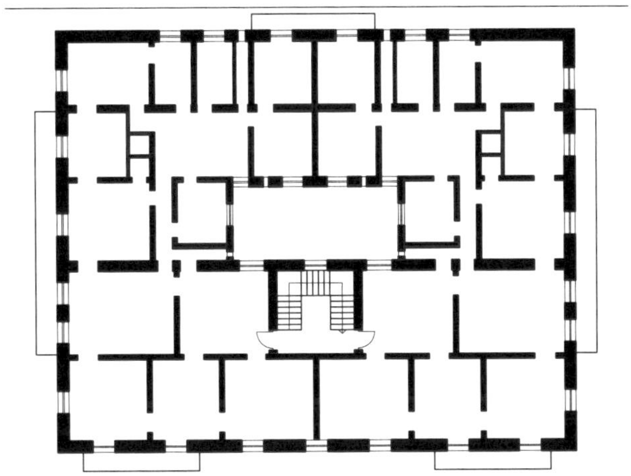

5.1
The bourgeois apartment type: Plan of Casa Blocco, Via Assarotti, Genoa, 1870

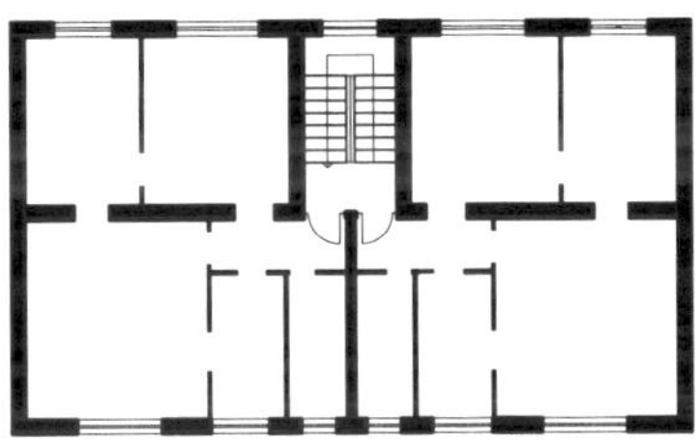

5.2
The working class apartment type: Plan of housing units, Bruchfeldstrasse Settlement, Frankfurt, 1926-27

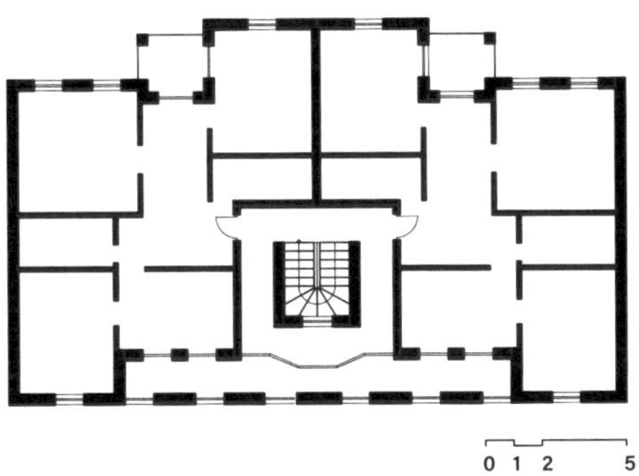

5.3
The middle class apartment type: Plan of housing units, Block 31, Ritterstrasse South, IBA Berlin, 1980-82

The final clue on abstraction, which has become particularly instrumentalized by neoliberalism as an acceleration of liberal philosophy, is introduced by Sohn-Rethel, who accords abstraction not as much in labor as in exchange. What his philosophical project offers to this account is the description of a process that also makes the private, like any product of labor, a commodity. His definition of "real abstraction" points at the necessary abstraction from the physical qualities involved in the objectification of an idea, which precedes the abstraction in the formation and circulation of the final object.[70] Thus, insofar as the idea of privacy is objectified into the (private) domestic object, while the subject of the exchange projects the qualitative properties of privacy on the object, the practice of exchange takes place in terms of the form of the *exchange value* of domesticity. Sohn-Rethel's historical narrative of the gradual expansion of exchange also links a genealogy from ancient Greece to the rise of modern capitalism, which is the crucial juncture in the separation of physical from intellectual labor —a society entirely defined by the sphere of exchange, circulation and distribution of commodities. Drawing an analogy according to this point, the private relationships and private labor involved in the (re)production of domesticity are subjugated to its commodification to the point of neutralization.[71] This leads to a truly capitalist form of conceptualization no longer derived from physical experience but from abstractions that are themselves derived from "a pattern of motion contained in the real abstraction of commodity exchange."[72] Thus, there is an inherent ambivalence in the construction of the private into a modern conceptual category denoting both a reassuring aura of "true" privacy that is individually attainable and an economic mechanism of appropriation of domestic space.

NEOLIBERALISM, HOUSING AND THE MARKET-STATE

Although, between the liberal state of the nineteenth century and the neoliberal state of the second half of the twentieth century there are many intermediate stages, they both rise as a pragmatic compromise to the monstrous idea and traumatic experience of absolute states.[73] Among the various political systems that have sought their own

70 Alfred Sohn-Rethel, *Intellectual and Manual Labour: A Critique of Epistemology* (London: Macmillan, 1979), 28–9.

71 Anselme Jappe, "Sohn-Rethel and the Origin of 'Real Abstraction': A Critique of Production or a Critique of Circulation?," *Historical Materialism* 21, no.1 (January 2013): 3–14.

72 Sohn-Rethel, *Intellectual and Manual Labour*, 128.

73 For a vivid portrayal of the medieval absolute monarchist state, see Thomas Hobbes, *Leviathan:Or the Matter, Forme, and Power of a Commonwealth Ecclesiasticall and Civill*, ed. Ian Shapiro (New Haven: Yale University Press, 2010 [1651]). For a portrayal of both the socialist and fascist states of the first half of the twentieth century as totalitarian, see Friedrich A. Hayek, *The Road to Serfdom* (London: Routledge Press, 1944).

philosophical justification of the powers that be, liberalism has stood for the utmost restriction of the material sphere of validity of the state legal order[74] by instrumentalizing the idea of individual freedom. Arendt, prophetically forecasting neoliberalism in 1958, argues that in all the cases since the advent of liberalism —Locke's "society of property-owners," Marx's "society of producers," the socialist and communist "society of laborers" and the current "society of job holders"— "it is the freedom (*or so-called freedom*) of society which requires and justifies the restraint of political authority. Freedom is located in the realm of the social, and force or violence becomes the monopoly of government."[75] The premises of liberal philosophy as a critique of totalitarian power and centralized planning make sense. The paradox, however, lies in the manner of pursuing the acclaimed liberation which became the instrument of state control: the abstraction of personal and material relations. Specifically, the transformation of the private into an individual, social and legal status propagated broadly within society as a measure of stability, led to an extreme proliferation of legislation. Neoliberalism resulted in the escalation of this phenomenon, a massive juridical structure whose rigid, rule-based control through policy-making instruments has been acknowledged by both liberal and neoliberal theorists.[76]

However, analyzing the implementation of the neoliberal ideology of the private solely in terms of policy, and not spatial configuration, is insufficient. It is necessary to explain why such housing policies continue to be in place, despite the wide catastrophic consequences they caused following 2008. The cultural appropriation of the private is based largely on its economic usage. Tied to the individual, the private is opposed to the collective. Based on a rightful title of ownership as a form of independence, the private is opposed to political governance. This mantra of personal autonomy undermined the inclusivity of political freedom —everybody's right to privacy— with the exclusivity of economic freedom, adopting a neoliberal meritocracy: privacy as a reward. The construction of an ambitious narrative of the exclusive and privileged nature of the private ought to acquire an almost one-to-one translation into design principles, if it were to cater for a wide spectrum of social and

74 On the sphere of validity of the state legal order, see footnote 9.

75 Emphasis added). Arendt, *The Human Condition*, 31.

76 See Waters and Waters, "Bureaucracy," in *Weber's Rationalism*, 73–128 and Ludwig Von Mises, *Bureaucracy* (New Haven: Yale University Press, 1944). Marx, in his critique of bureaucracy as the "mode of production" of civil rights, posited that corporate (private) and governmental (state) bureaucracy mutually rely on one another to exist. He maintained that "the bureaucracy is the state which has really made itself into civil society." Marx, "Critique of Hegel's Doctrine of the State", in *Early Writings*, 107.

economic statuses pursued by (neo)liberal society. Housing emerged as one of the main pillars and metrics of prosperity of the post-war economy in European capitals. Therefore, urban housing was envisioned at the scale of urban (strategic) planning, which sought to reconstruct the character of devastated cities out of their remaining historical and cultural cores rather than out of their debris, as tabula rasa. This was an attempt to enlist the exchange value of housing as part of the symbolic capital of the city. Housing was transformed from a provision of social welfare into a project of capitalist exploitation of urbanity through a very specific aspirational apparatus: being private in the heart of the city. The theoretical analysis that follows aims to disentangle the political and planning principles of neoliberalism which were translated into a widely successful image of the private. The policy and design analysis of the following case studies aims to illustrate the paradoxes and contradictions inherent to this rationale in addressing the idea of being private as true freedom.

The quest for economic freedom had reemerged as a trend before World War II as a revival of classical liberal ideals. The prestige of laissez-faire economics peaked in the 1920s but was quickly followed by their economic catastrophe in 1929. The restoration of monetary stability after the Great Depression was recognized as the touchstone of rationality in politics; no private suffering over the loss of constitutional liberties, no infringement of sovereignty, was deemed too great a cost in the balancing of sound budgets and currencies according to economic liberalism. The insistence of the two most powerful liberal states, Great Britain and the United States, on the fallacies of monetary orthodoxy gradually led to the rise of nationalism and socialism that took over Europe. The 1930s witnessed the absolutes of the 1920s called into question, while in the 1940s, economic liberalism suffered an even worse defeat. The term "neoliberalism" was coined at a meeting of liberal economists in Paris in 1938 as a rejection of collectivism, socialism and laissez-faire liberalism. Among the group, the two figures who came to define neoliberal ideology through the supremacy of the market were Ludwig von Mises and Friedrich Hayek.[77] Both denounced the socialism exemplified by Roosevelt's New Deal and Britain's devel-

77 Hayek, *The Road to Serfdom*, (Chicago, IL.: University of Chicago Press, 1944) and Von Mises, *Bureaucracy*.

oping welfare state, and viewed such policies as a manifestation of a collectivism akin to Nazism and communism. Instead, they championed for the "promise of a new freedom."[78] Exiled in London, their rigor of reasoning was intended to be a grim warning to Britons who expected their government to provide a way out from their individual economic difficulties. Echoing the desire of the bankrupt British state to empower a popultion to undertake investment in housing, they championed the role of the *private sector* —the market— into the economy and society.

As early as 1944, Friedrich Hayek and Karl Polanyi, prominent figures of the two Austrian schools of economic theory, had already written their seminal works on this political philosophy of the time: the first more discipline oriented, the second more socially critical. According to Polanyi, the great variety of forms in which the collectivist pre-war movement appeared, was due to the vital social interests affected by the expanding market; the shift to social and national protectionism was due to the manifestation of the weaknesses and perils inherent in a self-regulating market system.[79] Hayek, on the other hand, argued that the forms of collectivism were the inevitable results of the increasing growth of state control and state power, "national planning" and socialism, which he claimed was perfected in Germany at the cost of democracy.[80] Both agreed that the liberal-collectivist conflict could be resolved by restating the relationship between freedom and authority. In his position, which offered neoliberalism the moral ground it still defends today, Hayek conceived no personal freedom "in the absence of free markets, respect for private property rights and rule of law."[81]

The period immediately following World War II was described as "a time of hesitation" for Britain and the European continent as countries were faced with the daunting task of reconstruction and reconstitution. The widely accepted notion that the unpredictability of the free market had caused the depression, coupled with four years of centrally directed production driven by the war, had increased the mainstream acceptance of peace-time government planning for the economy. In 1947, Hayek found-

78 This book takes hints from a condensed version of the *The Road to Serfdom* published in the April 1945 edition of *Reader's Digest*, first published in Great Britain in 1999 and then in 2005 by *The Institute of Economic Affairs*. Friedrich A. Hayek, *The Road to Serfdom*, (London: The Institute of Economic Affairs, 2005 [1944]), 47.

79 Karl Polanyi, *The Great Transformation: The Political and Economic Origins of Our Time* (Boston: Beacon Press, 1957 [1944]).

80 Hayek, *The Road to Serfdom*, 61.

81 Ibid., 16.

ed the first organization that would spread the doctrine of neoliberalism —the Mont Pelerin Society. This was supported financially by wealthy people who saw an opportunity to exempt themselves from regulations and taxes. As it evolved, neoliberalism became more socially appealing. Its mantra suggested that competition be the superior method of automatic data recording, price coordination and, hence, economic problem solving. The principles it introduced against central, collectivist and faceless planning were "competition," "differentiation" and "flexibility" in the satisfaction of consumerist needs.[82] Among its American apostles, Milton Friedman exemplified the European Enlightenment term of "*individual* freedom"[83] against the "general welfare" or "the cry for an economic dictator,"[84] to contradict the American usage that he believed had been corrupted by Conservatives since the Great Depression.

Initially, neoliberalism did not enjoy widespread acceptance. The post-war Keynesian consensus was almost universal: governments in the United States and much of western Europe sought social outcomes by developing new public services and safety nets.[85] By the 1970s, when these policies began to fall apart and economic crises recurred on both sides of the Atlantic, neoliberal ideas had reached the peak of their popularity. With the support of sympathetic think-tanks, elements of neoliberalism —especially its prescriptions for financial policy— were adopted by Jimmy Carter's administration in the United States and Jim Callaghan's government in Britain. After Ronald Reagan and Margaret Thatcher rose to power, neoliberal policies were forcefully imposed: massive tax cuts for the rich, the crushing of trade unions, deregulation, privatization, outsourcing and competition in public services. During this transition the movement lost its name. While in 1951, Friedman, an arduous supporter of liberating the market from the governmental constraints of classical economic thought, had propagated neoliberalism as the way toward true freedom, soon after the term began to disappear.[86] Stranger still, as the movement became more coherent, the lost name was not replaced by any common alternative. Hayek's own ideas entered the mainstream of public policy debate as "Thatcherism," or "Adam-Smith liberalism," or "neo-conservatism" while the term "neoliberalism" was

82 Ibid., 59.

83 (Emphasis added). Milton Friedman, "Neo-liberalism and its prospects," *Farmand* (February 1951): 89–90.

84 Hayek devised the term "economic dictator" referring to the state. Hayek, *The Road to Serfdom*, 49–50.

85 One of the many influential contributions of economist John Maynard Keynes in the first half of the twentieth century is "The End of Laissez-Faire" (1926). As an adviser to the British treasury during both world wars, he agreed in principle that a marketplace of *free individuals* pursuing their *own self-interest* would stand a better chance of improving society's economic situation than the socialist state. However, he suggested that government should play a constructive role in protecting individuals from capitalism's cycles and crises, which, as neoliberal implementation proved, cannot guarantee social justice once the "redistribution of wealth" is predicated upon economic and not social criteria. See John Maynard Keynes, *The End of Laissez-Faire and the Economic Consequences of the Peace* (New York: Prometheus Books, 2003 [1926]).

86 Friedman was among the intellectual leaders of the Chicago school of economics, who rejected Keynesianism in favor of monetarism until the global crisis of the mid-1970s, when he turned to the concept of rational expectations. See Milton Friedman, *Capitalism and Freedom* (Chicago, IL: The University of Chicago Press, 2002 [1962]).

used pejoratively. However, these descriptions of the ideology as classical liberalism are misleading as they suggest that there is nothing novel about it. When Keynesian demand management melted down in the global crisis of the mid-1970s, there was an alternative ready to be picked up. It was a persistent philosophy that had been advocated by a network of theorists and activists since the late 1940s with a plan for the alleged absence of planning or, as Von Mises proposed, the liberation from the bureaucratic nightmare of central planning.[87] The doctrine promoted "the market," the place of unhindered *competition*, as the guarantor for the delivery of benefits that could never be achieved by central planning.[88] Warnings about the threats posed to society by allowing "the market mechanism to be sole director of the fate of human beings and their natural environment,"[89] could not be heard at that time.

Although one would expect that an ideology raising the ideals of society to utopian expectations would be essentially doubted, rarely in its history has neoliberalism been identified in such a manner. On the contrary, the proposition of this faith described as a natural force, a kind of biological law, was enhanced by the neo-Darwinian idea that individuals must compete among themselves for social survival.[90] The housing sector became "the wobbly pillar of the welfare state"[91] entrusted with the aspirations of the individuals in the race to climb the social and economic ladder. The function of the market in housing provision sounded like a natural mechanism generating a system that would cater to all people's needs, just like mother earth. Yet, Polanyi points out explicitly the implication that Keynes missed in his formulation of social protectionism from economic crises, which as a trend resists the self-regulation of the market. The idea of satisfying existential needs (like the need for privacy) as social and economic betterment was, according to Polanyi, the result of social relations being embedded in the economic system, instead of the economy being embedded in social relations.[92] The hidden agenda of this kind of welfare lay in the mere fact that people would need to have a certain economic power to cover their needs and, thus, the post-war welfare state was initially a project tailored to the *middle classes*. Moreover, the state would need to finance anything that was unpro-

87 Von Mises, *Bureaucracy*.
88 Hayek, *The Road to Serfdom*, 59.
89 Polanyi, *The Great Transformation*, 73.
90 On the term "social Darwinism" emerging at the same time as a culture where "social instincts" were capable of neutralizing the eliminatory aspects of natural selection, see Richard Hofstadter, *Social Darwinism in American Thought* (Boston: Beacon Press, 1992 [1944]).
91 Torgersen describes the institutional peculiarity of housing as part of the welfare state and how welfare concerns suffered from contradictions in the nature of *egalitarian and redistributory purposes*. He does so by exploring the role housing tenures play in schemes in England and Scandinavia. Ulf Torgersen, "Housing: The Wobbly Pillar under the Welfare State," *Scandinavian Housing and Planning Research* 4, no. 1 (March 2014): 116–126.
92 Polanyi, *The Great Transformation*, 57.

ductive or could not be sustained otherwise. Hayek, in his fascination with neoliberalism, overlooked that vital national services cannot be allowed to collapse, which means that competition cannot run its course.[93] The state still had to deal with the risk of investment in basic welfare services, like housing, and therefore, the narrative of the private had to be really successful to ensure financial return. Since "the companion task of politics is to devise forms of government within a democracy which shall be capable of accomplishing the [state] Agenda," [94] in fact, this narrative became a form of governmentality, in the Foucauldian sense. The idea of *middle-classness,*[95] while central to this state agenda for social betterment and modernization, in the full realization of the neoliberal state, deregulated and cancelled out itself (the existence of a middle class) through the competitive processes it adopted.

Privatization,[96] as an economic policy, took a systematic form in the welfare state and was justified by the need to provide increased financial resources to local authorities. Hence, the idea of individual home ownership as the "natural" tenure, that everyone should aspire to, conditioned the design and typology of housing and gave rise to a mass petit-bourgeois consumerism that fragmentized cities to an extreme level (or, in the course of neoliberalism, did not resist the fragmentation already underway). However, the economic asymmetries were the outcome of the social and spatial asymmetries and not vice versa. Privatization is discussed here as a process of extrapolation of the right to privacy into the economic freedom to be private and into the spatial configuration of housing that is able to reflect this status as a symbol of social upgrade. It is examined, as a spatial policy and practice propagating the private as a privilege that (re)produces asymmetries and hierarchies in the domestic and urban realm: individualization, alienation of care, gentrification, displacement. It shares Harvey's description "as one among the policies of dispossession pursued in the name of neo-liberal orthodoxy,"[97] which applies both to those included in and excluded from these processes. Dispossession has effectively taken place *a priori* in the neoliberal signification of the private, therefore, the etymological rootedness of privacy into *deprivation* of individual rights recurs as a powerful mechanism in the framework of this thesis.

93 Tony Judt, *Ill Fares the Land: A Treatise on Our Present Discontents* (New York: Penguin Books, 2010).
94 Keynes, *The End of Laissez-Faire*, 37.
95 De Angelis, *Omnia Sunt Communia*, 280.
96 The term was first attested in reference to German economic policies in the 1930s or a variant of liberalism called *ordoliberalism*, which advocated the need for a strong state to ensure the free market produces results within "rational expectations."
97 David Harvey, "The 'New Imperialism': Accumulation by Dispossession," *Socialist Register* 40 (2004): 75.

Neoliberalism has failed to address privacy as an essential personal freedom as it fell victim to what it reproached its opponents for. In theory, it advocated the naturalness of the market in achieving equilibrium, stability and growth, and thus the well-being of society without government intervention. However, it became the state's tool for its own undermining as social provider and the organization of its retreat to operate in the background. Kelsen, in his theory of the state, acknowledges the inherent incompetence of law to limit the material sphere of validity of the state legal order. He admits that "nothing in the nature of the State prevents the legal order from regulating any subject matter in any field of social life, from restricting the freedom of the individual to any degree."[98] In the moment when the state was supposedly withdrawn, it became intertwined with the market to associate the economic rationale of the private with planning methods and design principles of housing. This realization points at the cultural implementation of neoliberalism as a productive system of certain subjectivities, social relations and certain ways of living. In other words, it put forward "a certain existential norm in western societies and, far beyond them, in all those societies that follow them on the path of 'modernity.'"[99] Dardot and Laval's point underlines the extrapolation of competition on a global scale which increased tensions between the internal class conflicts and international politics of European states due to their structured framework of interlocking financial and governmental institutions. This made European capital cities explicit examples in the realization of the neoliberal housing project, as it will be discussed through the case studies that follow.

In policy and in practice, then, neoliberalism involves "coercive, disciplinary forms of state intervention in order to impose market rule upon all aspects of social life."[100] The ever-expanding volume of regulation empowered by the institutions actually unites neoliberal philosophy with its predecessors, revealing the latent aspects of control and exploitation that have been constitutive of the concept of the private since its inception. Neoliberalism does not bear witness to the collapse of an ideal privacy so much as it tests, quite literally, the powers of suggestion in a new muta-

98 Kelsen, *General Theory of Law and State*, 242.

99 Pierre Dardot and Christian Laval, *The New Way of the World: On Neoliberal Society*, trans. Gregory Elliott (London: Verso, 2013), 3.

100 Neil Brenner and Nik Theodore, "Cities and Geographies of Actually Existing Neoliberalism," in *Spaces of Neoliberalism: Urban Restructuring in North America and Western Europe* (London: Blackwell Publishers Ltd, 2002), 5.

tion of the private as a process. The more the private became a permeable structure for neoliberal motives, the more society was shaped in such a manner so as to allow the function of speculation as industry, which led to the valorization of the risk that comes along with the "freedom of choice."[101] What marks neoliberalism as being more influential than its predecessors in the construction of the private narrative is the utopian promise encrypted in the image of domesticity: to transform risks into securities. It does so by offering "new" choices while, at the same time, mobilizing historically established architectural references and social hierarchies. However, already at the time when Hayek theorizes the decentralization of planning, Polanyi writes a cautionary tale of the market not as a self-regulating but, rather a governed apparatus. Housing privatization is not the result of any inherent tendency of markets towards self-regulation or excrescence, but is instead the effect of "an artificial set of values administered to the body social in order to meet the no less artificial demands of the economy."[102] It is to the awareness of the theorists of the time that the lack of an effective control mechanism of the economy would soon lead to a shortcoming. To argue that this control mechanism has diachronically been the state is to argue that we have never been private.

101 Hayek, *The Road to Serfdom*, 63.
102 Polanyi, *The Great Transformation*, 57.

II. From Housing to Neoliberal Living

A Review of Case Studies in London, Berlin and Athens

The Living Suburb: The Barbican's Neoliberal Ideal for an Urban Society

Since the turn of twenty-first century, the Barbican estate[1] in London has enjoyed recognition as one of the most remarkable post-war redevelopment schemes in Britain, embodying a utopian ideal of inner-city living. **(Fig. 1)** Developed in the 1950s as a council estate in the City of London's east end,[2] the Barbican is a special case, designed by a partnership of three ambitious young architects, Peter Chamberlin, Geoffry Powell and Christoph Bon. What distinguished the Barbican as exceptional from the start was the local government's investment in such a large-scale housing scheme. Elsewhere in Britain at that time the approach was very different. Capital expenditures of local authorities were eliminated due to the Suez Crisis and public housing was limited to slum clearance programs. The scale of the Barbican investment was not only meant to address a housing shortage in the City, but to also realize a vision of urban growth, social progress and the future of living in London.[3] The combination of innovation and variety, drama and grandeur, historicity and modernity in the architecture illustrated a deliberate break from the uniformity and standardization of the council housing tradition. The medieval weightiness, the inner "countryside" landscape, the residential towers and the rough concrete vocabulary became architectural symbols of a new landmark for London. **(Fig. 2)** The integration of recreational spaces and gardens as well as cultural facilities and shops captured an idea of urban living beyond a residential community; it was an independent microcosm. Indicative of the social transformation it accommodated, "people with little interest in medieval cities and Georgian country houses found they cared passionately for cinemas and lidos, because they were a part of their neighbourhood, their culture." [4] Indeed, the unprecedented variation of housing morphologies and flat typologies was intended to attract a wide spectrum of the social strata. However, the standards of this package of provisions made the

1 Barbican (from the French *barbacane*): an outwork for the defense of a gate or drawbridge; also a sort of penthouse or construction of timber to shelter warders or sentries from arrows or other missiles. The Barbican takes its name in memory from the Roman wall that once stood in the area. *Encyclopaedia Britannica*, s.v. "Barbican", https://www.britannica.com.

2 The City of London is a local government district in the County of London founded within London's medieval walled settlement initially constituted by the Romans in the first century AD. The area, which is also colloquially known as the Square Mile, contains the historic center and the primary central business district of London. The modern city has since grown far beyond the formal City of London borders, but this area remains a notable part of central London, which became a focal area of post-war redevelopment. David Mills, *Dictionary of London Place Names*, (Oxford: Oxford University Press, 2010).

3 Architecture critic Worsley acknowledged that "the Barbican provided the Gold Standard for those who believe Modern architecture failed in the decades after World War II." Giles Worsley, "A well-aged conceit," *The Telegraph*, February 27, 2002, https://www.telegraph.co.uk/culture/art/3573757/A-well-aged-conceit.html.

4 Elain Harwood and James O. Davis, *England's Post-War Listed Buildings* (Newcastle: Batsford Ltd, 2015), 2.

1
Living at the Barbican

2
View of the Barbican from the Shakespeare Tower

Barbican primarily accessible to the middle- and upper-classes, thereby earning its unique character as "not a typical council estate!"[5]

These principles illustrated in the scheme echoed the ongoing struggle of London society to escape the rigidity of the welfare state, a challenge with which it was continually confronted. The Barbican embodies an attempt to be both architecturally innovative and financially competitive enough to enter a new socio-economic order. The political supporters of this new order had already begun to attack the intellectual foundations of the collective state. The 1942 redevelopment plan for the City of London still emulated the desire to build a grand vision for the capital —a vision conditioned by an imperial image of Britain as a social democratic commonwealth.[6] The redevelopment scheme aimed to propagate a form of urbanism that was planned rather than one which evolved from the nineteenth-century laissez faire attitude. Thus, the 1944 Greater London Plan continued efforts to depopulate the centre of London, creating an expanding metropolis of suburbs (Greater London), while instead regarding the City itself as a business and commercial district.[7] However, by 1952, the Ministry of Housing and Local Government was considering ways in which the City could benefit from a residential population. The hope was for the city to take advantage of its daily influx of workers who, as a type, were seen as more sophisticated than industrial workers. According to the liberal democratic voices, there was no apparent reason why a society which aspires to a general level of wealth should restrict itself to only planning for standard council housing. Instead, they believed it could grant its members the "freedom" to improve their position and acquire a suburban standard of living within the City. Still, there was no apparent reason why the state should not maintain the responsibility to guarantee, without endangering "individual freedom," the certainty of a minimum of sustenance for all. As early as 1956, the first Barbican proposal managed to incorporate and translate the ambition of monumentality, found in the 1942 imperial vision of the City of London, into a modern vision of a unique standard of living in the City.

5 Reyner Banham, "A Walled City: The Barbican in the City of London," *New Society* 30, no. 629 (1974): 222.

6 The 1942, "London Replanned," campaign was organized by the Royal Academy Planning Committee.

7 The Greater London Plan, put forward by the London County Council, proposed the Green Belt as a limit to the physical growth of London and the distribution of over 1 million of its industrial population to the expanded towns beyond its limit. Zoning should be very clear and each part of the city should perform its proper function as a member of the urban body. Peter Hall, *Great Planning Disasters* (Berkeley & Los Angeles: California University Press, 1980), 58–60.

Accommodating this transition, the history of the Barbican is as much about the idealization as it is about the demystification regarding the stakes of urban housing. Throughout the nearly 30-year span of its realization, and still today, the Barbican has sparked controversy with the public and the press as a housing statement. From the modern affluence of the 1950s that promoted the benefits of compact, high-rise housing in the City to the global oil crisis of the 1970s, when architecture critic Reyner Banham criticized it as "Britain's largest voluntary ghetto,"[8] from the 1960s, when the middle-class nature of the estate was celebrated by 4,300 people on the waiting list, to the 1990s, when it finally fell out of fashion and was almost forgotten by the press, the Barbican evoked mixed feelings. However, it always had an appeal to the popular imagination as a place for living, especially among people working in the cultural and creative industries. The complex's award of Grade II listed status in 2001, officially marked the period of its revival as the object of desire in new generations whose only experience of the City was as a locus of real estate interest. In terms of architectural vocabulary, the requirements had never been for yet another modernist estate, but rather for an evocation of the intimate scale of the residential traditions of the City. To these, the architects responded with a revised version that was "not intimate, but grand and monumental."[9] Therefore, it seems the Barbican has been praised and dismissed for the exact same reasons. It has been admired for its grandeur, spacious accommodation and lavish urban landscaping in times of economic prosperity, while its fancy style, expensive maintenance and high rental rates were deemed socially unsustainable in times of economic austerity. Monumental yet domestic, modern yet historically suggestive, coherent yet diverse, urban yet secluded, the Barbican was never meant to be just a housing estate. Instead, it embodied a recapitalization of tropes found in the place-making goals for successful development.[10]

Seven decades later, the measurement of success transcends the consolation of post-war housing projects which have resisted redevelopment strategies driven by demolition or have not degenerated into desolated plots.[11] Amidst the pragmatic conditions

8 Banham, "A Walled City," 222.

9 Architecture critic Jonathan Glancey, who spent four years living at the Barbican, argues that "there is nothing like [it] in scale, intelligence, ingenuity, quality, urban landscaping and sheer abstract artistry anywhere else in Britain, perhaps even the world." See Jonathan Glancey, "Barbican: the critics' verdict," *Time Out*, February 6, 2007, https://www.timeout.com/london/things-to-do/barbican-the-critics-verdict.

10 The Barbican inspired a whole generation of modernist council housing projects built in the 1960s and early 1970s, such as the Balfron Tower by Erno Goldfinger (1968) and the Robin Hood Gardens by Alison and Peter Smithson (1972).

11 In the 1980s, after Margaret Thatcher abolished the Greater London Council—the governing body that had overseen the Balfron project— the site began to deteriorate. Balfron's Grade II listing protected it against demolition but not against a displacement-based regeneration strategy to sell Balfron and build new private high-end flats. This was undertaken by the Harca housing association set up by the local government (Tower Hamlets) in 1996. On the contrary, Robin Hood Gardens was denied listed status and an investment plan in renovations to liven the building. In 2017, a demolition plan put forward by developers was implemented, although renovations would come at a much lower cost. See Tim Burrows, "Balfron 2.0: How Goldfinger's utopian tower became luxury flats," *The Guardian*, September 19, 2019, https://www.theguardian.com/cities/2019/sep/19/balfron-20-how-goldfingers-utopian-tower-became-luxury-flats; and Jessica Mairs, "Bulldozers move in on Robin Hood Gardens," *Dezeen*, August 25, 2017, https://www.dezeen.com/2017/08/25/bulldozers-demolition-robin-hood-gardens-alison-peter-smithson-brutalist-estate.

of the ongoing housing crisis in London, and many other European cities, the Barbican tower flats and penthouse suites remain extremely sought after, achieving record high sales prices.[12] The following aims to demystify the Barbican's success as a pioneer of neoliberal development which has inspired a generation of European housing projects ever since. It is reassessed here not as the outcome of, but the introduction to, principles of an urbanism that educated a market society by promoting competition in urban living overt the demand for affordable housing in the city center. A critical reflection of the Barbican's legacy is necessary to understand a neoliberal housing agenda that was only fully realized in Britain and Europe in the 1980s. Such a reading renders privatization as an issue of policy and design that precedes, and, in fact, anticipates a market society.

To understand what is at stake in the Barbican as a housing project, one must contextualize it as part of an urban, social and national policy. Among the areas of London decimated by the 1945 bombardment and in serious decline in terms of their residential population, was the Ward of Cripplegate.[13] Historically dividing the City from its moorland suburbs, the Barbican site, as part of Cripplegate, was included in London's post-war reconstruction scheme. **(Fig. 3)** By 1952, a general shortage of accommodation —affecting industrial workers as much as the middle and professional classes— put severe pressure on the policy of no housing within the City. Consequently, a new local legislation linking the power of an authority to the size of its resident electorate raised housing among the "national priorities."[14] By 1954 the local authority —the City of London Corporation— was already collaborating with the London County Council[15] to develop a residential, rather than commercial, scheme for the Barbican. The aim was, to both propose a successful development for the massive 40-acre site which, left vacant, cost the City a fortune and to also accommodate the new council tenant profile; a typical corporate employee in the City giving preference to young families and professionals who were jointly considered as the main consumer force.

12 *Barbicania*, directed by Ila Bêka and Louise Lemoine, (London: Barbican Centre, 2014), DVD. At the request of the Barbican Centre Art Gallery, Ila Bêka and Louise Lemoine, cinematographers of architecture, produced a film in 2014, as a daily documentary of the estate's life for a month, following an urban trip from the top floors of the towers to the underground levels of the art center. The film draws an intimate as well as critical map of the place in order to question its durability as a utopia since the 1950s.

13 The City of London is divided into 25 wards. Cripplegate was an area of the City, outside the homonymous wall gate, which had been decimated by the Blitz. According to the Barbican architects' report in 1951, only 48 people lived in the Ward of Cripplegate. Chamberlin Powell & Bon Architects, *Barbican Redevelopment: Report to the Court of Common Council of the Corporation of the City of London on Residential Redevelopment within the Barbican Area* (Bolton and London: Tillotsons Bolton Ltd., 1959), 1.

14 The main electorate of the City consisted until then of businessmen with voting rights, not residents.

15 The LCC was the authority in charge of the redevelopment plans for 'the Greater London' until the Greater London Council was founded in 1962. Until 1954, when the Corporation put forward a new vision of urban development with the Barbican scheme, the LCC had invested in infrastructural plans rather than a discussion on the City, which fell outside its full responsibility.

3
The Barbican site within the City's re-development area, Town and Country Planning Act, 1947

Chamberlin Powell & Bon Architects, Barbican Redevelopment: Report to the Court of Common Council of the Corporation of the City of London on Residential Redevelopment within the Barbican Area (Bolton and London: Tillotsons Bolton Ltd, 1959)

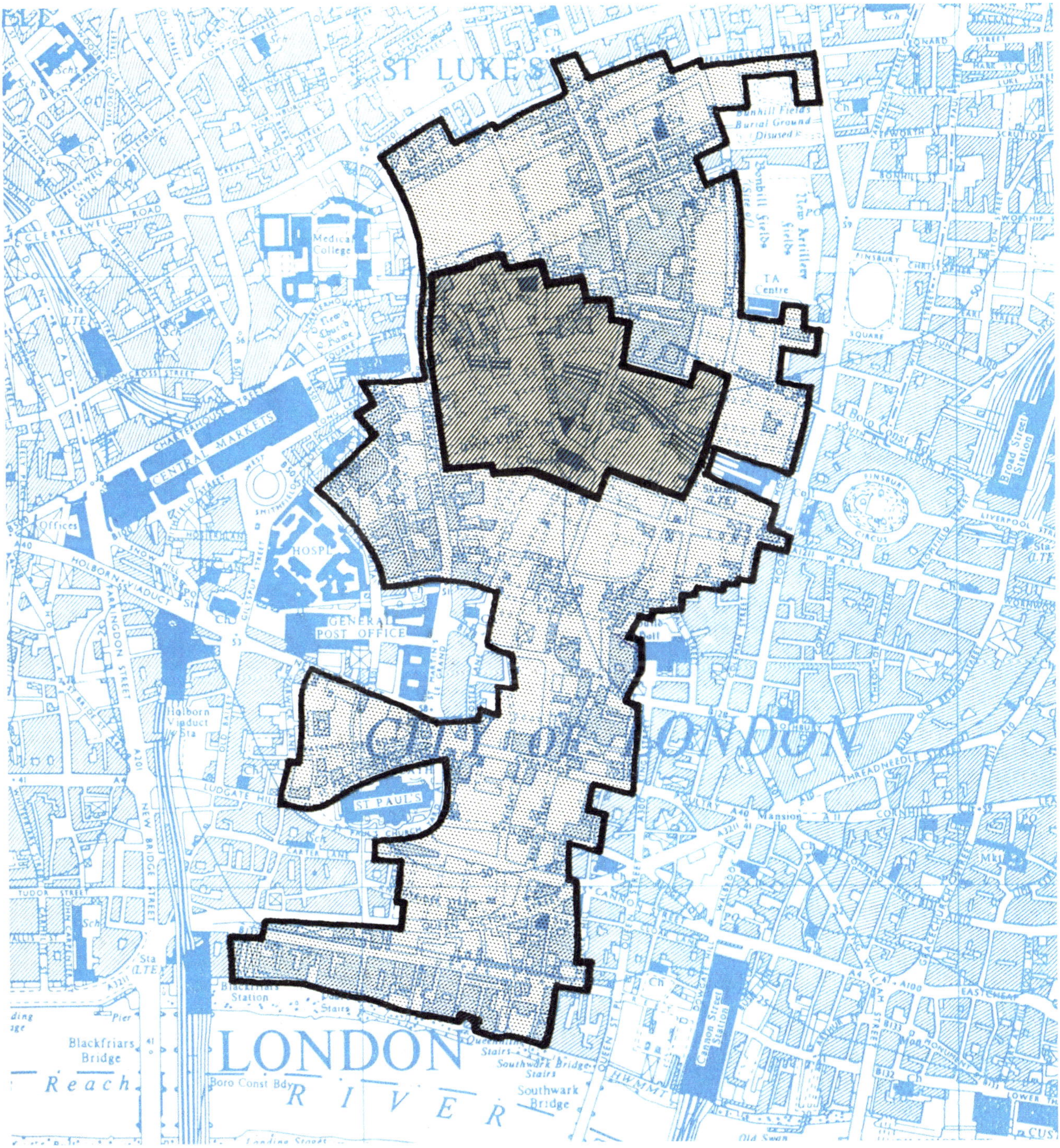

In terms of scale and policy, the Barbican reflects the state's desire to empower both local authorities and the market to undertake the investment in housing, or more precisely, to address housing as an investment. This is identified as a key process of the *urban governance* rising in post-war Western Europe, which involved a downscaling of the state and an upscaling of welfare projects —like housing— as a way to promote urban and regional growth.[16] Neoliberal critic Neil Brenner argues that each configuration of urban governance since the early 1960s has been crystallized in a historically specific, state-led, "scale-making project."[17] The Barbican pioneered this process in the 1950s, initiating an era when urban policies were assigned to local governments.[18] These policies targeted underdeveloped areas and peripheral zones, like the Barbican site, that would constitute London's new metropolitan area. Stripped of any pretense surrounding the issue of financial viability, the main political question behind the policies tested at the Barbican was how the redevelopment could attract market interest to compensate for the estate's long-term expenditures. This question was translated into regulatory frameworks for urban planning and housing intended to raise the place-bound reputation and market value of the City as a residential area. However, this subdivision of regulatory frameworks did not always succeed in making them work harmoniously with each other. In 1954 opposition to the promotion of a housing scheme for the Barbican still persisted and it was finally transferred from the Improvements and Town Planning Committee to the Public Health Committee.[19] The latter advocated for a higher standard of housing for more residents, opposing the sub-standard homes that millions had been living in throughout the country. In order to isolate the Planning Committee, the Barbican Committee was founded to oversee the development, a desicion that marked the total separation between planning and housing, each under different administrations. This separation caused many problems in the completion of the Barbican and became a key strategy of neoliberal piecemeal development in the future.

Unlike other local authorities, the Corporation decided to validate the aspirations of an emerging young generation in "a self-consciously elitist pursuit of quality,"[20]

16 Neil Brenner, "Urban Governance and the Production of New State Spaces in Western Europe, 1960-2000," *Review of International Political Economy* 11, no. 3 (August 2004): 457.

17 Ibid., 458.

18 Ioanna Piniara, "Housing policy as a form of urban governance: The Barbican Estate and the enclosure of the urban commons," in *Housing as Commons: Housing Alternatives as Response to the Current Urban Crisis*, eds. Stavros Stavrides and Penny Travlou (London: Bloomsbury Academic, 2022), 279–94.

19 David Heathcote, *Barbican: Penthouse over the City*, (Chichester: Wiley-Blackwell Publishing, 2004), 67–8.

20 Ibid., 34.

promoting urban living as a means of escaping the gloominess of the economy and the City. **(Fig. 4,5)** Thus, the new Barbican Committee commissioned Chamberlin, Powell & Bon (CPB), architects of the nearby Golden Lane estate, for the New Barbican residential development. CPB's material for the Committee's planning permit application and promotion was quite sophisticated in its portrayal of a vision of urban and social upgrade. Since the Corporation did not have the financial means of realizing the scheme itself, the idea of a high-density elite quarter that would be more likely to guarantee financial returns became the key objective of the Barbican's development. CPB were faced with the challenge of suggesting ways in which the development would ensure "continuing demand" among wealthy tenants, "have some characteristics that are outstanding and unique," "reflect the prestige of the City" and also achieve "a definite formality in the layout."[21] These characteristics marked the Barbican as a council estate for the "more than just moderately well-off"[22] from the outset.

At the same time, the architects tried to combine policy requirements, historical referencing and personal taste into the formulation of their own theoretical and design discourse. The prototype for the Barbican as a social condenser was addressed through the City of London Plan's idea for, *a new inner-city suburb*. In order to reincarnate a suburban atmosphere in the city, the strategy of reducing ground density was reinterpreted in a grand scale through a combination of courts and terraces, creating intimate spaces on the ground and high-rise structures above. Another quality of suburban life that was to be reconfigured in the new urban model suggested by the Ministry of Housing and Local Government prioritized "the quiet sense of seclusion which should be characteristic of a residential neighbourhood."[23] Such ideas that would affirm that, "cities were worth living in," informed CPB's 1958 theoretical project, the "Living Suburb," developed further for the Society for Promotion of Urban Renewal.[24] In the Barbican brief, the urban aspects of this model were articulated in planning requirements as "respect for the historical associations, traditions and monuments of the City" and "buildings in a form worthy of the

21 Chamberlin Powell & Bon Architects, *Barbican Redevelopment*, 2.

22 Banham, "Walled City," 222.

23 Chamberlin Powell & Bon Architects, *Barbican Redevelopment*, 4.

24 On Lionel Brett's statement (BrL/4/1, RIBA Archives) and CPB's intimate involvement with the SPUR's policy making and planning, see John R. Gold, "Towards Renewal," in *The Practice of Modernism: Modern Architects and Urban Transformation, 1954-1972* (London: Routledge, 2007), 77–104.

4
Interior view of the complex showing surviving fragments of the ancient Roman wall and a later 13th-century bastion running parallel to a canal of the central lake

5
View of the Frobisher crescent block and Cromwell Tower

finest City monuments in contemporary material and in the service of contemporary necessities." Suburban aspects were articulated in the requirements for "gardens and open spaces" and "a sense of community." [25]

The formal take on the Barbican layout was described by Chamberlin as, "a landscaped environment with community facilities" that would "turn this desert [the Barbican site] into a garden."[26] The core design concept was the provision of housing in dense blocks and towers structured within a landscape that would incorporate a system of courts and water elements, the surviving twelfth-century St. Giles church[27] as well as modern community facilities. **(Figs. 6.1- 6.2)** A programmatic study reveals that the Barbican scheme aspired to provide far more amenities than typical council housing. It was an 'all-inclusive' community, with neighborhood services (schools, cafeterias, restaurants, car parks), cultural facilities (arts center, concert hall, cinema) and recreation facilities with overtones of exoticism (from the central two-acre water garden with fountains to the glass conservatory with rare tropical plants). On the other hand, the three towers would dramatize the otherwise horizontal treatment of the complex and, by their outstanding form and relationship to each other, would give an identity to the neighborhood legible from a distance.[28] The concept that was carried forward to the final 1959 residential plan was an idea of "good-class" development, a cross between London's high-end inner suburbs and its modern 'loft' apartments —a balance between Englishness and International Style.

The references inspired ideas for the configuration of enclosures with focal points of interest and navigation creating a theatrical experience. Instead of a central 'stage' with a singular character, the composition employed an interplay of sceneries and themes "which people may walk without feeling that they are treading the same path too often; this deliberate intention of the design is epitomised in the evergreen labyrinth."[29] The architects were also fascinated by mechanisms of successful isolation from the surroundings and lavish landscaping with the exclusive privilege of the residents to be granted access into certain areas of the complex

25 "New Barbican," *The Architects' Journal* (14 October 1954): 458–9.

26 *The Times*, 53541, May 26, 1956, 4. See also, *Barbican Development: Report to the Court of Common Council of the Corporation of the City of London on residential development within the Barbican Area* by Chamberlin Powell & Bon, May 31, 1956, https://www.barbicanliving.co.uk/1956-scheme.

27 St Giles of Cripplegate is one of the few medieval churches in the City of London that survived the Great Fire of 1666 and the 1945 bombardment. See Christopher Hibbert, Ben Weinreb, John Keay and Julia Keay, *The London Encyclopaedia*, third edition (London: Pan Macmillan, 2010).

28 Cromwell Tower, completed in 1973, Lauderdale Tower, completed in 1974, and Shakespeare Tower, completed in 1976, all at 123 meters (404 ft), remained London's tallest residential structures until the turn of the twenty-first century.

29 Chamberlin Powell & Bon, *Barbican Development*.

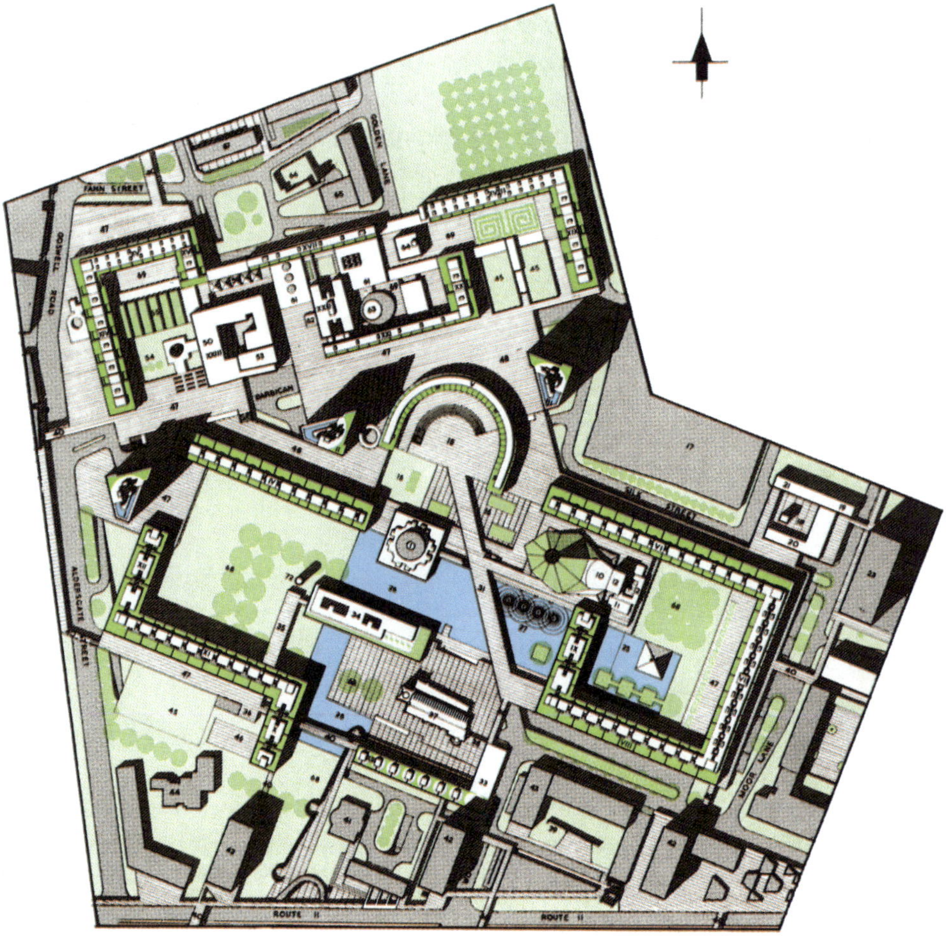

6.1
1959 General layout

Chamberlin Powell & Bon Architects, Barbican Redevelopment: Report to the Court of Common Council of the Corporation of the City of London on Residential Redevelopment within the Barbican Area (Bolton and London: Tillotsons Bolton Ltd, 1959)

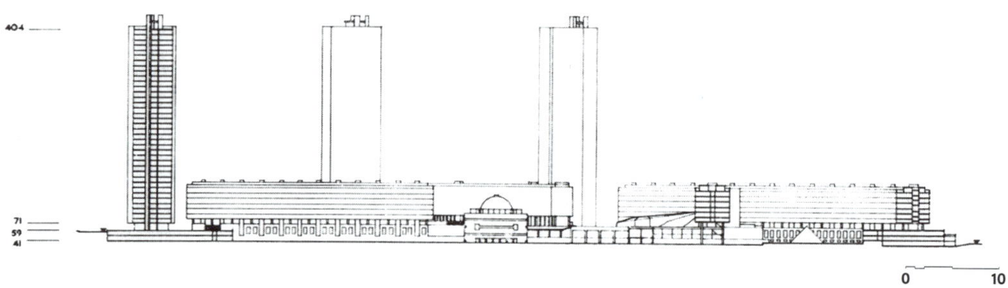

6.2
Longitudinal section

where their daily lives could, "unwind in private."[30] The final composition of the Barbican scheme abided by the LCC's requirement that it be included in the urban plan of elevated walkways separating pedestrian and automotive traffic.[31] The requirement of the podium, and subsequent need to elevate some of the housing blocks six meters above street level, led to a monumental version of the pilotis, further dramatized by the use of water below.

CPB tried to reference both historical and contemporary types of international housing culture, and of their preferred travel destinations, into a new luxurious residential architectural vocabulary. They all belonged to a generation of practicing architects in Britain that was still under the spell of Corbusian modernism but also retained a commitment to the Arts and Crafts movement and garden-city planning. Their style matured at the Barbican housing project as an application of a sculpturally expressive method to the contemporary canon of modernism, one which introduced a symbolic language of successful marketing. On the one hand, it employed suggestive forms to symbolize status. On the other, it created dramatic effects out of the mundane to trigger private market interest.

Thus, the final 1959 Barbican plan consisted of a collection of residential typologies: three 43-to-44-story tower blocks, 13 8-storey terrace blocks, a row of townhouses (a type of terraced housing with multiple floors), a cluster of 14 "mews" (terraces of small two-story houses) and a crescent block. The Barbican towers were monoolithic triangular forms with an imposing massing of pre-cast concrete paneling that stressed the medieval character of 'permanence' desired for the new "City Monument." The material treatment of exposed concrete extended to the terrace blocks, which were architecturally inspired by Le Corbusier's vision of a "vertical garden city" constituting, "the perfect receptacle for the family," realized in the Unite d'Habitation in Berlin the previous year.[32] Further adopting Corbusian references, a special crowning of white barrel vaults was devised to create a contrast with the underlying regularity. At the Barbican terrace blocks, this feature signaled

30 Interview with Barbican resident, Max Fraser, in Anton Rodriguez, *Residents: Inside the Iconic Barbican Estate*, (London: Barbican Centre, 2016), Foreword.

31 The City of London Pedway Scheme was devised as part of the post-war reconstruction plans to regulate traffic in London using elevated walkways. In 1947, architect Charles Holden and planner William Holford developed a proposal that envisaged a network of first-floor walkways that would connect buildings across the City. It was put into effect mainly during the 1950s, as the City of London Corporation had incorporated the scheme into its development plan, but it was dropped by the mid-1960s as part of a holistic approach to the City. See Oliver Wainwright, "Walkways in the sky: the return of London's forgotten pedways," *The Guardian*, October 2, 2018, https://www.theguardian.com/cities/2018/oct/02/walkways-in-the-sky-the-return-of-londons-forgotten-pedways. See also *The Pedway: Elevating London*, directed by Chris Bevan Lee in 2013, video, https://vimeo.com/80787092.

32 Peter Blake, *Le Corbusier: Architecture and Form* (London: Penguin Books, 1964), 124.

a geometric interpretation of the roofline of a two-and-a-half story penthouse type. The synthetic language of white vaulted roof tops was employed also at the Frobisher crescent block, a historical urban form, that had been assigned an imperial character in town-planning by the nineteenth-century architect John Nash. Metaphors for exceptionality had to be devised in the case of the townhouses as well, compensating for their rather disadvantageous location below the podium. Creating a picturesque surrounding landscape and framing spectacular views from the interior of these houses became a priority which in turn gave birth to another iconic feature of the Barbican's architecture: the large windows with a reversed arch in the bottom, designed as a reflection of the barrel vaults at the top. However, the ultimate suburban dream was reconfigured in the mews: the small terraced houses with individual parking spaces and separate access from a private garden at the west side for Barbican residents only. The dream of seclusion was realized through their placement at the level below the podium which made them almost invisible from the western, street-level entrance to the complex.

The estate's overall isolation from its surroundings was the culmination of the architects' conception of exclusivity which the synthesis exuded by turning its back to the City. The etymological root of the Barbican as a fortified outpost or defensive tower signified a safe haven where inhabitants could satisfy all their needs. Its inward-looking layout resembled the self-referential character of a palace or a mansion, a gesture which reintroduced the urban type of the *precinct,* where everything was to be found within its boundary or close at hand. This implied from the outset a civic community with an intended autonomy, both social and spatial, settting it apart from the typical concept of council housing. While open communal spaces as a part or extension of the public realm had been central to the design of council housing complexes, at the Barbican, extraordinary provisions were wrapped up in an envelope that disrupted a visual continuity and seamless connection with the City. The precinct signaled a new urban *enclosure,* where the main theme of suburban luxury as privacy and personal character was reconfigured as an extrapolation of interiors from the domestic to the urban scale within the boundaries of the Barbican's medieval wall. Architectural idiosyncrasies, such as unintuitive thresholds and hidden entrances, discouraged passers-by from wandering in. The contradiction between the exterior impenetrable impression and the interior welcoming atmosphere, enhanced the idea of an exclusive experience that was supposed to be lacking from traditional council housing. The view from most of the flats, overlooking aspects of this internal world, almost obliterated any sense of the City while being in its heart. On the contrary, they were meant to invoke the naturalness and serenity of living in the countryside. Effort was invested in the transformation of the urban experience through the transition from the congestion, air pollution and industrial grimness of London to a beautiful, spacious, quiet piece of urban land. Domestic privacy was inscribed in this experiential framework as a quality of the modern, "living suburb," that should be as much connected to the City, as secluded and exclusive. **(Figs. 7,8)**

For Pevsner, the Barbican was the epitome of "townscape."[33] His theory of the townscape was an idiosyncratic attempt to domesticate European modernism by assimilating it with *the picturesque* as the essence of English culture.[34] Pevsner saw it as an attack on the uniform, inhuman character of doctrinaire modernism and as a refuge "in autochthonous urban forms, building heritage and the countryside."[35] He considered the Barbican as an exercise, where history was not a repository of forms and ideals but, instead, the practice of imagination in a surprising conjunction of old and new forms that creates interesting yet intimate environments. Banham, on the other hand, criticized the Barbican's, "townscape of large scale rhetoric and heroic architectural forms," as having, "the swagger, gravitas and indifference to small scale effects of Imperial Rome."[36] Considering the Barbican site from today's standpoint, Stephen Gardiner stated that, "such a position of importance, in the middle of the capital, requires a landmark of distinction that has the weight of *permanence* and *security*."[37] But the idea that the inner city could be a desirable place to live was, at the time the Barbican was conceived, completely undermined,

33 Mathew Aitchison ed., *Nikolaus Pevsner: On Visual Planning and the Picturesque*, (Santa Monica: Getty Research Institute, 2010). See also John Macarthur, "Townscape, anti-scrape and surrealism: Paul Nash and John Piper in The Architectural Review," *The Journal of Architecture* 14, no. 3 (2009): 387–406.

34 Nikolaus Pevsner, "Price on Picturesque Planning," *The Architectural Review*, 95, (1944): 47–50.

35 Aitchison, *Nikolaus Pevsner*, 406.

36 Banham, "Walled City," 222. See also Reyner Banham, "Revenge of the Picturesque: English Architectural Polemics, 1945-1965," in John Summerson, *Concerning Architecture: Essays on Architectural Writers and Writing Presented to Nikolaus Pevsner*, (London: Penguin Books, 1968), 265–73.

37 (Emphasis added). Stephen Gardiner, "A Landmark of Distinction," *Observer* 9924, 1981, 32.

7
Exterior view of the Barbican

8
Interior view of the Barbican showing the monumental staircase connecting the podium to the lakeside entrance to the recreation and arts complex

while the "center of the capital" lay in the west rather than the east end of the City. The ambition behind the Barbican's objectives followed the reverse course of strategic thinking; "a landmark of distinction" could play a definite part in establishing a character that would raise the status and value of the area into "a position of importance."[38] This definition of townscape would create a new *experience* of urban pleasure for Londoners and a living environment for the most privileged.

At the Barbican, more than any of their projects, CPB acted as proponents for the reversal of (sub)urban sprawl, reinstating both the idea of domestic privacy and view of urbanity as a city center worth living in. However, this cordial invite was not addressed to the typical council housing tenant in any stage of the urban reconstruction process. The 'recentralization' rhetoric, developed by architects and urban planners of the time and picked up by the Barbican Committee, obscures the brutal class politics involved in the urban renewal of the City.[39] Sociologist Ruth Glass coined the term, *gentrification,* in 1964 to describe the nature of the transformation of the city's social character through the demographic replacement of many of the working class quarters of London by the middle classes.[40] The phenomenon witnessed the upgrade of modest mews, cottages and old Victorian houses into, "elegant, expensive residences," becoming accessible to only "the financially fittest, who can still afford to live and work there."[41] The idea that the Barbican was a 'ghetto' of high culture, of a 'private' character assigned to the public experience of the development, could be seen as the first such instance. Although there was no pre-existing community to be displaced, the high demand demonstrated by the waiting list for the 2,100 Barbican units in 1968[42] led to the cancellation of plans for small subsidized flats in the North Barbican[43] leaving all dwellings to be leased at market rates. The idea of, "caretakers and cleaners rub[bing] shoulders with clerks and clergymen,"[44] in what was seen as a model of social integration, faded away. This kind of welfare did not attempt to cater to basic needs, rather it constructed the domestic subjectivity and the image of urban society it aspired to serve.

38 Ibid.

39 CIAM 8, themed "The Heart of the City," was concerned about "unplanned decentralization" and called for planned "recentralization" that would save "the core" of the cities in their process of renewal. CIAM 8, Hoddesdon, "Summary of Needs at the Core," in *Architecture Culture 1943-1968: A Documentary Anthology*, ed. Joan Ockman (New York: Rizzoli International Publications, 1993), 135–136.

40 "Once this process of 'gentrification' starts in a district, it goes on until all or most of the original working-class occupiers are displaced, and the whole social character of the district is changed." Glass, by pointing out a new form of social distinction that was fracturing society, described a process of spatialization of class struggle. By using this characterization, she subverted the image of the British upper-class 'gentry.' Ruth Glass, "Introduction," in *London: Aspects of Change*, (London: MacGibbon & Kee Ltd, 1964).

41 Ibid., 17.

42 "London: Living in the City," *Architects' Journal* 148, no. 40 (October 1968): 704.

43 The subsidized flats of the North Barbican were aimed at poorer young people at lower rents reflecting their size and remoteness. "Bed-sits" was the snob real estate jargon for these flats at the time.

44 Anton Rodriguez, *Residents: Inside the Iconic Barbican Estate*, (London: Barbican Centre, 2016), 6.

The rhetoric of the Barbican project marked the beginning of a new policy of *embourgoisement* of the City. The challenge was never to be just a housing estate, but a community of those who had benefited from the 1950s affluence. Access to this kind of urban privacy became a matter of entitlement to those who had 'earned' it. The design of the estate set the stage for a new international lifestyle, combining elements of Baroque formality, Mediterranean leitmotifs, penthouse Americanism and Corbusian avant-gardism. However incongruous, this combination underlined the intention to build a narrative around the rather technical term, 'reconstruction.' This narrative expressed the fetish of a sociality that takes over and reinvents the center and, at the same time, the idea of differentiation that removes the stigma of standardized housing and supports the claim for a better life. Thus, it encapsulated in the most refined way, the subjection of the welfare state housing project in the service of the upper-middle classes. Sociologist Andrew Webster described the social criteria for the prospective Barbican tenant as asking oneself whether one fits in the following categories; "a merchant banker who frequently plays host to international visitors," or, "an intellectual couple with a musically-trained daughter who returns home often when not on tour."[45] If one affords to admit to one or the other, then the architects of the Barbican had them in mind for one of their apartments.

The consistent attempt to demonstrate the theme of variation as luxury was further elaborated in the integration of over 100 different dwelling types and individualized services. Dramatization rather than functionality of living space, was the main requirement at the Barbican. These dwellings should passively flatter their prospective owners through a combination of architectural signifiers of wealth and Modernist gestures such as open-plan living spaces and customized design for the service areas. Each of the different types of dwellings was meant to signify luxury and modernity in an exclusive manner. It was, however, in the main —long— terrace blocks and towers that the architects chose to illustrate their clearest statement of living at the Barbican; the universal provision of large living areas with various compositions, views and ambiences, renouncing standardized living. The tower

45 Andrew Webster, "Barbican goes back to the future," *BBC News*, February, 15, 2002, http://news.bbc.co.uk/2/hi/entertainment/1822863.stm.

flats offered the most dramatic spaces with their irregularly shaped living areas and the continuous, latticed balconies running the full-length of the flat's perimeter. **(Fig. 9)** The top units literally set a new high in the city along with new hierarchies. The largest bedroom and the living room occupied the dramatically pointed corners of the flat with breath-taking views of the city, thus were promoted as places of extraction of symbolic capital. Services, both internal —bathrooms— and external —lifts— were individualized to the extreme. Even kitchens, which were reduced to dark functional corridors, were not communal. If tower flats symbolized the idea of living above all others at the top of the City, the penthouses attracted the attention in the crowning of the medium-rise blocks. They provided a leitmotif for the terraces, marking them as a locus of exoticism and creating a unique view looking down from the towers. Emblematic of the avant-garde and luxurious designs, both the tower flats and vaulted penthouses of the terrace blocks instigated class differences, each creating vectors toward the top.

The Barbican is perhaps the pinnacle of a project for the return to capitalism from the command economy. It grew out of a moment of political theory that ever-increasing economic growth would provide the basis for uninterrupted social progress. Therefore, architecture and planning should channel growth towards a vision of a better society. This ethos was embedded in a new breed of large-scale development, initiated by the Barbican, which ultimately succumbed to an all-encompassing aspiration as "a machine for living": it was equally committed to pedestrianization as to the generous provision for car-ownership, to large open spaces as to high-density structures, to cosmopolitanism as to the reconfiguration of traditional living. CPB were faced with the design of something beyond their experience; the task to give form to a housing development through a process of, "re-imagining and recreating urban space primarily for the investor, the developer, the business person or cash-laden tourist."[46] Critics rightly contrasted the wealthy exclusivity of the estate with the residential deprivation surrounding it and the inward-looking nature of what was supposed to be an urban scheme. Designed to shield its residents

46 Friend of Zanetti, "Constructing Neoliberal Glasgow: The Privatisation of Space," *Variant* 25 (Spring 2006): 19.

9
Tower flats: Layout and floor plans

1 Bedroom
2 Wardrobe
3 Bathroom
4 Shower
5 W.C.
6 Kitchen
7 Dining and living room
8 Study

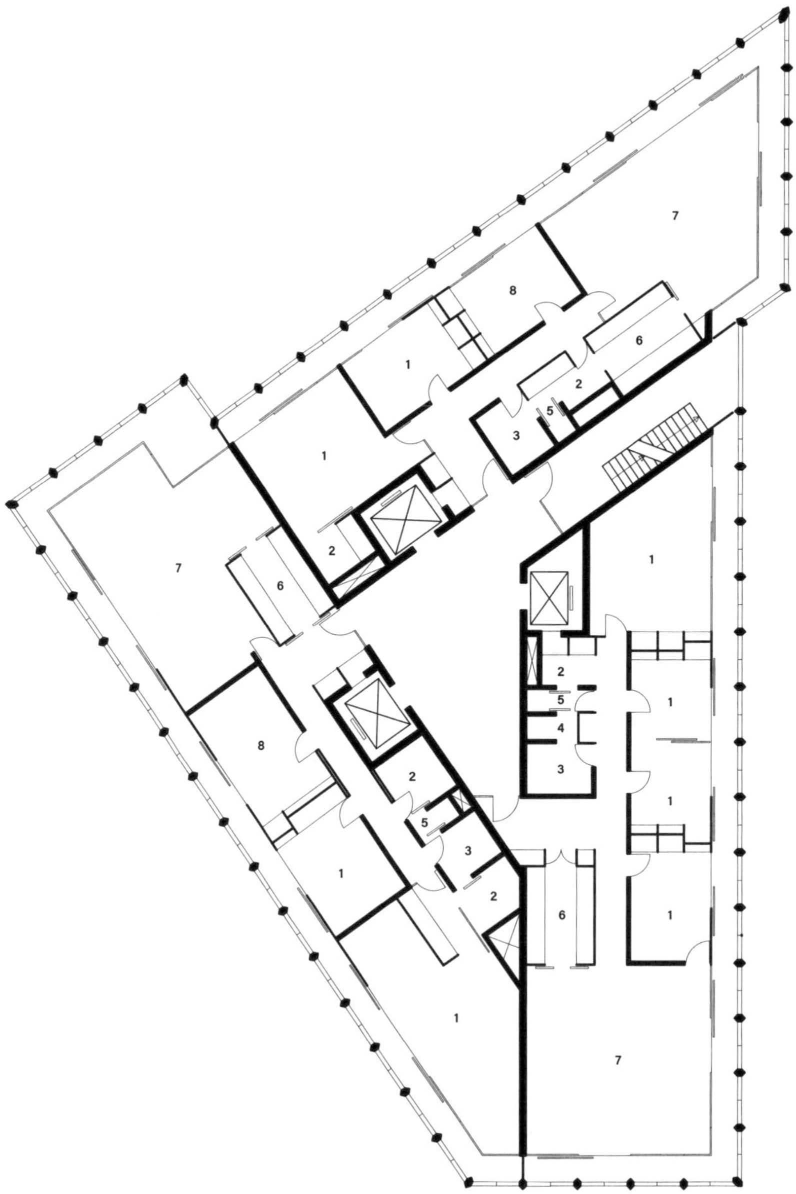

from the grimness of the outside world, this holistic experiment in urban housing was both from within the city and apart from it. These residents could now enjoy "the kind of privacy and mono-cultural, one-class community that has previously been available only in purpose-built suburbs; but without the pains and frustrations of long-distance commuting."[47]

The Barbican's ambition was to capture all aspects of its possible clientele by offering this extreme diversification of dwelling types. The whole puzzle of variations, from the bed-sit to the six-bed-house and from the studio flat to the penthouse, offered the impression of a 'custom-made' home that the standard housing was lacking. What was undoubtedly an innovation at the time, is today seamlessly entwined in the neoliberal mentality; a condition where the typological gradience simultaneously flaunts and sooths the class cleavage so that no one drops out of the process. The internal contradiction of neoliberalism, however, lies in that recanting, "the power of the planner over our private lives,"[48] it, nevertheless, promotes a highly designed palette of options in the provision of housing. As much as the Barbican flat catalogue was meant to nominally allow inclusivity and differentiation, it illustrated a highly suggestive condition of lifestyle, where residents were only allowed to decide for the interior arrangements in their flats (and this lasted only until the estate became listed in 2001). Not only did this architecture accept the reproduction of a rigid model of a stratified society, but also the language of emphatic and historically signifying forms created a kind of pastiche as a way to transcend the housing project. The use of contrast, allegory and metaphor in the design exuded the intention to incarnate the urban vision of Wilkins and his group and to convince the Corporation to support it; the Barbican plan was more a coherent exercise in brainstorming than an implementation design —it was more *a story* than a plan. Thus, it introduced an approach to housing development that became the norm in the neoliberal years; the design proposition of a narrative of living to attract market interest as the indicator for subsequent support by planning authorities.

47 Banham, "Walled City," 222.
48 Hayek, *The Road to Serfdom*, 63.

Deeming the success of the Barbican based on its capacity, "for generating future growth and for waging a competitive struggle to attract investment capital," internalizes the neoliberal fascination with "mega-projects" and "place-marketing."[49] At the Barbican, competition as a planning principle was invested in a new architectural glossary to address urban domestic privacy as a luxury and a reward or, as neoliberal critic Brenner puts it, a "projected space." According to his analysis, "the production of new spaces [...] combines elements of the old geographical order with aspects of the 'projected spaces' sought by the advocates of neoliberal and/or progressive modernization."[50] This combination also introduces a pattern of social reproduction that is meant to ensure market demand and, thus, capital accumulation. The Barbican development grew out of the framework of council housing as a safety net of standard housing and transformed it into housing as 'projected space' that everyone should be constantly chasing after. This asserts Polanyi's neoliberal insight, that a market economy can only operate within a market society.

The Barbican simultaneously anticipated and tested tropes of place-making and social restructuring that became the role model for housing development in neoliberal Europe. The year 1980 was a turning point for the fate of the Barbican as it is being discussed here marked by the election of Thatcher's conservative government. While the development was near completion and almost half of the population relied on council housing for affordable accommodation, the Barbican flats began to be sold on the market or to the tenants at a discount following the, Right-to-Buy, legislation in 1981.[51] What neoliberalism as a discourse adds to contemporary capitalism is not the ownership culture, which is not new, but rather a different conceptualization of social equality. According to the political philosopher Balibar, the idea of class struggle is in question as the displacement of antagonism into all scales of everyday life and social relations renders the protection from precariousness impossible from the class point of view.[52] The Thatcherite policy infused council housing with the development of new class divisions, such as the one between owners and tenants or ground floor and penthouse tenants. Thus, the new domestic subjectivity would be tied to preconceived ideas of domestic privacy offered as a commodity. The Right-to-Buy scheme became the self-fulfilling prophecy for providing the ideal of privacy for future owners that the Barbican had designed and promoted.

49 Neil Brenner and Nik Theodore, *Spaces of Neoliberalism: Urban restructuring in North America and Western Europe* (Oxford: Blackwell Publishing, 2002), 199.

50 Neil Brenner, "Urban Governance and the Production of New State Spaces," 462.

51 The Right-to-Buy scheme was a Thatcherite policy giving tenants of councils and some housing associations the right to buy, at a large discount, the council house they lived in. Critics claim that the policy fueled a housing shortage for people of low income, initiated a housing price bubble and ultimately led to what had already been recognised by Ruth Glass as the displacement and gentrification of local communities. Jennifer Clarke, *The Barbican: Sitting on History* (London: City of London Corporation, Records Office, 1990), 68.

52 Étienne Balibar, "Towards a New Critique of Political Economy – Session 3," (lecture, The Birkbeck Institute for the Humanities London, March 6, 2017). For a critique of the tension between social equality and economic liberty in neoliberal democracy, see Étienne Balibar, *Equaliberty: Political Essays*, trans. James Ingram (Durham, NC: Duke University Press, 2014).

View from
Cromwell tower

The Inner City as a Place for Living: The IBA's Housing Policy and Marketing of Urban Identity

The International Building Exhibition (IBA) of 1987 was a long debated experiment to rethink Berlin using the inner city as both a preserved and a re-animated place for living ("Die Innenstadt als Wohnort"); a theme initially used in the urban planning of London and, ever since, had been applied in many other European cities as well. **(Fig. 1)** However, by that time, few European cities could have been characterized by comparable challenges: political and intellectual discontinuity as well as programmatic variation in urban development. In Berlin though, the impacts of World War II and the Berlin Wall, together with the city's subsequent failures in urban planning, remained tangible longer than elsewhere.[1] International calls to incorporate aspects of identity, collective memory and social welfare in the divided city's revival materialized in the IBA's federal planning decisions through policies which opposed the prevalent technocratic functionalism (reconstruction by demolition) of the 1950s and 60s.[2] This approach was conceived as an expression of optimism at a time of economic, spatial and cultural crisis; a time, "when a head wind threatens the continuation of economic abundance,"[3] and the destructive trends of urban renewal threaten the city as a form of reference. Therefore, the IBA was the final result of a decade long process from the 70s. This process was already responsible for instituting a new national housing policy, organizing a series of international competitions and, starting in 1979, for realizing selected projects, ultimately culminating in the final IBA exhibition in 1987. Politically, the exhibition promoted the city as a social condenser and mobilized social housing as a way to showcase the character of West Berlin as an alternative to the socialist architecture of East Berlin

The IBA's format of calling for ideas and solutions for the city was neither unprecedented nor unique. On the contrary, it continued the tradition of "Berlin's

1 Berlin suffered such damage that no city had experienced by then in a war. The loss of around 500,000 dwellings, the destruction or depreciation of all the important industrial and commercial infrastructure as well as the damage to numerous monuments produced more than 75 million cubic metres of debris. The size of the catastrophe marked, however, a unique possibility for the construction sector. Ewald Weitz and Jürgen Friedenberg, *Interbau Berlin 1957: Internationale Bauausstellung im Berliner Hansaviertel* [*Interbau Berlin 1957: International Building Exhibition in the Hansa Quarter in Berlin*] (Berlin : Internationale Werbe- und Anzeigen-Gesellschaft, 1957), 13–18. According to Peter Blake, the Interbaau exhibition inaugurated in 1957 in West Berlin and containing impressive buildings by Aalto, Markelius, Niemeyer, and Gropius was the "humble" forerunner of the ambitious IBA 1987. Peter Blake, "Berlin's IBA: A Critical Assessment," *Architectural Record* no. 8 (1993): 50–52.

2 Federal planning had started already in the early 1970s by commissioning architect Joseph Paul Kleihues with an analysis of the urban form, the famous "Berlin Atlas." The "new city" that had emerged from the reconstruction methods of the previous decades was considered in this framework as a destruction of "the historical city" of the nineteenth century. Joseph P. Kleihues, *Berlin-Atlas zu Stadtbild und Stadtraum - Versuchsgebiet Charlottenburg* (Berlin: Berlin Senate, 1973), 52. In this respect, Aldo Rossi's seminal work was a major theoretical reference for the IBA 1987 urban renewal approach and the post-Wall reconstruction of Berlin. See Aldo Rossi, *The Architecture of the City* (Cambridge, MA: The MIT Press, 1966). Ve influential have also been the following: Jane Jacob *The Life and Death of Great American Cities* (Ne York: Random House, 1961); Wolf J. Siedler, Elisabe Niggemeyer and Gina Angress, *Die Gemordete Sta* [*The Murdered City*] (Berlin: Herbig, 1967); and Fr Koetter and Colin Rowe, *Collage City* (Cambridge, M London: The MIT Press, 1978). On the cultural functic of memory as a reconstruction of the past based the mental images of the present, see Maurice Ha bwachs, *On Collective Memory* (Chicago, IL: The Ur versity of Chicago Press, 1992).

City map of the division between East and West Berlin and the IBA proposals in West Berlin, 1987

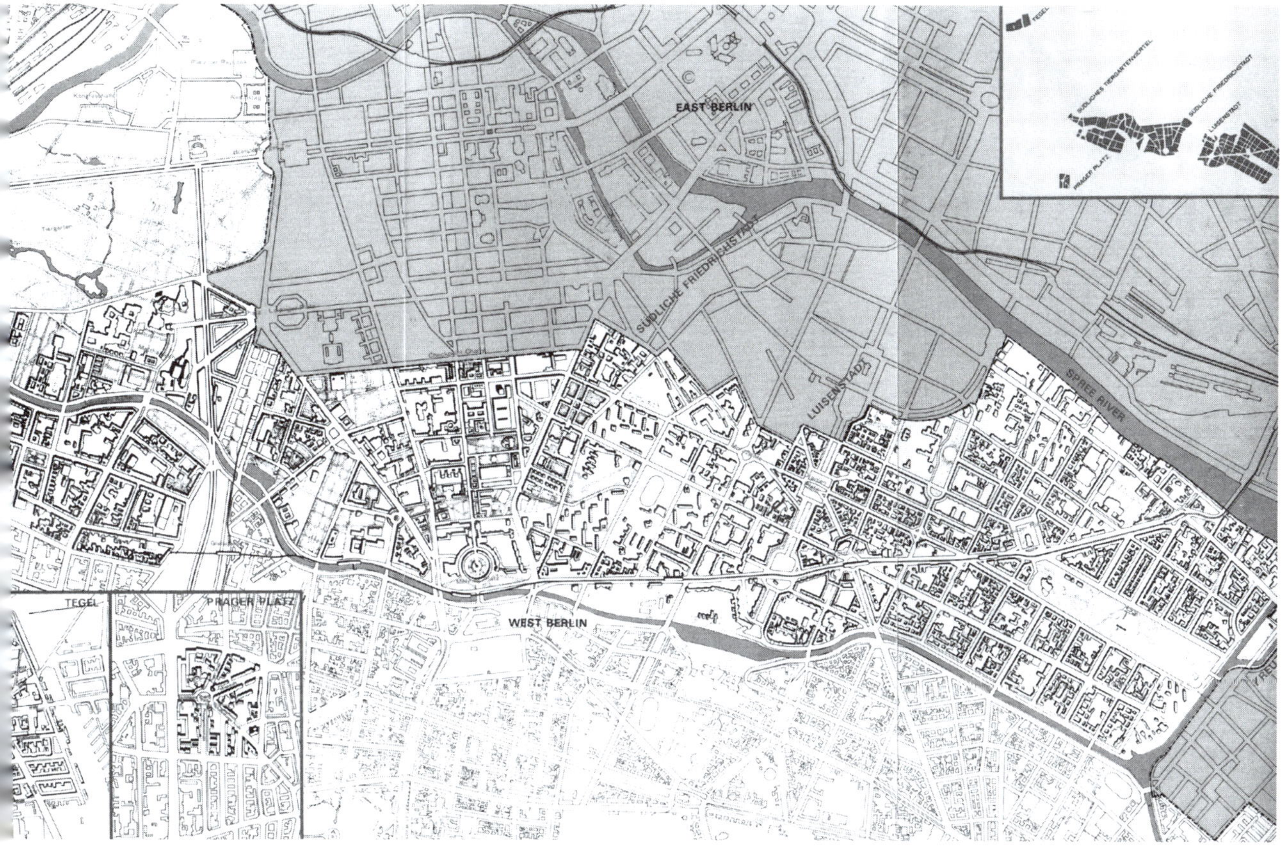

Wolfgang Braunfels, "Politics and Architecture: The International Building Exhibition and the Question of Berlin," in "Architecture in Progress: Internationalle Bauausstellung Berlin 1984," ed. Frank Russel, *Architectural Design and Academy Editions* (1983): 15–17.

varied panorama"[4] of pioneering ventures —exhibitions, competitions and publications— intended to determine, both programmatically and aesthetically, its architectural and urban development during the twentieth century. This genealogy can be traced back to the 1910 General Urban Development Exhibition ("Allgemeine Städtebauausstellung"), which was intended to attract public attention to the outcomes of the Greater Berlin Competition launched earlier the same year.[5] The proposals sought to provide both a new character and solutions to the city's housing shortage, as Berlin rapidly outgrew its nineteenth-century fabric, forming the capital of the newly established German Reich. In 1931, the German Building Exhibition ("Deutsche Bauausstellung") was organized to retrospectively showcase Berlin's architectural movements and exemplary housing developments from the 1920s. Together, these movements and projects signified the city's urban housing culture, involving the Social Democratic local government in the service of state-financed housing. The International Building Exhibition ("Interbau") in 1957 echoed the political unrest and ideological polarization found in East Berlin —the post-war capital of the German Democratic Republic. Within it a physical enclave had formed loyal to the political supremacy of the western allies (the Federal Republic of Germany): West Berlin. Indeed, the contrast between Interbau's reconstruction of West Berlin's Hansa-Quarter as a modernist residential area and the nationalist grandeur of the reconstructed Stalinallee (Karl-Marx-Allee) in East Berlin, highlights the ideological differences which led to Berlin's physical separation in 1961.[6] The IBA of 1987 attempted to correct this past via a radical yet rational strategy for the regeneration of, "the substance of the city," backed by considerable governmental subsidies.[7]

Berlin in the 1980s provided the motivations and circumstances for the IBA to rupture with its tradition and instead successfully establish different urban policy and planning approaches later identified as neoliberal. Two such tropes came to characterize the IBA in particular. First, the IBA introduced housing as a cultural, rather than an infrastructural, aspect in the construction of urban identity. The context around Berlin in the 1950s and 60s was hectic. The city was marked by post-war

4 Josef P. Kleihues, "Stations in the Architectural History of Berlin in the 20th Century: IBA", in Bauausstellung Berlin GmbH, *International Building Exhibition Berlin 1987*, Extra Edition (Tokyo: a+u Publishing Co.Ltd., May 1987), 222. See also Vittorio Magnago Lampugnani, "The Berlin Tradition of Architectural Exhibitions," in "Architecture in Progress," 10–14.

5 On the Competition and Exhibition of 1910 as the pinnacle of the new discipline of urbanism, see Katharina Borsi, "Drawing the region: Hermann Jansen's vision of Greater Berlin in 1910," *The Journal of Architecture* 20, no.1 (2015): 47–72.

6 The heavy, serious "architecture of oppression" was to be replaced by the light, bright, cheerful and serene "architecture of freedom", "totalitarian" historicism by "democratic" rationalism. Lampugnani, "The Berlin Tradition" in Russel, "Architecture in Progress," 13. See also Emily Pugh, *The Berlin Wall and the Urban Space and Experience of East and West Berlin, 1961-1989* (PhD Diss., City University of New York, 2008).

7 Lampugnani was a senior architect consultant in the development of the Building Exhibition. In his contracted survey of the history of Berlin exhibitions, he argues for the need for repeated reflection on the oppositions (innovation/tradition, change/conservation, exception/rule) with which the character of the city has been historically confronted. Within this discourse, radicality and rationality emerge also as an opposition against which Lampugnani's stance clearly prioritized a quest "to find some clear and rational answer to the political, technical, cultural and philosophical problems of the time." This reformist rather than radical agenda was particularly addressed in the contributions of a group of Neo-rationalist architects. See Lampugnani, "The Berlin Tradition" in Russel, "Architecture in Progress," 14.

depopulation, unemployment, post-traumatic stress, vacant and neglected plots and entire quarters, the construction of large tenement buildings as well as a growing social movement opposing demolition. Against this backdrop a radical reconsideration of urban planning and housing policy was undertaken in the mid-1970s.[8] It marked a departure from the grand modernist urban visions of the 1960s, whose strict separation of programs (housing and working, vehicular and pedestrian) was deemed as the main factor of fragmentation and de-humanization of cities. This evaluation led to the invention of the IBA's second trope. Its theme, "the inner city as a place for living," hoped to offer a wide spectrum of contemporary interpretations for the recuperation of "human urban design" and "urban character."[9] The question of a single character was particularly challenging, given the conflicts from the city's internal division. The IBA's choice to curate West Berlin as a pool for "models"[10] was itself subject to conflicts of orientation and aim, the result of a need to redevelop not only individual and regional identities, but also a common platform in anticipation of the time when the city would be re-united. This complexity led to the elaboration of a familiar operating process: the format of an architectural competition. The IBA directed the competition toward internationally renowned architects as a way to legitimize a diverse, yet superficial, reading of the city rather than towards local architects who they feared would be potentially too self-critical. These two aspects of the IBA are not considered to signal the rise of a new order, which this thesis posits occurred earlier, in Barbican's tentative introduction of a variety of urban living types as a new character for London. Rather, they are seen as a decisive step towards entrenching this order; the conscious intensification of the relationship between the image of housing and the marketing of an identity for the European city.

Thus, the aims and responsibilities of the IBA were split from the outset and assigned to two separate departments with different theories and approaches. The new building department ("Neubau"), led by Joseph Paul Kleihues, was concerned with the "Critical Reconstruction" ("kritische Rekonstruktion") of West Berlin's demonstration areas (Tegel Area, Prager Platz, Southern Tiergarten and Southern

The housing shortage and the subsequent protests had led to the illegal occupation of Kreuzberg at the end of the 1970s. Ulrich Kohlbrenner, "Umbruch in den siebziger Jahren – Grundlagen und Modelle zur bewahrenden Stadterneuerung [Disruption in the 1970s - Principles and Models for Sustainable Urban Renewal]", in *Stadterneuerung Berlin* (Berlin: Senatsverwaltung für Bau- und Wohnungswesen, 1990), 45–55. See also Carmen Hass-Klau, "Berlin: 'Soft' Urban Renewal in Kreuzberg," *Built Environment* 12, no. 3 (1986): 165–175.

Lore Ditzen, "A Warning About Pictures: A Companion to the International Building Exhibition, Berlin," in Bauausstellung Berlin GmbH, *International Building Exhibition*, 16–24.

10 Josef P. Kleihues and Wolf J. Siedler, "Modelle für eine Stadt," article series, *Berliner Morgenpost*, January 18, 1977, 1. See also Wallis Miller, "'IBA's Models for a City': Housing and the Image of Cold-War Berlin," *The Journal of Architectural Education* 46, no. 4 (1993): 202–18.

2
Map of the IBA demonstration areas for Critical Reconstruction (1-4) and Urban Renewal (5-6)

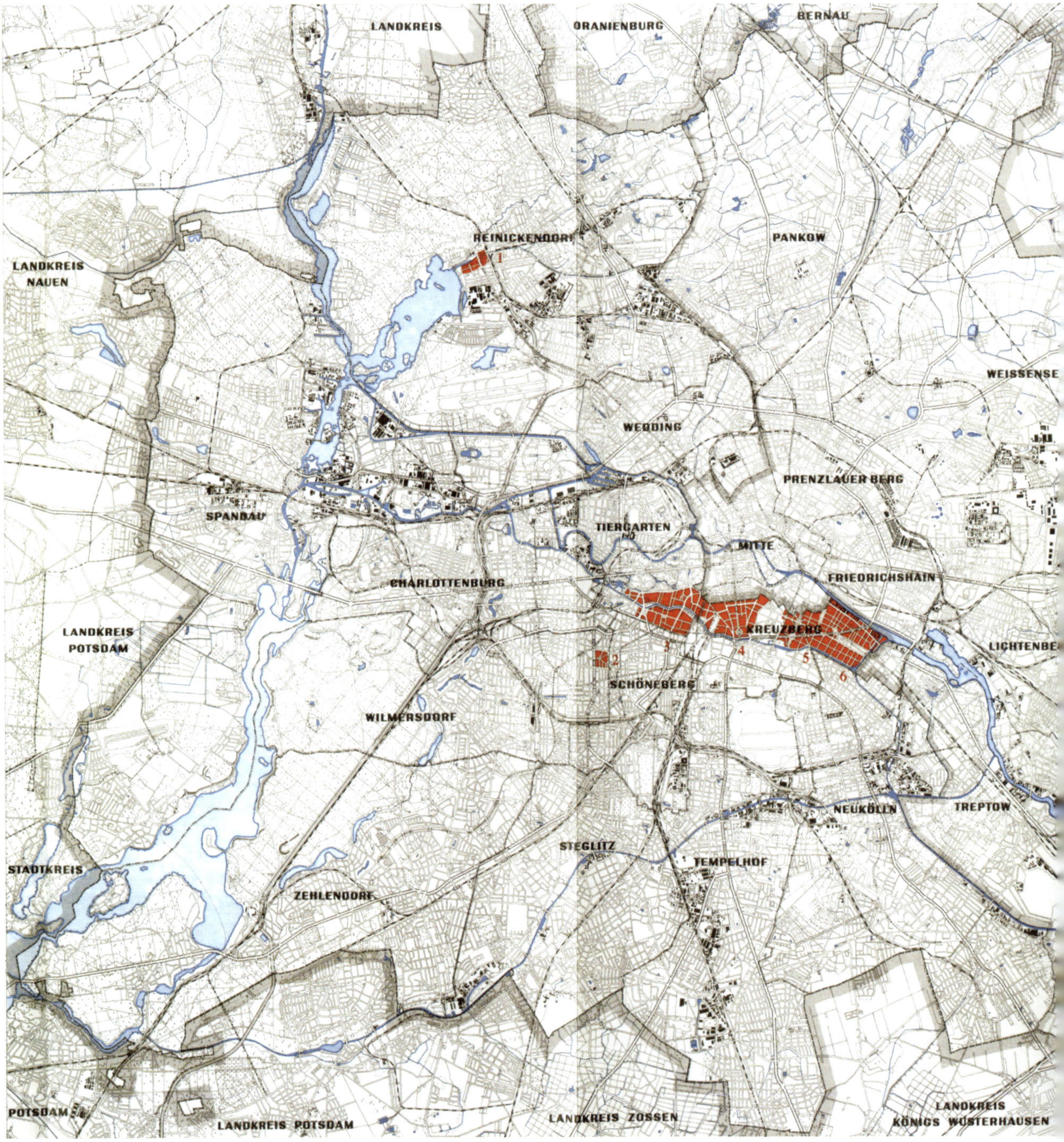

Friedrichstadt). **(Fig. 2)** This involved, on the one hand, realizing exemplary housing schemes by world-famous European and North American architects on derelict land left by the war. On the other, the re-contextualization of historical urban living typologies, cultural buildings and transportation networks in light of the city's newly marketed intellectual center. This new townscape was implemented with a spirit of "poetic rationalism"[11] to foster a dialogue between opposing forces. Questioning post-modernism as the misguided step forward from the disenchantment with modernity, it aimed at reviving an image of Berlin as a metropolis "whose appearance and versatility gives the feeling of the future whilst respecting the traces of history."[12] As a theoretical and political discourse, it sought a "collective consciousness" in urban living emerging from the perpetual struggle between oppositions: tradition and modernity, preservation and renewal, classicism and contemporaneity.

The second department of the IBA, the old building department ("Altbau") directed by Hardt-Waltherr Hämer, was concerned with the "Urban Renewal"("Stadterneuerung ") of areas in East Kreuzberg (Luisenstadt, Southern Kreuzberg). It was intended to increase the quality of housing and social amenities in areas that were deteriorating into urban slums by mainly refurbishing buildings that were deemed worthy of preservation. Despite primarily consisting of older and decaying buildings from the nineteenth and early twentieth centuries, the Urban Renewal initiative also included a number of new buildings. Interventions on such new buildings, however, focused on their integration into existing blocks so as to remodel the historic urban layout. The adjective "careful" ("behutsam") was added to the term "urban renewal" as a way to better describe the approach; it acknowledged the overlap between pragmatic forces in the development of this part of the city, implied the interaction of social, economic, ecological, political and architectural factors and prioritized the close collaboration with local residents.[13] "With the aim of harmonizing the overall and individual conditions" in coping with the "social issues of day-to-day life,"[14] Careful Urban Renewal became a prototype for coordination among authorities, administrative bodies, clients and interested parties, which, nevertheless, did not lack

Josef P. Kleihues, "Southern Tiergarten Quarter: Centre of Crisis, Solitary Modernist, Future as Forum," in Bauausstellung Berlin GmbH, *International Building Exhibition*, 35.

Josef P. Kleihues, "Prager Platz Area: Disarrayed Feathers, Aggressive Void, Historical Collage," in Bauausstellung Berlin GmbH, *International Building Exhibition*, 59–60.

Harald Bodenschatz and Cordelia Polinna, *Learning from IBA-die IBA 1987 in Berlin* (Berlin: Senatsverwaltung für Stadtentwicklung, 2010), 9–24.

Hardt-Waltherr Haemer, "Careful Urban Renewal: An Experiment and an Example," in Bauausstellung Berlin GmbH, *International Building Exhibition*, 243.

conflicts. Although this urban process proved more anthropocentric and socially conscious, in its site-specific interventions, it still did not provide a true alternative to the formalistic and historically-oriented approach of Critical Reconstruction.

The contradictions in approach between the two segments of the IBA were meant to be reconciled through their conscious and unified goal: to develop a reassuring discourse around privacy in inner-city living bound to historic urban forms. Despite taking on unique characteristics throughout the various districts, and their aesthetic experimentation, these forms were intended to act as unifying urban elements rather than disruptive infrastructural nodes (as in the 1960s). This realization shifts the familiar postmodern narrative, often linked to the IBA, away from the quest for a valid assessment of aesthetic forms. On the contrary, it points at the decoupling of aesthetic conventions from urban planning and regional specificity which define the institutional and cultural regime of the city. The intellectual orientation of the project, set by Kleihues and his peers, reveals a commitment to the historical European city and the use of architecture's disciplinary tools towards rationalism as more inviting than the provocative Anglo-Saxon post-modernism.[15] Moreover, Kleihues's belief, that "the outer appearance of architecture reveals its substance," resembles a Pythian oracle that can justify the discussion on the "right" decision for urban development and renewal in both cases.[16] However, if one of the three main political aims of the IBA was, "the experimentation with new forms of housing and city planning policies for Berlin which accommodate and test adaptations to changed socio-economic conditions,"[17] then the inability to separate rational building from the symbolic capital of the city reveals the "substance" of social housing. The latter became the "bed of Procrustes"[18] for the format of an international competition that asked outstanding international architects to design model individual solutions and came to be seen as the element of innovation in the urban fabric that was introduced by the IBA.

15 The selection of the architects for the realized projects confirms that key proponents of post-modernism in the United States such as Robert Venturi or Charles Jencks were not included or not even invited to participate. The trend can be described, in retrospect, as first-wave or continental post-modernism, but was not at the time a programmatic or stylistic intention.

16 Josef P. Kleihues, "Rudiments of History, Place of Contradictions, Critical Reconstruction," in Bauausstellung Berlin GmbH, *International Building Exhibition*, 147.

17 Bauausstellung Berlin GmbH, *The City Center as a Place to Live: Efforts in Careful Urban Renewal* (Berlin: Eigenverlag, 1984), 7.

18 Ditzen, "A Warning About Pictures," 24.

As an architectural event with such broad and prominent representation of the profession, the IBA gained unprecedented popularity and influence throughout European cities. As an urban initiative, it was inevitably confronted by the internal contradiction of neoliberalism: on one hand, the pluralism of models and, on the other, the need for coherence required to support the private as a dominant and, thus, instrumental narrative. It is telling that the structure of the agenda was based on three key aspects —The City as Program, the City as Exhibition and The City as Project. These aspects prioritize the comparison to "the development strategies and methods of different European cities with respect to their urban cores" and "a housing market analysis for Berlin which is to clarify the structural and spatial trends of housing requirements."[19] It is the framework that formulated the questions of urban development and renewal around image-making competition among cities for a place in the global market. It is also the framework that, by drawing wide-spread attention, popularized the trend of addressing the housing demand of a city in crisis through rebranding failing models in new packages rather than radically questioning them. This chapter interrogates the "critical" capacity of Critical Reconstruction to question the status quo and embrace experimentation as well as the promise of the "careful" Urban Renewal to make the city socially and economically livable. These questions attempt to understand the extent to which the IBA's social housing narrative retained the ethos of the socialist city within the rapidly changing palimpsest of Berlin. It is increasingly important to assess IBA's residential projects taking into account the historical configuration of urban form, the exchange value of housing and the specific objectives and strategies of the state's housing policy. Of these three factors, this analysis considers the latter to be the one orchestrating the whole and, thus, will be the main subject of investigation and critique.

The IBA Corporation ("Bauausstellung Berlin GmbH"), which belonged to the Berlin City Government, was commissioned by the Chamber of Deputies in 1979 to prepare the International Building Exhibition. The institution, created and financed by the city Senate of Berlin, dealt with the project first on the level of the city as pro-

19 Bauausstellung, Berlin GmbH, *The City Center as a Place to Live*, 12.

gram. In line with Berlin's institutional urban planning, the IBA organization relied on consulting contracts, competitions and advisory commissions with architects and planners. The Building Exhibition was seen as an open process initially planned for 1984 and finally inaugurated in 1987, when it had commissioned some 12,000 new and renovated apartments backed by governmental subsidies. Kleihues's programmatic proposal relied on West Berlin's varied context, which would host design proposals from internationally recognized architects as the objects of the exhibition. This panorama of architecture's latest developments would provide a "critical field" for the city to reflect on its identity and set the guidelines for development on city-owned sites. The land was leased by the city to private companies, investment societies or building cooperatives to develop the projects under the city's supervision.[20] At the same time, the urban strategy had to ensure a certain integrity of the designs by eliminating the impact of a potential refusal of privately-owned (or already built-upon) parcels to be conceded to the IBA scheme. Therefore, the procedural proposal reveals that a sense of identity had already been formed and was ready to be implemented. As a working method, the competition inverted the typical plot allocation process —where cities awarded sites to developers and later approved their financial and physical plans for housing. In this case, developers had to respond with financial proposals to the design-based recommendations of specific formal, social and economic criteria already defined by the city (design, cost estimates, and subsidy level) as part of a conscious urban vision.[21]

By principle, therefore, the IBA advocated a turn away from modernist urban development and claimed the revival of the value of historically dialectic and "culturalist" approaches to urbanism in the post-crisis (1973) western world. While, according to Kleihues, in the late 1970s and early 1980s the advance of global capitalism and an international modernist style jeopardized the cultural distinctiveness of capital cities,[22] Berlin re-introduced social housing as a concept of "urban culture" and the key to economic and social sustainability.[23] As such, the initiative was embedded within a political economy that was championed as being able to explore the capacity of the

20 Approximately two-thirds of the land zoned as housing and for which IBA commissioned design proposals were owned by the City of West Berlin. See Manfred Schonlau, "Die Berliner Wohnungsbauförderung," *Baumeister* (May 1987): 22.

21 Josef P. Kleihues, "Programmvorschlage fur eine internationale Bauausstellung zur Wiederbelebung des alten Berlin [Programmatic proposals for an International Building Exhibition for the Revival of the Old Berlin]," *Berliner Morgenpost*, January 18, 1977.

22 Kleihues argues that Modernism's grinding of fixed authoritative conventions with a convenient "Dialectic of the Enlightenment" is completely pretentious and that its confrontation with historicity was exhausted in its mere negation. See Nitsche, *Projektübersicht*, 7.

23 This capitalist idea of a cultural identity is framed within the field of urban sociology. Giddens illustrates how socialism, inspite or because of its contradictions, was exploited by capitalism in the framework of the welfare state, particularly as a form of political order to supposedly ameliorate class conflict and build a 'friendly' image of the cities. Anthony Giddens, *A Contemporary Critique of Historical Materialism*, Vol. I (Berkley: University of California Press, 1981). Mellor maintains that the themes of urban sociology have been the concerns of the welfare state in its effort to ensure a way of life, which has remained tied to the assumptions of liberalism. Therefore, urbanization should be analyzed in the framework of the political economy of regional development and local identity. J.R. Mellor, *Urban Sociology in an Urbanized Society* (London: Routledge & Kegan Paul, 1977). This theoretical framework, although not named as such, reflects the process of consolidation of the neoliberal strategy for the valorization of place identity.

relationship between history, memory, and the built environment in producing the *value* of the urban character.[24] The third political aim of the IBA —"the extension of the significance of Berlin as an international, scientific and cultural centre"[25]— was increasingly prioritized in order for Berlin to lead the Council of Europe's vision for reconstructing the identity of European cities.[26] The appointment of Kleihues as the director of the Critical Reconstruction department was essential for this goal. He was a leading figure of the so-called Berlin "rationalist school," which criticized post-war modernist urban planning and the destruction of historical urban structures as a depoliticized approach to the city. In his statements, Kleihues used diplomatic language regarding the search for an urban identity. He claimed that it was not a question of restoring the eighteenth- and nineteenth-century city but reconstructing the city, incorporating modern aspects of the urban layout, structure and morphology.[27] On the contrary, Hämer, the director of the "Careful Urban Renewal" group, was outspoken regarding "the main concern of preserving the existent building fabric developed in the nineteenth and early twentieth century."[28] However, once the aims were outlined into basic principles for the program, the aim of restoring the city's past character became clear.

Kleihues, at his introductory interview of the IBA publications, adopted Aldo Rossi's approach on the historical continuity of the city. He saw in Rossi's pre-IBA housing projects the character he envisioned for Berlin: "a revelation of the better Prussian tradition" as the historical relationship between the simplicity of architecture and the "landscape" of the city.[29] Drawing from that, he set the two main objectives of the IBA regarding the construction of an identity: the aesthetic experimentation that would refresh the city and the preservation of the urban layout as the intellectual and cultural foundation of the city. Despite his proclamations that the challenge would lie in the former, it was essentially predicated upon the latter. His definition of the "urban layout" as the regulator of "the conditions of economy, exchange, and traffic," which define the "basic character of a place," reveals the main parameters to maintain.[30] The design directives exude the gravity of the ties between the social, institutional

24 Such a complex interest in and examination of the 'urban' in Berlin was the legacy of Walter Benjamin's studies of the urban quest for cultural identity. Walter Benjamin, *One-Way Street and Other Writings*, trans. Edmund Jephcott and Kingsley Shorter (London: NLB, 1979), 177. Harvey theorizes the rise of globalization during this period. In his theory of rent, he emphasizes the instrumental role of the assignment of both cultural (identity) and technological (infrastructure) value to (urban) land as the basis for reproduction and extraction (and war as a method of devaluation). See David Harvey, *The Limits to Capital* (Oxford: Basil Blackwell Publisher Ltd, 1982).

25 Bauausstellung, Berlin GmbH, *The City Center as a Place to Live*, 7.

26 The trend for reassessing the surviving historical built stock in the European cities had led to the declaration of 1975 as the European Year for Monument Protection. The relevant campaign of the Council of Europe favored the preservation of *the historical European city* as the pre-industrial city against great new construction and modern urban planning. See Bodenschatz and Polinna, *Learning from IBA*, 25–27.

27 Josef P. Kleihues, "Stations in the Architectural History of Berlin in the 20th Century: IBA," in Bauausstellung Berlin GmbH, *International Building Exhibition*, 236.

28 Ibid., 235.

29 Josef P. Kleihues and Heinrich Klotz, *International Building Exhibition Berlin 1987: Examples of a New Architecture*, trans. Ian Robson (London: Academy Editions, 1986), 10. Prussia was a historically prominent German state that entered the ranks of the great powers of Europe shortly after becoming a kingdom at the beginning of the eighteenth century until the abdication of William II, at the end of World War I in 1918. It transformed Berlin from a relatively unknown backwater to a powerful and cosmopolitan European capital. This was the time when Berlin architecture was characterized by a spectacular revival of classicism represented by Karl Friedrich Schinkel, and became the object of retrospective attempts for the restoration of the city's historic royal appearance. See Geoffrey Barraclough, *The Origins of Modern Germany*, second edition (Oxford: Basil Blackwell Oxford, 1962).

30 Josef P. Kleihues, "Rudiments of History," in Bauausstellung Berlin GmbH, *International Building Exhibition*, 147.

3

Figure ground map of Critical Reconstruction areas exemplifying the urban layout as "the basic character of a place."

Oswald Mathias Ungers, "Friedrichvorstadt Study," in "Architecture in Progress: Internationalle Bauausstellung Berlin 1984," ed. Frank Russel, Architectural Design and Academy Editions (1983), 120.

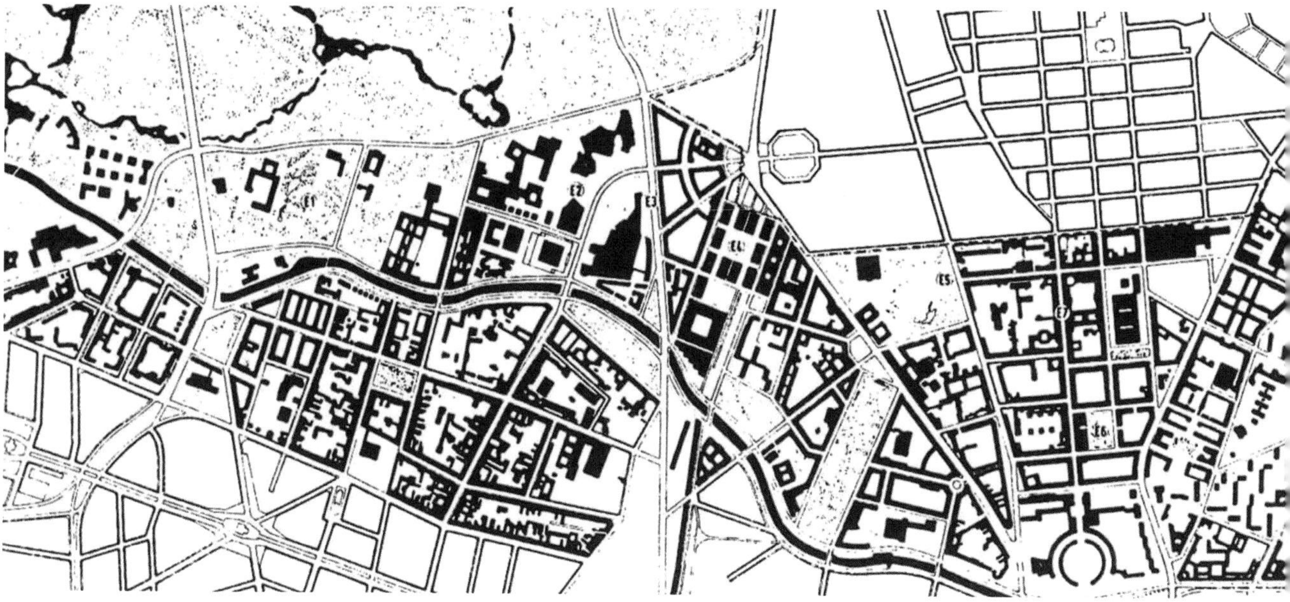

and formal aspects of the city against its aesthetic treatment: the preservation, renewal and improvement of "the urban layout" for the distribution of uses; the allocation of space and access from the basis of "the geometry of the urban structure," which defines the public, semi-public and private realms of the city; its "relationship to the countryside" as the basis and natural prerequisite of life in the city symbolically seen in urban landscaping projects; "the appearance of the city" as the physiognomy of its houses, which express the intellectual and cultural elements of its history.[31] Kleihues encapsulates the priority in one of his three theses according to which "everything that is necessary," as dictated by the urban morphology, "needs aesthetic intensification."[32] Thus he distinguishes the formal identity of the city, which is diachronic, and its visual or connotative identity, which depends on motivating the observer to notice.

Alan Colquhoun describes the formal strategy of the IBA as historically and spatially continuous, reading the city as a palimpsest.[33] The reconstruction of the historical Berliner layout, the repetitive street-based urban blocks, as a continuous fabric was meant to anonymously host a variety of functions alongside the housing. The new buildings would then contribute to the formal continuity of the fabric and to the connotative identity of the city through aesthetic contrast.[34] By also addressing IBA's take on public space in terms of "external rooms" (squares) and "corridors" (streets) with definite boundaries instead of "a limitless void within which buildings occur,"[35] Colquhoun unveils the formal idea of segregating the private and public realms: *the urban block's* perimeter and, where possible, the block's continuous façade. **(Fig. 3)** His analysis draws on Rob Krier's theory of the restoration of the urban structure as a response to the "crisis of the city" brought about by modern urbanism.[36] Krier, a proponent of the rationalist school, claimed that modernism's focus on buildings as isolated objects fragmented urban public space and civic life. Therefore, he believed the focus of the new approach should return to the historical continuity of the city.[37] His vision promoted the city as a unified composition, defining urban spaces in clearly articulated forms such as streets and squares. Inspired from Krier's discourse, Kleihues defined three typologies of public space,

31 Josef P. Kleihues, "Stations in the Architectural History," in Bauausstellung Berlin GmbH, *International Building Exhibition*, 236.

32 Josef P. Kleihues, "Architecture, as I wanted to say, needs the care and support of us all," in Russel, "Architecture in Progress," 8.

33 Alan Colquhoun, "Twentieth-Century Concepts of Urban Space," in *Modernity and the Classical Tradition: Architectural Essays 1980-1987* (London: The MIT Press, 1989), 223–34. See also Katharina Borsi, Nicole Porter and Megan Nottingham, "The Typology of the Berlin Block: History, Continuity and Spatial Performance," *Athens Journal of Architecture* 2, no.1 (January 2016): 45–47.

34 On formal continuity as historical continuity, see also Emily Pugh, "Beyond the Berlin Myth: The Local, the Global and the IBA 87," in Philip Broadbent and Sabine Hake, *Berlin Divided City, 1945-1989*, (New York: Berghahn, 2010), 156–167.

35 Colquhoun, *Modernity and the Classical Tradition*, 232.

36 Rob Krier, *Urban Space* (New York: Rizzoli International, 1979), 49.

37 "Raumkontinuum." In his work *Urban Space in Theory and Practice*, Krier provides a typological study of streets and squares arguing for historical continuity. See Rob Krier, *Stadtraum in Theorie und Praxis* (Stuttgart: Karl Kramer Verlag, 1975), 67.

"the street, the square, the park," that together predetermine the urban layout to which "the identity of the city as a three-dimensional model is bound."[38] What remains from such a formal fixation on the public is the designation of the private in the street-based apartment block, where diversification could only legitimize itself by artistic quality and social involvement.

In this respect, the demonstration areas of the New Building sector are representative of how individual housing projects support such clear-cut ideas of publicness and privateness and how certain urban areas and typologies were re-signified as places of *identification* in the city. Nowhere is the IBA's urban strategy for "the City as Project" clearer than in the Critical Reconstruction area of Southern Friedrichstadt, a district where all the histories of the city co-exist. **(Fig. 4)** On the one hand, it demonstrates the city's Baroque origins and is the place where the urban syntax, which Kleihues refers to as "typological clarity," was born in the eighteenth century —the street-based apartment block. On the other hand, still in the 1970s, it was reminiscent of the wounds of the city as the epicenter of the 1945 bombardment and suffered desolation and a melancholic atmosphere as a result of its adjacency to the Wall and Checkpoint Charlie. The eighteenth-century importance of the continuity of the street façade in planning concepts and the nineteenth century expropriation of plots for residential block developments peaked at huge complexes with hundreds-metres-long façades by the turn of the twentieth century.[39] At the end of the war, when the whole Friedrichstadt lay in ruins, the governmental institutions moved their premises to more attractive areas. Finally, the urban layout with the circular Mehringplatz and the cutting off of the circulation alignments at Checkpoint Charlie to separate from East Berlin was defined by Scharoun's design in 1962. The IBA aimed to change the "shipwrecked"[40] atmosphere of the area by reviving its monumental character and making it a safe and attractive place for living. **(Fig. 5)**

38 Josef P. Kleihues, "Rudiments of History," 147.
39 Thomas Biller and Wolfgang Schäche, "Notes on the Rise, Development and Destruction of a Block in Friedrichstadt," in Russel, "Architecture in Progress," 20.
40 Rem Koolhaas, "Shipwrecked," in *S M L XL* (New York: Monacelli Press, 1995), 254–69.

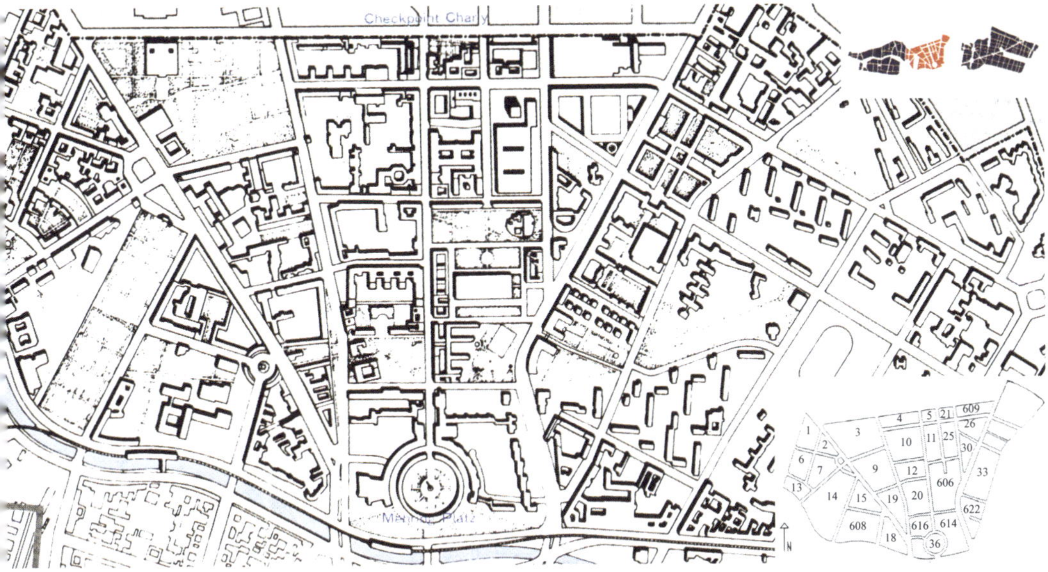

4
Map of the Critical Reconstruction projects in Southern Friedrichstadt

5
View of the Wall at Checkpoint Charlie facing East Berlin, 1980
© OMA

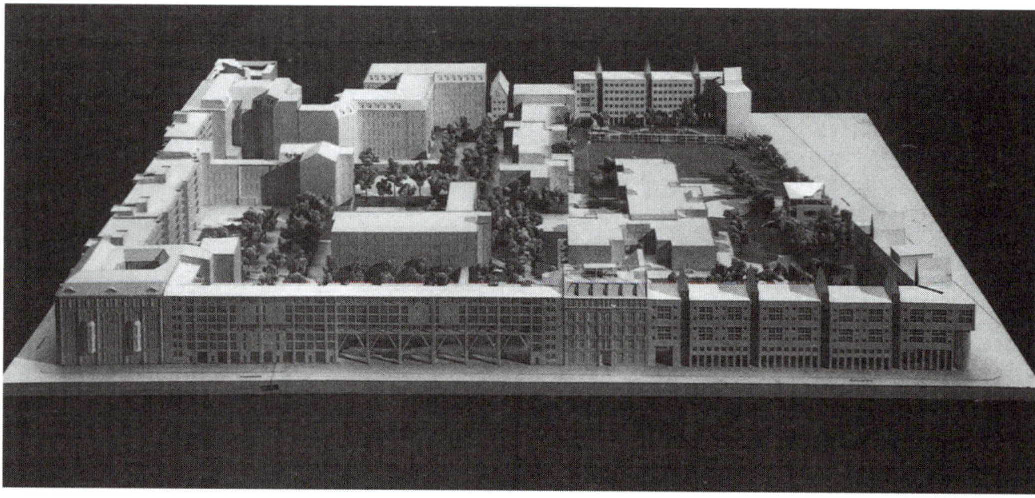

6.1
Aldo Rossi and Gianni Braghieri, model of proposal for block 10

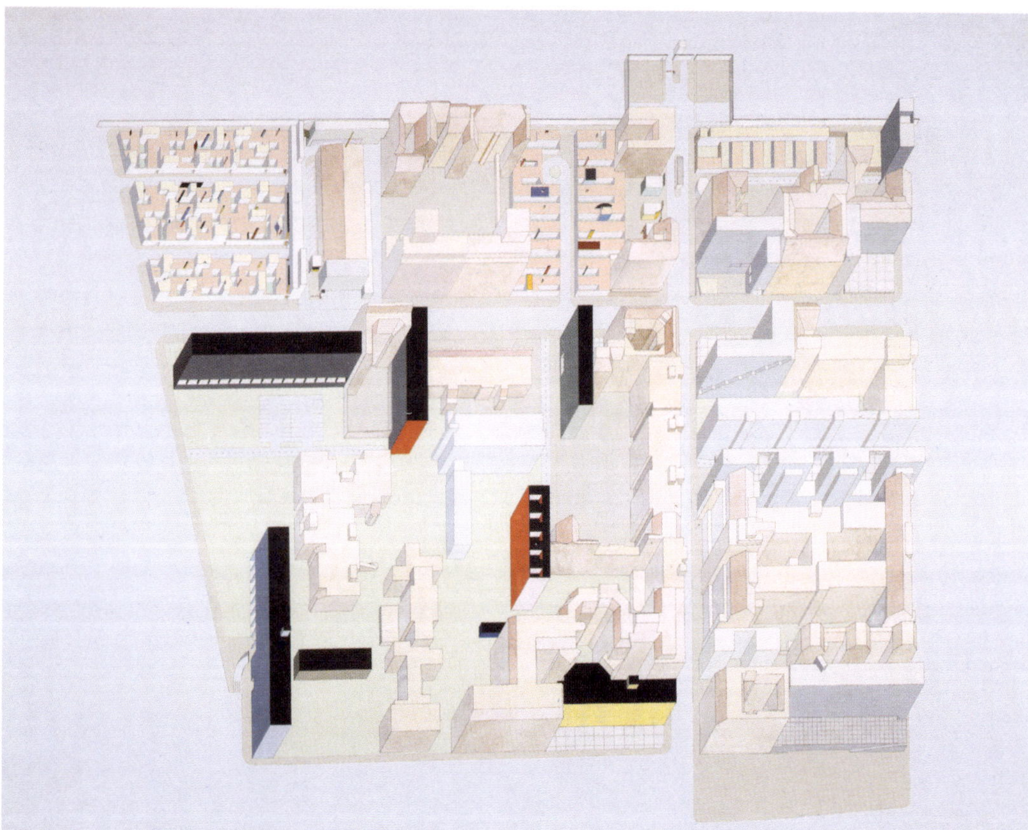

6.2
OMA axonometric plate
© OMA

In 1980, the administration invited 16 architects for a competition among to develop an urban concept for blocks 4, 5, 10 and 11 on the intersection of Friedrichstrasse and Kochstrasse —with blocks 4 and 5 directly facing Checkpoint Charlie— where the urban character had been profoundly damaged. (see legend in **(Fig. 4)**) Comparing the proposal from the Office for Metropolitan Architecture (OMA) with the realized project from Aldo Rossi and Gianni Braghieri for block 10,[41] reveals the IBA's pragmatic response to the theoretical opposition between a radical and a rational regeneration of "the substance of the city." **(Fig. 6.1)** In the discussion on the reconstruction of the European city, Rossi had dismissed functionalism since the 1960s. In one of his articles, he argued that Berlin's residential typology could truly respect urban continuity thanks to the city's fragmentation into smaller zones, fabrics and artefacts (such as the urban blocks), unlike the totalitarian masterplanning of modernists.[42] In their proposal, Rossi and Braghieri attempted to restore the area's historical urban fabric, by reinstating the eighteenth-century continuous façade. Rem Koolhaas, on the other hand, found it pretentious and ahistorical to adopt a specific architectural doctrine and silence mistaken ideologies of the past.[43] Rather than the mere restoration or reinterpretation of the eighteenth-century block, the OMA attitude set out to invest also in the latent, contradictory or even pessimistic characteristics of the urban context as a definition of contemporaneity. **(Fig. 6.2)** Therefore, their proposal introduced another type of conceptual continuity, beyond the literalness of the street plan, that would relate the existing buildings with qualities of iconic proposals for Friedrichstadt by Mendelsohn, Mies and Hilberseimer and, thus, create anchors for new insertions.[44] It is telling of the difference in the scope that Rossi's model is focused on depicting block 10 and its detailed particularities from a close viewpoint on Kochstrasse, while Koolhaas's model depicts a holistic approach for blocks 4, 5, 10 and 11 from a viewpoint facing the Wall in anticipation of a reunited city.

The selection of Rossi's proposal reveals an alignment with the IBA's true objectives, however it is also worth comparing the architectural tropes and the missed opportunities for typological experimentation. Rossi's effort to restore the street

41 Block 10 is surrounded to the North by Kochstrasse, to the East by Friedrichstrasse, to the West by Wilhelmstrasse, and to the South by Puttkamerstrasse. The Wall is one block away (block 4) to the North.

42 Aldo Rossi, "Aspetti della tipologia residenziale a Berlino [Aspects of Residential Typology in Berlin]," *Casabella Continuità* 288 (July 1964): 11–20.

43 Koolhaas, "Shipwrecked," in *S M L XL*, 259.

44 Ibid., 256. Koolhaas's references were Erich Mendelsohn's "Headquarters of the German Metallurgic Federation," 1929–30, Ludwig Hilberseimer's "City of Slabs," 1928, and Mies van der Rohe's project for Friedrichstrasse, 1921. These projects might well have been Rossi's frightful references of the "totalitarian master planning of modernists."

axis resulted in maintaining average heights along Friedrichstraße and using it as a guide to reconstruct the continuity of the façade in two parts: the first along Kochstrasse and around the corner partly on Wilhelmstrasse, in memory of the original building destroyed during World War II [45]; the second on the corner of Wilhelmstrasse and Puttkamerstrasse. **(Figs. 7.1-7.2)** The main design concept (for the two corners) consists of a housing building of brick and glass on the exterior façade and white plaster on the interior façade, separated with strips of vertical connections with prominent green copper pinched roofs, resembling Berlin's Gothic spiers. These references to the construction style of nineteenth-century Berlin and their visual symbolism; red-brick façades signaling housing, metallic green vertical segments signalling stairs, and glazed loggias signaling winter gardens (only in Wilhelmstrasse), accentuated the idea of individual housing very much like the urban villa type introduced in Tiergarten.[46] Although the colorful and varied façades intended to achieve the required stylistic diversity by "loosening up" the block prescription of Critical Reconstruction, in fact they managed to dissolve the idea of collective treatment of the building interiors as a whole. Indeed, only in the ground floor layout, where colonnades are designed to support shops along the front façades, can one see such a potential. The serial apposition of units serviced by two galleries running parallel —one in the front and one in the back— gave the possibility of unification into larger spaces up to a maximum span of 10 metres that lay between two stair cores. The glass façades on Wilhelmstrasse were conceived as additional flexible elements which could be removed, allowing a concession of private space to public space through open-air markets.

However, these qualities were exclusive to the commercial area on the ground floor. Connectivity and openness were sacrificed on the upper floors in order to grant each of the 83 apartments a private character. Individual apartments coverred the complete surface of each housing segment leaving the stairs as the only communal area, shared between two segments. **(Figs. 8.1 - 8.2)** Rear façades were favored for accommodating living spaces as their individual loggias enjoyed a sense of privacy

45 Zahara Chapra, "Rossi House - Block 10," *Architectuul*, June 9, 2020, http://architectuul.com. This iconic corner with the recognizable giant white four-storey column was featured as the cover image of an article in *New York Times* on April 14, 1988 with the title "Changing the Face of West Berlin" by Joseph Giovannini.

46 These blocks were based on the relevant discourse developed by Ungers in the 1970s, a period which had seen a trend of middle-class families moving to the suburbs or small towns. Oswald M. Ungers, "The Urban Villa: A Prototype for Inner-City Residences," in Oswald M. Ungers, Hans Kollhoff and Arthur Ovaska, *The Urban Villa: A multi-family dwelling type*, Cornell Summer Academy 77, (Berlin, Cologne: Studio Press for Architecture, 1977), 1–5.

7.1
Corner of Kochstrasse
and Wilhelmstrasse

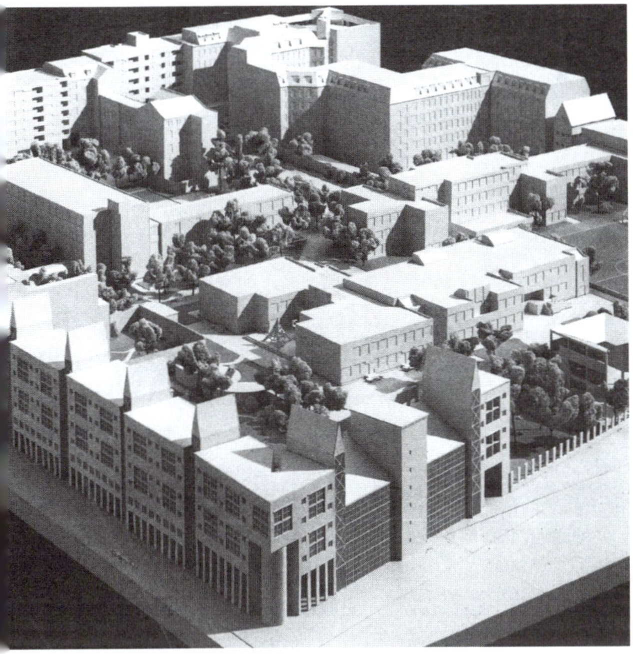

7.2
Axonometric drawing
and elevation study

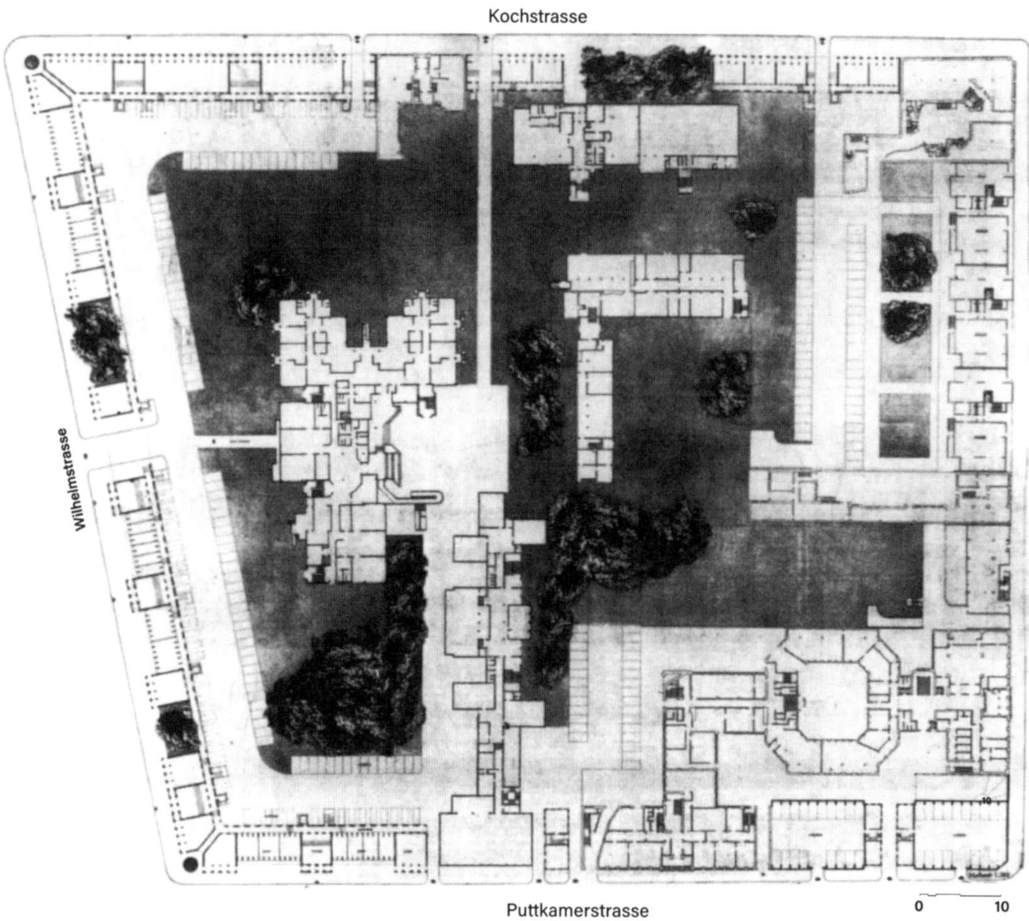

8.1
Block 10 layout, ground floor plan

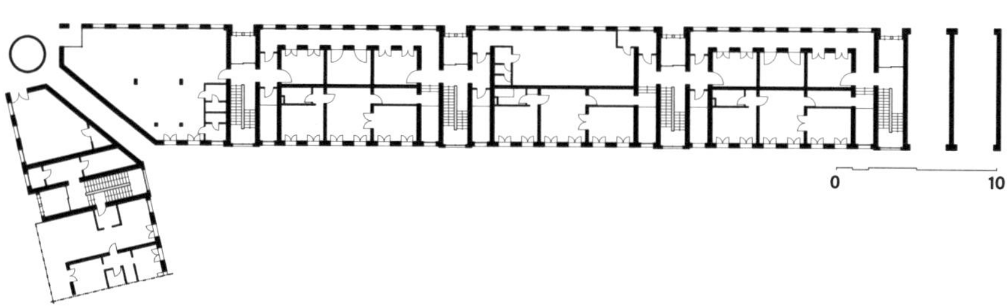

8.2
First floor plan along Kochstrasse

promoted by the "new interior" of the urban block. Despite the idea that calculated gaps on the block perimeter and the inner greenery would be seen as a form of fluidity between housing and the city, the block's massive continuous perimeter structure created the impression of an impenetrable boundary and the interior gardens were strictly for private use only.

The OMA proposal, on the other hand, by setting six main "anchor" buildings of administrative use to frame the existing ones, leaves block 10 as an iconographic condition of historical artefacts and posits the criticality of designing housing "in the shadow of the Berlin Wall and the border control facilities of Checkpoint Charlie" in block 4.[47] **(Fig. 9)** To separate the domestic from these facilities the project establishes it on a podium as an artificial surface over Friedrichstrasse. The originality of the design lies in a radical reinterpretation of the block through the subdivision by two new streets, an extreme fragmentation into individual plots and a total of 74 new units. **(Fig. 10)** Based on the block grid there is a typological gradient from the Wall towards Kochstrasse: the north housing section of 18 luxurious terrace houses with front yards intends to disperse the notorious link between social housing and the Wall; the middle housing section provides 56 identical plots with units of various sizes, terminating in a row of workshops in the last section. Another perpendicular row of villas is designed to play a role in the overall iconography of the Wall. Despite reinforcing the self-contained intimacy of each unit and its dissociation from the context, this proposal at least puts forward a form of architectural and urban dialectic by superimposing one on top of the other. Terrace houses are directly accessible from the podium while the street in the air provides collective access to the three upper stories and a deck leads to the flats in the penthouse. This generates an interplay that is not exhausted in the rearrangement of the kitchen and the bathroom, but also of other basic elements —chimney, balustrade, fenestration— which create a layering of the in-between spaces. Most importantly, it maintains a degree of open-endedness to transformation or future interpretation with minimal material display and the possibility of rearrangement of small components.

47 Koolhaas, "Shipwrecked," in *S M L XL*, 261.

9
Axonometric of the proposal for block 4, © OMA

10
View of the middle
housing section
© OMA

Kleihues admitted that "the IBA attempted to embrace widespread aims [...] in order to show that even within the narrowly restrictive framework of state-subsidized housing, the realization of ideas worthy in terms of both quality and variety is, in fact, attainable."[48] However, its goal was never to radicalize the process that produced government-subsidized housing as the IBA's jurisdiction was limited to the generation of ideas and their representation in a public exhibition. IBA's restricted budget allowance made it a part of the structure of the city bureaucracy which, as expected, compromised the contact with those who realized the proposals that did reach the street. It provoked theoretical discussions on architectural problems of housing regarding aesthetic production and making the city "livable," rather than proposing new typologies and structural changes to housing provision to benefit the socially disadvantaged. The prevalence of this neoliberal trend of selecting "calculated risks" among given options in housing development is still striking from today's point of view. Furthermore, it confirms Foucault's argument that neoliberalism is not as much about commodification as about competition.[49]

Already within the architectural critique of the time, Colin Rowe regarded the goals of the IBA as simply too ambitious and consumed by "a hostile examination of details" rather than applicable solutions.[50] Pierluigi Nicolin argued that the European inner city demanded an essential reconstruction of the planning and financial institutions ultimately responsible for housing.[51] The diversity that served to produce an image of urban identity for the city of West Berlin was only a superficial variation of façades that concealed the fact that social housing itself was to incarnate this identity; to (re)create the inner-city fabric. In his critique, Douglas Clelland, an English architect who participated in the IBA, translated the topic of IBA "Die Innenstadt als Wohnort" as "the inner city as a residential area" and not "as a place for living."[52] He criticized the predominance of the residential as a fixed program and the clear-cut distinction of private and public at the edge of the block as an extremely limited horizon of possibility for the city, as opposed to the full width of the term "living." This reflection of the architectural practice, although painful, was more incisive than

48 Josef P. Kleihues, "Apartment Buildings and Apartments," 72.

49 Foucault, *The Birth of Biopolitics*, 147, 226.

50 Colin Rowe, "IBA: Rowe reflects," *The Architectural Review* 1076 (1984): 92-3.

51 He characterized the theme of housing in the central areas of the city "to paraphrase Milizia [...] a big tumult in details within the disheartening modesty of the whole." Pierluigi Nicolin, "Abitare in città [Living in the City]," *Lotus International* no. 41 (1984): 5. Translation by Mauro Marzo in "Lotus. The first thirty years of an architectural magazine," *Magazine del Festival dell' Architettura* no. 43, (July-September 2018): 41–66.

52 Doug Clelland, "Architecture in Progress 2," in Russel, "Architecture in Progress," 2–4.

any criticism in its realization that architects, by accepting the limitation of the term "wohnen," accepted the architecture of privatization.

The IBA served as a stepping stone towards a discourse on urban renewal and the role of housing that bound them to a strict formal definition of the private-public template and its cultural exploitation, leading to processes such as gentrification and displacement. Henri Lefebvre, in the aftermath of the IBA, described the ubiquitous trend of urban redevelopment of ailing cities, which exploits the historic fabric, as an indispensable process in order to sell the myth of urbanity at a profit.[53] He did not attribute it to a progressive strategy employed by enlightened architects, instead to economic ambitions that subsume spaces "to the service of cultural consumption."[54] Yet, the IBA makes a strong case for such a bold and prolific architectural strategy as being necessary to serve these ambitions. Kleihues's clever promise of stylistic diversity guaranteed broad political support as well as the endorsement of the international design scene and domestic investment societies. This combination made IBA a resounding success, an unprecedented architectural spectacle that Time magazine called "the most ambitious showcase of world architecture in this generation."[55] Its format became a model synonymous with the desired upgrading into a "global city," a part of avant-garde architecture which attracts transnational capital while simultaneously reproducing a familiar physical framework in which "local" idiosyncrasies of living can crystallize. As such the IBA left a legacy and an example for the years to come: a planning system that is utilized to generate the exchange value of housing by suggesting a symbolic identity to cities, while also diffusing the impression of pluralism and diversity within an effectively regulated framework of housing provision.

53 Henri Lefebvre (from the *The Production of Space*, 1991) quoted in Neil Leach, *Rethinking Architecture* (London and New York: Routledge, 1997), 143.

54 Ibid.

55 Kurt Anderson, "Rebuilding Berlin — Yet Again," *Time*, June 1987, 66. See also Sebastian Schmaling, "Masked Nostalgia, Chic Regression: The "Critical" Reconstruction of Berlin," *Harvard Design Magazine* no. 23 (Fall-Winter 2005), http://www.harvarddesignmagazine.org/issues/23/masked-nostalgia-chic-regression-the-critical-reconstruction-of-berlin.

The Art of Living in the Heart of the City: From Ekistics to the Ultimate Domestication of the City Centre

1.1
General view of Doxiadis organization building, 1958–1972

Photographs 33406, Constantinos A. Doxiadis Archives

1.2
The One Athens conversion, 2007–2014

The late paradigm of neoliberal development —the "crisis response"— is investigated via the luxurious housing scheme called "One Athens," the 2014 conversion of the former Doxiadis Organization headquarter in Athens.[1] **(Figs. 1.1-1.2)** Architect and planner Constantinos A. Doxiadis (1913-1975) was a leading figure in post-war efforts for reconstruction in underdeveloped countries and, particularly, for the configuration of a modern system of planning in Greece.[2] The Doxiadis Associates (DA) building, was the built manifesto of Doxiadis's theory of Ekistics, a scientific approach to the human settlement as the structural unit of a global urban system.[3] Although the DA building was not a residential project, it embodied the principles of Ekistics, originating from the Greek verb *oikizo* (to settle in), as a dynamic process of development of a human community.[4] It was designed in the 1950s for a premium location on Lycabettus hill in the central area of Kolonaki and was established, in the collective memory of the city, as an iconic example of modernist architecture. Following Doxiadis's death and the dissolution of his organization, the building gradually fell into disrepair during the 1980s and 1990s, partly due to the fact that it had not been formally listed for preservation. This claim rose as the construction works for the One Athens conversion started after the outbreak of the global financial crisis in 2007–08. The appeals to state organs delayed, but did not compromise, the implementation of the developer's vision for the most contemporary and outstanding residential complex of the 21st century in Athens. The project proceeded according to the initial design by Divercity architects, an office with international experience in luxurious housing, and the complex was inaugurated in 2014. The project was welcomed with fascination —if not with hope— but the context of a collapsed market was particularly unfitting for "one of the largest residential investments in Athens."[5]

In fact, this case study presents both the starting and breaking point of the fundamental transition from the reformist to the neoliberal agenda of housing development in Greece. On the one hand, the Doxiadis building presents an attempt to apply a design canon to the informal housing development, which marked the urban

The Doxiadis Organization consisted of five firms: the Doxiadis Associates international consultancy on Development & Ekistics, the Computer Centre, the Institute of Mechanical Engineering, the 'Zygos' Real Estate Investment company, and the Athens Publishing Centre. It was also home to the Athens Technological Institute for architecture-related studies and the Athens Centre of Ekistics for advanced research. It was established in bibliography and publications as the Doxiadis Associates (DA) building.

Philip Deane, the single author of Doxiadis's biography, describes Doxiadis as "Greek in practice, yet a true internationalist," expressing the quest between "modernization" and "regionalism" that was typical of the intellectual generation of the 1930s. See Philip Deane, *Constantinos Doxiadis: Master Builder for Free Men* (New York: Oceana Publications, 1965), 57.

3 Constantinos A. Doxiadis, *Architecture in Transition* (London: Hutchinson & Co, 1963) and Constantinos A. Doxiadis, *Ekistics: An Introduction to the Science of Human Settlements* (London: Hutchinson & Co, 1968). Doxiadis considered the first book as his manifesto and the second as his established discourse of Ekistics.

4 Human community was regarded by Doxiadis as the social unit, dynamic and expandable across the scales of the human habitat (ekistics) and the fourth dimension, which is time. Doxiadis, *Architecture in Transition*, 175.

5 The total amount of investment reached EUR 70 million. Vasilis Kotsis, "Nea Yorki ginetai to Kolonaki [Kolonaki becomes New York]," *To Vima*, August 6, 2013, and Demetres Develegkos, "Spitia chlides sto Lycaveto [Luxurious residences at Lycabettus]," *capital.gr*, October 18, 2014, https://www.capital.gr/agora-akiniton/2134548/spitia-xlidis-sto-lukabitto.

history of the second half of the twentieth century. On the other hand, One Athens illustrates how neoliberal housing policies, in moments of general disenchantment with the capitalist system, use the power of architectural symbols in order to re-market the idea of the private. Before analyzing the two end points of this trajectory, the introduction provides a brief overview of the transition from reformism to neoliberalism, which is not as sharp as many people believe. As we have seen in previous case studies, this process was largely mediated by the welfare state, which mobilized housing toward the empowerment of the middle classes as the main consumerist force. In Greece it was a belated hybrid of "state, market and civil society" [6] that gradually transformed the housing mechanism from the engine of a domestic construction economy to a part of global financial capitalism. The transformation was not fully realized until the turn of the twenty-first century. Therefore, housing production improvising the neoliberal design agenda was short-lived, interrupted by a systemic collapse. To understand this transition is to unveil the political stakes of the private narrative in modern Greek state planning.

The claim for modernization became closely bound to the housing sector in post-war Greece.[7] Unlike the welfare state consensus established in Western Europe, in Greece the implementation of the Marshall Plan improvised an American concept for the developed world: "aided self-help housing."[8] This policy, introduced in 1949 by Doxiadis as Minister of Reconstruction, incentivized owner-beneficiaries to participate in the construction of custom-made homes.[9] **(Fig. 2)** Analyzing aspects of the program, architect Konstantina Kalfa reveals that what became a dominant pattern of access to housing by *one's own means* was not a culturally rooted preference for privately owned housing in Greece.[10] Instead, it was a pedagogical project for the population, massively migrating to the cities, to adopt the social behavior, ideals and mentality that would form their *modern* identity. Kalfa concludes that private housing became the main instrument through which a whole nation negotiated its transition to modernity. The increasing housing demand of the 1950s and 1960s enabled *antiparoche*, a system of land exchange with horizontal shares in the

6 James G. Barlow, Judith Allen, Jesus Leal, Thomas Maloutas and Liliana Padovani, *Housing and Welfare in Southern Europe* (London: Blackwell Publishing, 2004).

7 Yannis Aesopos and Yorgos Simeoforidis, *Landscapes of modernization: Greek architecture 1960's and 1990's* (Athens: Metapolis Press, 1999).

8 The American Housing and Home Finance Agency, which was founded in 1947, was responsible for implementing the housing policy abroad. Richard Harris, "The silence of the experts: "Aided self-help housing," 1939-1954," *Habitat International* 22, no.2 (1998): 165–189. See also Andreas Kakridis, "Deus ex machina?: Truman/Marshall Aid, Engineers, and Greece's Post-war Development Discourse," *Journal of Modern Greek Studies* 27, no. 2 (2009): 241–274.

9 Deane portrays Doxiadis as a Prometheus of housing: "Instead of building them houses immediately, Doxiadis was teaching the homeless how to be brick makers, stone masons and carpenters." Deane, *Constantinos Doxiadis*, 38-39. See also Nancy H. Kwak, *A World of Home-owners: American Power and the Politics of Housing Aid* (Chicago: University Chicago Press, 2015).

10 Kalfa describes this project as a clearly defined episode that posed the dilemma between the adoption of capitalism or communism in post-war Greece on the very intimate level of everyday life. Konstantina Kalfa, *Autostegasi, Tora! / Atheati Plevra tes Amerikanikes Voitheas stin Ellada* [*Self-help housing now! The invisible side of American help in Greece*] (Athens: Futura, 2019).

2
Dimitris Harissiadis, Construction works in Athens, August 1950.

3
Yiorgis Yerolympos, The polykatoikia of the antiparoche, Zografou, central Athens, 2012

new development, to define the urban character of Greek cities.[11] **(Fig. 3)** The state supported this system with tax allowances and the permission of greater building heights, which resulted in the massive production of *polykatoikia*, the multi-story apartment block. Architectural historian Theocharopoulou argues that the polykatoikia triggered a social transformation, "enabling the migrants who poured into Athens to become urban citizens, aspiring to a modern life."[12] The dream of this modern life was captured into the penthouse private apartment (ρετιρέ). Alongside apartments, the polykatoikia also became the receptacle of commercial and business uses, which led the researcher Wooditsch to describe it as an "osmotic sphere" of the private realm with the public space of the city.[13] However, social geographer Maloutas argued that the spatial integration of various social groups in the polykatoikia does not negate social segregation,[14] which differentiates co-existence from actual osmosis. Despite the exterior uniformity and the interior typical plan, his study suggests that the polykatoikia accommodated a clear social stratification along the vertical axis.

In the post-dictatorship era[15] the polykatoikia stood literally as the concrete form of democratization; a socially equitable distribution of a privately owned habitable space.[16] During these years the provision of welfare and housing was systematized and became accessible to a vast constellation of civil servants, which comprised the electorate of Papandreou's Centre Union. PASOK came to power with the promise that the state and the public sector would pave "the democratic road to socialism."[17] In 1981, it initiated a political era under the mantra of *modernization* with reforms promoting equality and the redistribution of wealth to "the people."[18] The key reform in the creation of a clientelist state was the liberalization of the banking system.[19] Housing remained at the top of the consumerist agenda by means of excessive loaning, which created a widespread euphoric illusion of affluence while inflating the national debt.[20] Under Simitis's leadership in 1996, the PASOK slogan was upgraded from "Modernization" to "European Integration."[21] Two key events of this period supported neoliberalism, a movement celebrated as a revived metropolitanism in

11 "Antiparoche" followed the revision of the 1929 condominium legislation and it was a system of exchange between land owners and contractors. The new development produced extra horizontal shares than that of the land owner in order to accommodate the demand. *On horizontal (per floor) ownership* (1929) N. 3741, FEK A 4 – 09.01.1929.

12 Theocharopoulou analyzes this social phenomenon as a cultural revolution, where the interiors of the polykatoikia apartments reflected the desire for modernity. See Ioanna Theocharopoulou, *Builders, Housewives and the Construction of Modern Athens* (London: Artifice Press, 2018).

13 Richard Wooditsch, *The Public Private House: Modern Athens and its Polykatoikia* (Zurich: Park Books, 2019).

14 Thomas Maloutas, *I Koinoniki Geographia tis Athinas: Koinonikes Omades kai Domimeno Perivallon se mia Notioeuropaiki Mitropoli* [*The Social Geography of Athens: Social Groups and Built Environment in a South-European Metropolis*] (Athens: Alexandria, 2018).

15 A military junta ruled Greece from 1967 to 1974. A group of colonels took power before the elections that Georgios Papandreou's Centre Union was predicted to win. The dictatorship was characterized by far-right policies, restriction of civil liberties, and exile of political opponents.

16 "The acquisition of housing by those deprived of it or inefficiently housed constitutes the subject of state welfare." Greek Constitution 1975, Article 21, Paragraph 4. See also Thomas Maloutas, Demetres Emmanuel and Maro Pantelidou-Malouta, *Social structures, practices and concepts: New parameters and changing trends 1980-2000* (Athens: National Centre for Social Research, 2006), 44.

17 The Marxist theorist Nicos Poulantzas formulated thi concept to refer to a form of democratic socialism tha commits to a pluralist representative democracy tha is not inherently bourgeois. He also concluded tha neoliberalism was only one facet of a broader turn h called "authoritarian statism": a combination of th managerial powers of the Keynesian state with a strategic retreat from some of its former economic func tions. Nicos Poulantzas, *State, Power, Socialism*, trans Patrick Camiller (London:NLB, 1978), 251.

18 George Th. Mavrogordatos, "From Traditional Cliertelism to Machine Politics: The Impact of PASOK Populism in Greece," *South European Society and Politic* 2, no. 3 (1997): 1–26.

Athens; first, the 1999 awarding of the 2004 Olympic Games and second the 2001 adoption of the Euro.[22] The 2004 Olympics masterplan settled for "realistic possibilities" and put forward a metropolitan idea based on the regeneration of the historic center. This was a piecemeal and superficial approach; it took place in selected areas of the center and was a project for either the refurbishment or concealment of façades in order to enhance the metropolitan image.[23] For housing this was a call for the return to the city center after successive waves of suburban sprawl. At the same time, the country's entry into the European Monetary Union unlocked access to inexpensive credit from the European Central Bank. Investment in housing was boosted once again and real estate prices soared to such an extent that, by 2006, access to privately-owned housing based on income was impossible. This was the ultimate pedagogical project; to educate the masses that debt was a small price to pay for the dream of life-long security through home ownership. This period marked the transition from demand-based housing provision to housing investment regulated by fictitious capital, from a contractual system of exchange to one of indebtedness.

According to statistics, not only asset prices but also dwelling sizes were disproportionate to purchasing power. **(Figs. 4.1-4.2)** This affluence dictated a renegotiation between economy and luxury, between the homogeneity of the polykatoikia and the desire for differentiation. Architecturally, the idea of individuality was expressed by a new generation of practices through design against the emphatic horizontality and uniformity of the polykatoikia. Experimentation with single-family housing types for apartment buildings in the city center resulted in the trend of the *poly/mono-katoikia* (multi/single-family house) during the first decade of the twenty-first century. Their architectural language improvised gestures to de-construct the continuous polykatoikia skin and address private living visually. The term *poly/mono-katoikia* was coined by Yannis Aesopos for his project in Nea Filothei (1999-2003), which combined a structure of single-family houses on the ground floor and the superstructure of a polykatoikia mediated by an elevated *pilotis* on the mezzanine floor. **(Fig. 5)** The attempt to infuse collective living with individual characteris-

19 Stathis Kalyvas, George Pagoulatos and Haridimos Tsoukas, *From Stagnation to Forced Adjustment: Reforms in Greece, 1974-2010* (Oxford: Oxford University Press, 2013).

20 It is important to note that Papandreou was aware that "if a state economy loses credibility" it would be forced to turn to the International Monetary Fund, which would offer help but in return "will dictate the government's economic policy and this will signal the end of the socialist experiment." Andreas Papandreou, 9th *Summit of the Central Committee of PASOK*, 1983.

21 Gerassimos Moschonas, "The Path of Modernisation: PASOK and European Integration," *Journal of Southern Europe and the Balkans* 3, no. 1 (2001): 11–24.

22 Giorgos Stathakis and Costis Chadjimichalis, "Athens as a "World" City: From the Anxiety of the Few to the Reality of the Majority," *Geographies* no. 7 (2004): 26–47.

23 The authors here describe a process of gentrification of selected areas of the city center. Ntina Vaiou et. al., "Athina 2004. Sta monopatia tis pagkosmiopoiesis [Athens 2004. In the track of globalization]," *Geographies* no. 7 (2004): 13–25.

4.1
Housing loans
in Greece, 1999-2009

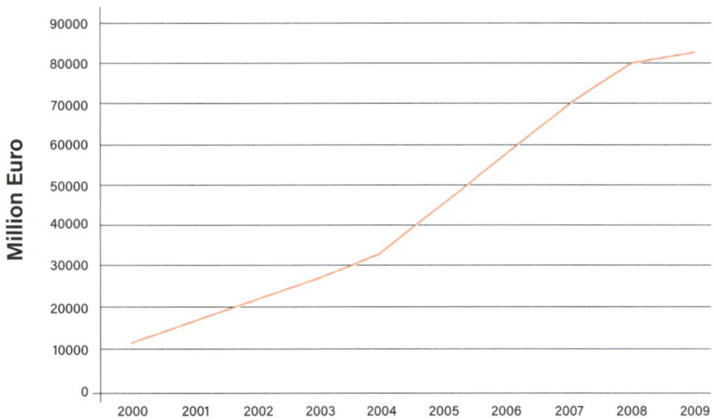

4.2
Size variation
of newly constructed
residences,1999-2009

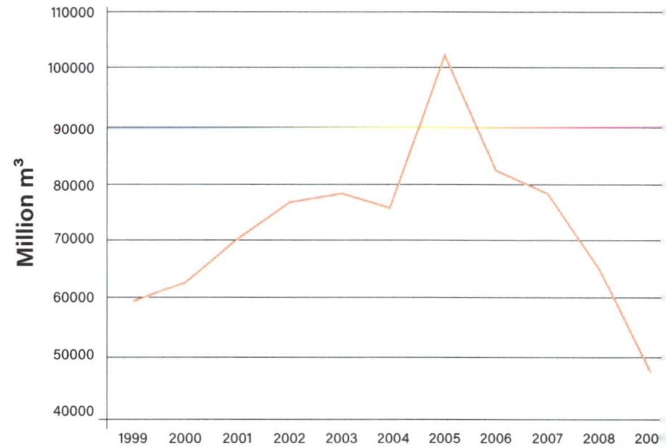

5
Poly/mono-katoikia,
Nea Filothei, 1999-2003
Architect: Yannis
Aesopos
Photo: Erieta Attali

6
The dissolution of the
box, Gazi, 2009-2013
Architect: Sofia Tsiraki
Photo: Babis Louizidis
and Katerina Glynou

7
Urban stripes, Koukaki,
2009-2013
Architect: K-Lab Architects
Photo: Panos Kokkinias

tics was also featured at "The dissolution of the box" in Gazi by Sofia Tsiraki (2009-2013). **(Fig. 6)** The free composition of slabs and structural elements challenged the powerful sense of repetition in plan and on the façade. A pattern of recessions of varying depths was meant to develop spacious urban terraces instead of narrow linear balconies. The introduction of double-height windows, different wall colors and exterior staircases reflected on the façade more a type of maisonette or an urban villa rather than a flat. In a similar spirit, *Urban Stripes* by K-Lab architects (2009-2013) created a different urban façade with irregularly sized openings and individual cubic balconies, counteracting the linearity of the typical polykatoikia elevation. **(Fig. 7)** According to the architects it addressed "flexibility" and "diversification" in providing solutions for different wallets and needs and, thus, different apartment layouts and sizes.

The *neoliberalization*[24] of housing was interrupted by the bursting of the real estate bubble in 2008, which led to unsustainable household debt. Greece entered the first economic adjustment program in 2010 which imposed heavy property taxes, salary cuts and the abolition of the legal protections for primary residences.[25] This brought about the collapse of the debt-based property regime and the dissolution of the middle class that had fueled it, as well as a significant disenchantment with the narrative of private housing. Neoliberalism sought to transcend this system that no longer provided a secure basis for capital accumulation, reverting to investment in luxury in order to appeal to an extremely restricted part of the population. In this context, the luxurious scheme One Athens was introduced to the public in 2014 as a "revolutionary new concept for living in downtown Athens,"[26] a revolution for the selected few. It will be assessed here not only against the principles of the symbolic architecture of its predecessor, but also in light of the power of the gestures to restore a neoliberal idea of private living within a crisis of neoliberal ideology.

The DA building epitomizes Doxiadis's theories that explored the dynamics of town planning as part of a global urban system. It stands for his radical vision to introduce

On neoliberalization as an open-ended process instead of a static concept, see Neil Brenner and Nik Theodore, *Spaces of Neoliberalism: Urban Restructuring in North America and Western Europe* (Oxford: Blackwell, 2002).

European Commission, *The Economic Adjustment Program for Greece –Third Review* (February 2011).

One Athens, *One Athens: Questions and Answers*, (press release, March 17, 2014), https://www.oneathens.gr/wp-content/uploads/2016/11/ONE-ATHENS-QA-eng-v10.pdf.

"a better-designed world"[27] and his belief that the alleviation of urban crises was a globally attainable ideal. The work and personality of Doxiadis was a controversial combination of a visionary approach and pragmatism.[28] The realization of his vision required the difficult task of operating in an extremely polarized domestic and international scene (including the Greek Civil War and the Cold War). He was largely involved in the post-war development doctrine, which brought about the implementation of the Marshall Plan in Europe, the Point Four Program in the Middle East and Organizational activity for social reformation according to the Western paradigm.[29] On the domestic front, the administrative restructuring he put forward as Vice Minister of Reconstruction (1945-1950) collided with the conservative bureaucratic apparatus and local guilds. In the battle for national sovereignty, Doxiadis's international affiliations and internal political neutrality led his opponents to undermine his epistemology as merely a technocracy or a business model. In response, he captured his political stance for the reconstruction program in the term "land planning"[3 which, however, was not able to reverse the tide of unplanned speculation-driven development of the 1950s in Greece. Nevertheless, it became the intellectual matrix for Doxiadis's theories of *Ekistics* and *Entopia*.

Born as a rational manner of action, Ekistics advanced from a state strategy for "the reformation of Greek settlements"[31] in the 1940s to "the science of human settlements"[32] in the 1960s. The theory provided a general framework "for every building to be built" as a hierarchy from "the smallest reasonable unit" to "the whole human habitat" expanding along its "fourth dimension," time.[33] As such, it sought to restore architecture's disciplinary role as the coordinator of an unprecedented complexity of input from various fields (community development, planning, economics, geography and the social sciences).[34] In 1966, Doxiadis coined the term Entopia in order to introduce a practicable concept between the utopian planning approaches and the existing dystopian conditions.[35] It put forward an idea of urban planning that pointec at a "new-centralization"[36] within the international (CIAM 8) spirit.[37] The "needs at th core" manifest the necessity of the city center to be developed as a space where th

27 "Forward to the better-designed world" is the title of a special editorial of the Pegasus journal from 1972, which accommodated Walter Ashley's illustrated article "Constantine Doxiadis: a new life style through Ekistics."

28 Professors Panayiotis Tournikiotis (History and Theory of Architecture) and Alexandros-Andreas Kyrtsis (Social Sciences and Regional Systems), in a 2006 documentary series on the portraits and careers of Greek architects, describe Doxiadis's personality as "a romantic pragmatist." See *Constantinos A. Doxiadis: A Romantic Pragmatist,* directed by Yorgos Tzirtzilakis (Athens: ERT S.A., 2006), tv broadcast. See also Panayiotis Tournikiotis, "Ancient and Modern Cities in the Work of Constantinos Doxiadis: The Modern City Facing the Future," (paper presented at the 6th International Docomomo Conference, Brasilia, 20–22 September 2000), 97–112, and Alexandros-Andreas Kyrtsis, *Constantinos A. Doxiadis: Texts, Design Drawings, Settlements* (Athens: Ikaros, 2006).

29 Doxiadis was a long-standing consultant to 20 governments and organizations, such as the United Nations, while the Ford Foundation commissioned his office for large-scale programs around the globe. Among these, the Point Four program addressed the escalating conflicts in the Middle East by offering technical assistance to underdeveloped areas in Iran, Iraq, Pakistan, Lebanon, Egypt, and Liberia.

30 He examined models and scales of organization of planning in Western Europe and the United States and adopted the German term *Landesplanung* or *Landesraumordnung*. See Constantinos A. Doxiadis, "Peri Chorotaxias [On Land-Planning]," *Technica Chronika* Year I' 20-21, no. 241-244 (January 1942): 1–12 and Co stantinos A. Doxiadis, "Contemporary Land Plannin *Chorotaxia-Poleodomia-Architektonike* [*Land Pla ning- Urban Planning- Architecture*] 1–B' (March 194

31 Constantinos A. Doxiadis, *Ekistic Policies for the R construction of the Country with a 20-Year Progra* (Athens: Ministry of Reconstruction, 1947) and Co stantinos A. Doxiadis, "Reconstruction and Arch tects," *O Architekton* [*The Architect*] 4, no. 8 (Janua 1948).

32 Constantinos A. Doxiadis, *Ekistics: An Introduction the Science of Human Settlements*, (London: Hutchi son & Co, 1968).

33 Constantinos A. Doxiadis, "New Solutions for Ne Problems," in Doxiadis, *Architecture in Transitic* 87–143.

"sense of community"[38] could be physically expressed. Soon, the World Society of Ekistics, would be contained in a single "human community" and the Entopia would find its application in the microcosm of the DA building in the heart of Athens.

In 1958, Doxiadis clustered the scattered departments of his Organization in a new building complex situated on the slope of Lycabettus hill in central Athens. The plot was simultaneously close to the city center and to nature, inside and above the city, overlooking it from a prominent spot. **(Fig. 8.1)** The building was designed by DA architects, T. Kouravelos and A. Scheepers under Doxiadis's instructions, and is considered one of the most authentic expressions of post-war modernism in Greece. **(Fig. 8.2)**
The building mass (15,000 m^3) was distributed in volumes of different heights according to the various programmatic requirements. The eight-story rear wing housed the DA headquarters, the five-story front wing accommodated the technical schools of the Athens Technological Institute (ATI) and the connecting wings hosted the Athens Center of Ekistics and the Computer Center. Not only did the architectural synthesis become the symbol of the Center of Ekistics as a "cosmopolitan"[39] human community. The hierarchy and articulation embodied the theory of gradual development from the smallest unit of human settlements, "the human room," to the largest unit, the city.[40] This dynamic evolutionary model should always be loyal to the original unit and adhere to key principles that foster a relationship between place and human community.

The first principle was maximizing the potential (quasi) contacts of the human community which was captured in the strategic selection of the site and the development of the synthesis. The effort to maintain the sweeping views of the city and the direct dialogue with the Acropolis,[41] engaged DA development in consecutive expansions between 1957 and 1972 to take up the whole block and to outgrow the height of apartment buildings in front of it. This new function of architecture, the lack of a final stage, was suggestive of a *living organism* always in a state of dynamic expansion and dialogue with the city. The second principle was to economically achieve the maximum contatcs. In this sense, the most symbolic element of the Ekistics spirit was the atrium

34 In an open letter, Doxiadis states that "Legislators, financiers, military men and scientists were asked to give their opinion on the reshaping of the post-war world, but architects and those responsible for physical planning have been ignored. This, however, is not wise, because the new world will be safe only after it has been reshaped on a new basis." Constantinos A. Doxiadis, *To Architects and to All Who Are Interested in Physical Planning for the Reconstruction of the World*, (Letter to the United Nations, October 12, 1945).

35 From the Greek words "en" (in) and "topos" (place), Entopia referred to a place that can be lived with applicable principles. Constantinos A. Doxiadis, *Between Dystopia and Utopia* (London: Faber and Faber Limited, 1966): 49–65.

36 Constantinos A. Doxiadis, *Building Entopia* (Athens: Athens Publishing Centre, 1975).

37 CIAM 8, themed "The Heart of the City" called for "planned recentralization" that would save "the core" of the cities in their process of renewal. CIAM 8, Hoddesdon, "Summary of Needs at the Core," in *Architecture Culture 1943-1968: A Documentary Anthology*, ed. Joan Ockman (New York: Rizzoli International Publications, 1993), 135–136.

38 Eric Mumford, *The CIAM Discourse on Urbanism, 1928–1960* (Cambridge, MA: MIT Press, 2000). The "sense of community" a few years later became one of the main requirements in the Barbican brief that meant to define its layout and ideology.

39 Constantinos A. Doxiadis, "Our Greek Headquarters," *DA Review* (July 1973): 1. The iconic building was massively featured in the DA publications, DA Review and Ekistics journals, but also in countless international journal and newspaper issues and covers.

40 Constantinos A. Doxiadis, "The Formation of Human Room," *Ekistics* 33, no. 196 (1972): 218–229.

41 Rita Reif, "The Acropolis is Backdrop for Modern Setting in Architect's Home," *The New York Times*, December 13, 1961, and "City Planner Constantinos Doxiadis: busy remodeler of the world," *Life*, American Edition, October 7, 1966, 55–60.

which, besides offering a welcoming space to the complex and direct access to all the wings, was meant, according to Doxiadis, to facilitate socialization, cross-circulation and visual contact among the different departments of the organization in the process of "community formation."[42] **(Figs. 8.3-8.4)** Designed to induce peace, harmony and inspiration, it welcomed students and staff to take a break from their daily routine and visitors to wander "like [in] a public garden."[43] Thus, it ultimately expressed Doxiadis' ideas on the architecture of Ekistics as engaging with archetypical procedures of creating space rather than forms.[44] The third principle was the standardization of space based on functionality[45] and comfort.[46] At the DA building the intention was to create large, open and convertible spaces to serve the various programmatic requirements: functional areas, parking spaces and an amphitheater in the basement; an exhibition hall, gallery spaces and computer labs on the ground floor; design studios, offices, libraries and archives on the upper floors. The design applied a 75 cm grid module based on the minimum working space for one person (determined by the width of a desk or drawing board), with a coordinated front façade rhythm of 3 meters. The working spaces could be converted into smaller or larger compartments using standardized moveable partitions. Such requirements for internal flexibility and uninterrupted views through the front and rear façades called for a "daring" structure.[47] This consisted of a system of reinforced concrete walls running perpendicular to the main elevations; the side walls of the building and parallel rows placed at 9-meter-wide intervals. **(Fig. 9.1)** The composition of the wings around the courtyard created also interior façades providing all spaces with direct natural lighting and ventilation. As a functional apparatus, it managed to accommodate the complex's growing needs and transformations while preserving the community's "inherent character."[48]

In his late years, Doxiadis realized that the Ekistics principles, formed by networks prioritizing economic growth and affluence, could not satisfy human needs.[49] His practice seems to have fallen victim to a "proto-neoliberalism" when "cities became flashpoints both for major economic dislocations and for various forms of sociopolitical struggle, particularly in the sphere of social reproduction."[50] Ekistics marked the final

42 Doxiadis, *Building Entopia*, 124.
43 Doxiadis wrote a letter to the film producers Rousopoulos and Lazaridis providing the script of a documentary on the DA atrium as a public space. See also Panayiota Pyla, "Gossip on the Doxiadis 'Gossip Square': Unpacking the Histories of an Unglamorous Public Space," *Architectural Histories* 1, no. 1 (2013): 1–6.
44 Doxiadis, *Architecture in Transition*, 195.
45 "Thoughts on Standardization," SD-DC 739/29.09.1969, Folder 19025, C. A. Doxiadis archives.
46 Constantinos A. Doxiadis, "The Doxiadis Associates Headquarters in Athens," *Architektonike* no. 13 (1959): 28–32.
47 Andreas Symeon, "Giati einai simantiko to ktiriako sygrotima Doxiadi [Why the Doxiadis complex is important]," *Greek Architects*, November 10, 2009, https://www.greekarchitects.gr.
48 "...to preserve at least our own inherent character." See "Apartment building on the intersection of Dimokritou-Str. Syndesmou streets and Lycabettus ring road," S-D 10154/22.11.1965, Folder 18961, C. A. Doxiadis Archives.
49 Constantinos A. Doxiadis, "Anthropocosmos: the world of man," *DA Review* no. 18 (1966): 2–8.
50 Brenner and Theodore, "Actually Existing Neoliberalism," 373.

8.1
ATI and Doxiadis Associates building with the Acropolis in the background

Archive Files 36399, Constantinos A. Doxiadis Archives

8.2
The modular system of the DA building, 1958

Archive Files 28989, Constantinos A. Doxiadis Archives

8.3
The DA atrium as a place for peace and harmony

Photographs 35835, Constantinos A. Doxiadis Archives

8.4
The DA atrium as a place for peace and harmony

C.A. Doxiadis, Architecture in Transition (London: Hutchinson & Co, 1963), 123.

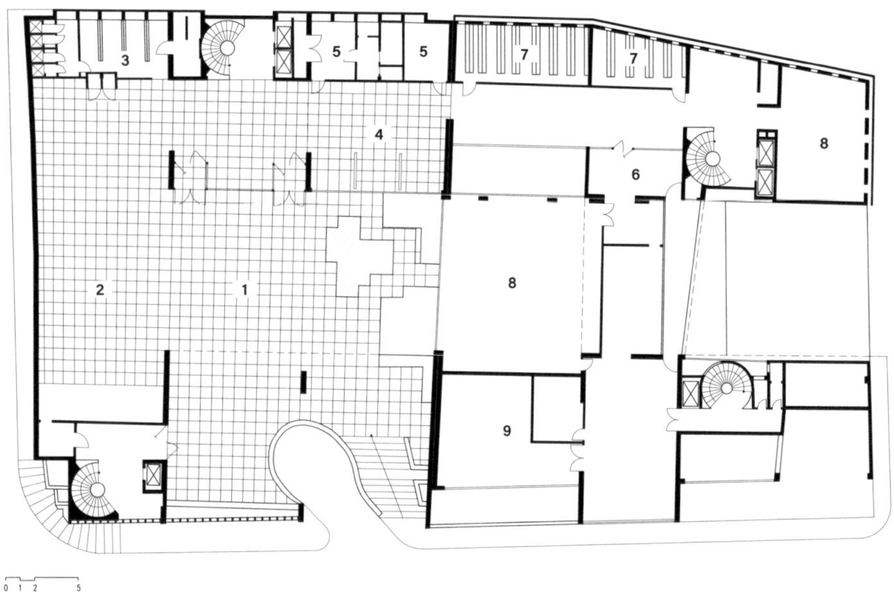

9.1
Ground floor plan, Doxiadis Associates and Athens Technological Organization building

1 Public atrium
2 Exhibition hall
3 Changing rooms
4 Gallery spaces
5 Auxiliary spaces
6 Reception area
7 Archives
8 Computer labs
9 Maintenance services

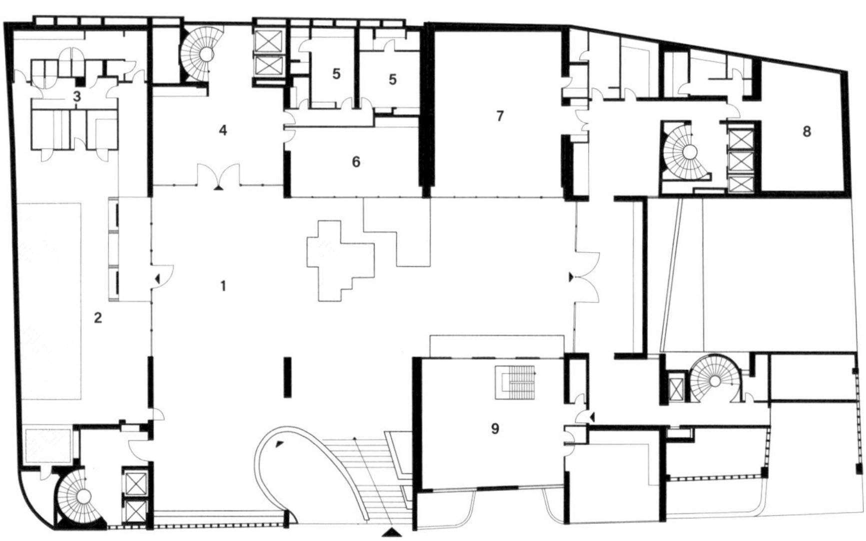

9.2
Ground floor plan, One Athens

1 Private atrium
2 Swimming pool hall
3 Hamam-sauna
4 Reception area
5 Treatment room
6 Gym
7 Playroom
8 Club/Screening
9 Private residence

methodological transition from a unifying theory to piecemeal opportunistic development, from housing as a functional container of human needs to housing as a territory for value extraction. Without his extraordinary leadership skills, his Organization soon fell apart after his death in 1975. The building gradually changed occupants, received a series of interventions and adjustments and "was unreservedly left to fall in disuse for decades."[51] In 2007 it was finally sold to Cyclamino S.A., a new developer, who commissioned its immediate conversion into "a high-standard residential complex,"[52] that would re-enact the landmark's "timeless existence."[53] As One Athens was under development, the legacy of the DA building returned to the foreground, calling into question the relation between the developer's ambition as experienced in private-public-partnership infrastructure projects,[54] and the creator's original vision.

It is important here to indicate the adoption of an international developmental trend according to which high-end residential investments operate within planned initiatives for the gentrification of the corresponding areas. In 2007, prior to the financial crisis, the developer purchased the DA building "with a very clear plan in mind [...] to create a fully serviced residential complex of international standards. It is typical of such residential developments in the metropolitan areas of London and New York, to provide communal spaces in their layout. The uniqueness of this building and its original communal use of the ground floor showed (us) the way."[55] The commissioning of the project sought to serve the developer's desire "to convert the building into the most contemporary and outstanding residential complex of the twenty-first century in Athens."[56] The conversion was assigned to Divercity Architects, an international architecture practice with experience in luxurious residential and retail complexes, such as the One Hyde Park in Knightsbridge, London, from which references were drawn.[57] Divercity defended the developer's view that "housing is the obvious answer" in the question of "how the private initiative can transform this building." In a statement, which would be characteristic of the intervention logic, they added that "*private space* cannot have aspirations [...] of bringing together activities far beyond this function."[58] The crisis and its consequences in

51 Dimitres Philippides, "Ena mythiko ktirio perna sten antipera oxthe [A Mythical Building breaks through to the Other Side]," *Triantafyllou Giorgos Architect*, January 12, 2014, http://triantafylloug.blogspot.com.

52 Dimitres Rigopoulos, "I nea epochi toy ktirioy doxiadi ston Lykavitto [The new era of the Doxiadis building at Lyvabettus]," *I Kathimerini*, March 16, 2014, https://www.kathimerini.gr/life/city/757912/i-nea-epochi-toy-ktirioy-doxiadi-ston-lykavitto.

53 One Athens, *ePresentation*, (March 17, 2014), https://www.oneathens.gr/ePresentation.pdf, 3.

54 A Greek version of private-public-partnership projects, "self-funded public works" or "state property development," were introduced as a state policy to boost real estate investment and equity funds. These projects just confirmed the trend of privatization of public services and infrastructure introduced in Greece after the establishment of neoliberal policies in Europe. See Pavlos M. Delladetsimas, "The current dynamics of the development of Athens: Conventional new model and infrastructure works," *Geographies* no. 7 (June 2004): 48–64.

55 Kyriakides, "Interview with Miltos Kampourides."

56 Ibid.

57 Divercity was selected by Wallpaper magazine as being among the world's leading young architecture practices in 2009 and was nominated for the Mies van der Rohe Award 2014 for the One Athens project.

58 (emphasis added) Marilena Astrapellou, "Interview with Nikolas Travasaros," *BH-Magazine*, June 16, 2013, 25–26.

the housing sector at that time did not seem to be able yet to challenge established concepts of private space. On the contrary, professional precariousness induced the idea that "architecture cannot survive anymore as an independent discipline"[59] and that "the final outcome is conditioned by the requirements of the contracting parties [...] while in the past [referring to Doxiadis] architects mastered the discussion on architecture."[60]

Such a compromised consideration of the architectural agency in the resolution between the history of the building and the new intervention sparked opposition within the profession. It also revealed the stance of the state regarding issues of architectural heritage, property rights and development interests in a time of economic recession and housing crisis. The intervention started quite aggressively and in 2009 the demolition of the façades of the building was already well underway. Following appeals by residents of the area to Monumenta, a non-profit organization for the protection of monuments, the architectural community was awakened to the duty of 'saving' the building in the last minute.[61] In December 2009, Monumenta appealed to the Ministries of Culture and Environment in order to take action in suspending the construction works. On the grounds of "the complete deterioration of the general layout" with the intention "to create a new elite community," Monumenta requested "the preservation of the facades at least."[62] The Association of Greek Architects bolstered the appeal to the Ministries and to the Urban Planning Authority of the Municipality of Athens with the request of "halting the intervention until the designation of a listed status to the building."[63] Meanwhile, the association's journal had started a campaign against the notion of "avant-garde monument protection" as a contradiction in terms, one prioritizing the preservation of the past and the other a future dependent on processes of destruction.[64] Although the article was not openly targeted at the One Athens intervention, it had clear references to the project.

The final decision was conditioned by the developer's intentions supported, not only by the project architects, but also by architects and members of the Central Council

59 Ibid., 26.
60 Ioanna Alexatou, "The Power of Collaboration. Interview with Divercity Architects," *Casa Viva*, July 2014, 39–40.
61 Dimitres Philippides, "A Mythical Building."
62 Monumenta, "To Ktirio Doxiadi aneke pia sto Parelthon [The Doxiadis Building Now Belongs to the Past]," (Letter to the Ministry of Culture and Tourism, December 1, 2009), https://www.greekarchitects.gr.
63 The appeal was supported by the School of Architecture of the National Technical University of Athens and the Technical Chamber of Greece. Evangelos Lyroudias (SADAS-PEA Director), "Sygrotima Grafeion Costa Doxiadi [C.A. Doxiadis Office Building]," in "Activity Log of the SADAS Board of Directors," *Architektones* (Journal of the Association of Greek Architects) 77 – B' (Nov-Dec 2009): 15.
64 Christos Theodoropoulos, "Pros mia avant-garde istorike prostasia [Towards an avant-garde monument protection]," *Architektones* 76 – B' (October 2009): 38–40.

for Modern Monuments. Symeon, a former DA partner, suggested alternative, less interventionist ways of façade treatment to preserve the outer shell while adjusting it for residential use.[65] At the council meeting, however, it was argued that the building had already been damaged by the subsequent occupation regimes and the initial design could not be saved. In a manner of appropriating Doxiadis's conceptualization of monuments as static, it was stressed that the conversion would boost the building's evolution as a "living organism" against its decay as "a monument – fossil."[66] Architectural arguments in favor of the new intervention were grounded in sheer faith in contemporary architecture. It was stressed that "objections against the conversion hamper the realization of a project extraordinary for the Greek standards and undoubtedly daring."[67] The struggle was acknowledged as "a conflict of two views on the treatment of architectural heritage: one dynamic and one static,"[68] where "the sole victim from an ex-post State intervention would be the building itself, which instead of moving forward in time would end up being one more modernist 'carcass.' "[69] This validation of the architectural intervention empowered arguments on the assessment of economic interest. The developer put further pressure, declaring that "the cost of the unfair pause of the construction works was too high," putting them in "a difficult position" within the crisis, despite their "faith in the value of the proposal."[70] What was actually at risk, when confronted with a possible annulment of the project, was the municipality's and the state's significant profit from property taxation upon the sale of the residences.[71] In April 2010, the council made a diplomatic decision to designate the building with a "partly-listed" status that did not disturb the premises of the One Athens proposal; it marked worthy of preservation only the load-bearing structure, the atrium, the staircases and the three-meter-grid, namely *the rhythm*, of the front façade.

The intervention was predicated upon the appropriation of Doxiadis's theories of place and powerful symbols by a new narrative: "The Art of Living in the Heart of the City."[72] Domestic privacy recurred as a powerful apparatus in the retrofitting of the *par excellence* office space into "the most sophisticated, luxurious and modern residences in the capital city." [73] It is important to note that this idea was conceived

65 Symeon here actually refers to the logic of the double skin at the Doxiadis's private apartment building on 2 Str. Syndesmou Street. Andreas Symeon, "Giati einai simantiko to ktiriako sygrotima Doxiadi [Why the Doxiadis complex is important]," *Greek Architects*, May 10, 2010, https://www.greekarchitects.gr.

66 Monumenta, "The Doxiadis Building."

67 Philippides, while admiring the new architecture, expressed reservations regarding the "consumption" of a lifestyle conceived a few years earlier under dramatically different circumstances. He thought of the project as, perhaps, prophetic of a future where inequalities rule. Giorgos Triantafyllou, "Syntome perigraphe tes istorias tou ktiriou kai tes mechri shmera diadromes tou ergou [Brief description of the history of Doxiadis building and its life course until today]," *Triantafyllou Giorgos Architect*, January 12, 2014, http://triantafylloug.blogspot.com.

68 Ibid.

69 By "State intervention" he is referring to the proper designation of a listed status to the building, which would cancel out or drastically reconfigure the submitted proposal for conversion. Ibid.

70 Kyriakides, "Interview with Miltos Kampourides."

71 "The owner will be liable to a property transfer tax (3%) to the corresponding tax authority (Tax Office I of the Athens Municipality) [...] One Athens owners should pay property tax, on an annual basis, which is subject to a rate based on the area and the apartment type". The Municipality would collect a real estate transfer tax upon purchase of the residences. The State would collect the annual property tax. According to the tax rates, apartment types and sizes given in the document, the total tax revenue would range between EUR 234,437 and 282,950 per year. One Athens, *One Athens*, 4.

72 "One Athens / Lifestyle," https://www.oneathens.gr/lifestyle.

73 Thanasis Charames, "One Athens: Mpikame ste nea schole Doxiadi [One Athens: Entering the New Doxiadis School]," *Lifo*, February 22, 2014, https://www.lifo.gr.

in the aftermath of the Olympic "regeneration" of the center, which had served to promote a metropolitan image of Athens. According to architectural historian James Ackerman, in periods of metropolitan growth, the impulse for "a fantasy which is impervious to the reality"[74] brings about the thriving of the villa type. As the quest for differentiation in mass housing had brought about a merging of private housing types and the multi-apartment building, here, the quest for luxury outrightly adopted the type of the villa. However, as Ackerman argues, the villa is not only a form, but quintessentially an ideology that fosters a dialogue between city and nature.[75] On that note, I argue that One Athens encapsulates this domestic ideology, which pursues "the new mythologies of the Athenian condition of meta-polis"[76] by re-introducing a relationship with the Attica landscape. On the one hand, it offers a panorama of the city "at a glance" and "dazzling" views of the Parthenon, while "the seaside and Saronic islands glimmer tantalizingly on the horizon all within easy reach."[77] **(Fig. 11)** At the same time, it offers proximity to a "vibrant, seductive and spontaneous Athens" which is "just a short walk downhill."[78] In the background, the pine-clad Lycabettus signifies a withdrawal from the noisy city and makes the complex "a serene oasis in the densely populated center —a rare luxury in any capital, but especially in Athens."[79] **(Fig. 10)** At the same time, it adopts the design of the villa in order to serve its ideology; it engages intimately with nature by "reflecting the setting," while it is separated "by a compact form cubic in outline" and an emphasis on plane surfaces that "disguise the nature of materials."[80] This explains why the issue of the façades was crucial in the negotiations for the parts of the DA building that were subject to alteration. The One Athens design "set out to reconnect the building with its surroundings"[81] and replaced all windows with floor-to-ceiling glass surfaces. By framing and reflecting the forest in the back, they allowed the uninterrupted flow of nature through the building and its connection to the city. On the other hand, the white compact outer shell with the large glossy surfaces was meant to stand out from its surroundings as opposed to the earthy color palette of its predecessor.

74 James S. Ackerman, *The Villa: Form and Ideology of Country Houses* (London: Thames and Hudson, 1990), 9.
75 Ibid., 10.
76 Aesopos and Simeoforides, *Landscapes of modernization*, 163.
77 "One Athens / Lifestyle."
78 "One Athens / Location," https://www.oneathens.gr/location.
79 Ibid.
80 Ackerman, *The Villa*, 30.
81 Divercity, "Conversion of Doxiadis Office Building-ATI into Apartment Building," *Archdaily*, February 8, 2015, https://www.archdaily.com/593057/conversion-of-doxiadis-office-building-ati-to-apartment-buildin-divercity.

10
Front view of the One Athens penthouses

11
Panoramic view from Lycabettus hill. In the foreground is One Athens complex during construction

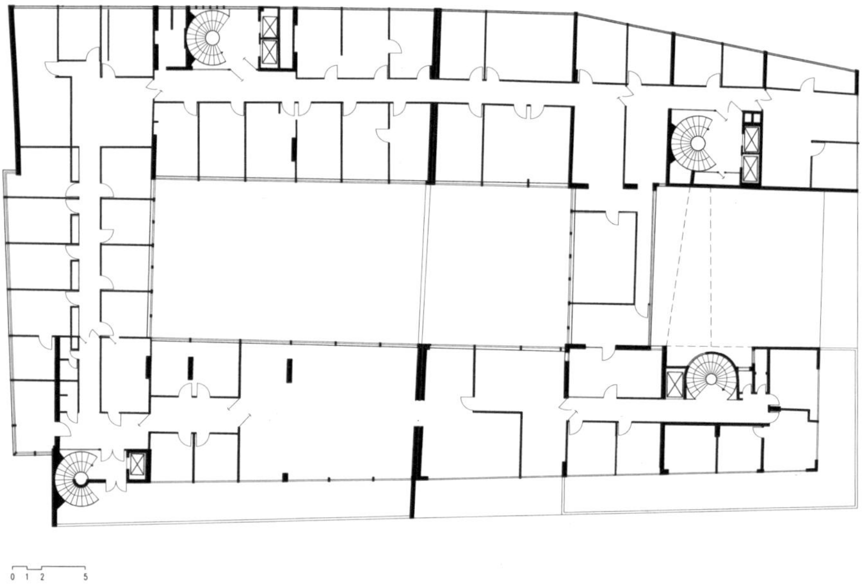

12.1
5th floor plan, Doxiadis Organization and Athens Technological Organization building

12.2
One Athens 5th floor plan

Furthermore, the treatment of the façades was meant to adopt internationally established trends in design and use of materials able to signify a modern and luxurious lifestyle. The retrofitting of office spaces into the desired new homes was considered a "dynamic"[82] design intervention, which stressed the need for "more versatile, *private*, and composite spaces."[83] The architects introduced a system of "pixellated" surfaces for the varying transparency of the façades, which enhanced the compact outlook of the building's volume. They retained the original modular grid as a framework filled with three components of different opacity in order to mark a gradient of *privacy* in the interior spaces. Private areas were earmarked by panels of the famous dark Aliveri marble that was popular among the proponents of a "delicate taste."[84] The marble pattern was supposed to provide "a snapshot of the landscape imprinted onto the building," a gesture that Ackerman describes as a paradoxical imitation of natural forms by manmade elements.[85] Translucent concrete was used for the "mid-zones" in order to spectacularize the view through "an interactive shadow theater created by the movement of the inhabitants."[86] The use of this material marked an innovation as it was the first application in a residential complex in Greece. Glass was used extensively to frame views of the landscape as "a window into an exclusive world."[87] Making the most of the capacities of these materials, One Athens aimed to act as the stage for day-by-night transformations, interplays and choreographies of a domesticity that becomes a living "experience." The more aspects of this domesticity became a spectacle for the city, the more privacy was offered as the luxury of concealment.

Programmatically, One Athens was dedicated to guaranteeing privileges in urban living comparable to those of "a five-star hotel."[88] Housing was distributed along the four wings and amenities, "not available anywhere else in Athens,"[89] were positioned on the ground floor around the atrium. These included a 100 square meter playroom in the place of the former Doxiadis archive, a club and a screening room in the former computer labs, and a gym with treatment rooms that taking up part of the former gallery. **(Fig. 9.2)** According to the architects, the structuring of the

82 Doxiadis's flair for dynamic instead of static concepts was repeatedly expropriated by the principles of the One Athens conversion. However, Doxiadis mainly referred to the dynamic expansion of the city (Dynapolis) as it stems from the need to plan for mass housing, not bespoke residences addressing a limited part of society.

83 "One Athens / Inspiration," 2020, https://www.oneathens.gr/inspiration.

84 Rigopoulos, "The new era of the Doxiadis building." According to Ackerman, the limitation within "the rule of taste" or "the sphere of taste" has often been motivated by the unchanging mythology of surplus wealth, see Ackerman, *The Villa*, 26–34.

85 Ibid.

86 "One Athens / Inspiration."

87 Ibid.

88 One Athens is still one of the largest investments in residential development in Athens, reaching a total cost of EUR 70 million. Ibid.

89 "One Athens / Concept," https://www.oneathens.gr/concept.

facilities around the atrium would retain its original spirit as a communal space. However, both the program and the architectural language reveal that the intended lifestyle was not that of "a community, typical of housing complexes of the Modern Movement,"[90] but of an exclusive, residents-only community with access to exceptional provisions. The 24-hour security service also attests this, making sure that no unauthorized visitor enters the complex. The project brief conceptualizes the atrium as "the lobby of a five-star hotel," a transition from the "clamor" of the city to the "serenity" of the complex, where "residents can have a massage, hold a meeting, or get to know their neighbor's children in the playroom." All they need is to "step inside," and automatically "enter a world where everything is accessible."[91]

At One Athens, according to the architects, "individuality is as important as a sense of community."[92] Therefore, the complex provides 26 luxury residences in "a range of sizes and types, depending on the resident's lifestyle and needs."[93] Each of the layouts is unique, while the apartments belong to five basic types and are offered only for sale[94]: two duplexes, four townhouses, three studios, twelve three- and four-bedroom apartments and five penthouses. Although all residents are granted exclusive access to "the most outstanding features on the top floor" —i.e. the roof garden,—the five upper residences encapsulate the ideal of the One Athens residential project: "the most spectacular penthouses the city has ever seen."[95] **(Fig. 10)** They all feature spacious interiors reaching over 600 square meters^2, large private garden terraces and outdoor jacuzzi tubs with "show-stopping views of the city"[96]: the ultimate domestic space for "all those fortunate enough to live here."[97]

The main challenge of the operation was generally considered the typological transformation of office spaces into a "revolutionary new concept for living in downtown Athens"[98] **(Figs. 12.1-12.2)** However, the consideration of the existing layout as an obstacle, especially in a conversion project that claims to value notions of memory and preservation, reveals how established ideas of domestic privacy are in residential typologies. Existing spatial concepts, like the canonical

90 Divercity, "Conversion of Doxiadis Office Building."
91 "One Athens / Concept."
92 Divercity, "Conversion of Doxiadis Office Building."
93 "One Athens / Concept."
94 One Athens, *One Athens*, 2.
95 "One Athens / Concept."
96 Kyriakos Spirou, "History Revisited: ONE ATHENS Apartment Building by C. A. Doxiadis and Divercity Architects," *Yatzer*, May 13, 2014, https://www.yatzer.com/one-athens.
97 "One Athens / Concept."
98 One Athens, *One Athens*, 1.

arrangement into equally sized rooms and the communal kitchen-canteen, did not challenge the new subdivision of floor areas into typical private apartments. The struggle was focused in ensuring that each apartment has individual services like terraces/balconies, staircases and lifts. A study of the floor plans further questions the intention for the provision of "open-plan apartments."[99] The original layout, which was essentially adjustable with moveable partitions and minimal structural elements, could ideally serve such a purpose. On the contrary, the resolution of the apartment layouts, regardless of the dwelling type, illustrates an extreme compartmentalization of interior spaces. Almost half of the total surface is dedicated to interior partitions, corridors, antechambers, storage rooms, and individual auxiliary spaces. The separation between serving and served areas marked by the closed kitchen, the maid's room placed by the kitchen, the master bedroom in the most isolated corner of the apartment with the most "privileged" view; they all echo an utterly conservative rather than revolutionary lifestyle and promote class and power relations. In particular, the *master bedroom* facing Lycabettus, as the hallmark of privacy and seclusion, exemplifies the hierarchical model of nuclear family domesticity. It renders the uneven distribution of qualities especially when compared to the existing layout, which provides a basis for equality and sharing. This differentiation among floors, types and rooms, and the subsequent issue of entitlement, point to the ideological pattern that made the "right to privacy" inaccessible to a growing part of society in the neoliberal years. What is more, this process took place at the start of the 2008 mortgage crisis, which paralyzed the credit system of housing provision and shattered the private narrative to its core.

The One Athens project, with the support of state organs, was an exemplary gesture to restore faith in the domestic dream by appealing to the city's collective memory through the Doxiadis building.[100] After its inauguration in 2014, the city celebrated the fact that the challenge to achieve "the residents' luxury of space in the city center"[101] was met. The lifestyle press heralded "the luxurious condominium One Athens, the first of its kind in the city"[102] where "we see how the private initiative once again

99 "One Athens / Concept."
100 Charames, "One Athens."
101 "One Athens / Lifestyle."
102 Spirou, "History Revisited."

prevents a historical building from decaying [...] and results in the aesthetic upgrade of *both private and public space*."[103] The invocation to a collective nostalgia of "the golden age of the Athenian apartment buildings of the 1960-70s" was attempted both conceptually and aesthetically. Doxiadis's theoretical concepts, such as *Ekistics* and *Ecumenopolis*, were twisted to fit the image of an "idealised metropolis" and "small communities within big cities."[104] The aesthetic of the interiors —the ribbed concrete slabs, "the herringbone timber floors and marble-clad bathrooms"[105]— became romanticized references to the period, which established the narrative of private housing in Greece. Overall, One Athens was promoted as an "ultra-modern residential complex which praises contemporary Greek architecture" and embodies the future of "a European metropolis like Athens."[106] The jargon, which acquired the dimensions of a campaign, even tried to rationalize the prices of these dwellings[107] to a society in the middle of crisis by means of common sense. This was based on the private sense construct as "luxury that makes living enjoyable and easy" and as provision of "choice [which] is not as self-evident as one may think."[108] In a moment of financial and cultural crisis, this private-public partnership paved the way for arguments on the symbolic content of architecture to be deliberately twisted. On the one hand, it promoted a fragmentary and filtered —if not embellished— version of the urban condition of Athens. On the other hand, it promoted the "villa" ideology as an apparatus for independence from the city, even when situated in the city center. Domesticity was mobilized to transform a highly symbolic architectural type and "to signal the regeneration of the Athenian center,"[109] that is, its ultimate *domestication*.

One Athens demonstrates in an illustrative way how neoliberal tactics on housing act inspite —or because of— their inevitable crises. That is, how international large-scale investment capital colonizes urban areas, where indigenous modes of production have been amputated, and attempts to re-market domesticity in terms of exchange value. In practice, it affirms the contradictions of the neoliberal project: while it claims the liberation from state intervention, it relies on the state to impose versions of market rule (e.g. regeneration processes) and manage the consequences

103 (Emphasis added) Soulis, "The New Jewel of Athens."
104 Ibid.
105 Rigopoulos, "The new era of the Doxiadis building."
106 Soulis, "The New Jewel of Athens."
107 Prices were estimated between EUR 15,000 and 18,000 per square metre according to the size and provisions of the dwelling. "Akinita: Times sto Kolonaki. Sto One Athens 18000 euro to tetragoniko! [Real estate prices in Kolonaki Area: At One Athens they reach up to EUR 18,000 per square metre!]," *Bank Wars*, April 22, 2014, http://www.bankwars.gr.
108 Rigopoulos, "The new era of the Doxiadis building."
109 Soulis, "The New Jewel of Athens."

of such marketization. The One Athens ambition was to "fill a considerable gap in Athens' luxury real estate market"[110] by making "the most sophisticated and cosmopolitan citizens feel at home."[111] The fact that the project failed, as a real estate investment against the reality of recession,[112] reinforces rather than weakens this account on the neoliberalization of urban living. The private as an aspirational apparatus is mobilized to instigate a sense of possession and rootedness, all the more in a traumatized society. It is meant to set the measure of a possible lifestyle against the odds: "young professionals, business people in need of a *pied à terre*, jet-setting couples, or parents enjoying a new lease of life now that their children have left home."[113] An interesting parallel between the Barbican and One Athens illustrates the evolution of the ideal of domestic privacy from one that encloses a part of the city, to one that encloses the whole city. The neoliberal project was not just communicated in One Athens by the internationally established tropes, such as the white glossy cubic envelope and the combination of soft modernism with classical materials. It was invested in the mythical nature of the private ideology, which liberates housing from the mundane restraints of utility and economy and makes it the locus of aspirations, as they were captured in the slogan:

> "One Athens is more than a home —it is an experience.
> This is the art of living in the heart of the city."[114]

110 One Athens, *One Athens*,1.
111 "One Athens / Lifestyle."
112 Only 7 out of the 26 residences were sold and the complex is still devoid of a community. Frixos Dracontides, "Giati stoixiose to Project Manhattan sto Kolonaki [Why the "Manhattan project" in Kolonaki failed]," *Proto Thema*, December 30, 2015, https://www.protothema.gr/stories/article/540574/giati-stoiheiose-to-project-manhatan-sto-kolonaki.
113 "One Athens / Lifestyle."
114 Ibid.

III. Epilogue — Towards an Ecology of the Private

A Manual for the Trigono Community Land Trust in Athens

The Right to Privacy as the Right to the City

In the previous chapters, I have traced the genealogical evolution of the private, its gradual dissociation from privacy as an essential social and physical condition of modernity, and its neoliberal extrapolation in the process of privatization as a new form o enclosure. The scrutiny of the private as a powerful category of neoliberalism, associated in principle with individualism and institutionally with property, hypothesizes the fallacy of its antithetical opposition to the public as state-driven or state-controlled. On the contrary, it posits the private, as a managerial paradigm, in direct and co-dependent relationship with the governmental apparatus. My case studies have provided a means of reading the neoliberal city by investigating the relationship between this economic rationale, housing policy and architectural typology. They also demonstrated the daunting failure of neoliberalism to secure accessibility to and sustainability of its urban domestic model, thus negating privacy as an affirmation of essentia autonomy and raising links with its classical concept of deprivation. This chapter, cou pled with a project, puts forward the political and spatial reinstatement of the private within the urban context addressing it in both ideological and design terms.

The struggle for the right to privacy needs to be framed through a strategy of decolonizing our imaginaries and mental infrastructures away from the private as an individual symbol of status and ownership. Instead, it resonates with Lefebvre's articulation of the right to the city, as the "demand [for] a transformed and renewe access to urban life."[1] Among the scholars who have revisited this concept in recen years,[2] Harvey most notably elaborates on its prefigurative dimension:

"The right to the city is far more than the individual liberty to access urban resource it is a right to change ourselves by changing the city. It is, moreover, a common rathe than an individual right since this transformation inevitably depends upon the exer-

1 Lefebvre proposed the idea of the "right to the city," in his 1968 book, *Le Droit à la Ville*, as a call for a political revolution intended to orient planning towards social needs and provide democratic control of both the State and of self-management as: "a permanent cultural revolution." For an English version, see Henri Lefebvre, *Writings on Cities*, trans. and eds. Eleonore Kofman and Elizabeth Lebas, (Oxford: Blackwell Publishers, 1996).

2 The concept has been revisited more recently by social movements, thinkers, and local authorities as a call for action to reclaim the city as a co-created space for living detached from the alarming effects of capitalism, commodification of social interaction and the rise of spatial inequalities in cities throughout the last two centuries. See David Pinder, "Reconstituting the Possible: Lefebvre, utopia and the urban question," *International Journal of Urban and Regional Research* 39, no. 1 (2013): 28–45 and Mark Purcell, "Possible Worlds: Henri Lefebvre and the Right to the City," *Journal of Urban Affairs* 36, no. 1 (2014): 141–54.

cise of a collective power to reshape the processes of urbanization. The freedom to make and remake our cities and ourselves is, I want to argue, one of the most precious yet most neglected of our human rights."[3]

There are three key insights in this process of claiming the right to the city, along which, I believe, the right to privacy has the potential to be regained: in terms of collective empowerment rather than individual entitlement; as an ongoing social practice rather than an established social status; and as an organic emergence of subjectivity rather than its deliberate construction. What these three insights share in common is that each renders the question of *reproduction* — "the freedom to make and remake our cities and ourselves"— central to the process of re-introducing the private as a civic discourse.[4] For this realization, Lefebvre argues, neither the organization of private enterprise, nor global planning, although necessary, would suffice. A leap forward is accomplished but neither the State, nor private enterprise – the Market– can provide an indispensable model of *rationality*.[5] Indeed, any model of rationality with an emancipatory perspective would need to escape this problematic binary logic and address the housing question politically and socially on the administrative level of the city.

I propose, therefore, that a new model of rationality be established through the conceptual shift from an economy of the private to *an ecology of the private*. Ecology, in this case, provides both an operational principle and spatial concept for addressing privacy as the possibility of preserving personal autonomy through a practice of commoning. To conceptualize this transition is to draw the radical use of the distinction between Nomos and Logos in the production of a domestic community and its subjects.[6] Nomos has been historically interpreted, from the ancient Greek city-state to modern international law, by Carl Schmitt, as the form of political and social order determined by a fundamental process of apportioning space.[7] The establishment of such an order implies an arbitrary act of (land) appropriation, which predicates any concomitant social category and system of governance on sovereign and property rights. On the

3 David Harvey, *Rebel Cities: From the right to the City to Urban Revolution*, (London: Verso, 2012), 5. See also David Harvey, "The right to the city," *New Left Review* no. 53 (September - October 2008): 23–40.

4 This will be key to my analysis later and refers to social reproduction as a historically collective process, one which has been completely subsumed by capitalism and yet remains implicit in any discourse of domesticity and housing commons. See Silvia Federici, *Revolution at Point Zero: Housework, Reproduction, and Feminist Struggle* (Oakland: PM Press: 2012).

5 Lefebvre, *Writings on Cities*, 177–184.

6 Expanding on the first chapter's etymological analysis of the word economy from oikos and nomos, the word "ecology" derives from oikos and lógos>légein (syllégein) : a) to utter or verbally articulate speech, to consider carefully, to deliberate, to argue convincingly b) to reflect, to collect. For a detailed etymological analysis, see H.G. Liddell and Robert Scott, *An Intermediate Greek-English Lexicon*, Revised Edition (Oxford: Clarendon Press, 1940).

7 Nomos as a concept of legal, and subsequently socio-spatial, order in ancient Greece (νόμος) was introduced in the first chapter. Here, Schmitt's analysis of the diachronic governance of nomos up to the very modern states is employed in order to be contested as the institutional principle of any emancipatory model. See Carl Schmitt, "On the Meaning of the Word Nomos," in *The Nomos of the Earth in the International Law of the Jus Publicum Europaeum*, trans. G. L. Ulmen (New York: Telos Press Publishing, 2006), 67–80.

other hand, the ancient Greek Logos ["word," "(right of) speech," "account," "reason," "proportion," "ground," "opinion," "law," "formula," and "discourse"] conveys a universal form of order and knowledge that is attainable through the fundamental principle of rationality, both as reason and dialectical capacity, common to the human condition.[8] It was introduced to pre-Socratic philosophy by Heraclitus and conceptualized as the link between (human) rational discourse and the world's rational structure.[9] Here, the principle of order is unifying rather than divisional, it is inherent to individuals but it only gains legitimacy by means of collective mobilization and exchange. When it comes to the management of domestic space (oikos), the idea of ecology is suggestive of an alternative form of agency in the institutionalization of the private and reframes the latter within the common discourse.

LOGOS AS THE REASON OF THE COMMON

To understand Logos as such, it is particularly important to dwell on Heraclitus's doctrine of independent reason governing the cosmos,[10] as it is the earliest theorization (sixth century BC) of a principle of order in relation to a primal universal *common*.[11]

"For this reason it is necessary to follow what is common. But although the Logos is common [τοῦ λόγου δ' ἐόντος ξυνοῦ], most people live as if they had their own *private* understanding [ὡς ἰδίαν ἔχοντες φρόνησιν]."[12]

The Heraclitan doctrine of Logos is framed by two theorems: the doctrine of Flux/Becoming and the Unity of Opposites. Opposites — or what we would call in contemporary philosophy the parts of a categorical distinction, like private and public — are unified in a system of balanced exchanges or a law-like interchange of elements. Thus, a category is not to be identified with any particular status quo, but with an ongoing process governed by a law of (ex)change. The point, however, is not that everything is subject to change, but that this quality of negotiation between elements or constituents supports the constancy of higher-level common structures.

8 *Encyclopaedia Britannica*, s.v. "Logos," https://www.britannica.com.To the Greek mind, Logos acquired a much more complex meaning than both its Latin counterpart "verbum" and the English "word." It stands for a cosmic constant through which the world's esoteric order, form and meaning are revealed to humans. Ever since, the term has been theorized in various fields, from ancient Greek tragedy to contemporary Western philosophy, from linguistics to theology, from Aristotle's rhetoric of "reasoned discourse" to Jung's analytical psychology of "objective interest." See Eugene Garver, *Aristotle's Rhetoric: An art of character* (Chicago: University of Chicago Press, 1994), 192 and Carl Jung, *Aspects of the Feminine* (Princeton, NJ: Princeton University Press,1982), 65.

9 Logos appears in Heraclitus's philosophical treatise *On Nature* (*Peri Physeos*), which was divided into three discourses: one on the universe, another on politics (and ethics), and the last on theology. These only survive in fragments. See Heraclitus, "Peri Physeos, 1–123," in L. Antzoule, G. Kritsele, St. Tsitirides and Th. K. Stefanopoulos, *Anthology of Ancient Greek Literature*, vol. I, pt. 4 (Athens: Ministry of Education, Research and Theology & Institute of Educational Policy, 2012), 218–223. Translated fragments from Richard D. McKirahan, *Philosophy before Socrates: An Introduction with Texts and Commentary*, second edition (Indianapolis: Hackett Publishing, 2011), 112–144.

10 Heraclitus of Ephesus (535–475 BC) was an Ionian philosopher and the acclaimed founder of many strands of scientific philosophy (cosmology, ethics, and metaphysics) as well as theoretical movements (dialectical materialism, empiricism, and rationalism). In these fields, he profoundly influenced the German philosophers Hegel, Nietzsche, Heidegger, and Schleiermacher.

11 The common (singular) is used here as a political principle of organization and action which is able to institute, govern and sustain the commons [plural], as the material and social outcome of common struggles. The common is not in itself a thing or a substance nor is it a quality belonging to a thing.

12 Heraclitus, "Peri Physeos," DK B2. Etymologically, the word ξυνός (xunós or k(s)unós or, as it evolved, koinós) derives from συν (con) and νόος [noos] (spirit, intellect, mentality) meaning common sense or understanding. The term appears frequently in contradistinction with ἰδιος-ἰδίαν (one's own) understanding, depending exactly on the way private consciousness is structured in relation to the common. See, G.S. Kirk, *Heraclitus: The Cosmic Fragments* (Cambridge: Cambridge University Press, 1954), 57–8.

Accordingly, when Heraclitus denies the reality of Being as a fixed status or condition, and declares Becoming, or eternal flux and change, to be the sole actuality, he enunciates the state of continuous transition from non-existence to existence.[13] To him, the embodiment of the process of Becoming, is in itself that divine rational process, the harmony of the law of the universe. Real knowledge consists in the comprehension of this permeating harmony, the common rhythm or measure embedded in the human perception, and the subordination of the individual to the laws of this universal reason.[14] Thus, Heraclitus does not recognize a Universal Flux, but rather a law-like flux of elements, and he does not argue for the Identity of Opposites, but for their Transformational Equivalence. He discerns, in the cosmic process, a Logos *analogous* to human reasoning power; a suggestion of agency is implied. Revisiting Heraclitus's philosophical concepts within the framework of the Enlightenment, Schleiermacher interprets Logos as a *relation*; the relationship between subjectivity, the particular or individual reason, and the universal or collective reason, which is one (common) state of rational consciousness.[15] The common modifies, or describes, Logos which in turn, gives order and rationality to the system.

A connection between Logos and Nomos is already drawn by Heraclitus in one of his most controversial fragments. Both are conceptualized in terms of a law, a principle or instruction of order which institutes rights that are inevitably grounded in the ultimate nature (physicality) of things:

"Speaking with sense [ξὺν νῷ λέγοντας] we must rely on what is common to all, in the same way as a city relies on its laws [ὅκωσπερ νόμῳ πόλις], *and much more reliably*. For all human laws [οἱ ἀνθρώπειοι νόμοι] are nourished by the one divine law. For it prevails as far as it will and suffices for all and overflows."[16]

On the basis of this terminological similarity, Schmitt supports his interpretation of a single, historically uninterrupted, constitutive act of spatial ordering by identifying both "human laws" and "the one divine law" with Nomos.[17] However, many pre-So-

13 For an important reassessment of Heraclitus, as a philosopher of the human condition, which delves into his linguistic complexity, see Charles H. Kahn, *The Art and Thought of Heraclitus* (Cambridge: Cambridge University Press, 1979).

14 According to Heraclitus the Logos holds always but humans are not always able to understand it. For a further study on Heraclitus's theory of knowledge see Edward Hussey, "Epistemology and Meaning in Heraclitus," in *Language and Logos*, eds. M. Schofield and M. C. Nussbaum (Cambridge: Cambridge University Press, 1982), 33–59.

15 Friedrich Schleiermacher, "Herakleitos der Dunkle, von Ephesos, dargestellt aus den Trümmern seines Werkes und den Zeugnissen der Alten," in P. Buttmann and F. A. Wolf, *Museum der Alterthums-Wissenschaft*, vol. I, pt. 3 (Berlin: Deutsche Forschungsgemeinschaft (DFG),1807), 313–533. See also Georg W. F. Hegel, *Lectures on the History of Philosophy 1825-6*, vol. II, pt. I. A.4., trans. and ed. R.F. Brown (Oxford: Oxford University Press, 2006), 70–82.

16 Heraclitus, "Peri Physeos," DK B114.

17 "The nomos can grow and multiply like land and property: all human nomoi are "nourished" by a single divine nomos. The word does not lose its connection to a historical process -to a constitutive act of spatial ordering. [...] In reality, the words of Heraclitus and Pindar mean only that all subsequent regulations of a written or unwritten kind derive their power from the inner measure of an original, constitutive act of spatial ordering. This original act is nomos." See Schmitt, *The Nomos of the Earth*, 70–78.

cratic scholars interpret the "divine law" as determinative of Logos, not Nomos, which has been able to provide a linguistic de-codification of Heraclitus's fragments as a whole.[18] The useful implication in reading the two fragments together is that Logos itself is the vessel to a common and that Nomos does not define or identify with its content, but relates to it by analogy. In fact, more careful attention to the analogy in the second fragment (Logos relies on the common as the city on its laws) demonstrates that the polis, not Nomos, is the analogue for Logos. Thus, Logos relies on a common but is not identical to it; it reflects the underlying order, the logic of which governs the community that the common presupposes —in the same way as the polis reflects the system that governs the political community that Nomos presupposes.

Logos, or what Dardot and Laval define as "the reason of the common," describes "a social process with a logic all its own": "a generalizable alternative rationality"[19] that is no more decreed from the outside as a form of enclosure or limit, like Nomos. It is, rather, the aggregate result of decisions and negotiations, measured against a common understanding, as a formula for organized action.[20] In this light, Schmitt's interpretation of the noos passage in The Odyssey as Nomos is questionable.[21] Odysseus might, indeed, have comprehended the noos of many cities and citadels as the existential understanding behind the operation of these urban communities, rather than their Nomos, the managerial paradigm of "divisional and distinguishing orders."[22] In fact, Schmitt dismisses noos precisely on the grounds of its universality —"common not just to many, but to all thinking people"— and accepts the normativistic, jurisprudential thinking of Nomos. To this, I juxtapose the non-normative sense of Heraclitan Logos, the law of becoming, which reflects a relationship between the individual and the collective, the part and the whole, the local and the global. This relationship is not instituted by the law of Nomos, an appropriated and walled space with a predetermined distinction between public and private, but through the law of Logos, the regulation of political action as a result of negotiation between opposites on the basis of the common principle.[23] Thus, the normative power of the 'factual' or the 'given' — the act of sovereign power — gives way to the constant struggle with normativistic

18 On the problematic equation of the Logos and Nomos fragments, and various arguments on their semantic estrangement, see Robin Reames, "Heraclitus' Doublespeak: The Paradoxical Origins of Rhetorical Logos," in *Logos without Rhetoric: The Arts of Language before Plato*, second edition (Columbia, SC: University of South Carolina Press, 2017).

19 Dardot and Laval concluded to the concept of the "reason of the common" as a response to their analysis of the operations of the "neoliberalism reason". See Pierre Dardot and Christian Laval, *The New Way of the World: On Neoliberal Society*, trans. G. Elliott (London: Verso, 2013). Then this concept became the project of their later work, see Pierre Dardot and Christian Laval, *Common: On Revolution in the 21st Century* (London: Bloomsbury Publishing, 2019), 103–104.

20 Heraclitus is the first to draw a parallel between nomos and the city wall to define an enclosed or walled, and sacred, space. For a further analysis of Nomos as a form of enclosure, besides Schmitt, see Hannah Arendt, "Introduction into Politics," in *The Promise of Politics*, ed. Cohn, J. (New York: Schoken Books, 2005), 93-200; Pier Vittorio Aureli, "Defining the Political and the Formal in Architecture," in *The Possibility of an Absolute Architecture* (Cambridge, MA: MIT Press, 2011), 1–13; and Pier Vittorio Aureli, "Appropriation, Subdivision, Abstraction: A Political History of the Urban Grid," *Log* no. 44 (2018): 139–67.

21 "Tell me, Muse, of the man of many devices, driven far astray after he had sacked the sacred citadel of Troy. Many were the men whose cities he saw and whose minds [noon] he learned, and many the woes he suffered in his heart upon the sea, seeking to win his own life and the return of his comrades." See Homer, *The Odyssey*, vol. I, book 1, verse 3, trans. A.T. Murray (Cambridge MA: Harvard University Press, 1995), 12–3.

22 Schmitt, *The Nomos of the Earth*, 78. For the etymological relation of noos and common, see footnote 12.

23 On the predetermined distinction between public and private in Nomos see Arendt, *The Promise of Politics* 186–7. On the normativistic nature of Nomos, Schmitt himself juxtaposes the non-normative sense of Heraclitus's statement and the need for the reader to work hard for the real fruits of his valuable treatise, Schmitt *The Nomos of the Earth*, 78, 342.

suppositions by keeping only, as Arendt described it, a normative core as a guide for action: a commitment to justice, plurality and solidarity.[24] Unlike economy, which Polanyi suggests is, as a rule, submerged to social relations forged through individual rights and values administered to the body social,[25] ecology provides a form of agency for theorizing modes of social relations based on a shared mode of existence.

LOGOS AS POLITICAL PRINCIPLE

Aristotle sublimates Logos as the instrument of political agency which enables the human to perceive, and make clear to others through reasoned discourse, the difference between what is advantageous and harmful, just and unjust, good and evil.[26] It is the full development of rational argument (ὁ δὲ λόγος) and cooperative action in accord with its dictates (ὁ δὲ βίος πρᾶξις), that constitute fully human life and it is the *sharing* of these things, Aristotle insists, that constitutes the household and the polis naturally as communities (ἡ δὲ τούτων κοινωνία ποιεῖ οἰκίαν καὶ πόλιν).[27] Posing the household realm in terms of private property (ἡ κτῆσις) and the public realm in terms of common use, Aristotle feeds his argument for the gradation of the intensity of care as labor (ἡ δ' ἐπιμέλεια), which is individual in the household while it is divided in the political community.[28] Therefore, I suggest it is precisely this fundamental prerogative of the political common, of Logos as opposed to Nomos, that should govern the household as a community; the premise of, "living together and sharing speech, thought, and actions," [29] against that of, "possessing as part of the economy (ἡ κτητικὴ μέρος τῆς οἰκονομίας)," [30] which automatically subordinates the subjects to "human relationships that are given, unchangeable and despotic." [31] Aubenque, one of the most important French Aristotelian scholars of the twentieth century, [32] concludes that the Aristotelian political act of commoning (κοινωνεῖν)[33] does not designate participation in the sense of belonging within an already existing order, like the proprietary order in the concept of economy (belonging-as-property), but in the sense of equal, active and reciprocal participation in collective deliberation that makes an order possible (belonging-becoming).

24 Arendt has provided substantial critique of Schmitt's conceptualization of Nomos in her work, directly questioning the source of law and the orientation of its measure, questions that this chapter also attempts to tackle through the concept of Logos. For this particular hint on the 'legitimacy' of a revised social contract, see Hannah Arendt, "The Social Question," in *On Revolution* (New York: Penguin, 2006), 59–114.

25 This concept of *embeddedness* of society to economy is, I would argue, Polanyi's most valuable contribution to economic theory, which he draws not only from the analysis of modern liberal economies, but also from his interpretation of the ancient Athenian economy. See Polanyi, *The Great Transformation*, 71–80 and Karl Polanyi, *The Livelihood of Man*, ed. H.W. Pearson (New York: Academic Press, 1977), 145–56.

26 Aristotelis, *Politica*, 1253a10–15.

27 Ibid., 1253a15–25 and 1254a.

28 Ibid., 1263a35 and 1337a25–30.

29 Aristotelis, *Ethica Nicomachea*, 1170b150.

30 Aristotelis, *Politica*, 1253b5–20.

31 Pier Vittorio Aureli, *The Possibility of an Absolute Architecture* (Cambridge, MA: MIT Press, 2011), 3.

32 Pierre Aubenque, *Le Problème de l'être chez Aristotle* [*The Problem of Being in Aristotle*], fifth edition (Paris: PUF, 2009).

33 The term *commoning* was introduced by historian Peter Linebough as the collective process that brings together and (re)produces the commons; these are the material and immaterial resources that constitute the wealth that is to be shared as well as the social relations and protocols of coordination, both formal and informal. See Peter Linebough, *The Magna Carta Manifesto: Liberties and Commons for All* (Berkeley: University of California Press, 2008).

Thus, the Logos transforms the household into a community, where belonging is the consequence of participation and care, not the cause or obligation thereof. [34]

Although Aristotle acknowledges conflict as an imminent threat to this process of exchange and decision making, it is by means of the Logos, as a mode of argumentative reasoning, that common places can emerge as instructions for the composition of a shared "body of persuasion." [35] And, while there is no attempted definition of place (τόπος [topos]) in his dedicated book, Topics, we can read his collection of commonly constructed places as not only an argumentative, but also a generative scheme of "find[ing] the *topos* from which to tackle," [36] denoting the emergence or making (ποίησις [poiesis]) of a common ground as a point of departure. Plato elaborates on the productive power of Logos, *poiesis*, as bringing forth and out of concealment, bringing forward to appearance and concrete imagery, while Heidegger dwells on its auto-poietic nature, the producing that brings forth.[37] Euripides further illustrates the institutive power of Logos, employing the metaphor of the body as the ground of privacy and Logos as the middle ground (τὸ μέσον) of confrontation, in which to weigh and determine what is measured, fitting, timely and necessary, and from which, rightful authority identified with the political community emanates.[38] Thus, Logos regulates the relationship between the private and the collective through this deliberative and poietic activity, which institutes a political common. It is the same practice that is able to modify the institutional rules it has itself established, radically placing the power of community governance prior to sovereign, individual or state power, the ruling authorities in the property-based regime of Nomos. This form of sharing that constitutes a political common does not deal with appropriation as it is radically outside of private property, at least in the sense of ownership, of a 'radical title' divorced from social conflicts and negotiations or a 'good' one can freely acquire, abuse, or dispose of (Heidegger stressed the accountability that comes along with such a poietic activity). Thus, Logos is the power to produce and reproduce *commons* that are not appropriable, only governed.[39]

34 Brian Massumi, "In becoming is belonging," in *Parables for the Virtual: Movement, Affect, Sensation* (Durham: Duke University Press, 2002), 68–88.

35 It is remarkable how Aristotle, after Heraclitus, qualifies not only the application of Logos but also the outcome of the rhetoric process, the deductive argument or conclusion (enthymême), as universal. The word enthymême suggests "memoria communis." See Aristotelis, *Rhetorike* [*Rhetoric*], I.1, 1–2, "Online Library of Ancient Greek Literature."

36 Aristotle, *Topics*, VIII.1, 155b4–5.

37 "He gar toi ek tou me ontos eis to on ionti hotooun aitia pasa esti poiesis." Plato, *Symposium (On Eros)*, 205b–c, "Online Library of Ancient Greek Literature." "Every occasion for whatever passes over and goes forward into presencing from that which is not presencing is *poiesis*, is bringing-forth [Her-vor-bringen]." Within the realm of modern philosophy, Heidegger illuminates all the nuances of poiesis, to bring forth or produce, to generate or beget, to utter, to elicit, evoking its relation to the common Logos as established by Heraclitus. See Martin Heidegger, *The Question Concerning Technology and Other Essays*, trans. W. Lovitt (London: Garland Publishing, 1977), 8–13.

38 Euripides's language is rich in formulations deriving from the archaic political ideology that describes class conflict as more typical of democracy than of oligarchy. Peter Burian, "Logos and Pathos: the Politics of the Suppliant Women," in *Directions in Euripidean criticism: A collection of essays* (Durham: Duke University Press, 1985), 136–142.

39 Dardot and Laval call this common deliberative and poietic activity that institutes the political common instituent praxis; the institutional act that puts in effect a form of governance instead of management. See "Instituting the Unappropriable," in Dardot and Laval, *Common*, 368–372.

LOGOS AS SOCIAL PRINCIPLE

The operational principle of Logos radically challenges the archetypical structure of the political and social order of Nomos, which Schmitt recognizes as the problematic sequence of three processes: appropriation, distribution, and production.[40] For centuries, appropriation was the precondition and foundation for any distribution and production. As soon as "the great appropriation" was completed, industrial capitalism opened up new and enormous possibilities of appropriation within the very process of production, as Marx has illustrated in detail.[41] Ever since, social sciences and economic philosophies have been concerned with the sequence of production and distribution, without directly addressing appropriation. Despite the claim for an unlimited increase in production, which would allegedly render distribution less precarious and appropriation economically irrational, liberalism reinforced the supremacy of ownership as the ultimate goal and prize of consumption. Neoliberalism, as I have critiqued, equated the social and the economic question, identifying social rights with economic freedoms, and consequently, purchasing power. The narrative of overabundance, freedom of choice, encouraged property ownership, while the issue of scarcity, always immanent in capitalism to sustain the supply-demand law, was not eradicated. On the contrary, neoliberal privatization became a mechanism for the *re-appropriation* and new enclosures of both social and material resources in order to ensure scarcity.[42] Socialism, on the other hand, posed the social question as such, through the doctrine of *redistribution* as a result of the reformation of property ownership. However, it did not revolutionize the economic order since it did not subvert appropriation as its precondition, instead amplifying it horizontally, making "future owners of former non-owners."[43]

Logos, as a revolutionary principle for the self-institutionalization of a political common,[44] recognizes social *reproduction* as a precondition for further production and distribution[45] and abolishes sovereign appropriation. Here, I adopt Federici's definition of social reproduction as being essential in the production of ourselves

40 See "Appropriation/Distribution/Production: An Attempt to Determine from Nomos the Basic Questions of Every Social and Economic Order," in Schmitt, *The Nomos of the Earth*, 324–335.

41 On the genesis of the industrial capitalist and the appropriation of the means of production, see Karl Marx, *Capital Volume I*, pt. VIII, trans. E. Aveling and S. Moore (London: Electric Book Co, (2001 [1887]), 914–940.

42 For further analysis of the mechanisms of "primitive accumulation" and re-appropriation in neoliberalism, see George Caffentzis, "Two Themes of Midnight Notes: Work/Refusal of Work and Enclosure/Commons," in *Towards the Last Jubilee! Midnight Notes at Thirty Years*, ed. Craig Hughes (New York: Autonomedia, 2010), 24–30; and Massimo De Angelis, "Separating the doing and the deed: capital and the continuous character of the enclosures," *Historical Materialism* 12, no. 2 (2004): 57–87. On "dispossession" as a typical mode of accumulation, "a new wave of enclosing the commons" in neoliberalism, see David Harvey, *The New Imperialism* (Oxford: Oxford University Press, 2005), 148–158.

43 "Every new age and every new epoch in the coexistence of peoples, empires, and countries, of rulers and power formations of every sort, is founded on new spatial divisions, new enclosures, and new spatial orders of the earth." Schmitt, *The Nomos of the Earth*, 327–335.

44 Revolution, Castoriadis argues, is not a war but the explicit self-transformation of society at the moment, when a community's majority engages with political —that is to say *instituting*— activity. See Cornelius Castoriadis, "What Revolution Is," in *A Society Adrift: Interviews and Debates, 1974–1994*, eds. Enrique Escobar, Myrto Gondicas and Pascal Vernay (New York: Fordham University Press, 2010), 144–51.

45 On the reciprocal conditioning of production and reproduction as social processes, see Karl Marx, *Capital Volume I*, 812–829. Hardt and Negri in *the Empire* envision this shift of standpoint as the critical moment (as Marx invites us to) when the most effective resistance to the social inequalities, which are born within the realm of production, arises. See Michael Hardt and Antonio Negri, *Empire* (Cambridge, MA: Harvard University Press, 2000), XI–XVIII.

as a common subject, our education for collective governance and the recognition of history as a collective project, which constitute, according to her, the main casualties of the neoliberal era of capitalism.[46] In particular, I return to its historical configuration to contradict the production of the familial and contractual subject of modern capitalism — the 'private individual'— through the ties of 'belonging-as-property' in the sphere of capitalist reproduction. Castoriadis argues that there is a simultaneity and reciprocity between the emergence of a collective movement and the transformation of its subjects,[47] which turns collective activity into a continuous process of commoning. This means, that the reproduction of the commons and the commons values both spring from and result in the shaping of *a commons subjectivity*.[48] When it comes to the self-institutionalization of a housing community as a political organization, the capacity of Logos in the "transformational equivalence of opposites" suggests an ecology of the private; the simultaneous and reciprocal fashioning of the private and commons subjectivity as the *ratio* for protocols of production, distribution and consumption.

The concept of social reproduction reinstates privacy as personal autonomy through the relational quality of ecology.[49] It considers belonging not as a privilege of identity but, rather, as the result of collective actualization. It signifies personal autonomy beyond the rigid framework of the unaccountable authority of appropriation and within the dynamic interdependence in the (re)production of commonality, which suggests a different logic of relating to land, to housing and to others. Whereas economy considers land as a territory to be conquered and exploited,[50] ecology positions land as a resource to be shared and perpetuated. The economy of the private subsumes and individualizes the labor of care and, thus, the very spaces of reproduction, within the framework of property. Meanwhile, the ecology of the private facilitates a broader circuit of common value production that is apt to secure common-pool resources in its name and socialize labor in terms of use rights. This makes the concept of self-valorization only intelligible in the sense of autonomy through collective empowerment.[51]

46 Federici, "Feminism and the Politics of the Common in an Era of Primitive Accumulation," in *Revolution at Point Zero*, 138–48.

47 Castoriadis, "A Society Adrift," in *Society Adrift*, 206-15.

48 On the formation of the commons subjectivity through an emancipatory collective 'in situ' praxis, see Dardot and Laval, *Common*, 266–74. On the commons subjectivity as the opposite of the individual capitalist subject known as Homo economicus and the strategic role of reproduction in a new politics, see De Angelis, "The Strategic Horizon of the Commons," in *Commoning with George Caffentzis and Silvia Federici*, eds. C. Barbagallo, N. Beuret and D. Harvie (London: Pluto Press, 2019), 209–221.

49 Berlant puts forward "nonsovereign relationality as the foundational quality of being in common" and defines "individuality as a genre carved from within dynamics of relation rather than a state prior to it or distinct from it." Lauren Berlant, "The commons: Infrastructures for troubling times," *Environment and Planning D: Society and Space* 34, no. 3 (2016): 393–419.

50 Aureli, "Appropriation, Subdivision, Abstraction," 165.

51 "An effective political ecology [which] can only come from a radical anti-capitalism," Dardot and Laval, *Common*, 1–7.

In the political struggle for reproduction commoning Federici identifies, not only the process of generating mutual bonds and collective interest but also a field of resistance against co-option by despotic (mainly patriarchal) relations and capitalist valorization.[52] Thus, generating a new political form of *autonomy* and *autopoiesis* as such,[53] includes the struggle of commoning communities not only to produce, sustain and protect their internal and immaterial relations, but also the material means that are necessary for their own reproduction.[54] That is the struggle to gain legal (*de jure*) recognition of commonality (the condition of being in common) beyond the *de facto* recognition of common resources and customary rights.[55]

ECOLOGY AS A PROTOCOL FOR URBAN HOUSING COMMONS

It comes as a paradox that commonality — the primal universal constant of human existence— would need to be legally claimed. However, to establish a paradigm shift, it needs to develop its ground within the framework of law, opposing the inherent perplexity of the legislative accommodation of collective subjectivity. In international law, *de facto* recognition does not override *de jure* recognition, which is a constitutive act of admission of legal rights to a community over a territory granted by the government in charge of the territory.[56] Rather, it is conceived as a 'certification of trust' between the government and the community, which can lead to *de jure* recognition on the precondition that the latter is recognized as a legal person. This parallel is very useful when it comes to the necessity of recognition of an urban housing community as a legal person. According to Lauterpacht, the necessary conditions of *de facto* recognition are that the community must be politically organized, have control over a defined territory, this definite control should tend towards performance, and the community thus constituted must be independent. After a period of *de facto* recognition, when the community is able to demonstrate reasonable assurance of stability and performance, as well as the general support of its population, it can move to de jure recognition; the final act of admission of the claimed territory by the state or the local authority. Thus, the recognition of a community as a legal person

52 Federici, "Part III: Reproducing Commons," in *Revolution at Point Zero*, 115–48.

53 For an in-depth analysis of commons as social systems and ecologies, see Massimo De Angelis, *Omnia Sunt Communia: On the Commons and the Transformation to Postcapitalism* (London: Zed Books, 2017).

54 On the commons, both as a material resource and a social product, pointing at an anti-sovereign political paradigm as the basis for a truly democratic global society, see Hardt and Negri, *Empire*, 393–414.

55 Linebough describes the notion of *de facto* recognition already in the thirteenth century, when the English commoners were able to maintain and develop certain customs in common —collecting wood in the forest, or setting up villages on the king's land— which the king was forced to recognize as rights. However, these rights were not "granted" by the sovereign, but were instead already existing customary rights acknowledged as de facto rights. See Linebough, "Two Charters," in *Magna Carta Manifesto*, 21–45.

56 On the concepts and terms of the international law in this paragraph, see H. Lauterpacht, "Recognition of States in International Law," *The Yale Law Journal* 53, no. 3 (1944): 385–458.

is the fundamental precondition for the constitution of its commonality because, by acknowledging a set of relationships among its subjects, it establishes its new spatial order in terms of territory, system of governance, performance and autonomy, in other words, its commons rights.[57] Autonomy, here, is not the result of sovereign power, but of accountability both within the community and a broader commons (such as the claim for a territory constituted as 'public space').

Concerning the legal recognition of material resources, the analytical framework of property — the normative protocol structuring social relations regarding things (real rights) — provides insights for an alternative regulation of duties, rights, powers, privileges, freedoms and limitations. The identification of the configuration of property with private property, largely undisputed by philosophical accounts, does not normally acknowledge commoning as property.[58] The commons is seen as the paradigmatic non-property case. Yet commoning, as common property, is concerned with the same questions of access to the resource, allowance and objective of use, responsibility, allocation of generated wealth, transfer of privileges, decision-making, organization of care, and, most importantly, the value system governing these rules. In the latter lies the difference of commoning, which is dedicated to distributing the "bundle of rights"[59] encrypted in the institution of property — ownership, custody, possession, use, enjoyment, disposal — as democratically and generously as possible among its subjects. This leads to an opening up of the spatial framework, whereby the physical boundaries of private property are challenged and the association of privacy with domesticity is refuted. This is an act of genuine interest for reinstating privacy as a social value; for aleviating the stress induced by the burden of reproduction and care, both of which have been inscribed within domesticity. The designation of private space, "a room of one's own," is negotiated upon protocols of expanded use of communal spaces and the sharing of domestic labor. At the same time, one's accountability to a collective subjectivity and shared resources undermines 'the right to abuse' the established common property. The predominance of the 'the right of use' in the commons cancels out the absolute

57 According to Linebaugh, the constitution and function of commons is always political and invested in counter-sovereignty, with performative aspirations to decolonize a physical and social space that has been inhabited by imperial, capitalist, and property-right power. Linebough, "The Constitution of the Commons," in *Magna Carta Manifesto*, 242–268.

58 J. Martin Pedersen, "Properties of Property: A Jurisprudential Analysis," *The Commoner*, no. 4 (Winter 2010): 139.

59 Schlager and Ostrom identify a bundle of five rights in property, that is, a bundle of five socially protected powers —access, withdrawal, management, exclusion, and alienation. See Elinor Ostrom and Edella Schlager, "Property-Rights Regimes and Natural Resources: A Conceptual Analysis," *Land Economics* 68, no. 3 (1992): 249–262.

privileges of property, but also the individual suffering from its economic burden and precariousness, the result of neoliberal privatization. Achieving common rights and resources becomes the means through which the right to privacy, as personal autonomy, can flourish. Illuminating this spectrum of relational modalities shifts the administration and the spatial organization of urban land and housing towards an ecology of the private.

Introduction to the Project of Athens

1
Central Athens and the neighbouring municipalities in the Attica basin

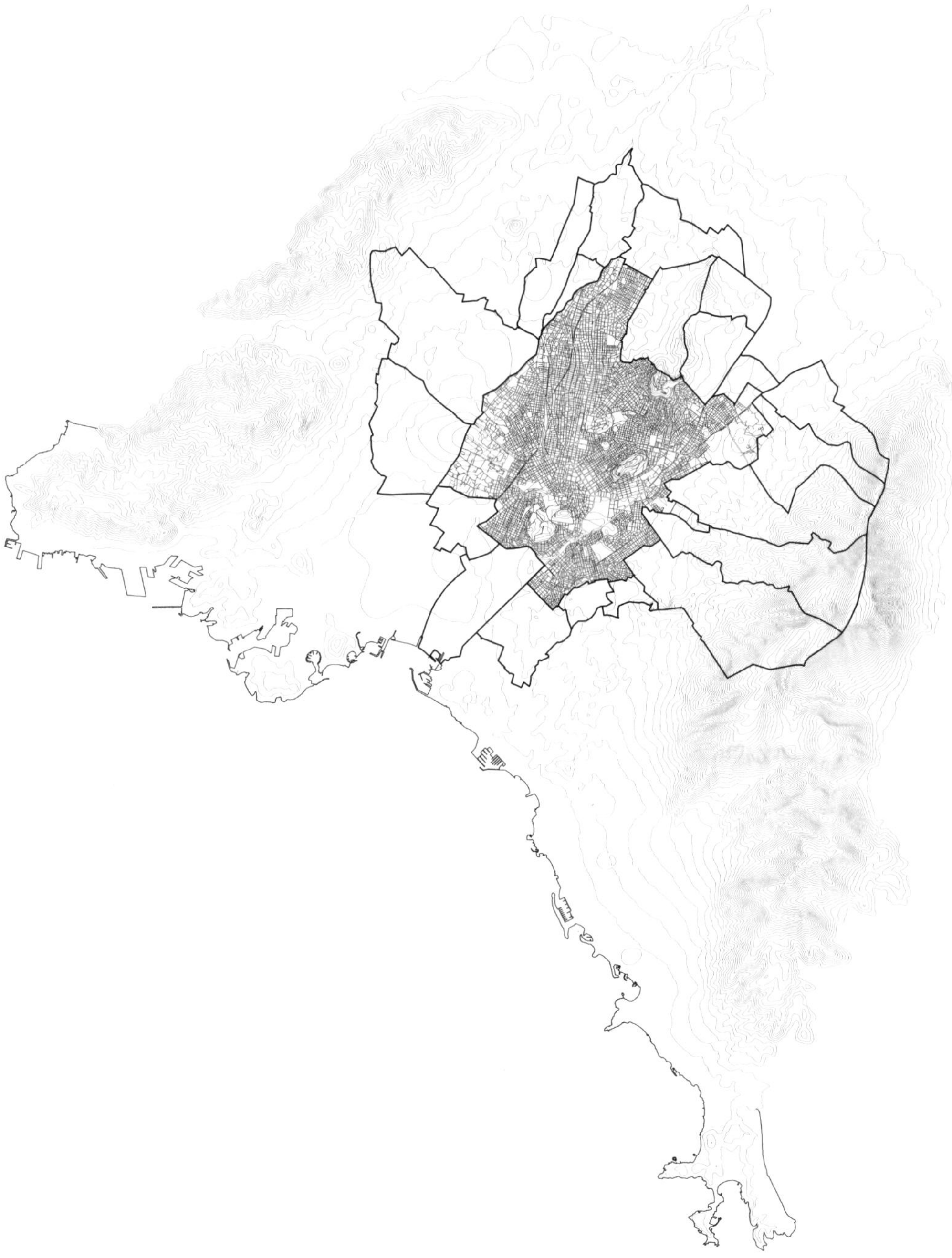

The project will be tested in the inner city of Athens, **(Fig. 1)** where the fallacies of the neoliberal housing system have been dauntingly exposed. The proposal aims to illustrate the transition to an alternative pedagogy of domestic privacy through commoning. I call it a transition because commoning is neither the mere outcome of recognition, nor *ex nihilo* creation, but of collective practices and procedures that create the new through the gradual transformation of what already exists. Stavrides describes commoning as an inventive process, which involves creation and produces new forms of social life, even though it appears as the result of adaptive practices.[1] The trope of adaptation is valued here architecturally, as a way to reinterpret once radical visions of domesticity; ecologically, as a way to minimize the market implication and the environmental footprint; and socially, as a way to, "find concealed in society as it is the material conditions of production and the corresponding relations prerequisite for a classless society."[2] However, commoning should not be viewed as the 'third way' between the state and the market, but rather as a model *in* and *by the making*; until the point, when a critical mass of society decides to adopt a new domestic culture "as a goal in itself and not as survival regulated by dominant power."[3] The design of commoning is a collaborative process: it orchestrates the coordination of state government, city administration and the community, it also facilitates the protocols of symbiosis and the networks of support and mutual aid. These parameters assume the state as the facilitator, the local government as the initiator and organizer, and the community as the executor.[4]

The proposal is developed along three scales: a juridical framework; an urban strategy; and an architectural project in the form of a manual, a step-by-step method for the typological adaptation of an existing community settlement. Carefully selected, the case study was chosen for its possibility to set a valuable social and typological paradigm for communities throughout the city. A thorough analysis illuminates the site's potential from an urban and architectural perspective, as well as for its social resiliency: the long-standing reproduction of its community. Therefore, community empowerment structures each level of the proposal: first, de-commodifying housing

1 Stavros Stavrides, "Housing and Urban Commoning," in *Common Space: The City as Commons* (London: Zed Books, 2016), 95–129.

2 Karl Marx, *Grundrisse: Foundations of the Critique of Political Economy* (London: Penguin Books, 1976), 158.

3 Stavrides, *Common Space*, 99.

4 "Whether it commands, acts, or supervises, the state is the initiator and ultimate director of change; if from time to time it involves itself in tasks directly, it does so by way of demonstration, to make a start and to set an example. Once a beginning has been made, the machinery established, the state withdraws, leaving the execution of the new task to local authorities and citizens." Pierre-Joseph Proudhon, "A Progressive Constitution," in *The Federative Principle: The Need to Reconstitute the Party of Revolution* [1863], http://theanarchistlibrary.org/library/pierre-joseph-proudhon-the-principle-of-federation.

and the corresponding land as a strategy to eliminate the precariousness of both private and state property; second, utilizing boundary commoning[5] as a strategy to create new commons from existing communities, sustaining them within a network of solidarity and co-governance; and third, decoupling construction labor from the market (private developers and the large-scale construction industry), educating inhabitants on environmentally conscious forms of building.[6] The strategic intelligence of the project will be measured by its capacity to challenge the rationale of the neoliberal city by challenging the relationship between economic condition and housing typology. In other words, I seek to address the ecology of the private both institutionally and spatially through an alternative system of values: participation instead of individualism as a form of empowerment, accountability instead of sovereignty as a form of governance, openness instead of enclosure as a form of sustainability, and trust instead of ownership as a precondition for the sense of security.

CASE STUDY: THE TRIGONO COMMUNITY SETTLEMENT IN KESSARIANI

My hypothesis concerns the Trigono community settlement in Kessariani, on its border with Athens. **(Fig. 2)** The Trigono belongs to the so-called "refugee block settlements," some of the few historical examples of social housing in Athens, which were part of a state program for the urban accommodation of a massive influx of Greek refugees.[7] The first and second phases of the program were implemented in collaboration with and using financial support from international institutions, for the provision of humanitarian aid and temporary accommodation for refugees.[8] In the meantime, the Greek state was responsible for devising and funding a new fiscal policy for the socio-economic integration of these populations. The block settlements belong to the third long-term phase of the scheme, which was launched by the Ministry of Welfare in 1933.[9] The legal-technical framework was a unique combination of planning and building regulations enacted to deal with the on-going high demand for housing, which set the groundwork for the respective

5 Massimo De Angelis, "Boundary Commoning," in *Omnia Sunt Communia: On the Commons and the Transformation to Postcapitalism* (London: Zed Books, 2017), 256–302.

6 Ostrom calls the social art of skilled work "crafting" and it differs from the mere application of rules imposed from the outside. The artisanal character of crafting defines the unique mode of government of every commons. See Elinor Ostrom, *Crafting Institutions for Self-Governing Irrigation Systems* (San Francisco: ICS Press, 1992), 32.

7 The unprecedented political and humanitarian act of a massive repatriation of war refugees in 1922 marked the twentieth century history of Greece. For a social analysis of the repercussions of the treaty of Lausanne, see Vika Gizele, *Koinonikoi Metaschimatismoi kai Proeleusi tis Koinonikis Katoikias stin Ellada (1920-1930)* [*Social Transformations and the Origins of Social Housing in Greece (1920-1930)*] (Athens: Epikairotita, 1984).

8 The League of Nations supported this gigantic project with a protocol series, see Société des Nations, *L'établissement des réfugiés en Grèce* (Genève: Publications de la Societe des Nations, 1926).

9 Nikolaos A. Lianos, "I Stegastiki Apokatastasi ton Prosfygon [Housing provision for the Refugees]," *Lifo*, December 2, 2016, https://www.lifo.gr/articles/greece_articles/123756.

2
The 'Trigono' settlement on the border of the municipalities of Athens and Kessariani

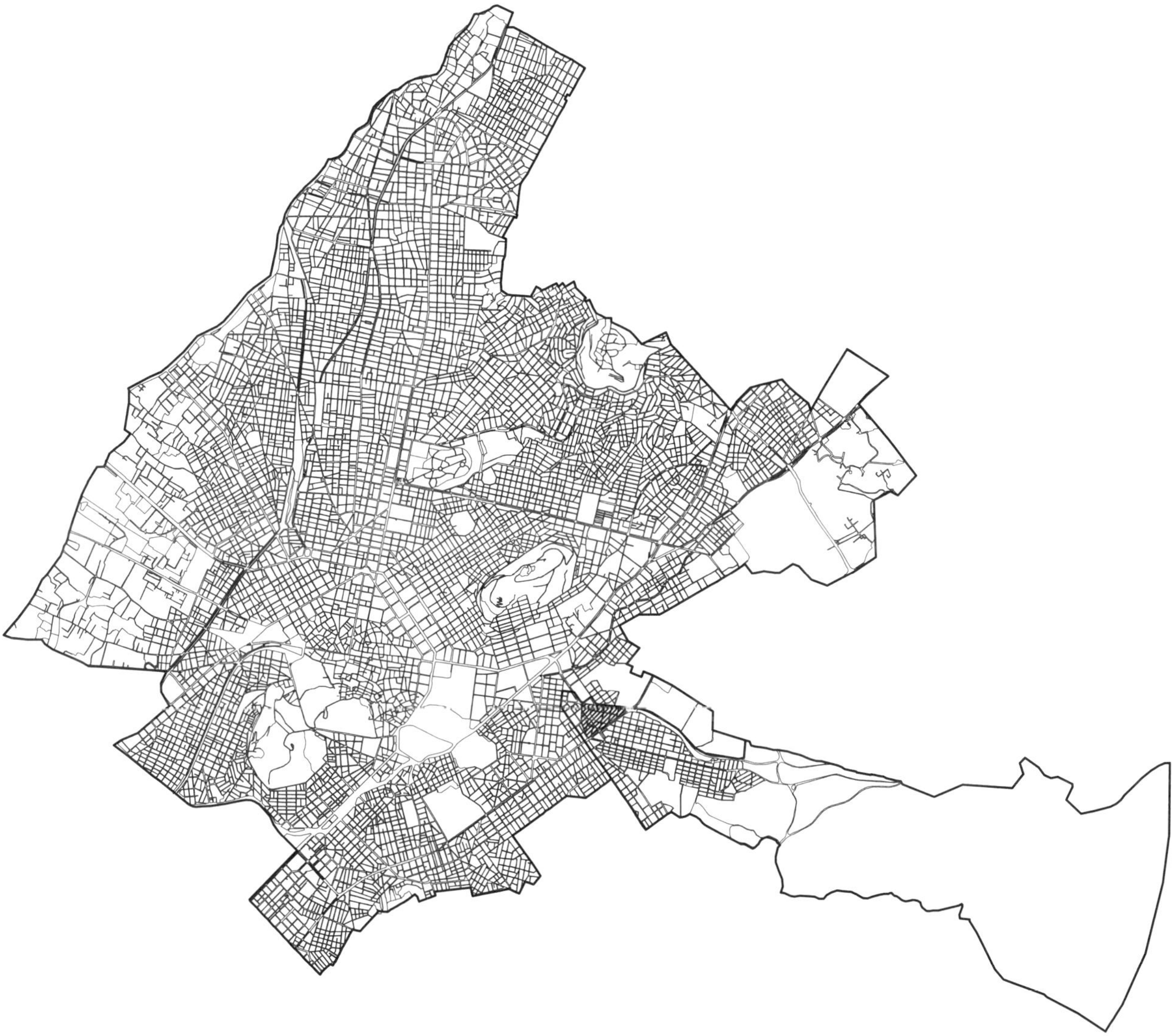

legislation of public and private property. Thus, it adopted the governmental land policy of, "expropriation of plots for the construction of refugee establishments," and the regulations of a typical multi-apartment building for, "private per floor (horizontal) ownership," "common, indivisible ownership of the plot, the building's infrastructure and facilities" and "absolute use rights of common areas."[10]

Kessariani was among the districts on the periphery of Athens and Piraeus dedicated to the urban accommodation of refugees.[11] The formerly peri-urban rural land at the foot of Hymettus mountain was compulsorily purchased by the state and added to the regulatory plan of Athens in 1931. The design of the settlement was, "a rudimentary urban plan based on a Hippodamian system,"[12] following on one side, the path of the "Big Stream" of Kessariani and, on the other side, the main longitudinal axis of the district, a former military boulevard leading to Hymettus. **(Fig. 3)** During the second phase, the urban blocks were further subdivided into parcels and conceded to the refugees in proportion to their "exchangeable" property.[13] It was an arrangement on the condition that they would then use their own means to self-build single-family homes within a fixed time, as a form of sweat equity to reduce the cost of home-ownership. The intense construction activity of the 1920s brought about the unionization of the refugee beneficiaries —land-owners— into associations of home builders and a boom in the domestic cement industry, where the majority of these populations were employed. Their participation in the construction process, both as stakeholders and labor, created a strong bond between housing construction and home-ownership.[14] Not only did this period establish a legacy of a petit-bourgeois society, but also the construction sector, particularly the concrete industry, became the foundation of the domestic economy for the rest of the twentieth century.

In 1932, the Ministry of Welfare's Technical Department organized a committee of renowned Greek architects to devise urban and housing typologies for the settlements that would enter the program's third phase: the apartment blocks.[15] Two

10 *On the requisition of properties for the accommodation of refugees and the expropriation of plots for the construction of refugee establishments* (1922) FEK A 243–23.11.1922. *On horizontal (per floor) ownership* (1929) N. 3741, FEK A 4–09.01.1929. The Acts, Decrees and Regulations of the Hellenic Parliament are published in the Official Government Gazette (FEK).

11 Eliza Papadopoulou and Georgios Sarigiannis, *Synoptike Ekthese gia tis Prosfygikes Perioches tou Lekanopediou Attikes* [*Brief Study on the Refugee Settlement Districts in Attica Basin*] (Athens: Faculty of Urban and Strategic Planning, National Technical University of Athens, 2006), 73–81. For the urban development of Kessariani as a juridical and urban entity, see Myrianthe Moussa et. al, "Kessariani: I 'Krise' os Diadikasia tes Chorikes Paragoges [Kessariani: Crisis as Spatial Process]," (paper presented at Attica in Crisis Conference, Athens, 20–22 October 2017), https://www.researchgate.net/publication/322006631_Kaisariane_E_Krise_os_diadikasia_tes_chorikes_paragoges.

12 Emmanuel Marmaras, "Poleodomikes kai Architektonikes Episimanseis apo tin Archaeotita os Simera" ["Urban and Architectural Notes from Antiquity to Today,"] (paper presented at Athens 1910–1940 Conference, Athens, 15–18 February 1996), 275.

13 Once it was established in the treaty of Lausanne that repatriation was permanent, the governments involved in the exchange of populations, registered the properties and land holdings of the latter in their place of origin. The estimated value was to be claimed nominally as a bond in the respective 'land bank' in the host country. This type of property was called "exchangeable." On the terms of socio-economic integration of the Greek bourgeois refugees from Asia Minor and the rootedness of social housing in private property and self-provision in Greece, see Gizele, *Koinonikoi Metaschimatismoi.*

3

General diagram of the Kessariani settlement, Engineer M. Scardis, 02/03/1931

Diagram 1299/1931, Department of Public Health and Social Welfare, Region of Attica

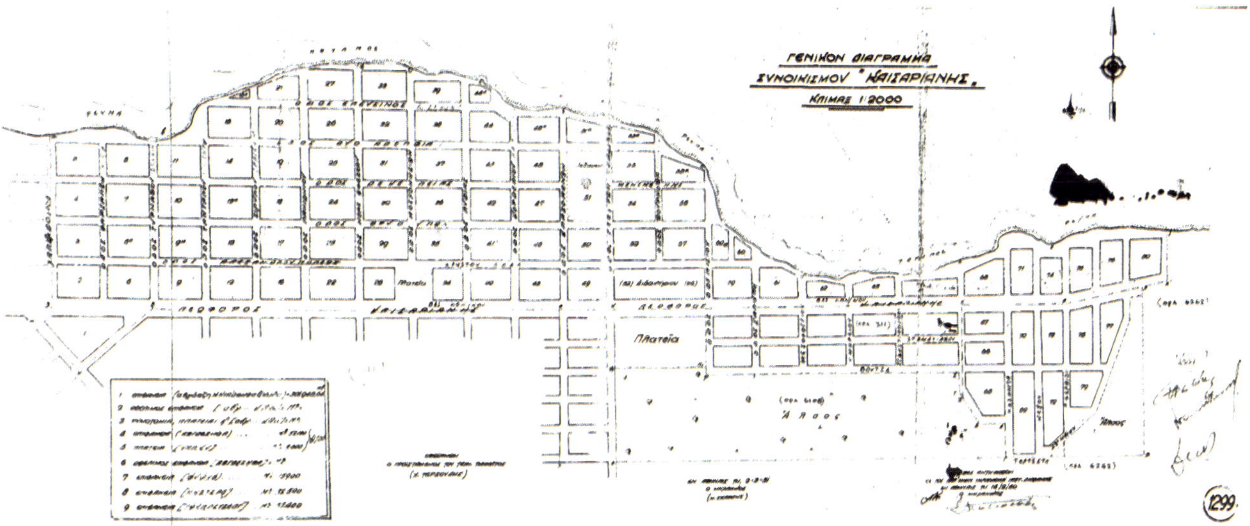

14 Until 1920 there were two cement factories in Greece and the demand in the market was very low. By the end of the 1920s, however, two more cement factories were created and still demand could not be met entirely by the domestic supply. During the 1930s, the increase in cement production allowed also for exports. See Stavros Malagkoniaris, "Apo tis Paragkes sta Prosfygika [From Refugee Camps to Refugee Block Settlements]," *I Efimerida ton Syntakton*, September 25, 2016, https://www.efsyn.gr/themata/istorika/83658_apo-tis-paragkes-sta-prosfygika. For a detailed analysis of the transformation of the refugee settlement clusters into working class suburbs which fueled the proliferation of industrial economy, see Lila Leontidou, *Poleis tes Siopes: Ergatikos epoikismos tis Athinas kai tou Peiraia, 1907-1940* [*Silent Cities: The proletarian colonization of Athens and Piraeus, 1907-1940*] (Athens: Cultural Technological Foundation ETBA, 1989).

15 Architects such as Kimon Laskaris, Dimitris Kyriakos, Patroklos Karantinos and Ioannis Despotopoulos, who had undertaken studies in Europe and had gained experience close to famous modernists of the time, such as Le Corbusier, were already experimenting with the application of the Bauhaus principles in Greece. Despotopoulos openly argued for the superiority of the "socialist city" and "the systematization of the function of group organization" against a city fragmented into small land holdings, see Ioannis Despotopoulos, "Poleodomike [Town Planning]," *Technika Chronika* IV, no. 39 (1933): 756–773.

years later, the Kessariani settlement was separated from the municipality of Athens and became legally recognized as an independent municipality within the Attica region.[16] Subsequently, in 1937, the plan of Kessariani was adjusted according to the block settlement in the Trigono area.[17] **(Fig. 4)** Its triangular form was the outcome of efforts to establish it as the link between the two jurisdictions; it was compromised by the municipal borderline, the extension of two major perpendicular traffic routes from Athens and the riverbed of the Big Stream. The new typological arrangement supplanted the existing grid and typical perimeter block structure, except for three instances along the northern side of the triangle, which followed the developmental logic of the antiparoche.[18] **(Figs. 5.1-2)** However, the implementation of the third phase was interrupted by the outbreak of World War II followed by the Greek Civil War. These conflicts brought about a long period of political instability and financial hardship, particularly for Kessariani, which played a key role in the resistance movements. The scheme for the construction of the apartment blocks in the Trigono area resumed in 1958 and was completed in phases by 1968. **(Fig. 6)** Planning decisions also involved the burial and sealing of the Big Stream and the pedestrianization of the avenue cutting through the Trigono district. **(Fig. 7)** The unbuilt green spaces, left as a result of these decisions, were unified and constituted as a park.

It is important to situate the ideas behind the block settlements here within the broader context of the Keynesian policies and modern movement occurring in inter-war Europe. It is also necessary to describe how their architecture was inevitably conditioned by the subsequent political and economic circumstances, as well as by the customs and rituals of the inhabitants, what Philippides called, "vernacular modernism," of this period.[19] If the second CIAM in Frankfurt in 1929 had successfully introduced the social aspects and standards for the minimal dwelling, then the fourth CIAM in Athens in 1933 emphatically promoted the principles of the functional city. The widespread demand for decent conditions in urban and housing environments called for central planning that addressed the issue of the optimal use of urban land as inextricable from the rational design of housing. These princi-

16 *On the recognition of municipalities and settlements in the Attica region* (1934) FEK A 22–18.01.1934. There was a strong political incentive behind the legislative decree to detach all peripheral refugee settlements from the municipal jurisdictions of Athens and Piraeus so as to diminish the electoral power of the refugee populations. It was also a reflection of their intentional geographic and social segregation by the State and the bourgeois elite. For an in-depth analysis of the urban transformation of Athens as a result of social and political struggles within the refugee crisis, see Evgenia Tousi, *O Astikos Choros os Pedio Metaschimatismon ypo to Prisma tou Prosfygikou Zitimatos* [*Urban Space as a Field of Transformations in the Light of the Refugee Issue*] (PhD Diss., Athens: National Technical University of Athens, 2014).

17 *On the approval of the regulatory plan of Kessariani (Attica)* (1937) FEK A 401–14.10.1937.

18 Antiparoche followed the revision of the 1929 condominium legislation and it was a system of exchange between landowners and contractors. The new development produced horizontal shares a portion of which were given back to the landowner and the rest were sold by the contractor to accommodate the high demand.

19 Dimitres Philippides, "Formal and Vernacular Architecture (1930-1960)," in *Moderna Architectonike stin Ellada* [*Modern Architecture in Greece*] (Athens: Melissa, 2001). See also Fotene Georgakopoulou, "Diereunisi tis epirrois tou modernou kinimatos ston sxediasmo kai tin anegersi ton prosfygikon katoikion stin Athina kai ton Peiraia (1930-1940) [Investigation of the influence of the modern movement in the design and construction of the refugee block settlements in Athens and Piraeus (1930–1940)]," https://www.greekarchitects.gr.

4
The regulatory plan of Kessariani, General Secretary of Athens K. Kotzias, 26/08/1937

Diagram 1974/1937, Department of Public Health and Social Welfare, Region of Attica

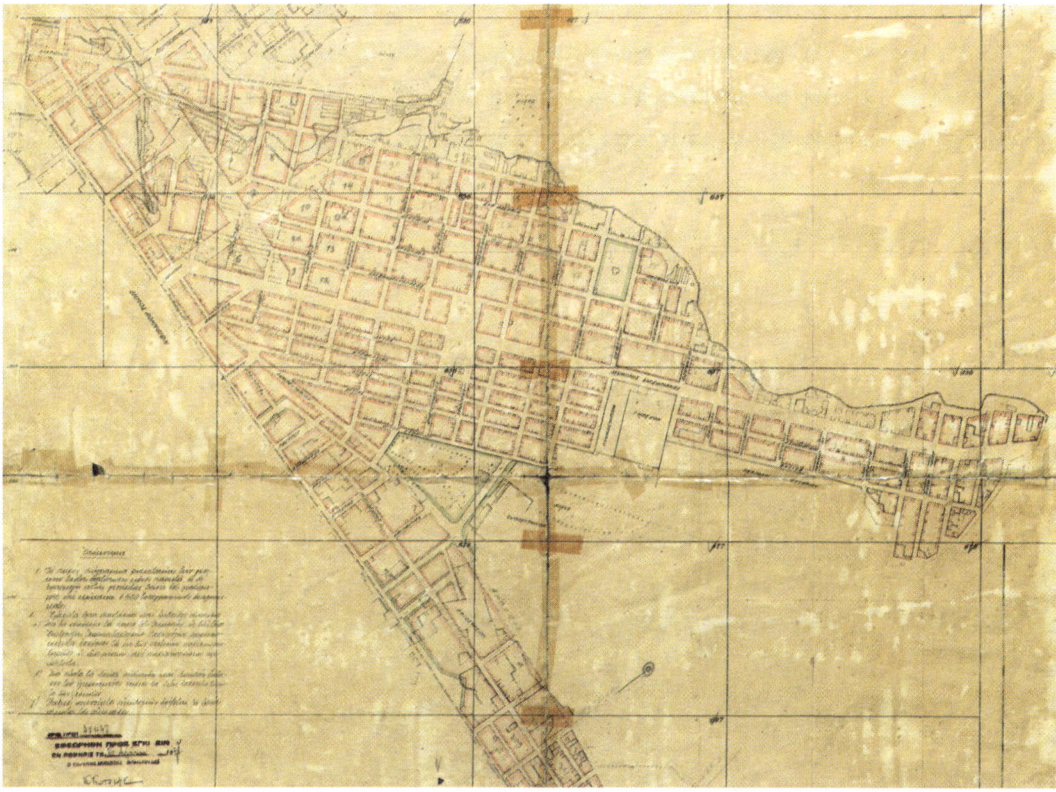

5.1
Areal photo of the Trigono area, 1930

5.1
Areal photo of the Trigono area, 2020

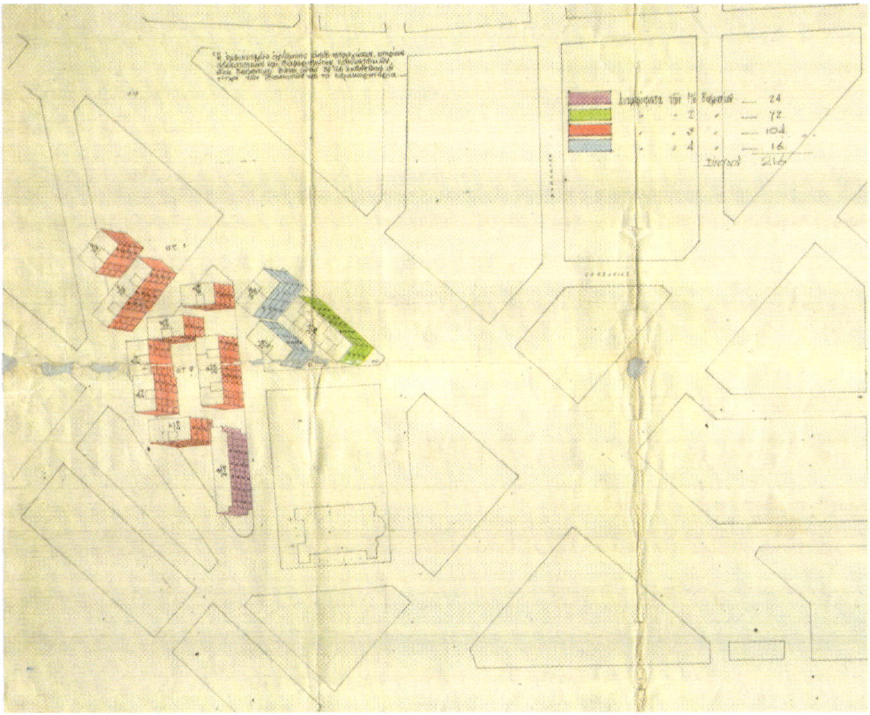

6
The St. Nicolas block cluster in the Trigono area, Architect: A. Sapounakis, 23/01/1964

Design 510/9, Department of Public Health and Social Welfare, Region of Attica

7
Final layout of the Trigono area

ples, however, were in stark contrast with the reality of Athens. The commercialization of residential developments, through the extreme subdivision of private property both in the working-class settlements and the bourgeois apartment buildings, had already fuelled the intensive exploitation of urban land. The Congress of Athens concluded that the regulation of the distribution of housing surface should prioritize the demands of the collectivist order and therefore, "the private interest should be subordinated to the interest of the totality."[20] Soon, the rise of totalitarianism in Europe and the establishment of the Metaxa dictatorship in Greece cast a shadow of negativity on the concepts of totality and central planning. The partial bankruptcy of the Greek economy in 1932 led to the final block settlement scheme, which was a combination of radicalism and conservatism. While the urban and architectural principles adhered to the directives of the Congresses, the idea of collective living was adjusted institutionally and typologically to match the nuclear family structure and homeownership.

The design of the blocks was inspired by the exemplary social housing settlements (Siedlungen) of the 1920s in Germany and Austria, adapted accordingly to the limitations of the Athenian scale and housing culture. Adhering to Scharoun's principle of, "neighborliness," as a spiritual quality, and Taut's concept of, "outdoor living space," the urban plan of the Trigono settlement grouped three- and four-story blocks in clusters around chunks of open space as a way to enhance the use value of the flats.[21] **(Figs. 8.1-8.7)** The arrangement of free-standing blocks in neighborhoods deescalates the experience of the large open public space, in which they are distributed, to "a space that corresponds to a child's joyfulness of experience, large enough to accommodate adventures, yet small enough to create a sense of home."[22] The plan is structured in such a way that narrow blocks (where the width of a flat equals the width of the block) are built in a north-south or east-west direction and positioned perpendicular to roads. **(Fig. 9)** This allows each unit to have the living room facing south or the bedroom(s) facing east, optimizing the conditions of lighting and ventilation, while minimizing noise pollution. Vasileiou, in his discussion

20 Van Eesteren, the president of the CIAM, defines the arrangement of the housing blocks as the main principle of functional town planning and then describes a series of principles for the rational design of housing such as the establishment of a certain population density per hectare and a minimum of natural lighting per housing unit. Cornelis Van Eesteren, "Methodoi organikes poleodomias kai efarmogai auton eis tin polin Amsterdam [Methods of functional town planning and their applications in Amsterdam]," *Technika Chronika* IV, no. 44–46 (1933): 1027–35.

21 These ideas were introduced in the design of the Weissenhof settlement in Stuttgart in 1927, to which Mies van Der Rohe invited, among others, Hans Scharoun and Bruno Taut to contribute. Hans Scharoun was then appointed architect in chief and urban planner of the Siemensstadt settlement in Berlin, built between 1929 and 1934. There, in collaboration with Walter Gropius, Hugo Haring, Bartning Otto, Fred Forbat and Paul Rudolf Henning, the principles were established. This marked a turning point in the urban reconceptualization of the Berliner enclosed "backyard" (Hof) as an open entity and as a new social architecture in favour of dense apartment blocks with large public spaces. See Martin Korda, *Städtebau* (Stuttgart: B.G. Teubner, 1999), 34 and Bruno Taut, "Der Außenwohnraum," *Einfa* 2, no. 4 (1931): 2–4. See also Peter B. Jones, "The Weissenhofsiedlung, Stuttgart," in *Modern Architecture through Case Studies 1945 to 1990*, eds. Peter B. Jones and Eamonn Canniffe (London: Architectural Press, 2002),10–46.

22 This quotes a part of Scharoun's description of "neighborliness" (Nachbarschaft). Ulrich Conrads, *Zeit des Labyrinths: beobachten, nachdenken, feststellen 1956-2006* [*Time of the Labyrinth: Observe, think determine 1956-2006*] (Berlin: Gütersloh, 2007), 152.

8.1
Bird's eye view of part of the Trigono complex depicting various types of blocks and their relationship to green open spaces. The Trigono synthesis in the foreground conrtadicts the typical urban development of Athens in the background.

8.2-8.7
Dominant Trigono
block types

9
Dominant Trigono block types

1 Trigono settlement, Athens 1938-1940
2 Part of the Hellerhof settlement, Mart Stam, Frankfurt 1929-1932
3 Part of the Haselhorst settlement, Fred ForbatBerlin 1928-1935

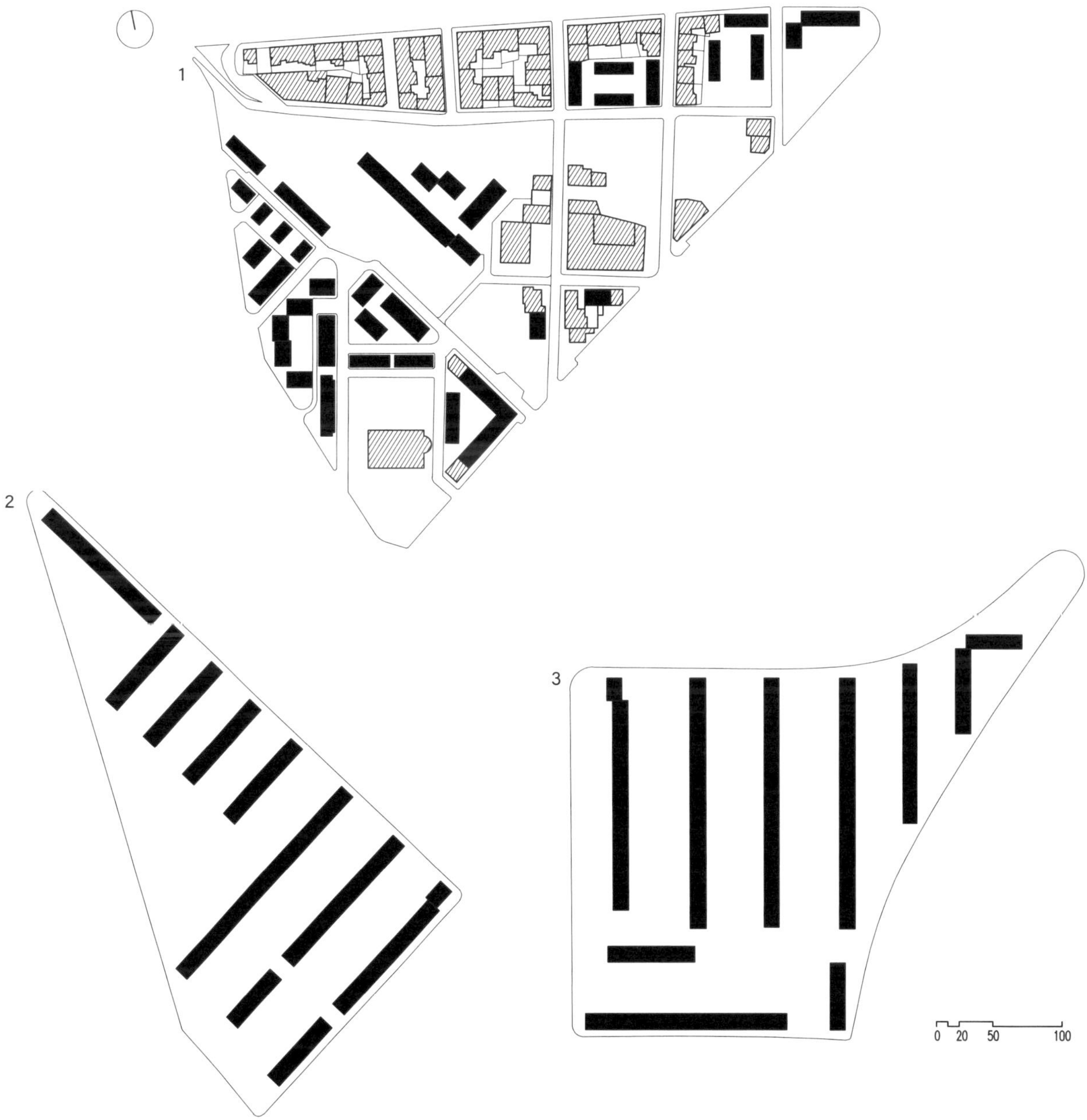

of these block settlements, argues that, "for their sunlit and airy openness alone, they would perhaps have been envied by many of those living in private apartment buildings in more spacious flats, but with windows overlooking gloomy shafts."[23] Translated into building standards, the built ratio of the Trigono area corresponding to these blocks, is 30% as opposed to that of the surrounding urban context, which may reach up to 80% of the respective plot. The openness and peacefulness of the settlement, in the heart of a very busy and dense area of the center, transmits the idea of a relaxed city, where privacy is predicated upon well-thought-out building ratios, proportions, and orientations.

The settlement has 411 homes, 24% of which are one-bed flats (35-45 m²), 66% are two-bed flats (55 m²) and 10% are three-bed flats (65 m²). The blocks have concrete structural systems and are equipped with staircases servicing two to twelve flats per floor, while most of them have accessible lower ground floors and roof terraces, which were used to host communal services in the past. Typologically, the flat layouts follow the organic tradition of their counterparts in Frankfurt, Berlin and Vienna, using the articulation of rooms to create separate wings according to function. However, they are adjusted to the Greek spatial, economic and climatic standards; they are scaled down, thus redefining the notion of minimal dwelling; they are strictly restrained to two flats per unit per floor, allowing for dual-aspect window openings to ensure the cross-ventilation and natural cooling of each flat; all types include a balcony, an essential element of Mediterranean domesticity. **(Fig. 10)** The Greek version also prioritizes the economy and simplicity of construction, therefore discarding the monumentality of the Viennese and the expressionism and plasticity of the German. On the contrary, it adopts the geometric, rational, and classicizing functionalism of Walter Gropius: the containment of all spaces within the perimeter of the plan —balconies are replaced by loggias of regulated depth— and the linear repetition of aligned, identical dwelling units.[24] Despite the rational subdivision overlaid on the plans, the design still maintains the objective of maximum variability, an ambition consciously embedded by Gropius.

23 Ioannis Vasileiou, *I Laiki Katoikia: Koinonikes Technikes kai Oikonomikes Apopseis* [*Mass Housing: Social Techniques and Economic Aspects*] (Athens: P.A. Dialisma, 1944), 82.

24 The flat types were standardized, codified and applied with minor adjustments in block combinations at a number of refugee settlements in Athens. In particular, the Type B of the Trigono settlement was very popular and had the code number 233 in the general system. The unit consists of two mirrored flats sharing a common staircase and entrance space. The linear block organization prevailed as the most efficient and dramatically influenced the relationship between private and public space in the blocks. See Stavros Stavrides et. al., *Metaschimatismoi tis schesis dimosiou-idiotikou chorou sta sygrotimata koinonikis katoikias ton ellinikon astikon kentron* [*Transformations of the relationship between public and private space in social housing blocks of Greek city centers*] (Athens: National Technical University of Athens, 2009), 67–68.

0
Principles of the flat typologies

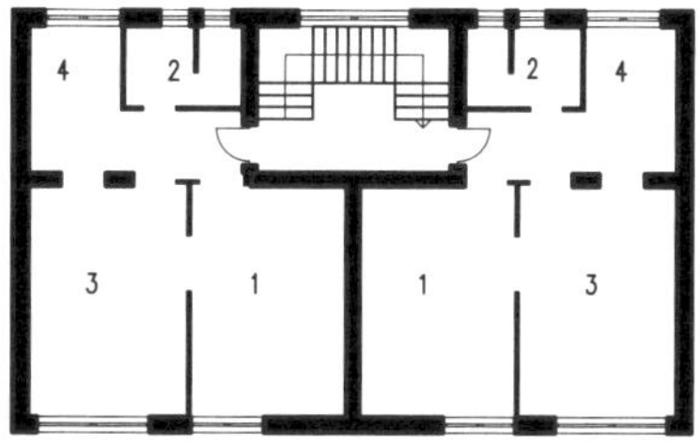

Römerstadt settlement, Frankfurt 1927-1928

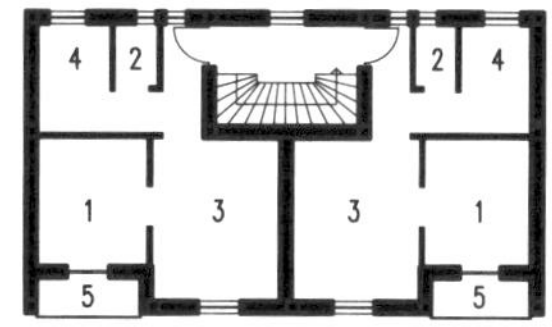

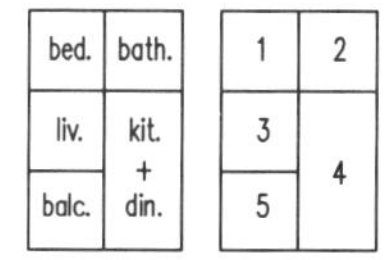

Trigono Settlement, type B1

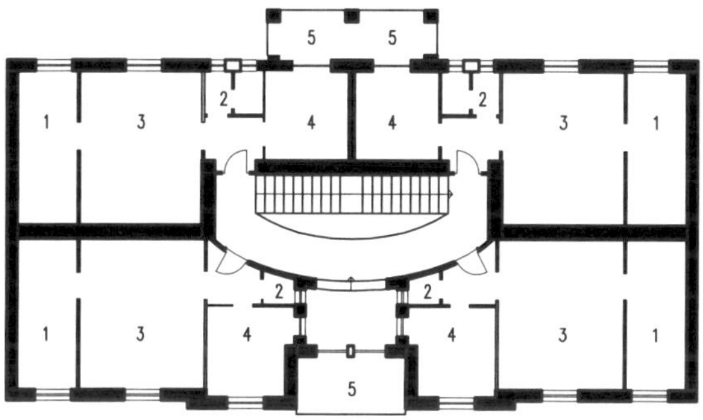

Karl-Seitz Hof settlement,Vienna 1926-1933

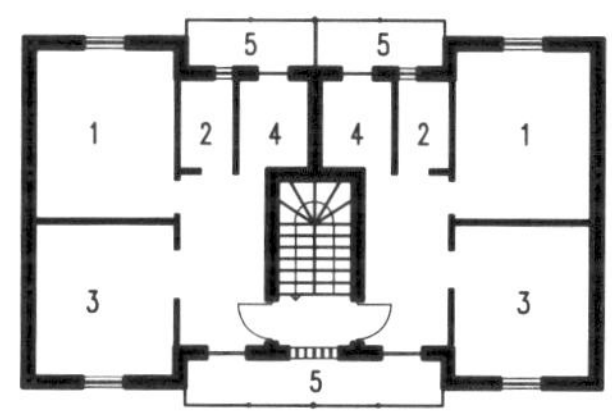

Trigono Settlement, type B2

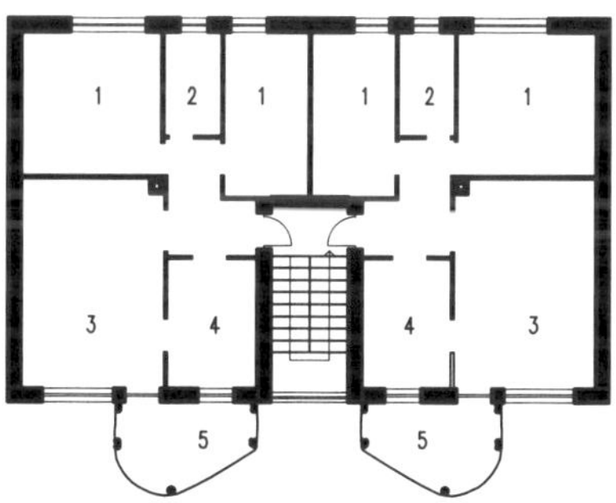

Siemensstadt settlement, Berlin 1929

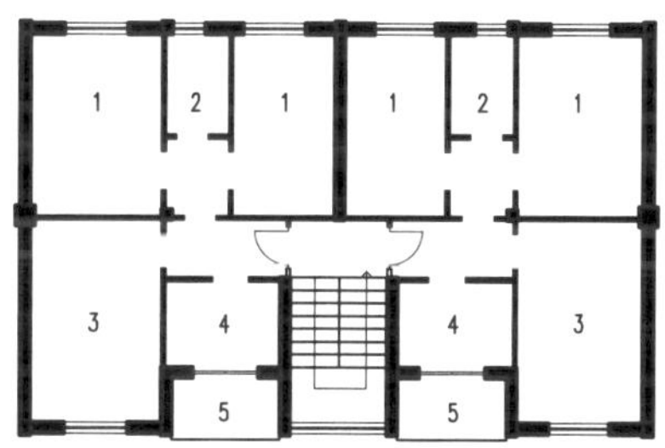

Trigono Settlement, type C

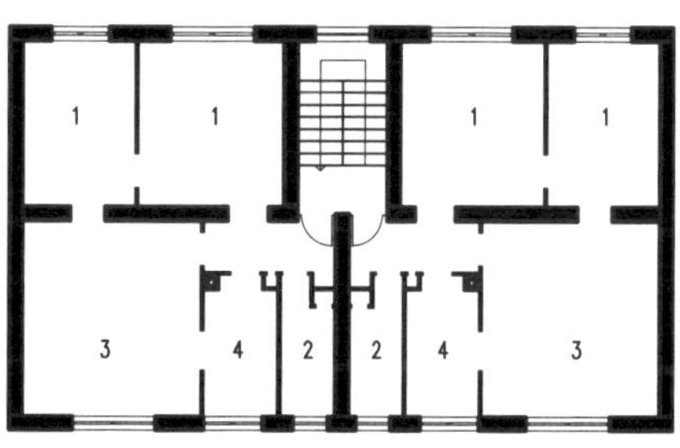

Bruchfeldstrasse settlement, Frankfurt 1926-1927

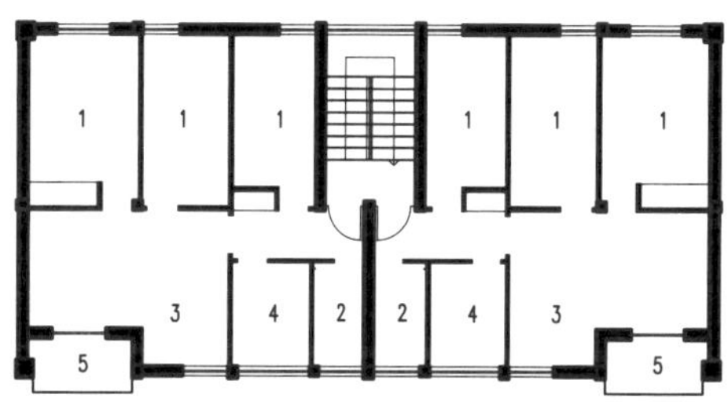

Trigono Settlement, type D

"Due to the varying conditions of those in need of dwellings, I argue that the form of the flexibly variable dwelling plan, where the determination of the individual rooms is not rigidly fixed, is the most efficient. According to the nature of occupation, number of members and individual needs, the family can exchange the rooms at will, since none of the rooms is a transit room."[25] **(Figs. 11.1-11.3)**

Although the suggested quality is limited to occupation-at-will within the nuclear family structure of a flat, Gropius's ingenuity —expressed in his typological exercise for the communal top floor— reveals the radical capacity of this variability to accommodate "the varying conditions of those in need of dwellings."

Externally, there is a clear intention for the massive integrity of the building as an object to perform the affective relationship with its adjoining space. The long elevation, with minimal plastic modulation, is meant to provide a uniform surface defined by the scale and weight of the object against which the space of the park flows. The suppression of any protruding element emphasizes the figuration of the façade as a skin stretched over a volume. The articulation of window openings and double loggias in the Gropius building underlines its geometry in a manner that is, "classically severe, rational and of a proportional brilliance."[26] However, while the symbolism of unity is achieved by Gropius's sharp contours and crisp lines, it is severely undermined in the façade of the Trigono version. The inclination of the ground leads to the subdivision of the solid into three volumes that escalate in height. The interruption of the continuity of loggias by the stair cores prevents their "formally and functionally distinct sphere" from mediating "between the individual parts of each block" and fostering a social interrelationship "as a transition between the private sphere of individual dwellings and the public one of the whole block."[27] Most notably, the slightly protruding structural skeleton of the building emphasizes the vertical rhythm and projects the underlying subdivision of individual units onto the surface, further highlighted by the *ad hoc* individual interventions on the façade. **(Fig. 12)**

25 Carl Gorgas, "Grossiedlung Siemensstadt," *Die Bauwelt* 21, (special supplement) no. 46 (1930): 9–10.
26 Karl-Heinz Hüter quoted in Katharina Borsi, "Hans Scharoun's 'Dwelling Cells' and the autonomy of architecture," *The Journal of Architecture* 23, no.7–8 (2018): 1124.
27 Gorgas, "Grossiedlung Siemensstadt," 11–12.

If the façade fails to transmit the unity of the object as a representation of the community it accommodates, that is because it is an honest reflection of the underlying typological and institutional regime. By adopting the design without sharing the vision for the production of a radically new model for living, the Greek program missed the opportunity to revolutionize the social and economic order of 'the private sphere.' On the contrary, this was inscribed within the surface of each flat, functionally with the individualization of all vital spaces, and institutionally with private property. The flats were designed, from the outset, to make, "future owners of former non-owners," rejecting vertical or collective articulations, instead favoring "per floor or apartment ownership" legislation and clearly prioritizing families with children. By law, every refugee family was eligible to acquire a flat in the block settlements upon evidence of absence of other property title of residence or land in Attica. Housing was subsidized by the State in the form of deferred payment, forgivable (interest-free) loans. The price of a flat was proportionally fixed at 70% of the State's expenditure —land and construction— less the face value of the bond issued to the refugees for their exchangeable property.[28] Once 10% of the price was submitted, the Ministry of Welfare would grant a temporary concessionaire that acted as a title of ownership and a registration of mortgage by the State. The final concessionaire was granted upon the completion of installment payments. Property rights were limited vertically, compared to a commercial apartment building, and horizontally, compared to the single-family refugee houses; the regulations forbid any extension beyond the existing height and perimeter of the building. Most notably, the homeowners' share of the plot, which in this case coincided with the building's ground surface, was only valid for the lifespan of the building, since the title of land in the area of the settlement was state property.[29] The inherent precariousness of this model was downplayed by the conscious strategy for social integration through ownership upon which, a sense of security was predicated in compensation for the pain of displacement.

On a symbolic level, the embodiment of 'the private' in the flat, as the recognizable structural unit of the block, and its hermetic distinction from "the public domain,"

28 For an explanation of exchangeable property see footnote 13. For a detailed description of the state's financial scheme regarding the pricing and payment strategy for the flats, see Vasileiou, *I Laiki Katoikia*, 77–78.

29 This model ensured ownership of a flat as an object in its current conditions detached from the territory that accommodated it. In challenging circumstances, though, such as earthquakes that caused serious damages to the buildings, the residents were faced with the risk of compulsory demolition and homelessness with no claim on the land. For an in-depth analysis of the institutional framework and the property regime in the block settlements, see Stavrides et. al., *Metaschimatismoi dimosiou-idiotikou*, 29–35.

11.1-11.3
Principles of unit arrangement

TYPE C

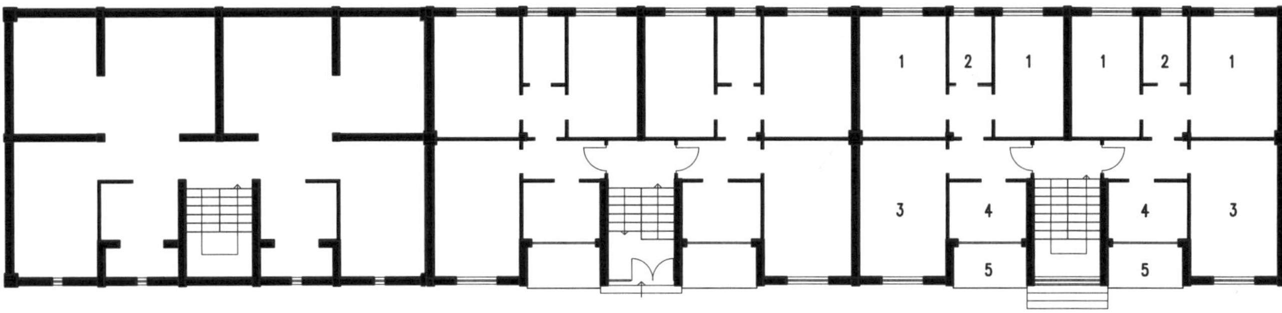

semi-basement floor plan 1st floor plan typical floor plan

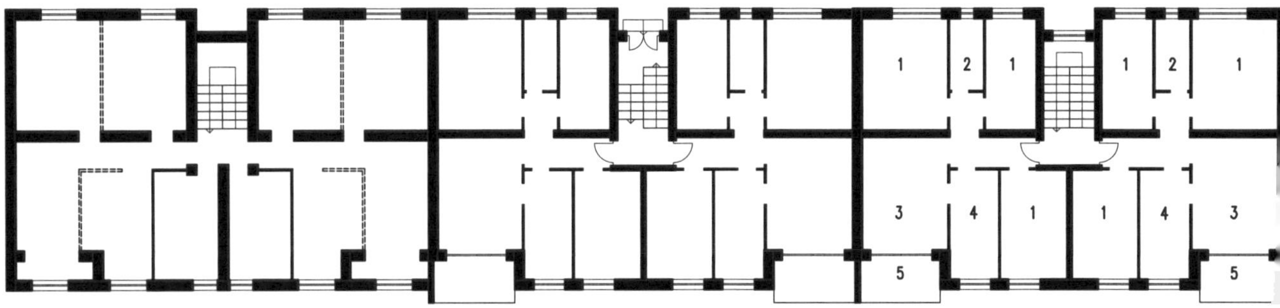

semi-basement floor plan 1st floor plan typical floor plan

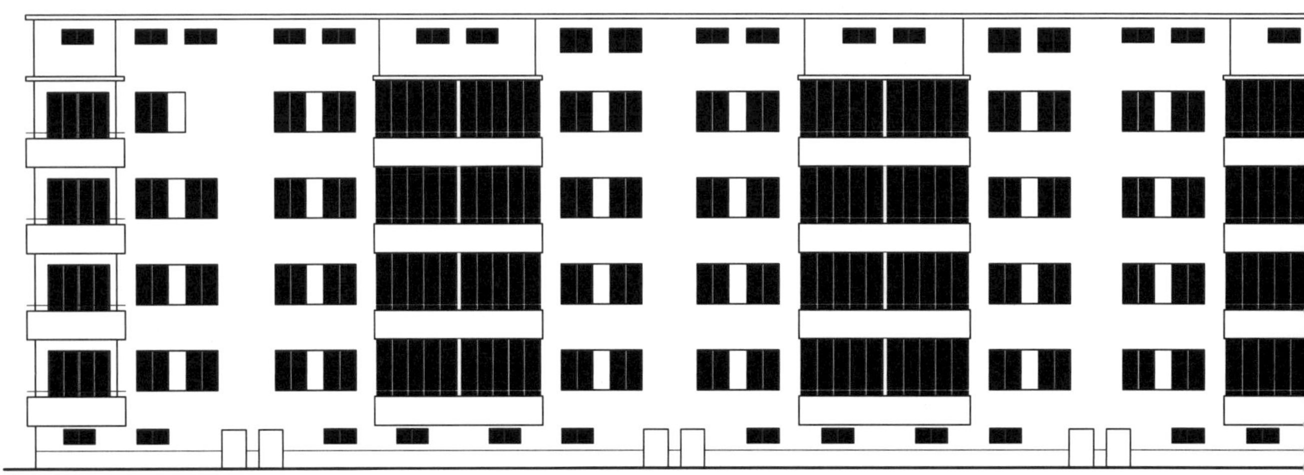

11.1

ical floor plan

Type D

Trigono settlement

11.2

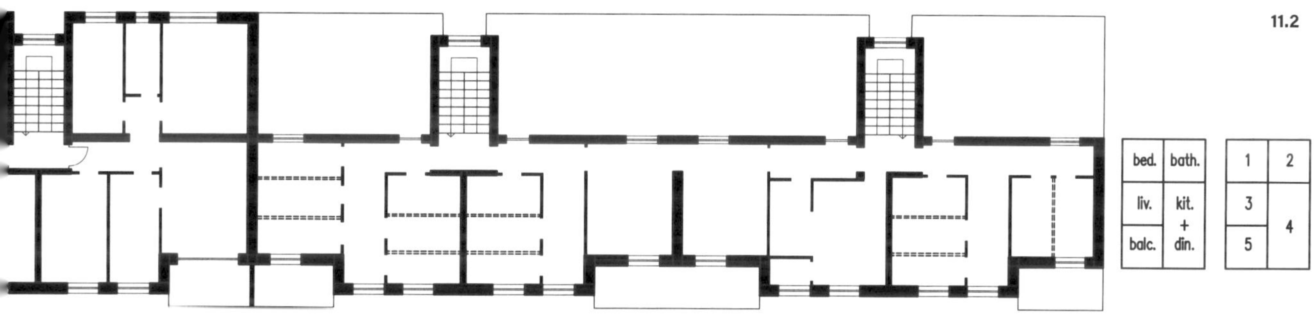

ical floor plan

top floor plan / variation

Siemensstadt settlement, Walter Gropius

11.3

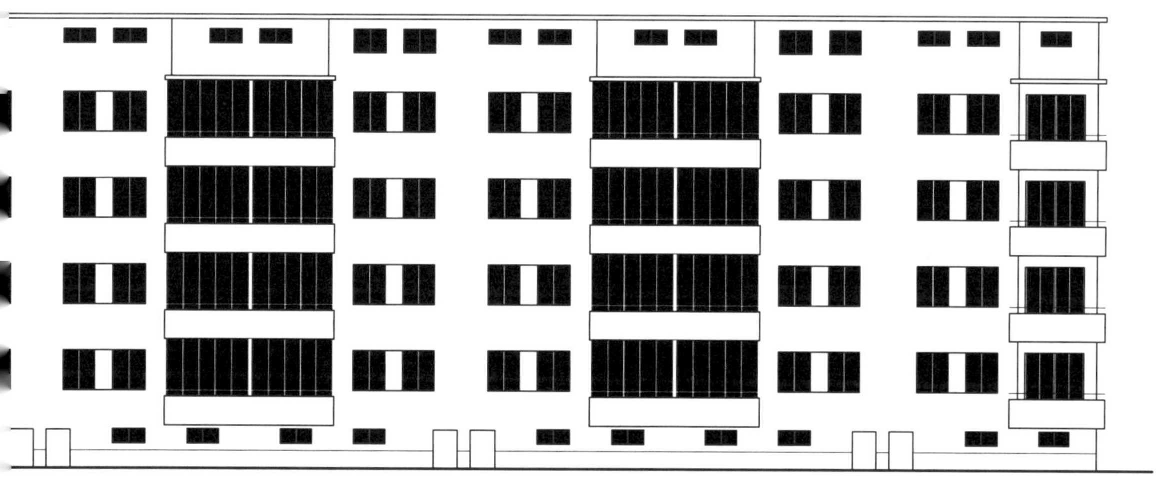

elevation

12
Trigono Settlement,
Type C and D elevation

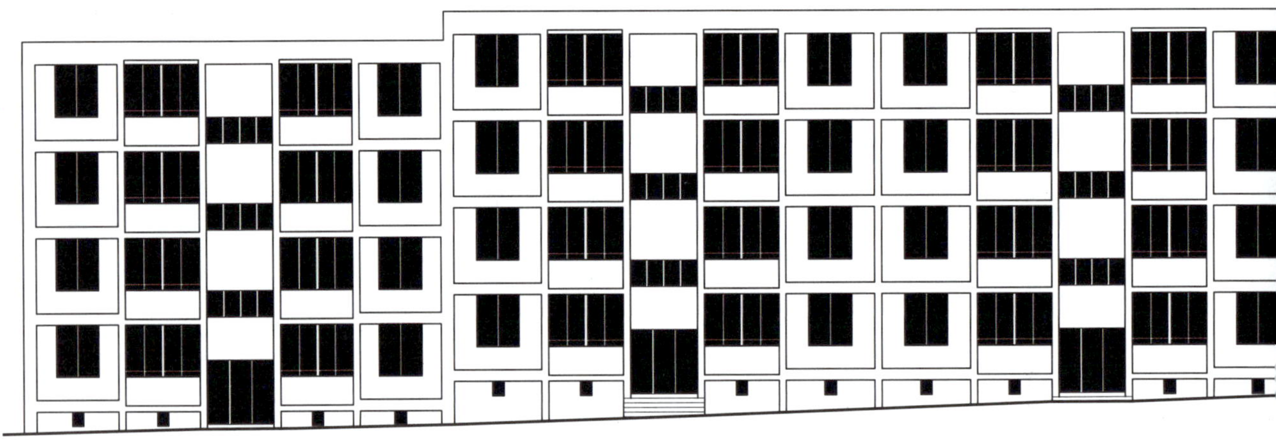

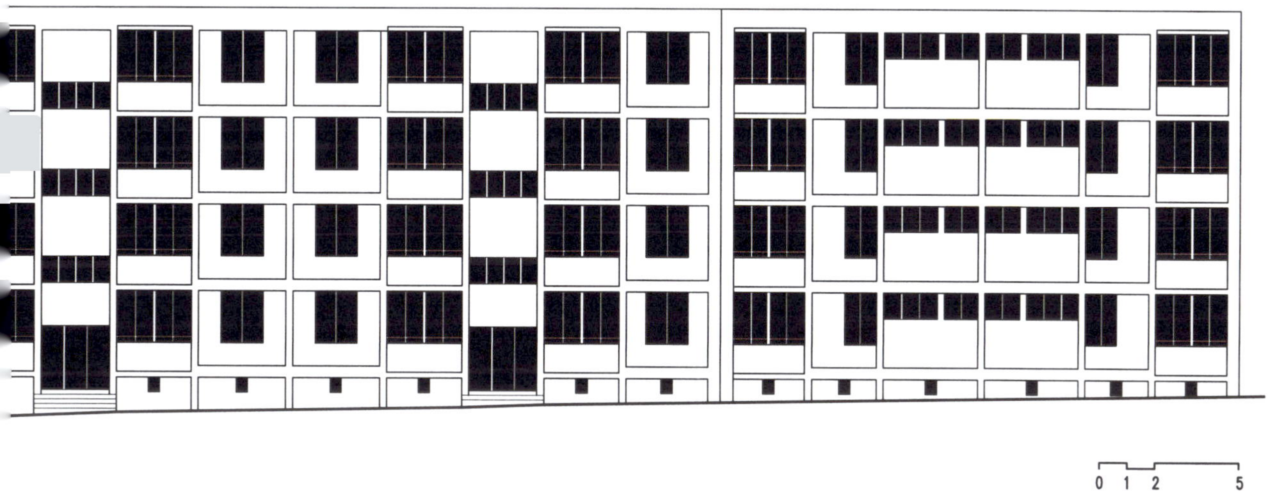
0 1 2 5

compromised the potential that could have otherwise been yielded for collective life. Initially, flats were allocated based principally on residents' place of origin, as a way to reinforce existing social and cultural bonds in the new communities. These bonds were especially visible in the shared space around the base of the building. Indeed, the 'ground datum' of the settlement was endowed with the trust of the residents, acting as a place for relaxation, encounter and play, collective gatherings and festivities. On the other hand, the blocks were designed as assemblies of private units explicitly connected by minimal enclosed service spaces (staircases, entrances, and doorsteps). Soon, the need for additional living space had a significant impact on the visual uniformity of the larger communal surfaces of the blocks; the façades and the roof terraces. The scope of this impact was made particularly visible through the *ad hoc* enclosure of the loggias and terrace space. In the absence o any instruction for collective mobilization, inhabitants of the ground floors engaged in idiosyncratic practices of occupying the front spaces in the form of gardens or courtyards, which overrode the legal and symbolic border of private space. Even when shared, these interventions were spatially developed in a way that stressed the individuality and differentiation of each flat as an extension through private appropriation.[30] Again it becomes clear, that the perception of private space, and the 'entitlement' to it, is a planned interpretation of the ties the State-Market partnership chooses to inflict on citizens.[31] The refugee settlements were the product of a housing policy intended not so much towards experimentation with forms of social housing in the spacious outskirts of the city, but rather, towards the marginalizatior of these populations from the city center. The blocks were less the product of a design endeavor on collective living as they were on "collective privacy,"[32] an indica tion of how privacy, as a social value, was promoted and identified with the flat as a whole —both as a living unit and as an asset.

So, where then does the resilience of the Trigono settlement as a long-standing urban housing community lie, if not in insightful planning? The answer includes a number of contingencies in the urban development and the economy, but its most

30 This practice constitutes 'adverse possession,' but since it was in the interest of the State to show tolerance to these communities, the claiming of some 'squatters rights' had to attain the objectives of legality and remedy defects in title. The legal term for public property coming under private ownership after 20 consecutive years of use *in good faith*, is called usucaption (Latin usucapio).

31 Gizele notes that "the transition from the rental to the property regime was undertaken by the Committee of Refugee Accommodation consciously and intentionally," Gizele, *Koinonikoi Metaschimatismoi*, 291. Leontidou concludes that "the geographical segregation of the refugee populations was intentionally organized and planned by the State." Leontidou, *Poleis tes Siopes*, 209. Stavrides et.al. argue that "the State housing programs were treated as opportunities for the granting of premiums to the private construction sector, rather than models of living for the weakest members of society." Stavrides et. al., *Metaschimatismoi dimosiou-idiotikou*, 61.

32 Stavrides et. al., *Metaschimatismoi dimosiou-idiotikou*, 66.

striking feature is, I argue, the capacity of the community to reproduce itself, riding the waves of social mobility and transformation which confront the city. To begin with, it is characteristic of the naivety of pre-war planning that the post-war urban sprawl of Athens would surround and transform these settlements from marginalized neighborhoods into islands of generous spatiality within the overbuilt city. Due to its proximity with historically bourgeois areas of the center, such as Pagrati and Kolonaki, the Trigono particularly 'subverted' the spatial segregation otherwise intended for the refugee settlements. The nearby construction of the Hilton hotel (1958-1963), a future landmark of modernism in Athens, designated the surrounding area as one of the most desirable in the city center, identifying the residential districts neighboring the Trigono with 'middle class.' In the following years, the radical innovation that the settlement model introduced to the housing sector resisted the sweeping current of the antiparoche, since the restrictions of land and building regulations would render such a choice unprofitable to developers. Similarly, the distinct legal titles separating land and buildings, safeguarded the project against the neoliberal policies of the Real Estate Company of the State (DEK S.A.) in the early 2000s and the national privatization program undertaken by its successor, the Treasury for the Development of the Private Property of the State (TAIPED S.A.) in 2011.[33]

Not only has the State diachronically neglected to appreciate or enhance the strengths of this model, but, on the rare occasions when it has declared an interest it has not been towards its reinforcement, but towards its replacement with something more financially lucrative. Throughout the Trigono's history, there have only been two state-driven initiatives which commissioned studies of the area in 1983 and 2009. Their aims were both addressed in terms of "urban renewal," a concept that has proved quite troubled in the neoliberal years in regards to the core objectives of such projects. The first study was undertaken by the State Corporation of Urban Planning, Settlements and Housing,[34] which carried out a thorough analysis of the urban and social background of the area. However, it resulted in a quite brutal proposal to demolish the Trigono blocks, replacing them with a higher and

33 The title "Private Property of the State," although an oxymoron, is quite telling in terms of the sovereign management of "public property" in the name of "indirectly serving the public interest" through "public income." This property is the outcome of the transactional activity of the government (investment in real estate or the stock market) that can be legally conceded to private parties as opposed to the "Public Property of the State," the material and immaterial public assets that are directly used and enjoyed by the public. Public assets that are the result of compulsory expropriation, such as the land of the "refugee block settlements," are classified as Private Property of the State. In 2011, the attempt to sell refugee block settlement land to private developers was cancelled due to the refusal of private owners to sell their flats.

34 The Corporation was founded in 1976 as a private-law legal person under the supervision of the Ministry of Land Planning and Public Infrastructure for the provision of affordable housing blocks or units to the middle- and low-income classes. It was also responsible for the provision of public infrastructure and support networks as well as urban renewal interventions for existing settlements. The land for new housing construction would become available by compulsory expropriations by the State, while funding would be secured by the corporation's rental properties and other royalties under its management. *On the constitution of the State Corporation of Urban Planning, Settlements and Housing*, N.446, FEK A 264, (1976). State Corporation of Urban Planning, Settlements and Housing, *Report on the Urban Study and Renewal Proposal in the Municipality of Kessariani / Final Phase* (Athens: Municipality of Kessariani, 1983).

more solid mixed-use arrangement of commercial, office and residential programs, which was rejected by the municipality of Kessariani. The urban study of 2009 was undertaken by the Ministry of Built Environment, Land Planning and Public Projects in a closer collaboration with the municipality. Working together, the study carried out an interesting analysis including the categorization of the apartment blocks into a collection of types.[35] Despite coming up with a friendlier approach to their modernization, the second proposal was also eventually abandoned and left the blocks without refurbishment in their current poor state.

Despite the stigma of their address, the "refugee block settlements" managed to retain their liveliness and build their identity as local communities rather than mobile and marginalized subjects. In Kessariani the motives behind the phenomenon which Maloutas describes as "the spatial entrapment of social mobility in traditional working-class suburbs,"[36] gradually became less class-based and more 'clan'-based. Although the population was comprised of a substantial industrial labor force, they were not spatially organized based on affiliation with a specific industrial establishment like in the case of industrial towns. On the contrary, housing, as the institutional expression of familial and property ties, retained a much more significant role in the process of spatial integration and social reproduction within the borders of the settlement and the municipality. Certainly, as a typical working-class district with affordable property and rental values, the area received waves of employment migration during the massive urbanization of Athens in the 1950–60s, and during the 90s with populations from Balkan and former socialist countries. The social mixture at Trigono was particularly conditioned by the second wave, when the economic gap between the block settlements and the commercial apartment building had become wider; the former had suffered decades-long state neglect and poor maintenance and the latter fell victim to neoliberal speculation. It is remarkable how, for the majority of newcomers who abided by the community's accepted social protocols, integration has been seamless. The settlement today accommodates a typical contemporary urban mixture in peaceful symbiosis: an aging part of the original popula-

35 Ministry of Environment, *Urban Renewal in the Municipality of Kessariani: Preservation and Rehabilitation of Existing Blocks/ Preliminary Study-Proposal: Alternative Regeneration* (Athens: Municipality of Kessariani, 2009).

36 Thomas Maloutas, *I Koinoniki Geographia tis Athinas: Koinonikes Omades kai Domimeno Perivallon se mia Notioeuropaiki Mitropoli* [*The Social Geography of Athens: Social Groups and Built Environment in a South-european Metropolis*] (Athens: Alexandria, 2018), 171–190.

tion and their descendants, to whom it has always been a home; immigrant families, to whom it has become a home; as well as students and young professionals, who seek a home they can afford in the city center.

Almost a century since their conception, these community settlements are still predominantly addressed through a historicist lens, which tends to obscure any possibility of intervening within —what I find— a rigid approach to treating them as monuments. While respecting their historical charge, I address them in my research through a more dynamic framework of their present and future potential as communities which demonstrate an extraordinary capacity for social integration and reproduction. The fact that they constitute an urban phenomenon of accreted abandoned visions makes them a parable of urban planning and typological investigation. They offer an ideal encounter to slow down and think about how we could live in cities. The selection of a case study, where utopian plans and heroic architectural visions of domesticity were once invested, can be liberating. It subverts both the state's and the market's claim on the neoliberal city; they have been incapable of molding the place to their will. The project is an attempt to mobilize the community to re-evaluate the idea of 'private space' in order to reclaim and release the spatial capacity of this architecture on the basis of collective actualization and self-governance of commonality. Based on De Angelis's idea of "boundary commoning,"[37] the mechanism which produces structural coupling between commons will allow the boundaries of the existing system to be included in the operational domain of the new commons. By employing this mechanism and radicalizing the premises of the existing, it aims to trigger the restructuring of the idea of being private in a twenty-first-century urban housing model.

37 De Angelis, *Omnia Sunt Communia*, 291–2.

JURIDICAL FRAMEWORK: THE TRIGONO COMMUNITY LAND TRUST

The description of urban planning and residential architecture's subordination to market speculation reveals that the housing question is inextricable from juridical and administrative issues of land. It also reveals the precariousness of both public and private property vis-a-vis market gains. Therefore, any attempt to claim territorial, governmental and performative rights on land 'secured' for community purposes, would require the legal recognition of this community in the name of which, freedoms and duties of acting outside the market logic are enshrined. Such a political constitution, as Dardot and Laval argue, is most effectively administered on a territorial level, whose integrative rules ensure the coordination of the resources that fall within them,[38] although its *socio-ecological* commons transcend the territorial logic. Therefore, the administration of a housing community of the settlement scale would best be implemented in co-operation with the municipality, as the elementary form of local government with a certain degree of decision-making freedoms within its jurisdiction. Such a relationship will allow the city administration to recognize and protect the fundamental right to privacy as the right to the city, a refusal to exclude (price out) this community from the urban reality. This entails a shift away from a state-market partnership towards a city-community partnership in a dedicated effort for affordable community-led housing, with the involvement of residents at all possible levels (grassroots organizing). It is the community that turns to the local authority for support of their administrative and spatial claims and it is the local authority that is responsible for crafting a model of "participatory and inclusive democracy"[39] to address the community's terms of sharing and forms of horizontal social relations. To have a chance as a model, in its very foundational process, the city-community partnership and the passage from individual to communal administration must be predicated upon trust.

38 On the notion of political organization as fundamentally territorial and geographic in nature, see "Political Proposition 9: We Must Institute a Federation of Commons," in Dardot and Laval, *Common*, Pt III.

39 De Angelis, *Omnia Sunt Communia*, 270.

The policy adopts the radical novel form of land tenure and community governance found in the institution of the *Community Land Trust* (CLT). Started in the 1960s as a land reform movement —and part of the American civil rights movement— the CLT has gained increasing popularity over the last decade in European cities, such as Brussels and London. Land is held in a trust for the exclusive use of a community and is therefore treated as common heritage, not an individual possession. Never to be resold, the property is managed by the non-profit organization instituted and governed in its name, the Community Land Trust.[40] As a model for urban housing communities, it promotes a combination of community-owned land, permanently removed from the market, and publicly assisted privately-owned housing. However, the thesis aspires to move beyond the home ownership aspect of the CLT [41] by gradually substituting property claims with expanded use rights as an incentive to housing. In order to draw the juridical framework for the operation of the Trigono model, key principles and institutional guidelines are adopted from the classic CLT structure, whereas terms of financial and technical assistance are extrapolated from its urban counterpart, the City-CLT partnership branch. There, the municipality is seen as the driving force in instigating and regulating CLT activity in its jurisdiction. Then, the CLT's strength in protecting the municipality's investment and the community's interests in the long run is exercised through the ethic of *stewardship*, towards the socialization of captured gains for the betterment of community life.[42] As city administrations take on a leading role and a special promise for testing and tailoring CLTs to their scale and residents' needs, numerous trends in City-CLT partnerships have emerged to challenge the ways in which the model has traditionally been structured, championed and applied.[43] Historically, the Municipality of Kessariani has been known for pioneering social advocacy, being close to its electorate and rejecting proposals for the gentrification of the Trigono area. This opens the opportunity for the CLT model to be introduced and adjusted to the Athenian context, by setting up the Kessariani-Trigono CLT partnership.

40 John E. Davis, *The Community Land Trust Reader* (Cambridge, MA: Lincoln Institute of Land Policy, 2010), 3–5.

41 Ibid., 10.

42 This ethic resonates with pre-colonial Native American attitudes and the New England custom of town commons and is epitomized in the right use and smart development of land toward social gains for the common good. Ibid., 48–65.

43 John E. Davis and Rick Jacobus, *The City-CLT Partnership: Municipal Support for Community Land Trusts* (Cambridge, MA: Lincoln Institute of Land Policy, 2008), 33.

The main juridical objective is the legal representation of the community and the administrative separation and interdependence of powers through which the community model can preserve autonomy.[44] Thus, the aim is to detach administrative and use rights of the land and buildings from absolute public and private property rights respectively. For the land, this signifies a crucial change of status: shifting from public to common, or collective, property. **(Fig. 13)** According to Waldron's account, they are both understood as referring to resources, with access and use privileges open to all and any member of the society or community on the basis of legal accountability. However, common property should not be identified with public, or state, property, which refers to resources that are administered by the government of a state for the benefit of "the public".[45] The public is an elusive unit, referring usually to an indeterminate group of people that, as a body, cannot actively participate in the administration of the resource at its disposal. Therefore, in public property, although use privileges are separated from title, the public authority is supposed to control how the property is disposed of in the "public interest", which, more often than not, has led to the power of exploiting or transferring resources for economic interest. On the other hand, *common property,* refers to resources whereby decisions are made collectively by the members of the community in whose name the property is held. Decision-making is based on a determination of the 'social interest.' This means that the administration of a collective resource is conditioned by collective decisions over the prioritization or benefit of a social need (e.g. structural improvements to the housing and land) or a social category (e.g. the elderly or a minority) towards the best interest of all members. Therefore, common property is characterized by the control of power and designation of rights having to be legitimized by, and assigned on, the grounds of the *objective of use* towards the social interest.[46]

This criterion, which is entrenched in Greek law as the "social benefit purpose,"[47] opens up a much wider field of possibilities for public assets than the rigid framework of property. The law provides for "the possibility for a public asset to be transferred to a legal person, which has been founded or constituted to pursue a

44 Proudhon calls it "one of the greatest ideas of science: that of the division or separation of powers." See Proudhon, "Forms of Government," in *The Federative Principle*, Ch. III.

45 Although Waldron is determined to justify private property, he provides original analyses of the concept of ownership, the ideas of access and use rights, and the relation to equality in all types of property. See James Waldron, *The Right to Private Property* (Oxford: Oxford University Press, 1988), Pt. 1.

46 Here, Stavrides's problematization on the danger of strengthening communities to define "their own" commons resulting in the creation of closed communities is challenging. See An Architektur, "On the Commons: A Public Interview with Massimo De Angelis and Stavros Stavrides," *e-flux journal* no. 17 (June 2010), https://www.e-flux.com/journal/17/67351/on-the-commons-a-public-interview-with-massimo-de-angelis-and-stavros-stavrides. Still, the primary struggle lies in representation and governance, which, in the proposed model involves "the public" through representatives of the local government and open citizen membership. The resolution of more complex prospects of sharing among different communities can only be achieved through a more direct democracy, which defines the rules of belonging on assessment of the objective of public use, not by qualification of 'public identity.' According to this, the common is nothing but a non-state public.

47 As "social benefit purpose" is regarded any purpose that is charitable, educational, cultural and generally beneficial to the society, in total or in part. When a public asset is disposed of for the purpose of social benefit, both the asset and the legal person representing it are regarded "social property." *Social Property Code*, Articles1–3, N.4182, FEK A 185 (2013).

13
The separation of powers

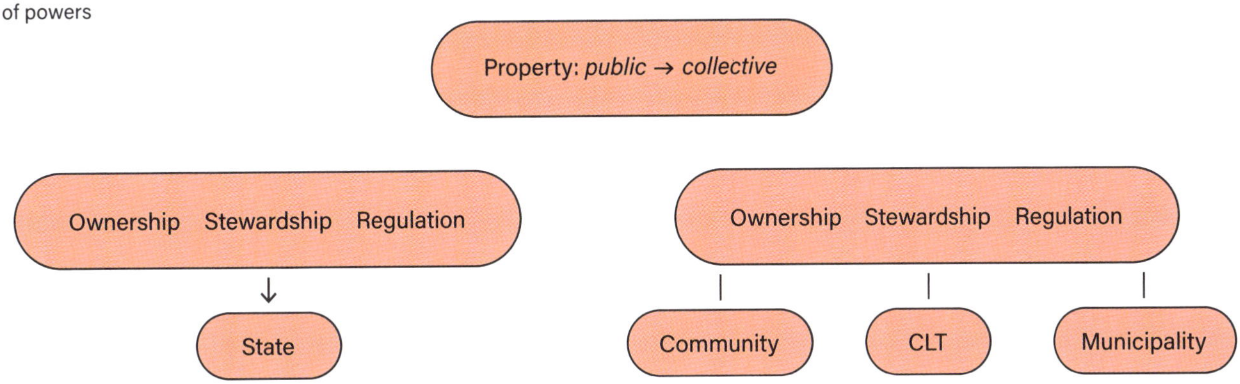

14
The Trigono CLT area

social benefit purpose, and the concession aims at supporting the implementation of this sole purpose."[48] According to this law, the Trigono settlement, an area of 31.7 acres **(Fig. 14)**, can be transferred to the Trigono Community Land Trust. Founded as a non-profit, tax-exempt corporation, the Trigono CLT holds the purpose of organizing the community of the blocks through modes of self-build cooperative housing, stewarding the adaptation of the blocks in pursuit of common objectives and any intervention to the land with respect of common heritage, ensuring the long-term affordability of accommodation. The municipality acts as the guarantor for the implementation of this social benefit purpose, the particularities of which fall under its juridical responsibilities "based on the principles of subsidiarity and proximity."[49] This is not, however, an invocation of municipal responsibilities toward the built environment, codified in terms of "urban and housing development," "land planning and zoning" and "urban renewal". As neoliberal practices, these have traditionally been keen on the demolition of blighted buildings with their reconstruction geared towards maximizing market profit on the land, something the CLT is legally bound against. Rather, the Kessariani-Trigono CLT partnership is predicated upon municipal responsibilities towards social protection and welfare, and particularly for "the financial support of self-help housing," "the regulation of issues of social housing,"[50] including "building regulations" and "any activity affecting the architectural environment and aesthetic physiognomy of settlements," and "the recognition of beneficiaries of housing provision."[51] "Structural improvement" within a social policy involves renovation, maintenance and even partial demolition for a typological transformation toward social change rather than economic opportunity. Self-building is proposed not simply to mitigate construction and labor costs but also as a means of bolstering people's confidence regarding the creation of their private space independent from industrial and market lobbies.

Thus, this tract of land is conceded in full real rights and free of charge to the new Trigono CLT, in order to undertake, in partnership with the municipality of Kessariani, the construction and maintenance of the works proposed in the planning application

48 The ministerial decree, in this case, is to be signed jointly by the Ministry of Finance, responsible for the management of public assets, and the Ministry of Health and Welfare, to which the refugee settlements, as assets, are registered. *On the Concession of Public Property and the Amendment of Bylaws on Public Assets*, Article 5, N. 1331, FEK A 330 (1949). *Concessions for Social Benefit Purposes*, Article 66, N. 330, FEK A 69 (1960).

49 *Municipal and Local Government Code*, Articles 94–5, N.3852 (2010).

50 Ibid. The very architectural notion of social housing is challenged here in order to overcome its strong legal entanglement with the State as the sole provider and to be addressed on the level of local government.

51 Ibid.

and to fulfill the social benefit purposes of the policy. The same terms are applied for the concession, as if it had been issued to the municipal authority; the works need to be carried out on the conceded land, insofar as there is no conflict with public or third-party rights, within a timeline of five years, and if, for any reason, the purposes cease to be fulfilled, the State is entitled to revoke the concession act.[52] To achieve feasibility in this timeframe, the planning application concerns the self-build adaptation of the different block types of the Trigono CLT toward the objective of common use. However, the CLT model is dedicated to retaining land ownership, and thus affordability and responsibility, permanently. This means that the Trigono CLT can expand its portfolio of common objective and stewardship activities to non-residential buildings and the natural resources of the area and resubmit proposals to renew the concession clause.[53] While, in the long run, the CLT can generate ground lease fees and revenues of stewardship and rentals in the service area to support the cost of managing the housing stock, during the foundational stage, it relies on start-up grants from the local government, private foundations and other donors. The city-CLT partnership plays the role of a developer, using their own officials, employees, members and volunteers to prepare, initiate, and manage the CLT projects. For the preparation of the housing project, for example, it is responsible for monitoring supply and demand by setting up an inventory of flats to acquire and a registry of eligible applicants for housing that becomes available. To initiate it, the municipality issues the direct allocation of 25% of council tax and infrastructure levy funds, which based on council-led self-build experience in England, can cover one-third of the expenditure on building materials over the project's duration.[54]

The classic CLT model does not provide a non-home-ownership alternative. Instead of leasing out parcels to homeowners, the Trigono CLT will administer its freehold rights on the land as a commonhold.[55] Furthermore, the gradual substitution of individual ownership titles of flats with use rights of expanded areas is central to the policy, in order to release the collective spatial capacity of the blocks and apply protocols of domesticity beyond property barriers. The main objective is considered

52 *On the Concession of Public Assets to Municipal and Local Governments*, Articles 200 & 277, N.3463, FEK A 114 (2006). *On the Concession of the Respective Refugee Block Settlement Land to the Municipality of Keratsini-Drapetsona*, Supreme Court, Public Law Decision (23 March 2012).

53 These projects will not be developed within the scope of this thesis.

54 Following the *Localism Act* (2011) and the *Neighbourhood Planning Legislation* (2012), amended reforms toward funding for community self-builders were put in place at *The Community Infrastructure Levy (Amendment) Regulations* (2012) and the *Self-build and custom housebuilding. Housing and Planning Act*, Pt. I, Ch. 2 (2016).

55 A Commonhold Association is a company that is itself owned by the freeholders and/or owners of the flats in order to manage the common and external parts of the property jointly so that they can control maintenance fees and service charges. *Leasehold Reform Act* (2002).

a reversal of the neoliberal "right to buy,"[56] i.e. the urge for council tenants to gain ownership of the restricted area of their homes, into "the right to transfer and the right to manage regulations,"[57] i.e. the urge for homeowners to submit individual ownership to the CLT in order to gain expanded use and collective administration rights of the whole neighborhood. At the beginning, a pilot period is required for the inhabitants to get familiar with the new model, while they still hold limited ownership powers, and for the CLT to collect the necessary funds to purchase the properties. Thus, the mid-term policy introduces the separation between ownership rights and use rights, which have so far acted indivisibly in the institution of private property. The "transformational equivalence of opposites" in the concept of ecology suggests that while the former shrink, the latter will expand.

It is useful to clarify the legal notions and terms, as defined in Greek Property Law, necessary for understanding the separation of rights. The legal structure of property is constituted in three fundamental rights —ownership, possession and occupation— which each defines a different form of power over things. Recognized by a legal title, the right of ownership is the direct and absolute power of the subject to dispose of the thing at will and excludes any other subject from taking action therein, insofar as these actions do not offend the law or other rights therein.[58] Possession is the exercise of physical power over a thing by a subject with the will for constant, unlimited and exclusive domination (*corpore animus*), which can only be recognized as a right insofar as it is exercised in good faith. Occupation is the exercise of physical power over a thing, which cannot claim exclusionary or other rights.[59] These forms of power designate three different relational modalities between subject and object; in ownership through dominion, in possession through disposal, and in occupation through use and enjoyment.

The rights of property can be legally separated, by contractual agreement, into: *bare ownership*, ownership severed from its full absolute power to dispose the thing at will; and *usufruct*, the right to use and enjoy the thing, to possess while maintaining

56 The *Housing Act* (1980), which gave five million council house tenants in England and Wales the Right to Buy their house from their local authority, is seen as a defining policy of Thatcherism.

57 The Right to Transfer under Section 34A of the *Housing Act* (1985), which is central to the Community Land Trust institution, is the right of council tenants to come together as a neighborhood, form a not-for-profit organization and request collective ownership and control of their own homes. A recent amendment includes proposals to make it easier for tenants to take the lead locally —either by taking over responsibility for managing housing services, or by exploring options for transfer from their local authority. *Giving tenants control: Right to Transfer and Right to Manage regulations consultation: summary of responses on the Right to Manage Regulations* (July 2012) Ministry of Housing, Communities & Local Government, Great Britain.

58 *The Content of Ownership*, Article 1000, Property Law, Greek Civil Code, Book III, Ch.3.

59 *Possession and Occupation*, Article 974, Property Law, Greek Civil Code, Book III, Ch. 2.

its substance.[60] Usufruct is a servitude in civil law, which is a subordinate real right that provides the benefit of possession and occupancy, especially as a result of a service on the property, such as infrastructural and building works.[61] On the other hand, the right implicates real burdens —property taxes, security fees— and is not transferrable. This type of agreement, which is a personal contract between the bare owner and the usufructuary —be it a natural or a legal person— opens a wide range of mutually beneficial potential arrangements on the property.[62] The mid-term goal for the Trigono CLT is to act as the steward of collective usufructuary rights in the buildings, in order to realize the spatial intervention in full potential and be able to expand the overall capacity for accommodation. Practically, for the majority of the Trigono flat owners, who are also the residents, the socialization of use rights of designated communal areas in their flat grants them expanded use rights of all newly designated indoor and outdoor communal areas of the building, once added to the CLT scheme. Both resident and non-resident flat owners are incentivized to transfer the usufruct through major property tax exemption and guarantee of intervention in the event of mortgage default.[63] Instead, they are urged to invest this money to the community through membership fees and donation funds. The long-term policy makes use of the operational term of a CLT to impose contractual controls over the resale, or transfer, of properties. This means that the owners, or bare owners, are allowed to either pass their property on to their heirs on the precondition that they will inhabit it or to sell it to the CLT based on a formula-determined, non-market price (e.g. considering the average income in the municipality). Instead of separating privately owned buildings from communally owned land,[64] the long-term goal of the Trigono CLT is to eradicate private property at the Trigono settlement and treat land and housing as an independent entity. That is, the CLT seeks to acquire the total built stock under its stewardship in order to fix the rents, in consultation with the local government, and ensure affordability in perpetuity.

The city-CLT partnership model has a tripartite governance and a membership logic, encouraging both communitarian and public representation and, thus,

60 *The Concept of Usufruct*, Article 1142, Property Law, Greek Civil Code, Book III, Ch.8.

61 *Real Servitude*, Articles 1118–20, Property Law, Greek Civil Code, Book III, Ch.7.

62 The bare owner retains the right to alienate bare ownership, e.g. by selling it, but usufruct terms still apply for the agreed course, which would make such a transaction very unlikely.

63 By law, the usufructuary, when it is a legal person, is obliged to submit 80% of the full property tax. *Single Property Tax*, Article 2, N. 4223, FEK A΄287 (31 December 2013). This is practically a state subsidy in the form of an 80% suspension on full property tax of the properties of the service area for the duration of the project. If, in the meantime, as is planned, most of these properties are acquired by the CLT, they enter a special equitable taxation scheme with value assessment of resale-restricted homes and land when they first entered the tax rolls, not on current market rates. See "Taxing CLT Property," in Davis and Jacobus, *The City-CLT Partnership*, 23–27.
This formula is based on the nineteenth century political thinking that pervades the CLT logic in its inception. Henry George's "single tax" (*Progress and Poverty*, 1879) was a proposition for a tax on the appreciating value of land, which would suffice to cover governmental expenditure, whereas this formula proposes a tax on the initial value of the property, which in this case is very low. At the same time, a portion of the municipality's revenue on the appreciating value of the surrounding area created by the CLT land (e.g as a natural reserve in the city) is ploughed back to the CLT according to John Stuart Mill's "social increment." See Davis, *The Community Land Trust Reader*, 66–75. In fact, this is the reinstatement of the social increment in the twenty first century city, where the appreciating value of land is not created by the growth and development of the surrounding society, but rather the appreciating value of the surrounding land is created by the de-growth and un-development of the CLT land, its socio-ecological commons. On "economic growth" as an indispensable requirement for the sustainability of capital, not commons systems, see De Angelis, (2017), *op.cit.*, 239–243. On the concept of de-growth, see Anitra Nelson and François Schneider, *Housing for Degrowth: Principles, Models, Challenges and Opportunities* (London: Routledge, 2019).

64 Davis, *The Community Land Trust Reader*, 3–5.

15
The City-CLT governance structure

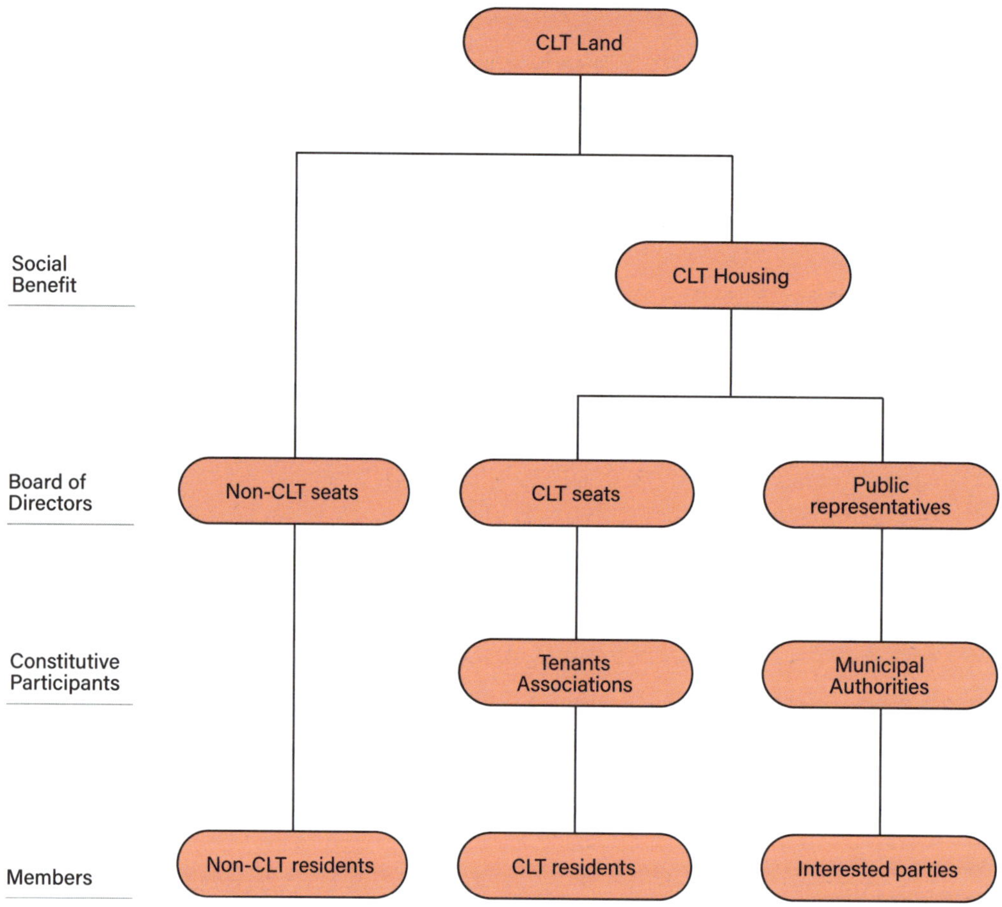

democratic administration. **(Fig. 15)** The board of directors consists of three parts, each with an equal number of seats:[65] one-third represents the interests of residents under the CLT housing scheme (CLT residents); one-third represents the interests of residents of the Trigono and the surrounding area who are not on the CLT housing scheme (non-CLT residents); and one-third is made up of municipal officials, local funders, non-profit providers of housing and social services, and other representatives of the public interest. Through a membership fee, CLT-resident and non-CLT-resident members can nominate and elect two-thirds of the board of directors, while the third designated as public representatives, is appointed by the rest of the CLT directors and the municipal authority (seats can be split among several cooperating municipalities). Therefore, a representative part of the city can have a say on decisions concerning the non-residential social benefit projects of the CLT.[66] Further, CLT residents are also members of the Tenants Association for their respective block, whose representatives appoint a Tenants Association Director to have a seat among the CLT directors. Although the general objectives of the residential project are decided among the aforementioned structure, the Tenants Association is the instrument to conclude the final configuration and new protocols in each building, by crafting the Block Constitution. Based on the particular block type and tenants' needs, during the project development an expert is appointed to the Board of the Association by the municipality, to consult the Constitution on issues of health and safety, insurance policy and financial management. Such inclusive participation opens up the possibility of not only radical pluralization, but also transversal horizontality —and solidarity— that can render the CLT a distinct paradigm in the city, both institutionally and formally.

URBAN STRATEGY: THE CLT ARCHIPELAGO OF ATHENS

If the CLT model is to radically challenge the established tropes of value production in urban domesticity, then, as an episodic gesture, it would be almost impossible to resist the risk of capitalist co-option and valorization. The reproduction of the

65 Davis and Jacobus, *The City-CLT Partnership*, 5.
66 Such projects could put forward the resurfacing of the Big Stream or the repurposing of public buildings in the Trigono area into communal facilities. According to the Civil Code, naturally flowing bodies of water, waterfronts, and riverbanks are regarded as common property of the city. See *Common Property.* Article 967, Property Law, Greek Civil Code.

private as part of the commons subjectivity, the auto-poietic mechanism of ecology, would need to be extrapolated to a CLT circuit in order to maintain and increase autonomy vis-à-vis the market-state system. The inner-city is exactly the frontline within which a CLT "critical mass" needs to proliferate, as if there is insufficient friction or counterforce, since it is viewed as offering the best chances for "a social revolution" of how to be private in the heart of the city.[67] It makes sense, then, that a CLT network is undertaken by the municipality of Athens, the juridical instrument responsible for monitoring the potential opportunities and instigating CLTs in the central domain of the city. Initially, the juridical report provides a selection of settlements in the Athens municipality, which hold the basic premise to enter the scheme; their land is public property and, in most cases, the housing blocks have survived and retained a substantial community core. **(Fig. 16.1)** The idea of boundary commoning recurs here as a form of CLT reproduction, which not only involves sharing and solidarity, but also "the construction of a commoning sense" and the constitution of an environment in which the CLTs depend on one another for continuing their auto-poiesis.[68] The Trigono CLT is exemplary in making its own complexity available for constructing other CLT identities, making the paradigm visible in the city both operationally and figuratively. Its location on the juridical border of Athens and Kessariani makes advanced claims on negotiation and cooperative administration between neighboring municipalities. Its urban and geographical characteristics unravel an atlas of topological and subterranean 'commonwealth' of the city able to suggest different ecologies.

These settlements are introduced as islands to the urban fabric, a fabric which has accommodated a very specific neoliberal project of domestic privacy within the organizational principles of a proprietary logic of urbanization. The urban fabric enclosing an island acts as the carrier of forms of life, which, once established in their new home, frequently develop alternative modes and protocols of living in their isolated surroundings.[69] However, not only are these islands not 'contained' in the abstract, repetitive system, but, amid their surrounding uniformity, they exhibit wha

67 On the notion of a "critical mass" of commons and the "tipping point," beyond which a "social revolution" can be real, see De Angelis, *Omnia Sunt Communia*, 289–91.

68 Ibid., 292.

69 *Encyclopaedia Britannica*, s.v. "Island," https://www.britannica.com.

may seem like the most imaginative ways of inhabiting space, although, they are, in fact, archetypical. **(Fig. 16.2)** In their direct engagement with particular features of topography and nature, lies a certain sensibility in the selection of location by the initial settlers in the 1920s to take advantage of a natural resource or topological asset. The concretization of the rivers of Athens during the speculative development of the 1960s, and the eradication of some settlements to facilitate the construction of roads, stresses the need to return to a rationality of reclaiming these ecologies in urban living.[70] As islands,[71] they demonstrate distinct geometries and scales that do not conform to the Athenian pixel (polykatoikia) and the urban block. **(Figs. 17.1-17.2)** Thus, they disrupt the grid, as the canonical order that has inflicted the clear-cut distinction and mutual exclusion of private and public. Their density and taxonomy can reinstate the idea of boundary in openness rather than enclosure, as the "filter [of] the relation between a system and its environment"[72] rather than a hermetic exclusionary border. **(Fig. 18)** The low ratio of built to open space and the relaxed arrangement of buildings on the land, define the typology of the boundary, which "reflects the operational and relational processes within the system."[73] Rather than reducing the territory to the sum of quantifiable, profit-driven relationships, these islands suggest alternative rules for measuring space and the produced value of the built environment and thus, alternative protocols of negotiation with urban space, which are automatically visible as a different rhythm in the city.

"The condition of insularity as a mode of relationships" suggests not only alternative urban forms, but also an "essential political form."[74] As entities, the islands can only resist the struggles against the capitalistic city under a common system of governance, which is a 'confederation of islands' on a supra-neighborhood and inter-municipal scale. According to Proudhon, the federal principle is the only political principle that respects the autonomy of local governments, by setting up "the contract of federation," whose essence is always to reserve more powers for the citizen and the municipal authorities than for the central power.[75] He contrasts this contract, which binds the citizen to the state on the basis of reciprocity and

A recent initiative, undertaken by the Urban Environment Laboratory of the National Technical University of Athens in collaboration with the State Corporation for Urban Renewal "Anaplasis" in 2019, proposed the resurfacing of a part of the Ilissos riverbed, which was unfortunately not implemented. See Nikos Belavilas, Katerina Christoforaki, and Polina Prentou, "Urban Environment Laboratory," Projective Cities MPhil in Architecture and Urban Design, AA (Athens workshop lecture, National Technical University of Athens, December 19, 2019).

On the characteristics of the "island" as a counter-colonial figure that challenges the ubiquity and abstraction of the grid, see Aureli, "Appropriation, Subdivision, Abstraction," 165–7.

De Angelis, *Omnia Sunt Communia*, 247.

Ibid.

74 Pier Vittorio Aureli, *The Possibility of an Absolute Architecture* (Cambridge, MA: MIT Press, 2010), 5.

75 Proudhon, "A Progressive Constitution," in *The Federative Principle*, Ch. VIII.

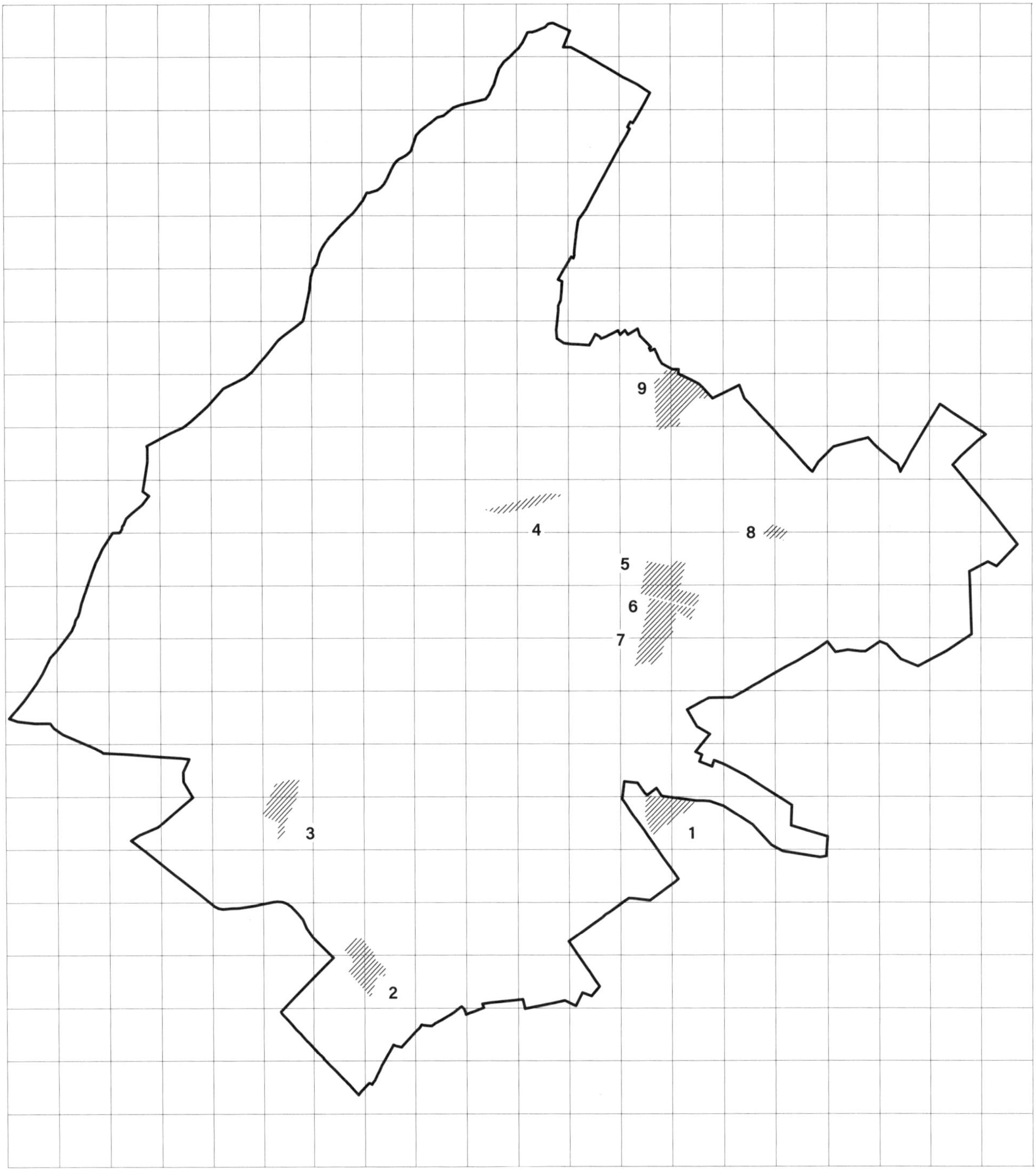

16.1
Municipality of Athens
Land concessions
to CLTs

State Property Settlements

1 Trigono
2 Aghios Sostis-Dourgouti
3 Neos Asyrmatos
4 Gkyzi (demolished)
5 Alexandras
6 Kountouriotika (demolished)
7 Stegi Patridos
8 Panormou
9 Oikismos Papandreo

.2
sland Ecologies

1 Trigono (The Big Stream of Kessariani)
2 Aghios Sostis - Dourgouti (Ilissos river)
3 Neos Asyrmatos (Philopappou hill)
4 Gkyzi (Cyclovoros stream)
5 Alexandras
6 Kountouriotika - (Lycabettus hill)
7 Stegi Patridos
8 Panormou (Ilissos river)
9 Oikismos Papandreou (Tourkovounia mountain)

Underlying rivers

a Kifissos
b Eridanos
c Ilissos
d The Big Stream of Kessariani

17.1
Island geometry

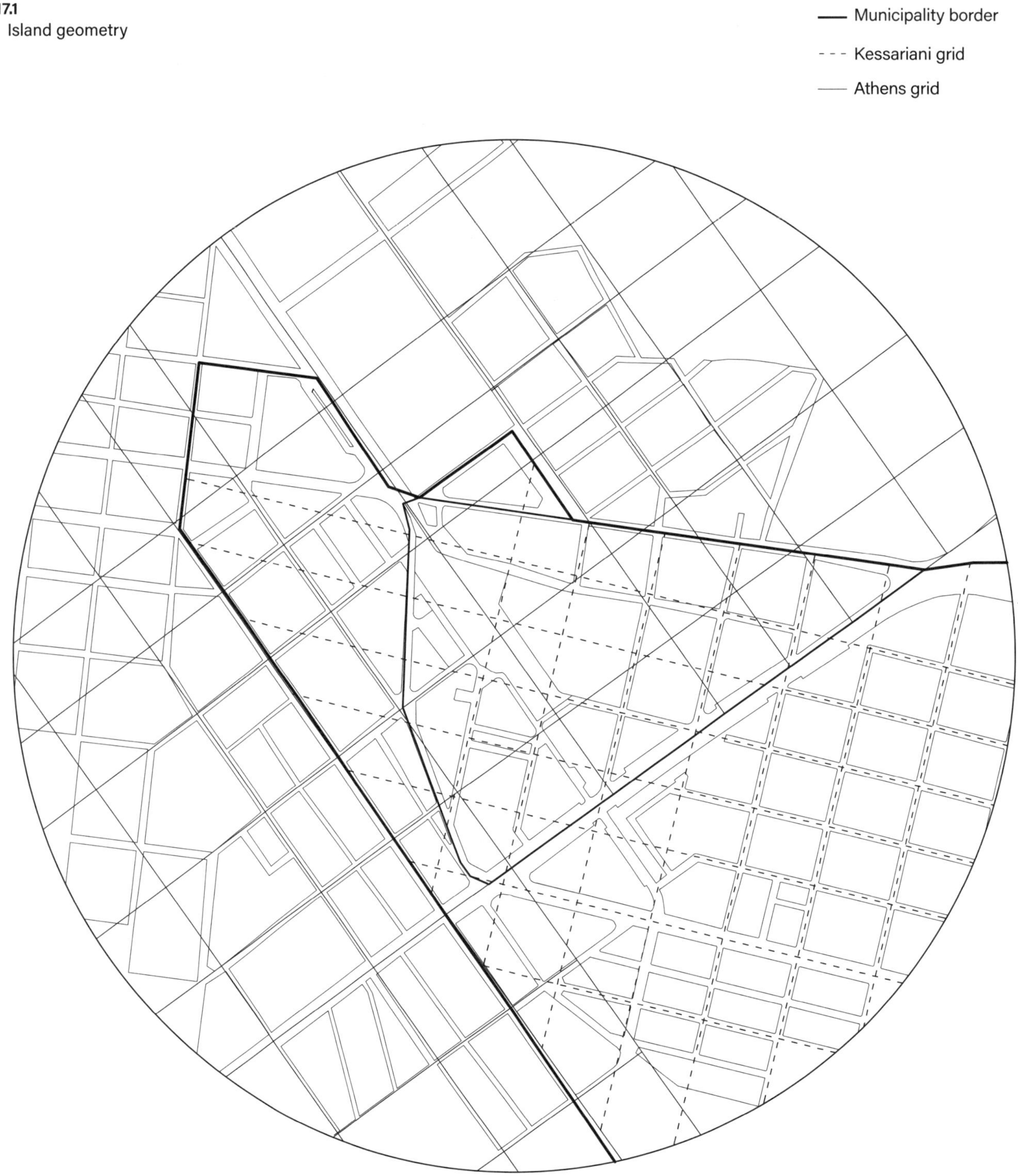

17.2
Island density

18
The CLT archipelago of Athens - Island typologies

Island typologies

1 Trigono
2 Aghios Sostis - Dourgouti
3 Neos Asyrmatos
4 Gkyzi (demolished)
5 Alexandras
6 Kountouriotika (demolished)
7 Stegi Patridos
8 Panormou
9 Oikismos Papandreou

equality of obligation, to "the society of private property," which he calls "the replica in miniature of all absolute states." It is basically a re-enactment of the Civil Code, which here reconnects the private, as a social sphere, with the public domain, as the field of pure politics. The CLT islands, the federated units, can mutually check and control their powers through what Arendt calls, "the emergence of the council system,"[76] where the concerned bodies of the CLT structures participate in different types of councils, i.e. tenant councils, professional councils, economic councils and joint councils. This radical pluralization of the ecology of the private in urban housing constitutes the CLT *archipelago*[77] of Athens. "Pluralization," Cacciari argues, does not suggest "the 'anarchic' emergence of singularities, rather [...] an order and a dialectic relationship."[78] By its nature, then, the archipelago, does not conform to hierarchical relationships, but rather harmonizes, without violently reducing to unity, the different figures, the different islands, in the individuality of their own character.

ARCHITECTURAL PROJECT: A MANUAL FOR SELF-BUILT ADAPTATION

The spatial resolution of ecology does not seek to disturb the urban form with new housing development, but instead aims to adapt the form of life in the blocks to the principles of commoning. According to architectural theorist Colquhoun, this is exactly the methodological instrumentality of typology; "a knowledge of past solutions applied to related problems," which informs creation as "a process of adapting forms derived either from past needs or from past aesthetic ideologies to the needs of the present."[79] He views this process as a mode of repetition, *experimentation* and transformation. Thus, the first pilot project for the Trigono CLT is a self-built experiment toward a typological transformation from within the living units. Unlike the neoliberal project, the spatial mediation of the ideological apparatus needs to be reconciled with the social mediation of lived experience. For the social benefit purpose to be achieved, the CLT will need to hire a local architect to engage in a deep study of the settlement's character and spatial needs, to collaborate closely with the community and devise design scenarios that are responsive to their

76 Hannah Arendt, "Thoughts on Politics and Revolution," in *Crises of the Republic: Lying in Politics, Civil Disobedience on Violence, Thoughts on Politics and Revolution* (New York: Harcourt Brace Jovanovich, 1972), 232.

77 Cacciari links the notion of the archipelago directly with Logos: "And of all the travels in the Archipelago, the idea of Travel will be born, of ultimate agonism, of contest, of ultimate struggle —of the Travel toward the common Logos, toward the unity which demonstrates multiplicity but as lost, it reveals it within its absence." Translation from the Greek edition, Massimo Cacciari, *Archipelago*, trans. Nasos Kyriazopoulos (Athens: P. Travlos, 1999), 21.

78 Ibid., 22.

79 Alan Colquhoun, "Typology and Design Method," in *Essays in Architectural Criticism; Modern Architecture and Historical Change* (Cambridge, MA.: Oppositions Books, 1981), 46.

social roles and the daily organization of their lives. This process provides powerful insights and arguments as much on the 'social' aspect of the project, the architectural practice as a social service, as on the 'benefit' aspect, the reasons why the inhabitants would engage in such a radical and laborious act.

The project is developed through the format of a manual that rejects architecture's objectification as a final photogenic image and instead highlights its commitment to the process of making and the aesthetic that the depiction of the process yields. However, this is not an attempt to nullify the exchange value of the iconic form of architecture in the phenomenological world. On the contrary, the purpose of this "aesthetic organization" of the objective reality of a participatory mode of production is, as Colquhoun suggests, to "capitalize on this subjective schematization [of exchange value]" and provide "an artificial construct which represents" this reality "in a socially recognizable way."[80] The manual invites the inhabitant into "a process of discovery that is never preempted by some image or style of a future building."[81] At the same time, it is a shift of the role of the architect towards "a 'facilitator' who can bring the needs of the people to the attention of manufacturers, government agencies and the like."[82] Papanek elaborates on the issue of education through design, where the designer attempts to educate the manufacturer and the client to overcome the indoctrination by the market for "gleaming, glistening, useless" design and the shaming of the 'low income,' which essentially constitutes the blaming of its victims.[83] This way of working is not easy. It demands good faith as much between the architect and the community as among the residents. Furthermore, it demands the complementary function of trust to shape a vision of privacy against market precarity.

The process starts with the identification of the flat types in the Trigono blocks and of the living patterns the residents have developed in them over the years. The dominant flat types, as has been discussed, imply from the outset minimum living for nuclear families, except for type A, presented in a unique block and initially addressed to couples or any other combination of two people. **(Figs. 19,20)**

80 Ibid., 44–5.
81 Stephen Kieran and James Timberlake, *Manual: The Architecture of Kieran Timberlake* (New York: Princeton Architectural Press, 2002), 6.
82 Victor Papanek, *Design for the Real World: Human Ecology and Social Change* (London: Bantam Books, 1970), 116.
83 See Papanek, "Snake Oil and Thalidomide: Mass Leisure, and Phony Fads in the Abundant Society," in *Design for the Real World*, 107–56.

Although this flat type is the least responsive to the 'recognized need' for typical family apartments, as a block structure, is today one of the most popular and liveliest examples in the area.[84] **(Figs. 21,22)** Interestingly, its liveliness is not the outcome of a policy preference toward young families, but rather of an established ethic of sharing among its predominantly single, middle-aged and elderly female population. The investigation into their living pattern reveals a configuration of private and communal spaces within the same structure and on each floor which is facilitated by the layout. **(Figs. 23,24)** The block demonstrates a linear arrangement of six small flats (35 m²) per floor and two communal staircases, one internal and one external or public, united by an external service corridor. The flats are essentially constituted as one large room (25 m²), the so-called "one-and-a-half-room"[85] unified, with minimum individual service spaces —bathroom, kitchen, hall. **(Figs. 25.1-25.3)** The private rooms are all facing the back side while the rest of the activities spill onto the corridor. For the longest part of the day, and year, as I have observed on my various site visits, the corridor becomes a terrace —an essential element in Greek domesticity— a dining and living room, a storage room, a garden, a laundry room, and basically a space for the socialization of care. Although a few of its oldest members, with demanding health conditions, have live-in caregivers (in this case the large room still functions as one-and-a-half-room to accommodate both), does not negate the fact that this terrace is effectively their living space. **(Figs. 26.1-26.3)** This layout becomes paradigmatic as an organizational principle that can variably accommodate not only a currently recognized need or a preferred social category, but "the varying conditions of those in need of dwellings" brought on by choice, or by the course of life itself: single living or single parenthood; the departure of adult children; or the loss of a partner. It provides a relatively generous room for privacy and solitude for each member without the assumption that the burden of loneliness, care and financial sustainability is to be undertaken by a nuclear family structure.

84 All information provided for the current situation and living patterns in the settlement is the product of site visits, personal observations and interviews conducted by the author as part of her field research.

85 This is based on Gropius's "two-and-a-half-room" flat, where the half-room is dedicated as a bedroom but the scheme is flexibly interchangeable for occupation at will. The type was launched at the Siemenstadt settlement (see Fig. 11), was repeated at the Gropius city social housing project in the 1960s, and was notoriously linked to the anarchist culture of Berlin after the fall of the Wall. See Paul Hockenos, "Bowie's Berlin," in *Berlin Calling: A Story of Anarchy, Music, the Wall and the Birth of the New Berlin* (New York: The New Press, 2017).

19
Identification and nomenclature of types

Name	Nr.	Flat Unit			Block Unit			
		Type	Size (sqm)	Layout	Type	Terrace	Floors	Roofing
A		1–bed	35	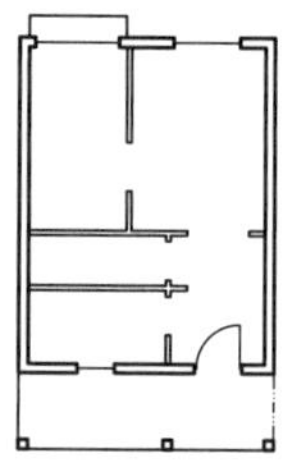	6–fold	shared	4	terraced
B	1	1–bed	35	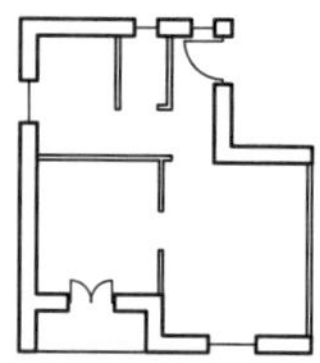	4–fold	individual	4	terraced
	2t	1–bed	45	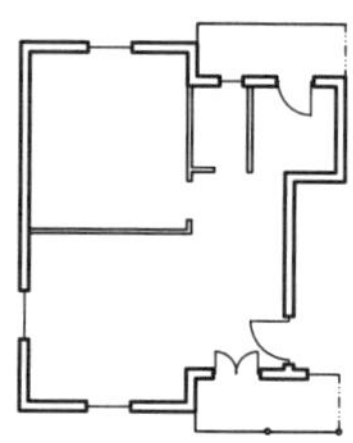	4–fold	individual	4	terraced
	2r				6–fold	individual	3	roofed
C		2–bed	55	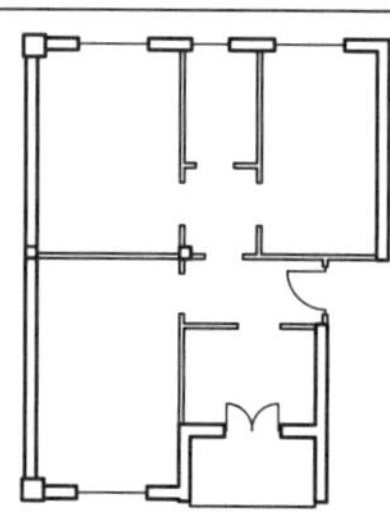	10–fold	individual	4	terraced
D		3–bed	65	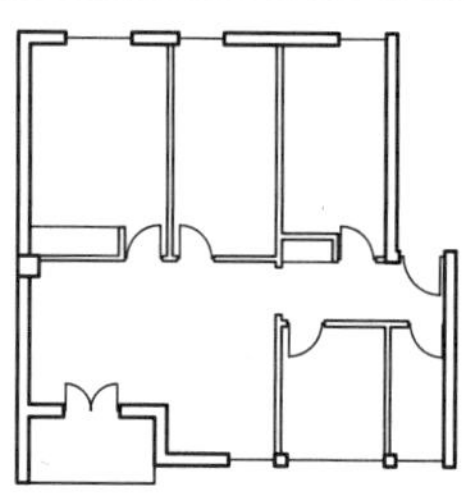	2–fold	individual	4	terraced

20
Type A block
in site plan

21
View of the block

23.1-23.2
The corridor as communal space

2
Type A in block -
Typical floor plan

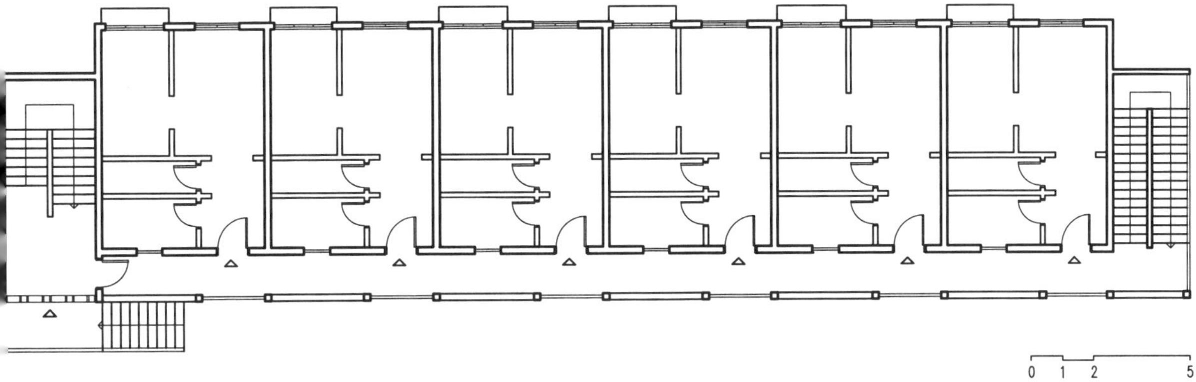

4
The configuration
of private and
communal spaces

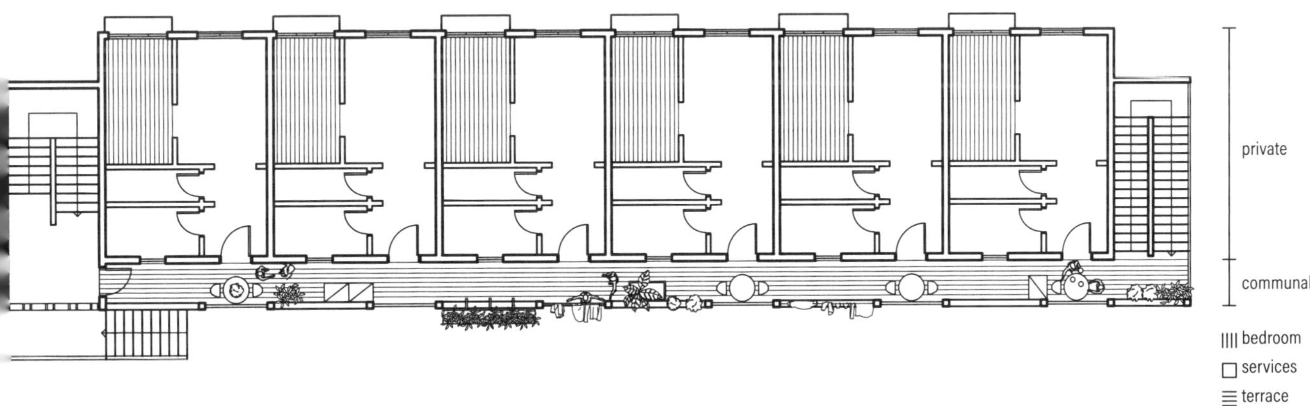

25.1-25.3
One-and-a-half-room
as one room

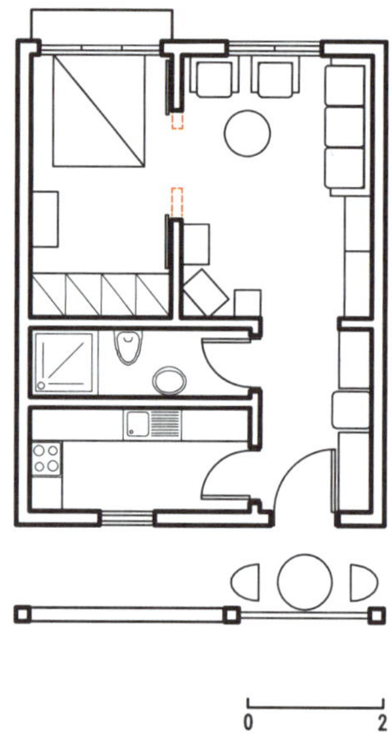

Vaso (40) is the granddaughter of the original refugee resident-owners who moved in the apartment in 1966. This is where her parents raised her and lived together for forty years until her father passed away. Following her mother's passing last year, Vaso became the owner and moved back with her husband. During her years of living alone, her mother had decided to have the partition wall between the two rooms partly demolished and the rooms unified into one private space which the couple has maintained. Vaso, who is a part-time employee at a supermarket, spends most of her time at home on the terrace (corridor) in the company of Elpida and her mother.

26.1-26.3
One-and-a-half-room
as two rooms

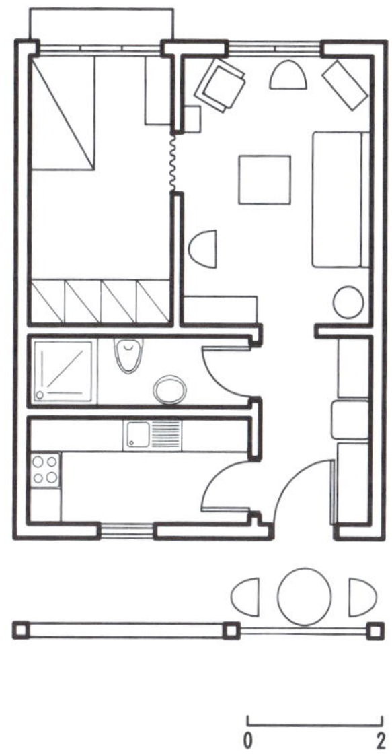

lpida (60) and her mother Georgia are resident-owners who bought this flat from an original refugee owner in the 980s. They maintained the existing layout and have lived together since Elpida's father passed away. The existing sub-ivision provides each with a room separated by a partition wall with a curtain hanging at the door opening; a clinic for ne necessary privacy and quietness for Mrs Georgia and a room for Elpida to sleep which also serves as a living room uring the day. They both benefit in spending most of their time on the terrace where meals are served and playtime vith their dog is shared with the neighbors.

Thus, the experimentation begins with infusing this paradigmatic logic into the linear blocks of the settlement, particularly, the longest compound of Types-C and -D, two-bed and three-bed flats, whose principles of arrangement have been described in the analysis. **(Fig. 27)** The structural system of reinforced concrete without load-bearing walls allows for flexibility in the management of the interior. **(Fig. 28)** The typological transformation proposes equally dimensioned private rooms to be arranged along one side of the building, ensuring good circulation and isolation, while in return allowing for the living and auxiliary spaces to become spatially more generous and shared communally. **(Fig. 29)** Phasing, in what I call the transitional stage, is a crucial aspect of this project that will take years to complete and will be constantly conditioned by the units added to the scheme and through negotiation with the needs of the new residents. Therefore, the manual starts by illustrating the most basic design scenario of two Type-C units merging, originally intended for families with one or two children. However, the existing scenario always shows a divergence from the original intention. Unit 1 is inhabited by Manolis and Evgenia, a couple around 65 years old, who have been living there for at least 35 years and whose children have left home. Unit 2 is inhabited by Yiannis and Mimoza, immigrants from Albania aged 55, who have been living there with their younger son for the last three years. **(Fig. 30)** In both flats, the original kitchen has expanded to take up the terrace (loggia) space that, especially in Mimoza's home, is extremely important; it is also used as a dining room and a study room due to the quality of natural light coming from the large south-facing window. **(Figs. 31.1-32.4)** The living room is used as a bedroom for their two grandchildren who spend frequent nights there after their son was divorced from the children's mother. **(Figs. 32.1-32.4)** The unit operation aims to redistribute private space equally, while collectivizing the rest of the services, in an attempt to enhance the capacities of both.

The project addresses the issue of privacy essentially as the treatment of the partition wall by radically challenging the material manifestation of the existing ideological apparatus of the private. As has been described, this settlement is the example *par'excellence* of a twentieth-century political economy committed to the proliferation of the concrete industry resulting in a strong working class. This very community has embodied the wage worker or the unskilled builder who has intentionally been robbed of the choice, and specialized knowledge, to invest their sweat into building their own home. Instead, by being tempted to serve an abstract system of housing provision in exchange for homeownership, they were granted the 'ticket' to the petit-bourgeois mentality. This powerful state-market lobby, the mechanism of *middle-classness,*[86] rendered alternative modes of housing construction at best traditional and at worst obsolete, an obstacle to the modernization of society and to the change of social status. De Angelis, in his point of view of a radical social transformation, proposes the "explosion of the middle class" as "a sudden increase in the social cooperation and a corresponding release of playful energies,"[87] which problematizes fixed perceptions of system boundaries, domestic economies and wage hierarchies. This project is dedicated to avoiding the pitfalls of gentrification and market exploitation by remaining a non-displacement process[88] and by introducing self-building as a way of self-valorization through community co-operation. The physical and mental engagement required in self-building acts against the alienation brought about by the abstraction of the property system and involves learning as a method of subsistence. Thus, the CLT is responsible for providing the community with the necessary equipment and specialized training before the works commence as well as on-going consultation during the process. **(Fig. 33)**

The selection of cross-laminated timber, a product not yet established in the Greek market, as the primary construction material, is key to the process. Cross-laminated timber has a documented track record in Europe — Scandinavia, Austria, Germany— which exceeds 20 years and has lately propelled wood again to a favorable place in design and construction, especially after its recognition by the International Building Code in 2015.[89] Not only does this engineered timber product perform better than concrete, brick and steel on structural, thermal, economic and environmental aspects,[90] but it also provides unique advantages for custom-made

86 My description of how this mechanism has functioned within the welfare state and the neoliberal state is successfully captured by De Angelis's term "middle-classness" and its definition as "constituted through an idea of betterment and order achieved within the boundaries of capitalist system." De Angelis, *Omnia Sunt Communia*, 280.

87 De Angelis understands this explosion in a way that will create a socio-cultural shock wave corresponding to the emergence of commoning through which boundaries, borders and the wage hierarchy are dissipated as result of social cooperation and a common platform of struggles.

88 "Development without Displacement: Organizational and Operational Choices in Starting a Community Land Trust," in Davis, *The Community Land Trust Reader*, 259–68.

89 Layne Evans, *Cross-Laminated-Timber: Taking wood buildings to the next level*, (*reThink Wood*: American Wood Council and FPInnovations, 2015), 1–12.The reThink Wood initiative is a coalition of interests representing America's wood products such as the American Wood Council, the leading developer for engineering data, technology and standards on structural wood products, and the FPInnovations research organization. Together they publish a peer-reviewed technical resource, the US CLT Handbook, on the cross-laminated timber system as the "alternate design" path. The Swedish suppliers of cross-laminated timber and the industrial body Swedish Wood have also recently published a handbook for the product. See Swedish Wood, *The CLT Handbook: CLT structures – facts and planning*, first edition (Stockholm: Föreningen Sveriges Skogsindustrier, 2019).

90 For an overview of the benefits of using cross-laminated timber see Evans, *Cross-Laminated-Timber*, 2–11. For a detailed description of the product standards, specifications and characteristics see the technical folder of the German renewable materials company Stora Enso, *Wood Products / Building Solutions*, (2015), https://issuu.com/storaenso/docs/01_technical_folder_-_stora_enso_bu/300. On the advances in carbon management in CLT production and applications see Erol Karacabeyli and Brad Douglas, *CLT Handbook* (Montreal: FPInnovations and Binational Softwood Lumber Council, 2013).

27
Types C and D
in site plan

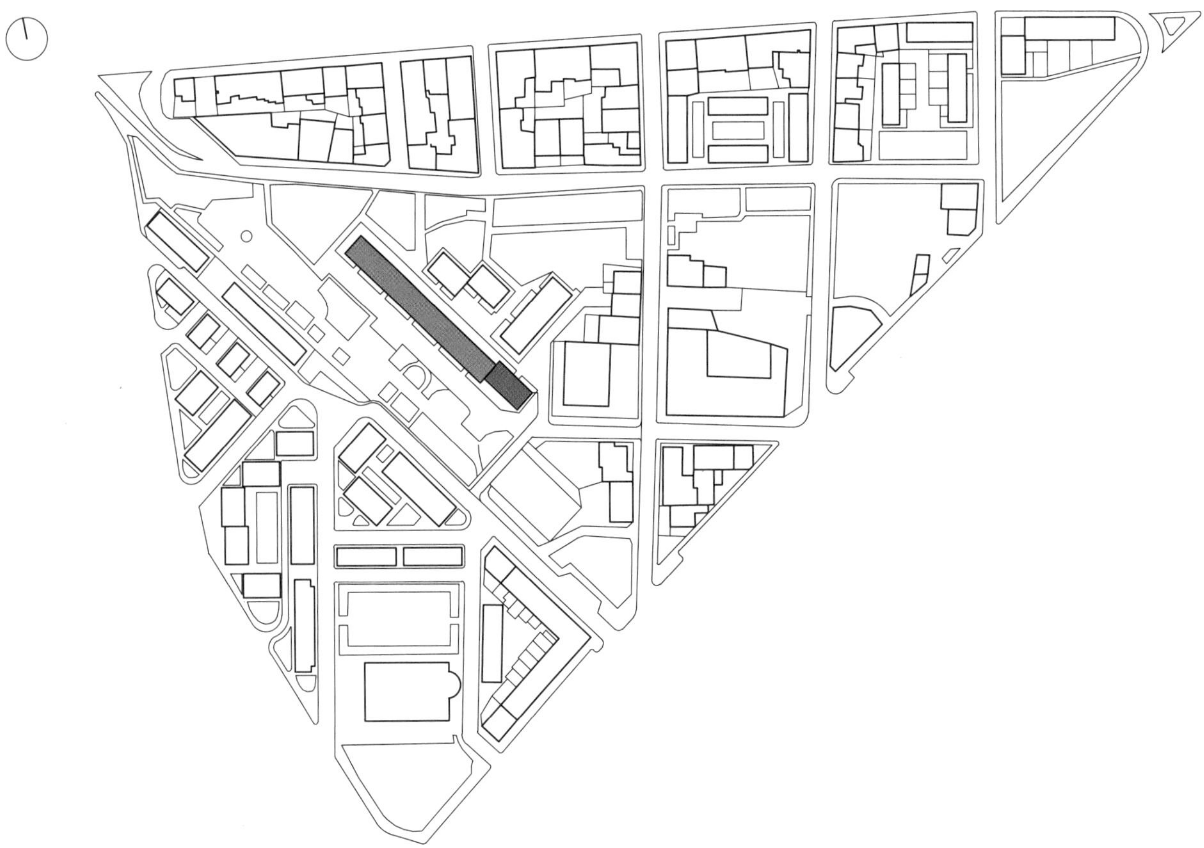

28
Structural system

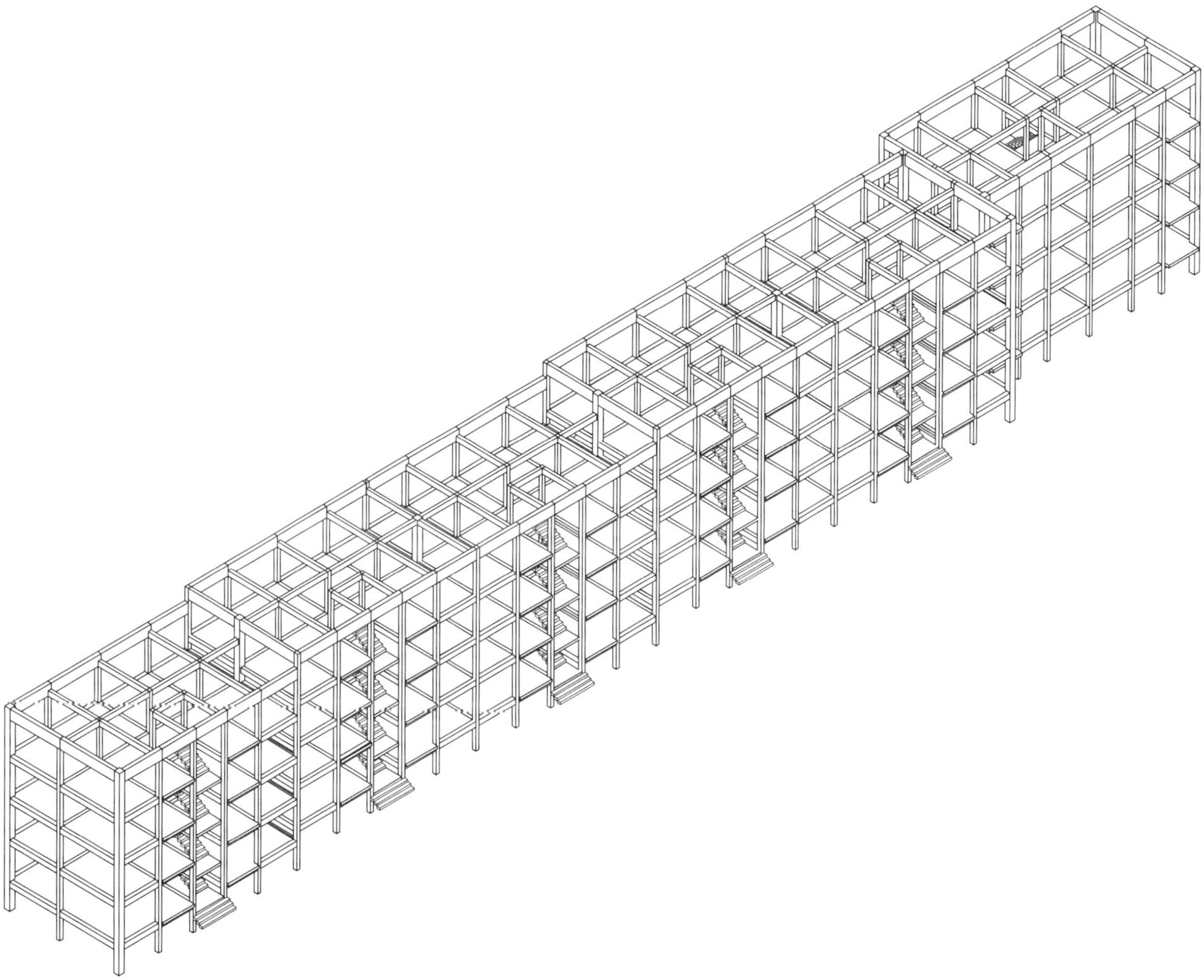

29
Diagrams
of typological
transformation

self-build purposes; these include design versatility, its lightweight and rapid installation. Thus, demolition and reconstruction can be undertaken by two trained people, once the materials are delivered on site, in collaboration with specialists for the re-fitting of the electrical and plumbing installations. **(Fig. 34)** The operation for the merging of the two units begins from the communal spaces. The removed mass of brick walls is calculated and replaced by cross-laminated timber panels, which consist of three equally thick single-layer panels arranged at right angles to each other and face-glued with structural adhesives. **(Fig. 35)**

To date, the advanced research and application of this technology in Europe is focused on conifers, like pine, for the inner layer and spruce, for the external layers. Since there is an abundance of pine forests in Greece which provide 51.7% of the total timber production,[91] this technology could also be introduced to the domestic industry. In particular, a group of small-scale manufacturers in north-western Greece (Epirus), who, during the decade of financial crisis, have invested in the processing of the local pine species (*pinus sylvestris*) of the Pindos mountain, practice with the same sawing, drying, pressing and planning equipment, necessary for cross-lamination, in their fabrication techniques (sawn timber, fiberboards, particleboards, firewood).[92] The provider of this project would need to acquire European Technical Approval[93] but, despite the added cost of accreditation, the price of the final product would still be lower than the average sales price provided by the Centre for the Promotion of Imports of the European Union. The overall cost of domestic supply instead of import would also benefit from the dramatic difference in shipping costs. The dimensions and lightness of the components have a further positive impact on the structural relief of the building and on the budget, as they are easily handled by ordinary tools and a small crane. The manufacturer can provide a carrier truck with an embedded crane of this scale for the direct application of the large external panels, preventing further labor and storage costs as well as safeguarding against material damage from misuse or exposure. The total delivery cost can be optimized, based on the capacity of the truck, for an opera-

91 Elias Voulgarides, "Production and Utilisation of Wood," in *I Poiotites kai i chreses tou xulou* [*The Qualities and Uses of Wood*], (Athens: Association of Greek Academic Libraries, 2015), 1–26. Voulgarides, a Professor of Forestry and Wood Science at the Aristotle University of Thessaloniki, has been arguing for the utilization of the abundant indigenous pine wood in domestic timber production, which covers only 30-35% of the demand in the construction sector. Thus, he points out the crucial deficit in domestic timber production and the major expenditure on timber imports. With his team he has conducted research on the potential of wood production in the pine and spruce forests of Northern Greece. See Elias Voulgarides, "Forest Production," in *Forestry in Changing Societies in Europe-Information for teaching module*, Part II, eds. Pelkonen, P., Pitkanen, P. Schmidt, G. Desten, P. Pinssi and E. Rojas (SILVA Network, 1999), 144–147.

92 Voulgarides, *I Poiotites kai i chreses tou xulou*, 8–10.

93 ETA regulates the manufacture and use of CLT in Europe and is the basis for the CE mark, which is a certification for the application of cross-laminated timber technology. Stora Enso, *Wood Products*, 7. The selected manufacturer would also need to indicate the PEFC mark —Program for the Endorsement of Forest Certification Schemes— which confirms that the purchase of a product guarantees and supports environmentally sound forestry management.

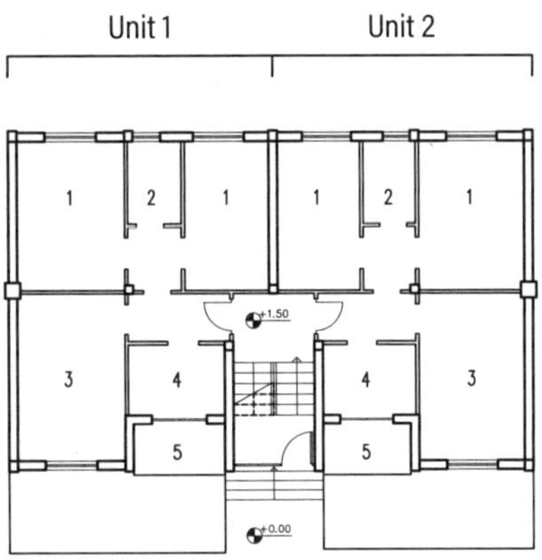

original intention

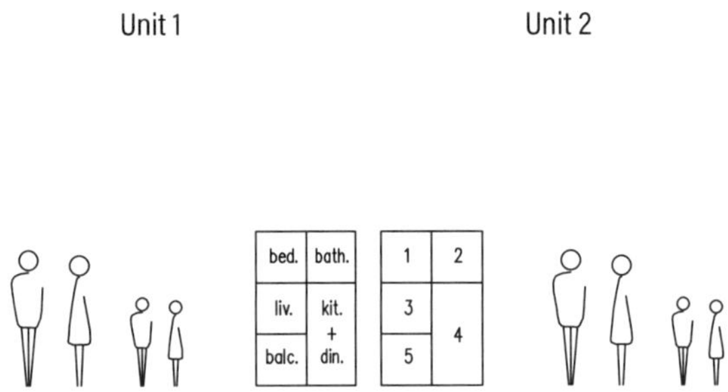

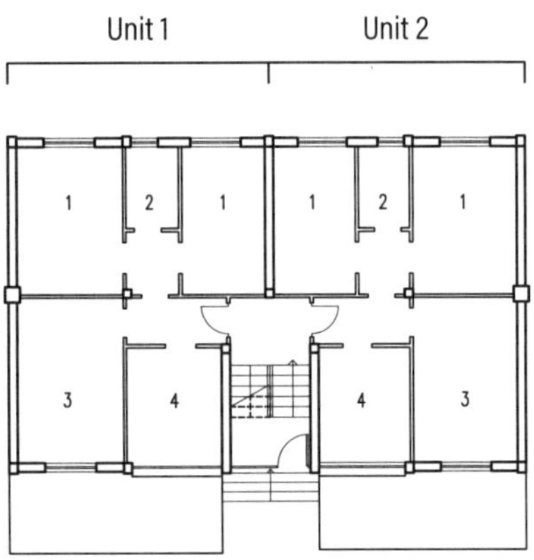

existing situation

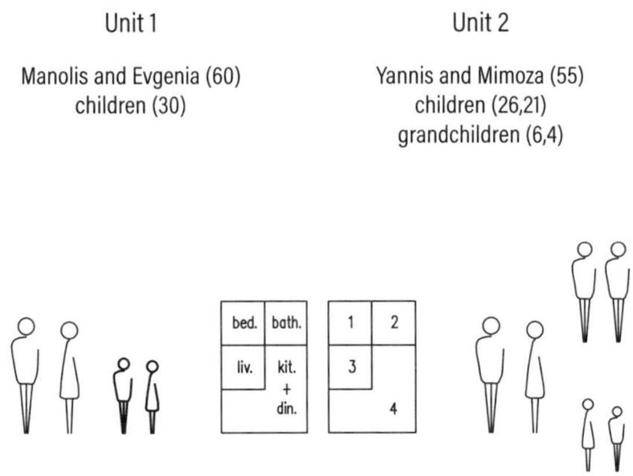

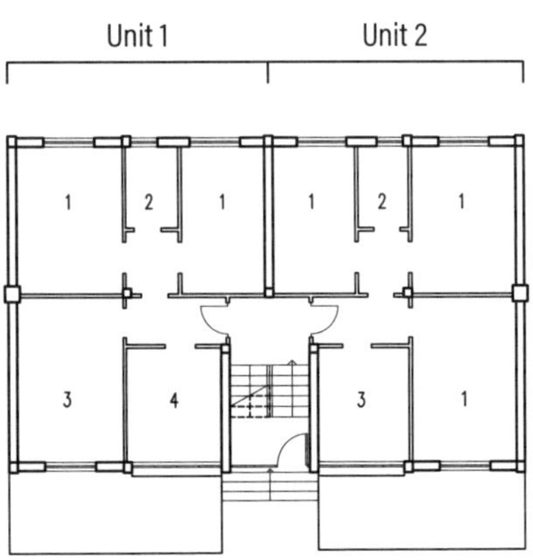

current use

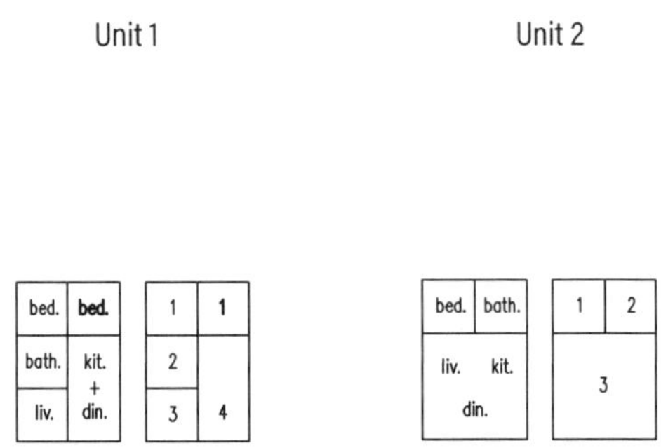

31.1-31.4

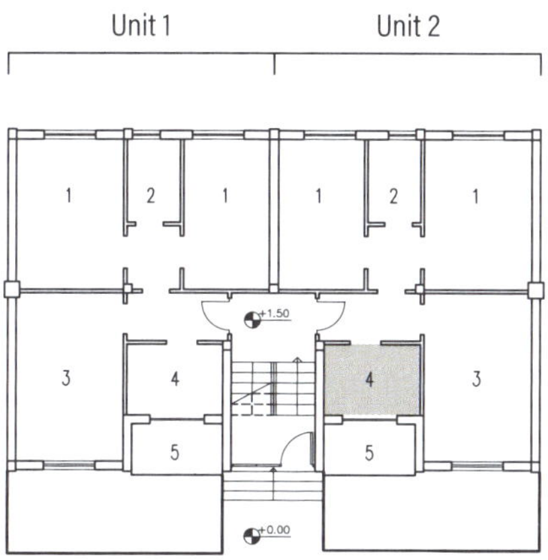

original intention

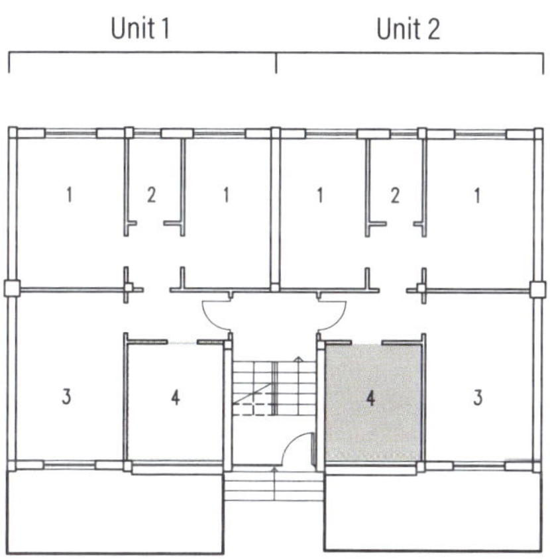

existing situation

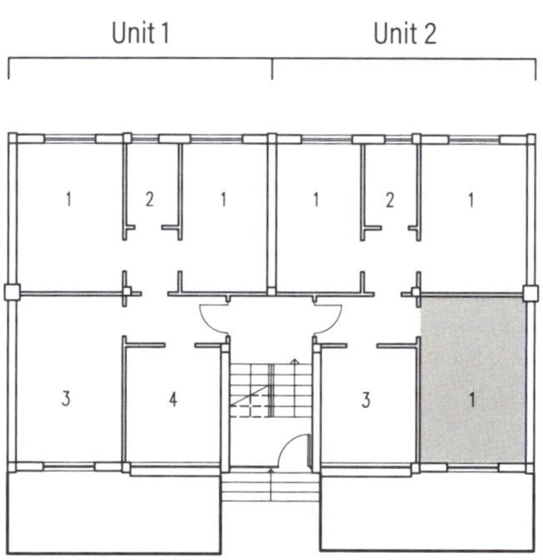

current use

32.1-32.4

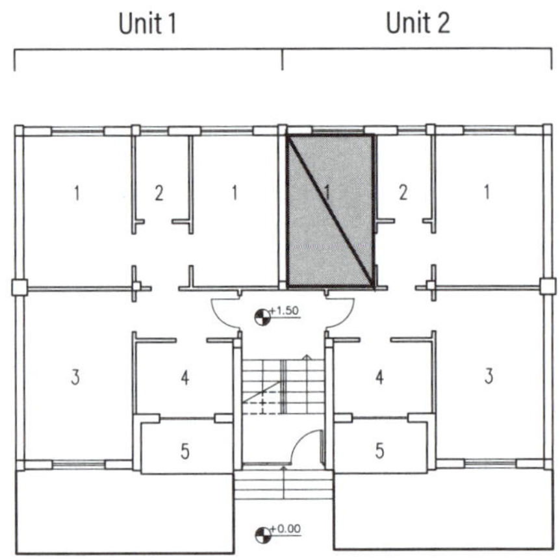

existing situation

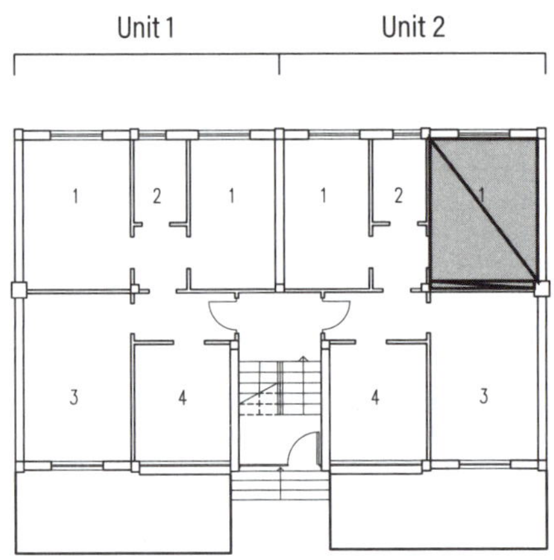

existing situation

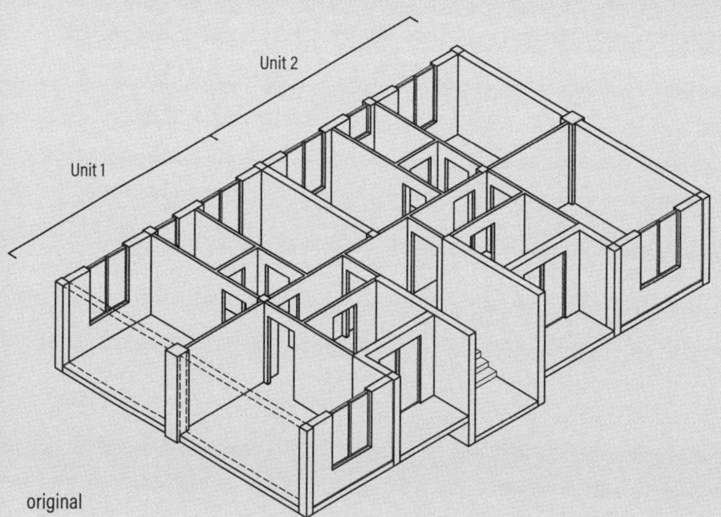

original

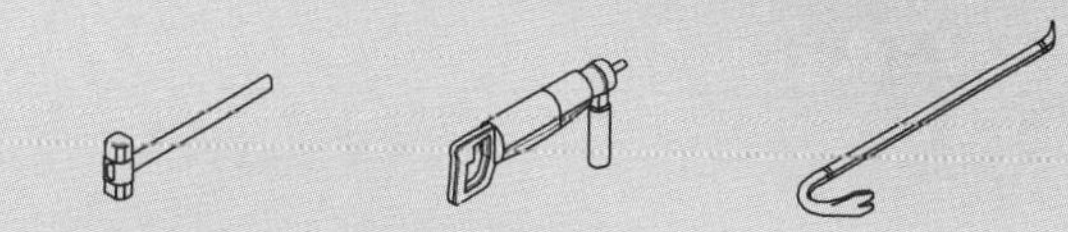

SLEDGEHAMMER PERCUSSIVE POWER TOOL CROWBAR

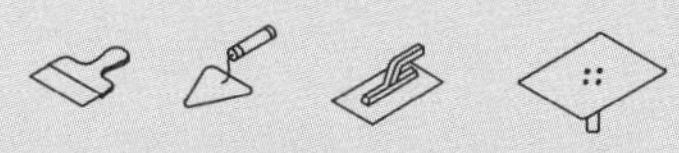

TROWEL SET HAWK

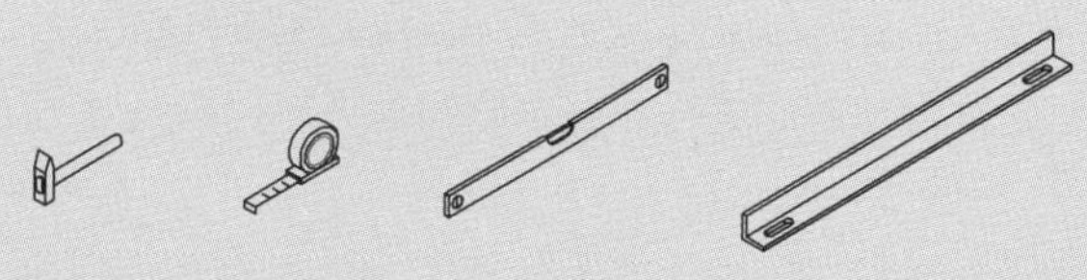

HAMMER TAPE MEASURE SPIRIT LEVEL STRAIGHTEDGE

PAINTROLLER SET STEP LADDER

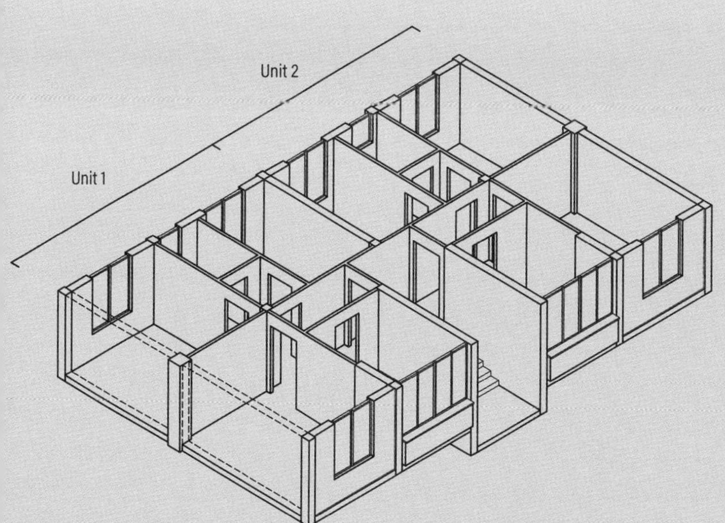

existing

DISPOSAL

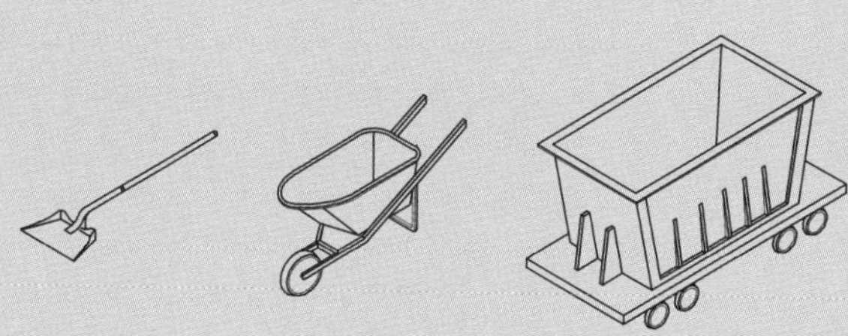

SHOVEL WHEELBARROW CONTAINER

MAN POWER SPECIALISTS

UNIT OPERATION TYPE C

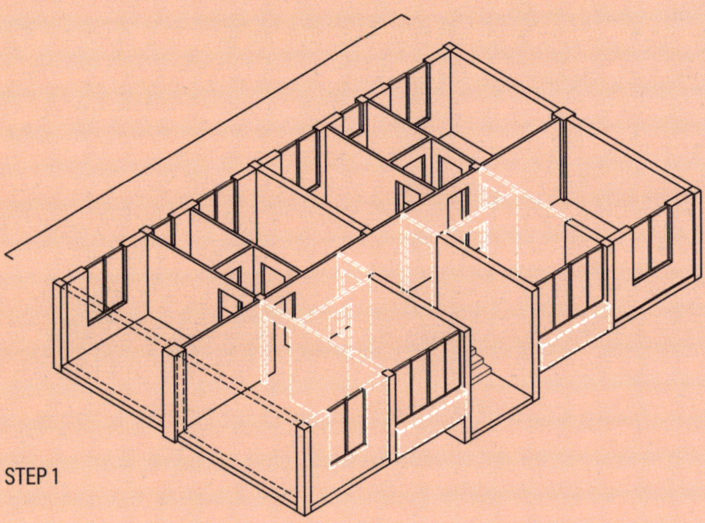

STEP 1

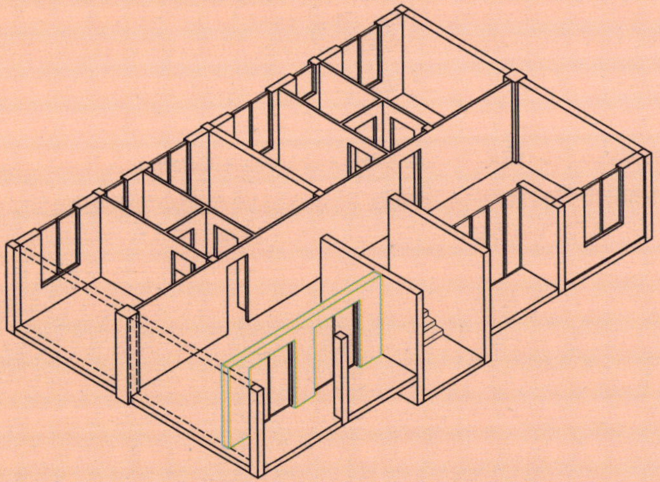

STEP 2

JOB DESCRIPTION

DEMOLITION

DRILLING

DEBRIS DISPOSAL

RECONSTRUCTION

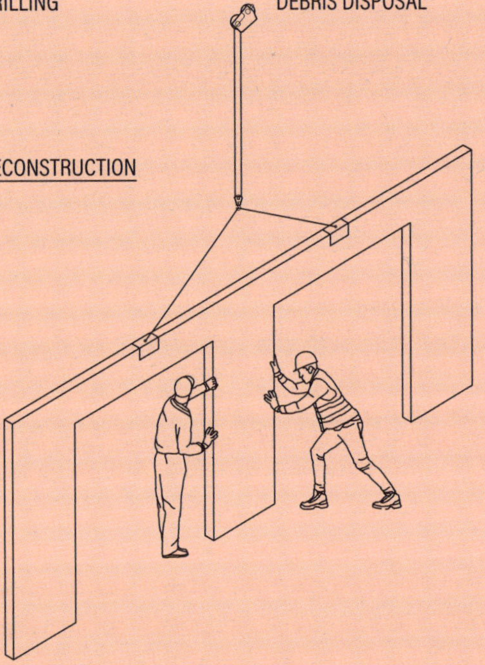

EXTERNAL WALL FITTING

WINDOW FRAME FITTING

WALL PAINTING

1-LAYER BRICK WALL (INTERNAL)

CUBIC CAPACITY

REMOVED

X 4 ~632 kg

X 2 ~2360 kg

X 1 ~2650 kg

~5642 kg

ADDED

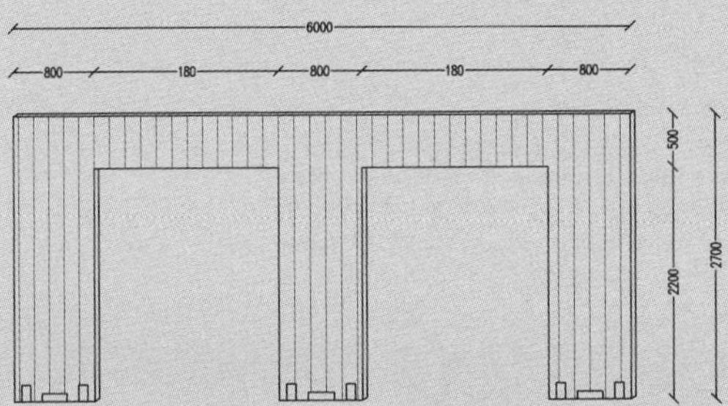

~330 kg

(471 kg/m³)

CLT PRICE: 350€/m³ [Average price (CBI, EU): 500€/m³]

SHIPPING COST: 500€/itinerary [Ioannina (Epirus) - via highways A5 and A8 / Truck capacity: 10t]

RENTAL EQUIPMENT : 100 €/h

TOTAL COST = MATERIAL + DELIVERY + EQUIPMENT

CLT WALL BOARD: TWO OPENINGS - DOOR TYPE (1S6 - C)

CONSTRUCTION DETAILS

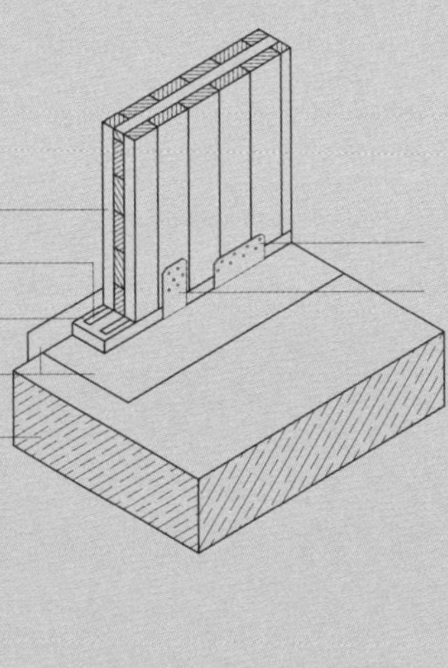

INTERIOR

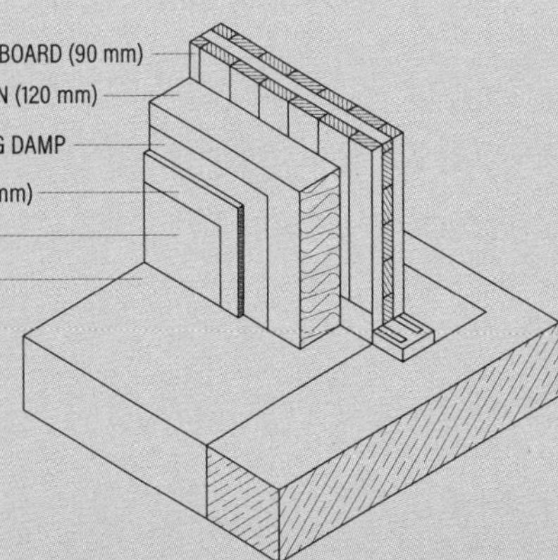

EXTERIOR

tion of eight to ten units at a time (or per itinerary). Cross-laminated timber manufacturers typically work closely with the project design team, and particularly with the assigned engineer of record, whose specifications they should try to meet by providing shop drawings and calculations on material efficiency.[94]

A similar process is undertaken in the private areas. **(Fig. 36)** External walls are replaced by floor to ceiling folding windows that are intended, as a façade system, to function independently from the internal partitioning for two main reasons. Morphologically, it serves the intention not to reflect any internal subdivision, apart from the structural system, on the façade; typologically, it allows for flexibility in arrangement during the transitional stage. Once measurements are taken and partition marking is completed, the private rooms, which measure 4.25 by 2.40 meters each, can be assembled by two skilled residents in half an hour. **(Fig. 37)** Thus, the new configuration provides each set of users in the scenario with a private room of a fixed size, which is an average of the two previous sizes, and challenges the social norms designed to facilitate nuclear family hierarchies. **(Fig. 38.1)** The inhabitants might well use their own furniture but the manual also proposes a standard set of wooden parts, based on the dimensions of the room, from which they can easily assemble beds, desks, closets and custom-made fittings. **(Figs. 38.2-38.5)** The private room is generic in its geometry but user-determined in its application in order to host various living combinations and arrangements. It can be interconnected with other rooms through sliding partition panels, which can also be entirely removed from their hanging rails for a particular occasion or, alternatively, locked in place by their handle to ensure privacy. Each room directly engages the tree alley in the back and can open up during the summer months, almost becoming a terrace. Thus, private space is not an indicator of social status, but rather a platform for the varying configurations and types of privacy.

As a socio-spatial strategy, the ecology of the private instrumentalizes the collective capacity of the block, as the domestic module, to cater to the generosity of commu-

94 Evans, *Cross-Laminated-Timber,* 5.

UNIT OPERATION TYPE C

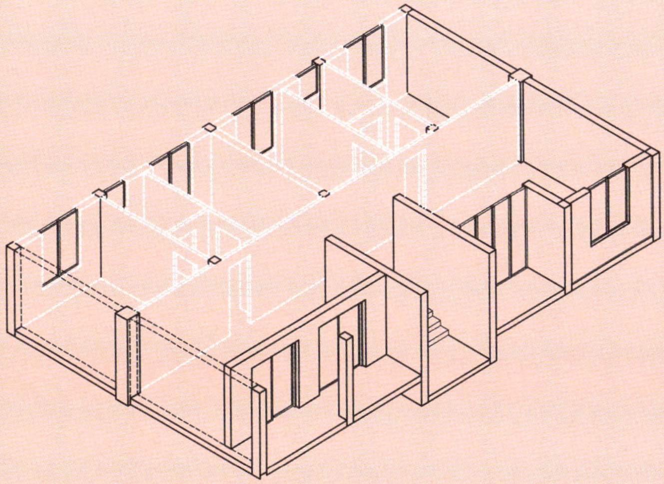

STEP 3

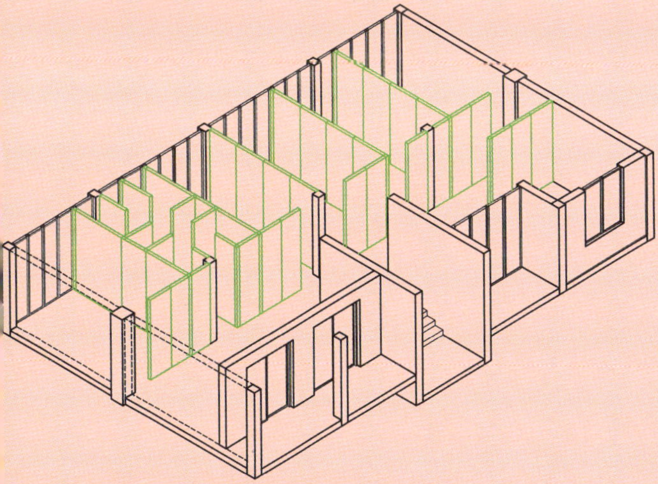

STEP 4

JOB DESCRIPTION

DEMOLITION

DRILLING

DEBRIS DISPOSAL

RECONSTRUCTION

WINDOW FRAME FITTING

PARTITION MARKING

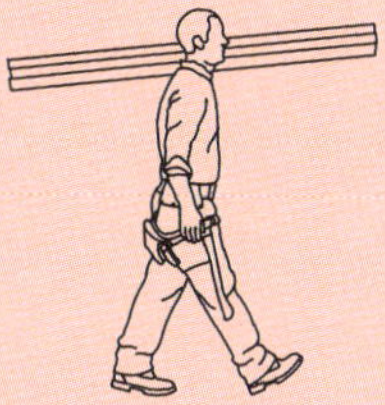

POST SETTING

PARTITION PANEL FITTING

PRIVATE ROOM OPERATION

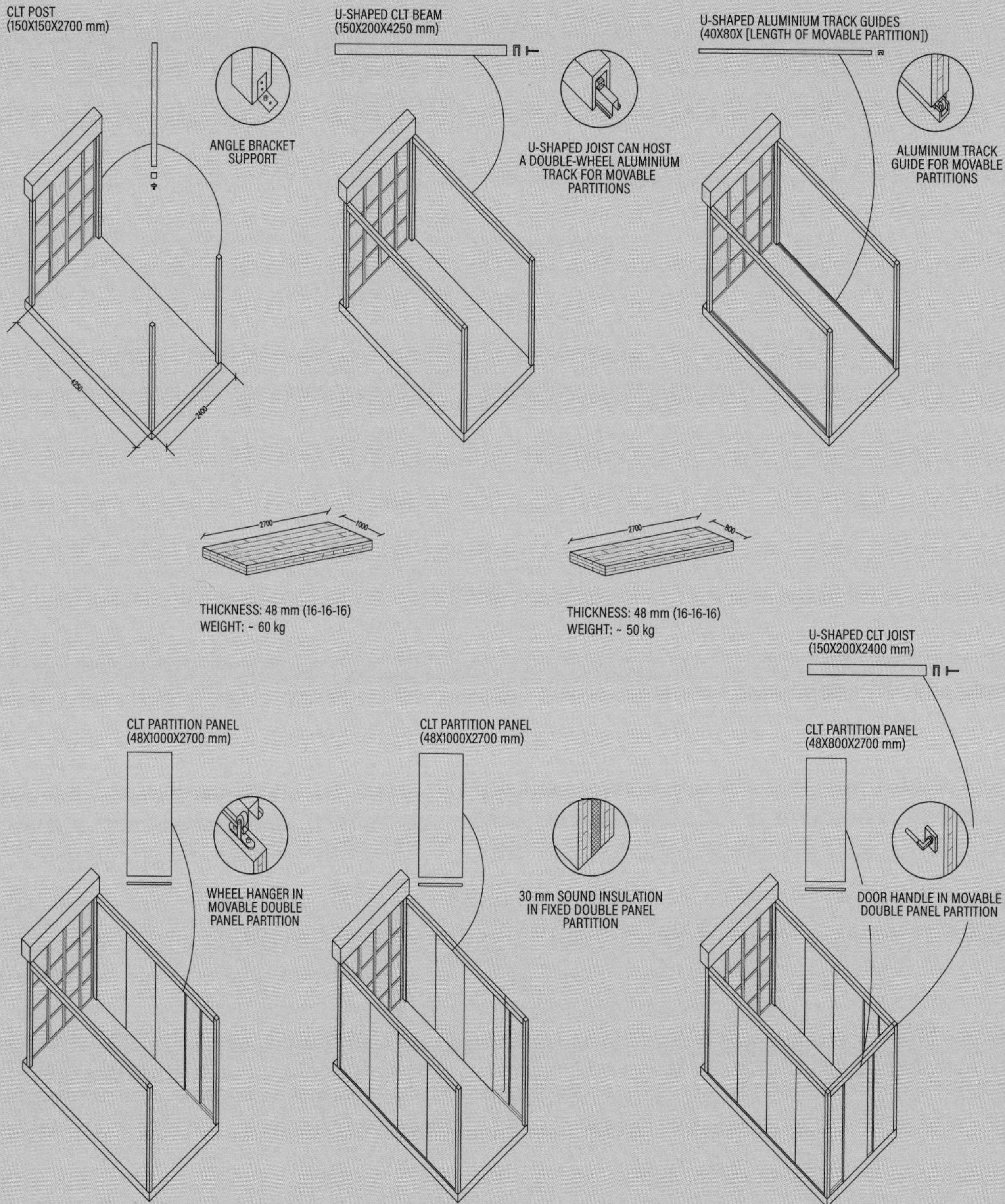

2.00
1.00
0.80
0.40

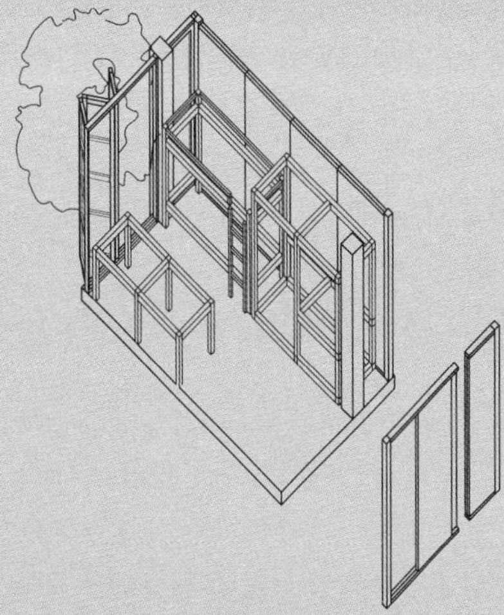

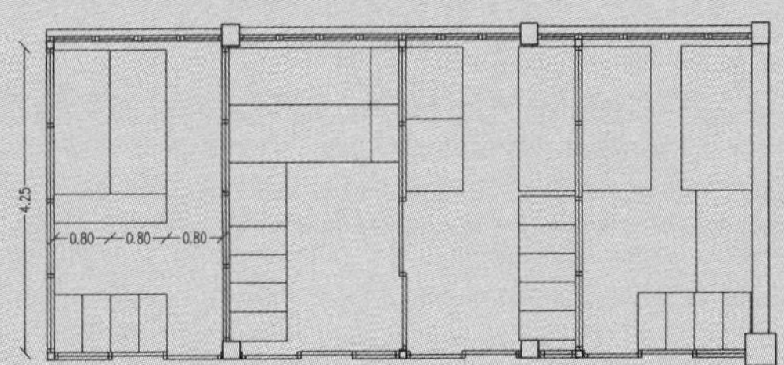
4.25
0.80
0.80
0.80

nal spaces and the particular social needs, while maintaining the *ratio* of the private. According to this logic, once a new unit is added to the scheme, the extra potential of spatial configuration is released, especially for communal spaces. **(Figs. 39.1-39.2)** When enough units on different floors are accumulated, there is a possibility for internal migration, for example the first semi-floor can be designed particularly for the elderly and people of restricted mobility. **(Figs. 40.1-40.2)** For every two or four flats added to the scheme, there is an extra private room created. In general, availability becomes more flexible and periodic as it is detached from the rigid, life-long ties of property and becomes contingent on changes of social circumstances. It is an open-ended project with various propositional stages but lacking a final state. **(Fig. 41)** However, any spatial configuration in this process of commoning should aim at securing privacy and rendering it visible in the domestic sphere. **(Fig. 42)** Contrary to the external walls, which will eventually be clad with topcoats and paint, the internal walls of the private rooms are now the only solid opaque partitions of the interior, retaining the bare wood aesthetic as a demarcation of privacy.

However, this does not imply that domesticity is limited within the perimeter of the building. Commonality opens up the spatial framework of the domestic module in order to compensate for the spatial restriction of the private. The following design scenario for Type-B1 and -B2, aims to show how the organizational principle could work in smaller-scale blocks by taking advantage of the composition of a cluster and the freedom of use of in-between areas for common purposes. **(Figs. 43, 44)** The existing scenarios here are compromised of the minimal configuration of spaces in these small types, and therefore dining and any other type of daily activity takes place in the living room. The Type-B1 unit is inhabited by Erene, aged 84, a widower who moved to this neighborhood as a young teenager with her refugee family in 1958 and has spent her whole adult life in this flat, inherited by her mother, as a married woman with three children. **(Figs. 45.1-45.4)** She has been living alone for the last 15 years in what appears to her now as "too much space for a single person." She is still capable of taking care of herself and she would be happy to cook more often, if only she had a company next-door (the flat next to hers has been empty for many years) to share a meal instead of spending the day on her little terrace watching the passers-by. The Type-B2 unit is inhabited by 65-year-old Stelios, a single man whose small-scale enterprise was devastated by the long-lasting recession and who moved into the neighborhood in search of affordable rent downtown. **(Figs. 46.1-46.4)** He has established the kitchen door in the back as the main entrance to the flat for practical reasons since the day of moving in and he has his niece and her boyfriend helping him to paint and clean the flat. During this process, he has had his bed set in the living room, while he is "keen on keeping it this way" even after the painting of the bedroom since "he is just by himself" and "prefers the view to the park" from the living room. Despite, or because of, their small size, both block types and their composition provide privileged open-air spaces for communal facilities: generous parterres in the in-between spaces of the ground floor and spacious sunlit roof terraces with views of the park and the city. However, they are either privately appropriated, the parterres as gardens by owners on the ground floor and the roof terraces as laundry or storage rooms by the top floor residents, or abandoned in decay. **(Figs. 47,48)**

The socio-spatial analysis reveals that the issue here is not a lack of appropriate spaces for privacy, but rather for socializing. The typological commitment to individuality, from the accessibility of the flats to the absolute minimum of service spaces, does not cultivate an ethic of sharing what is at the disposal of all residents to enjoy. Thus, the unit operation aims to redistribute private rooms toward the periphery of the cluster and to collectivize entrances and communal facilities towards its center in an attempt to activate the rear facades and these immediate outdoor spaces as places of encounter. **(Fig. 49)** For this purpose, an installation is designed at the center of the composition, a structural system of cross-laminated timber posts and joists as, an extension of the structural grid of Type-B1. Some frames are left blank while others are furnished with rotating screens to be regulated according to the weather conditions. This large canopy is meant to 'shelter' collective gatherings that cannot be accommodated in the restricted capacity of the blocks, as well as house-

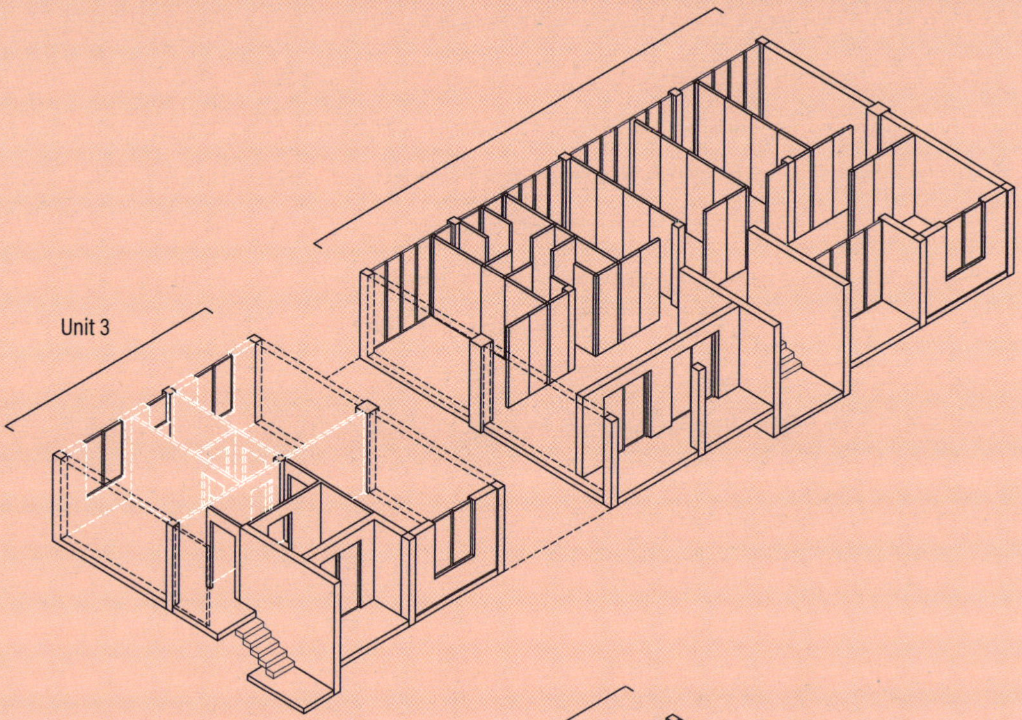

STEP 5

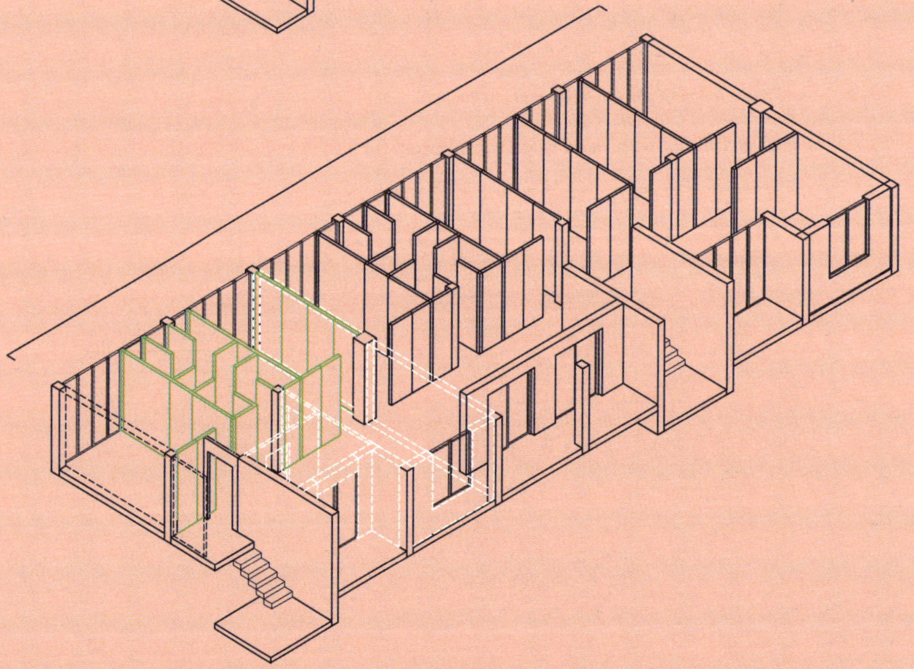

STEP 6

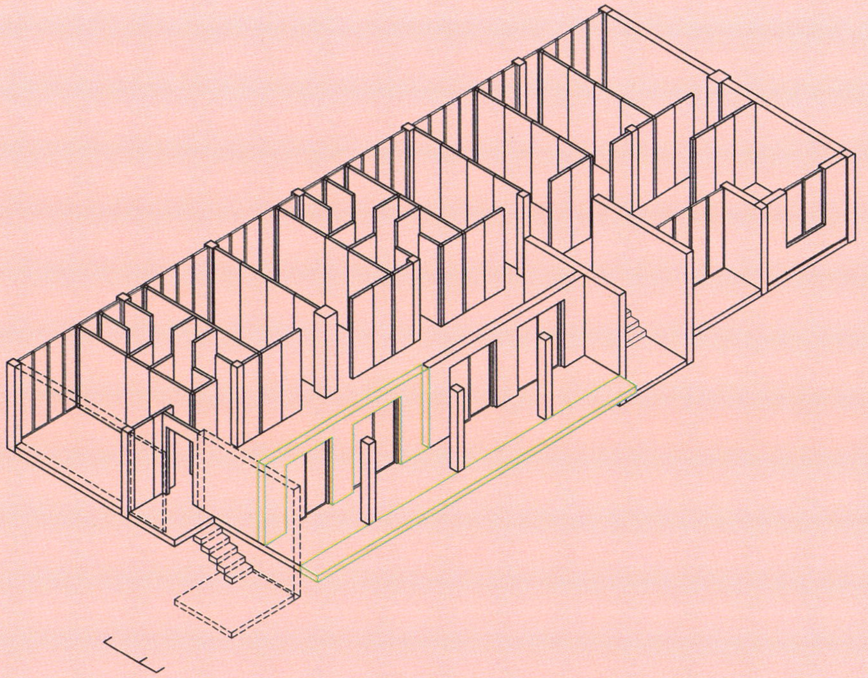

TEP 7

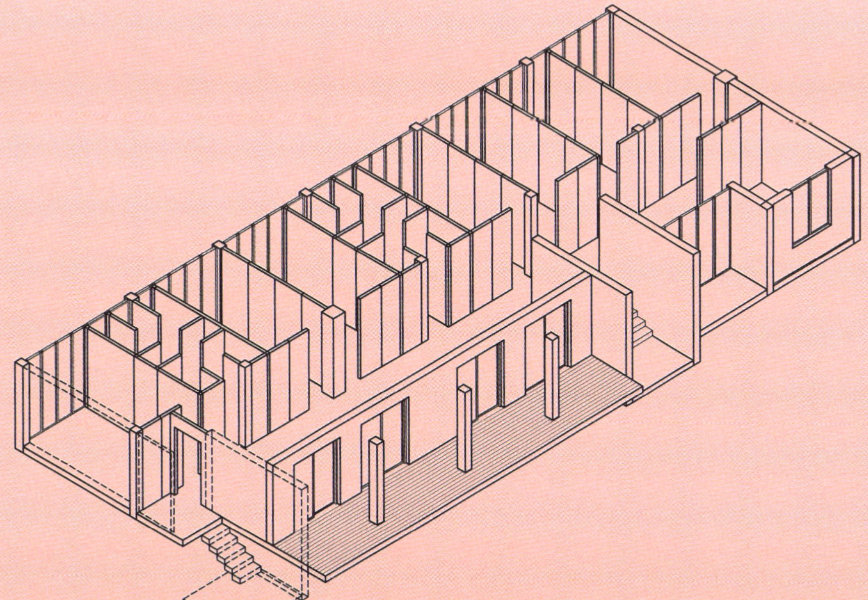

TEP 8

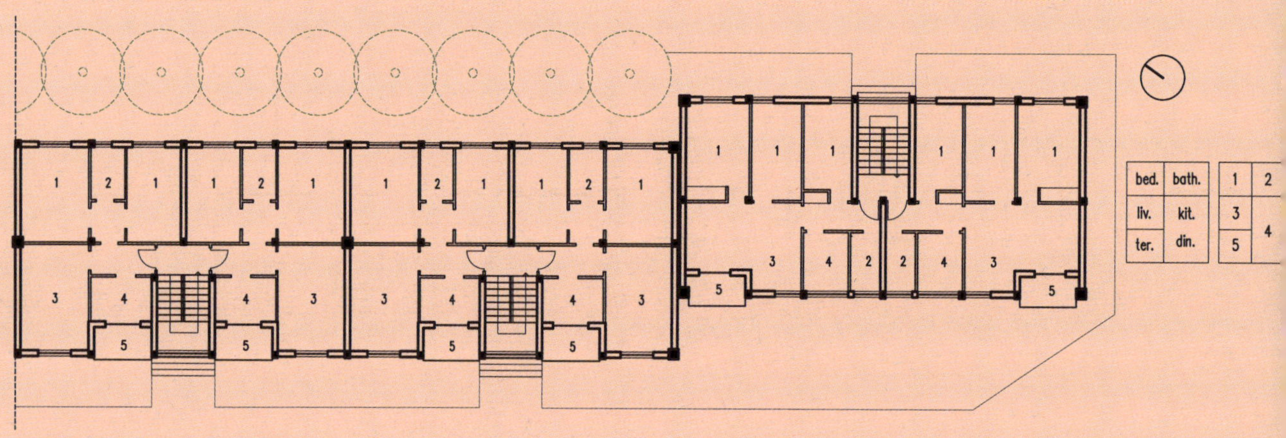

TYPICAL FLOOR PLAN / EXISTING

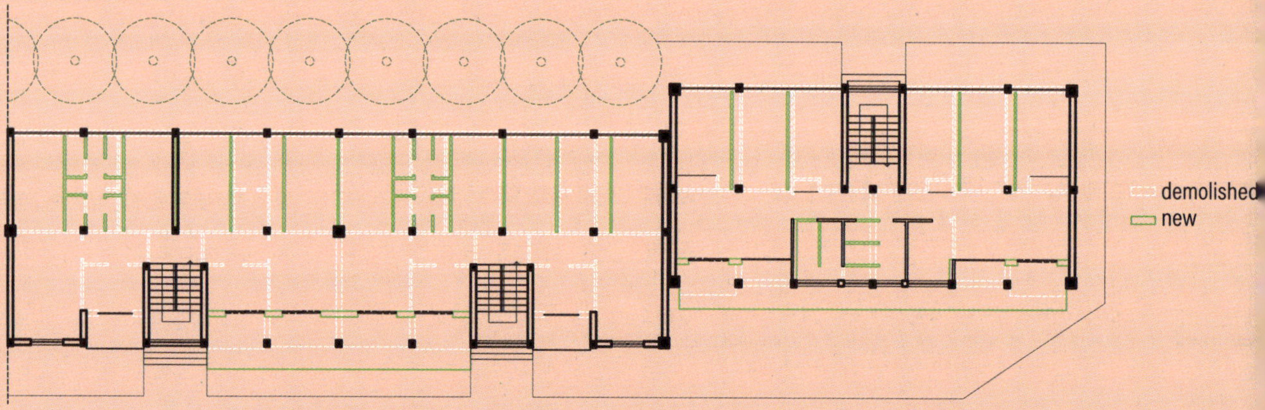

TYPICAL FLOOR PLAN / TRANSITIONAL

transitional

40.2

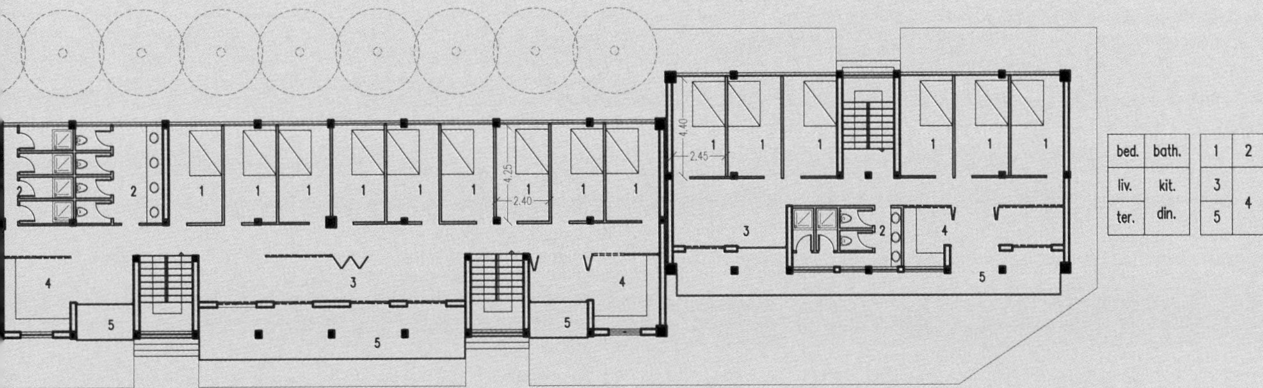

TYPICAL FLOOR PLAN / PROPOSITIONAL

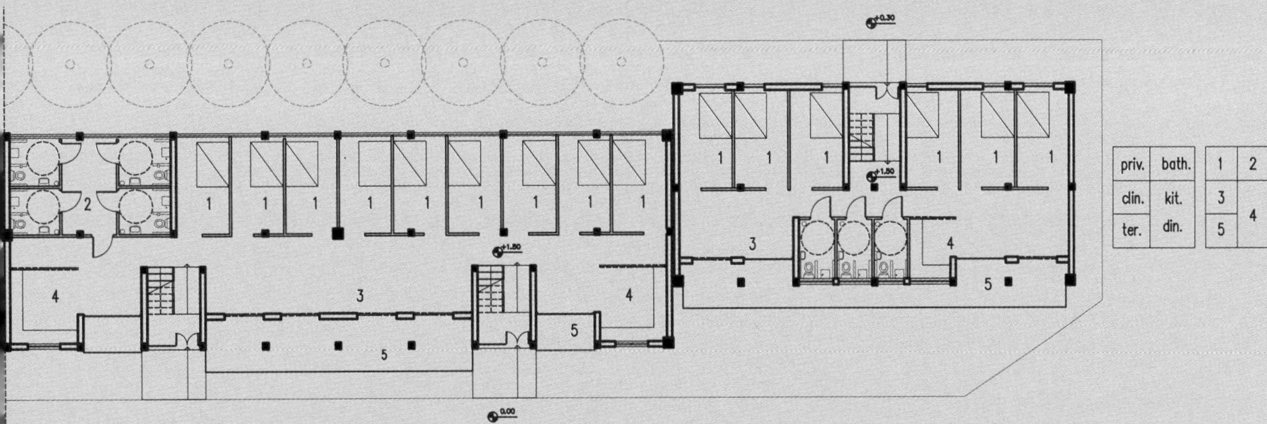

FIRST FLOOR PLAN / PROPOSITIONAL

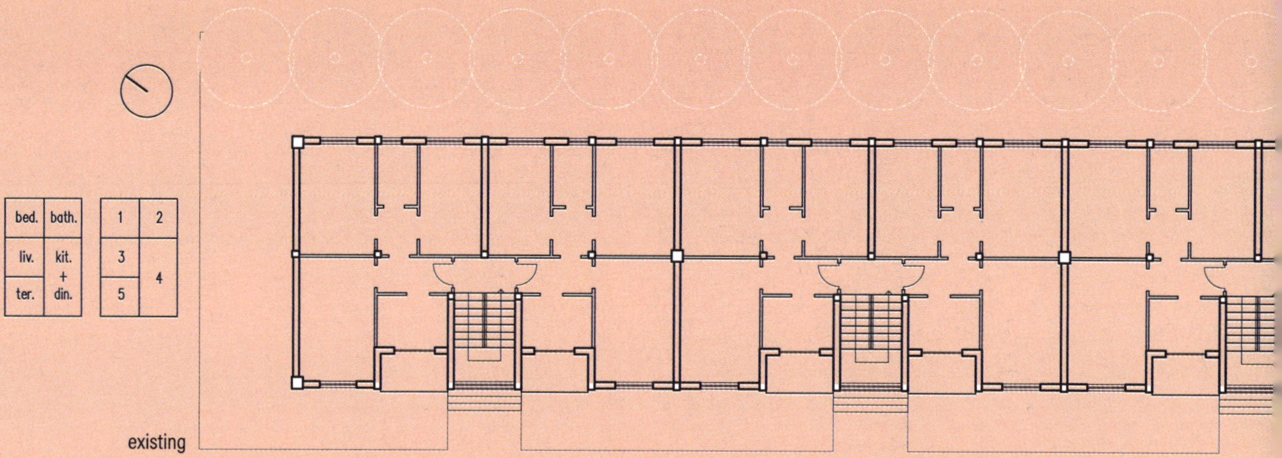

existing

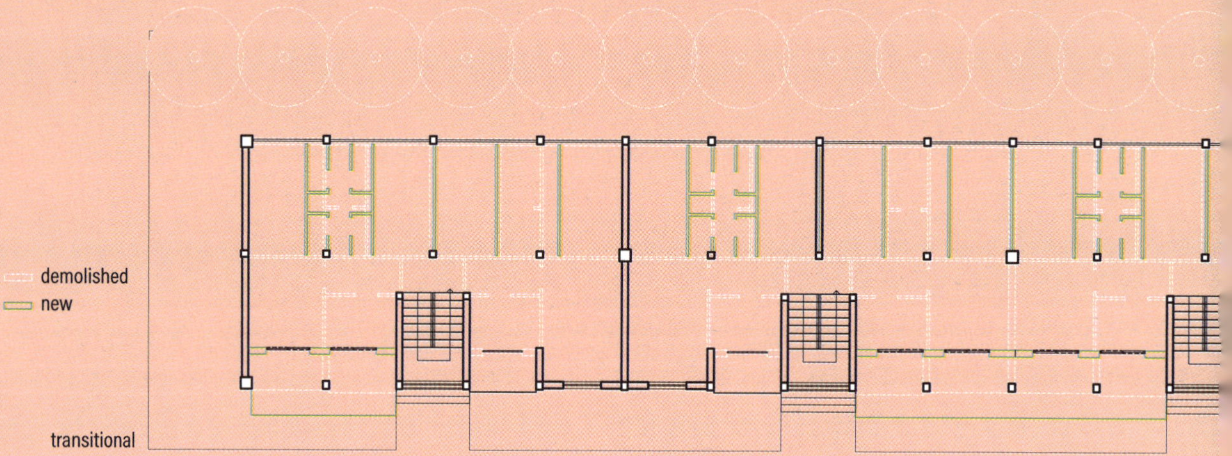

transitional

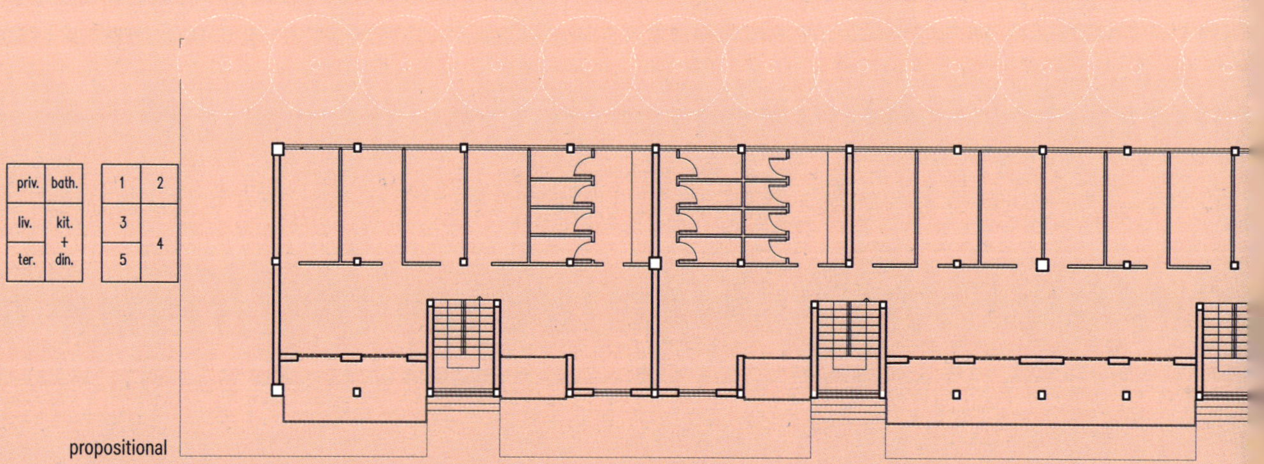

propositional

4.40
2.45
4.25
2.40
0 1 2 5 10

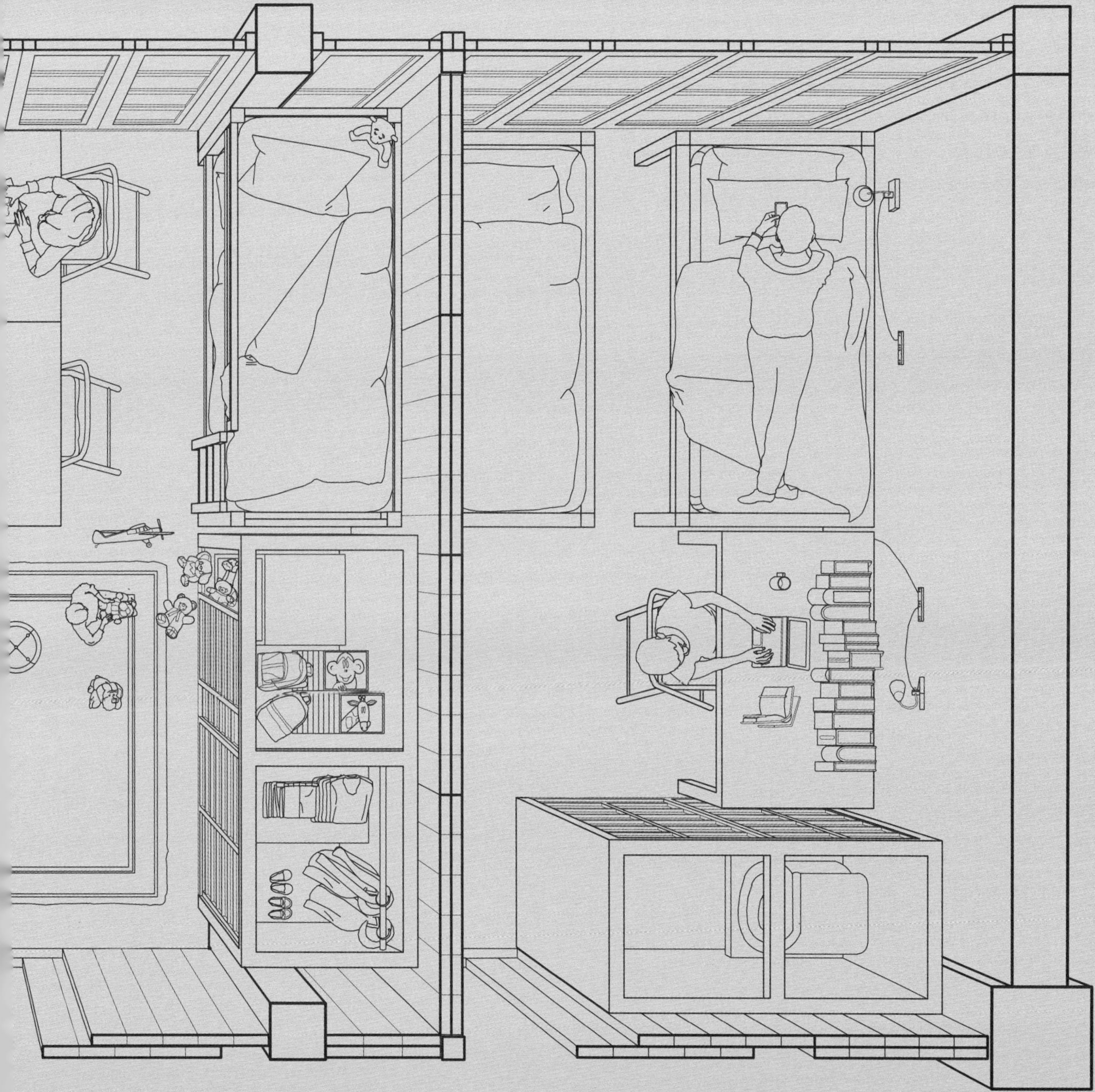

hold tasks, everyday rituals and recreational activities that are better performed outdoors and in company. The side parterres are dedicated to communalizing and organizing the legacy of gardening and small-scale cultivation. Thus, the garden ceases to be an extension of domestic space and becomes a collective practice of subsistence or recreation. Large communal kitchens are placed centrally in each block, symmetrically to the parterres, and are equipped with floor-to-ceiling folding windows to ensure direct access (ground floor) or visual contact (upper floors) with these spaces. **(Fig. 50)** In fact, the interval between every kitchen on the ground floor and the parterre in front of it is paved with a wooden deck and sheltered by a smaller scale installation, which can also be perimetrically closed with sliding panels or windows, as a porch attached to the building. **(Fig. 51)** This space acts as a vestibule or a living area, but is mainly meant to establish a transition to the outdoor, a connection with the gardens and the communal facilities through participatory processes of production and consumption, leisure and care. The accommodation of collective life is shared between these spaces and the roof terraces. The latter accommodate living areas, laundry rooms and, most importantly, working and studying areas, with a great quality of light to facilitate the increasing need for working from home against the habit of working from the bedroom. The outdoor spaces are similarly sheltered by pergola structures that regulate the brightness and heat for the top floors, especially during the summer months. This type of implementation confirms that the typological calibration between privacy and collectivity, and ultimately the domestic space, obtains a vast potential when devised through the lens of community empowerment.

Papanek argues that design as a problem-solving activity can never yield a single right answer, but will always produce an infinite number of answers. The 'rightness' of any design solution will, then, depend on the meaning which is invested in the arrangement.[95] Thus, the value of the manual lies in proposing a methodology of arrangement to achieve a 'meaningfulness' of the private as an existential quality which does not stand in antagonism, rather in transformational equivalence with

95 Papanek, *Design for the Real World*, 25.

the collective in domesticity. It endows the private room with a phenomenological capacity of its own and privacy with the social power of self-actualization, through everyday procedures and tools. Echoing the Italian radical innovation of the 1970s, these objects of "simple use" offer countermodels with which to embark on a new journey against the economic and legal abstraction of living, towards an *urban material culture*.[96] According to Natalini, one of the pioneers of the radical architecture movement of the 1970s, the teaching and exchange of experiences around themes, like the working of wood, can constitute an approach to the ideal point at which, education coincides with life itself.[97] It is only through egalitarian access to this 'learning' of how to be private that the possibility of living together is envisioned.

96 On the importance of subaltern and marginalized cultures of tools and procedures as the "extra-urban material culture," see Adolfo Natalini et. al., "Viaggio con la matita tra gli artefatti del mondo contadino [Journey with the pencil amidst the artifacts of the farming world]," *Modo* no. 7 (1978): 49–53.

97 Global Tools, "Documento 1," *Casabella* 377, no. 5 (1973): 4. Global Tools was a collective founded on January 12, 1973 by radical practitioners and groups, such as Archizoom, Superstudio and the Casabella editorial team.

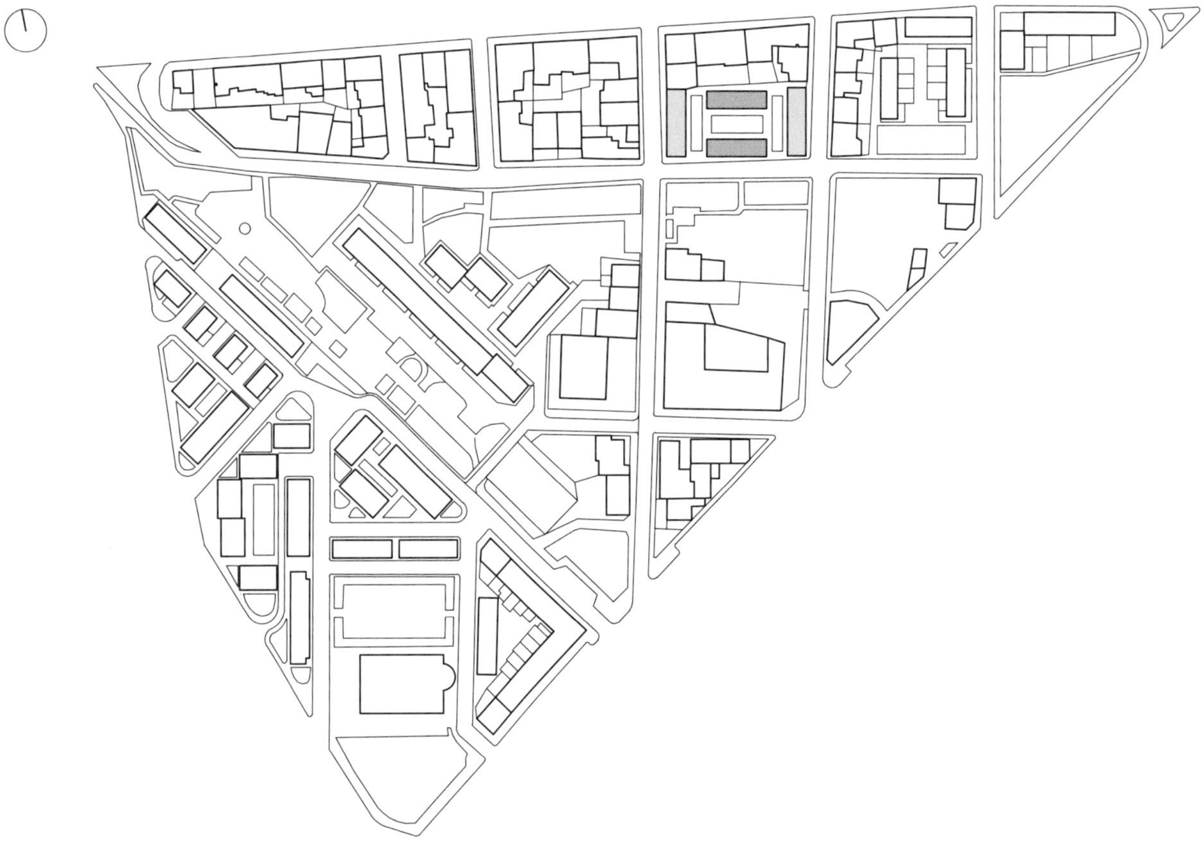

GROUND FLOOR PLAN

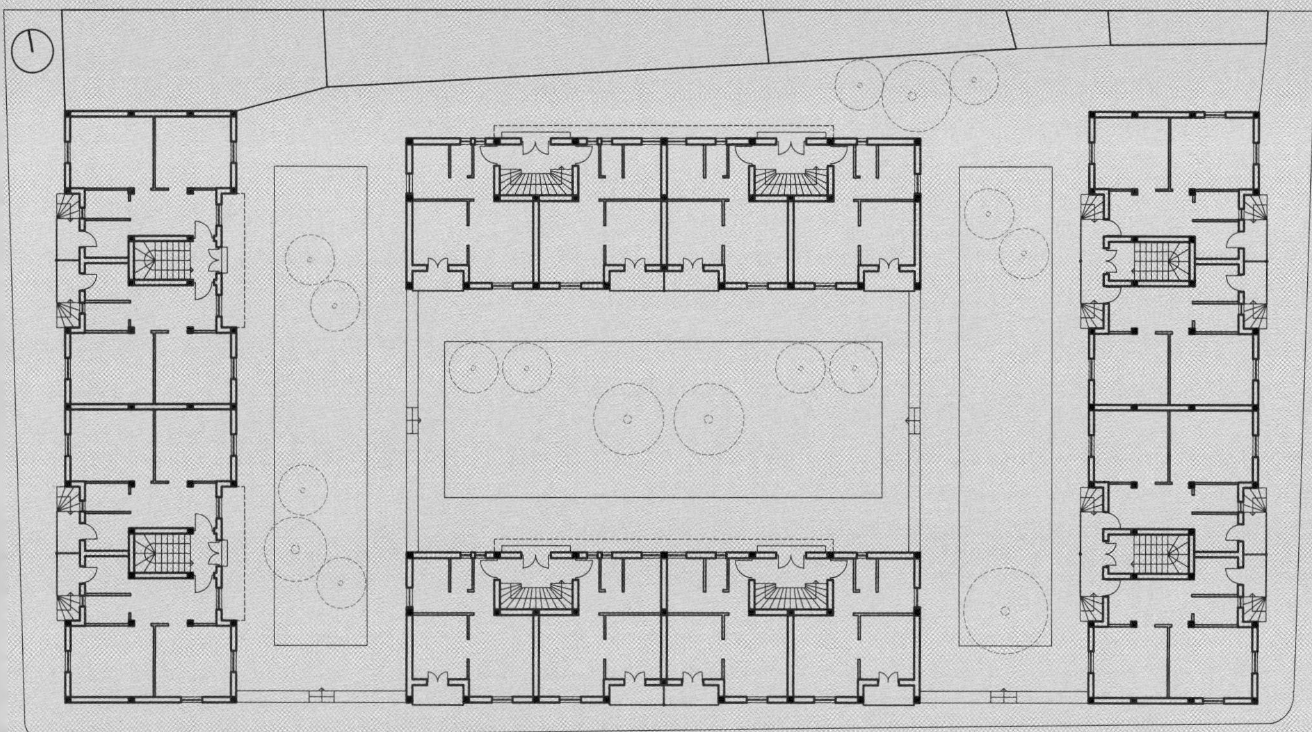

TYPE B2 TYPE B1 TYPE B2

TYPICAL FLOOR PLAN

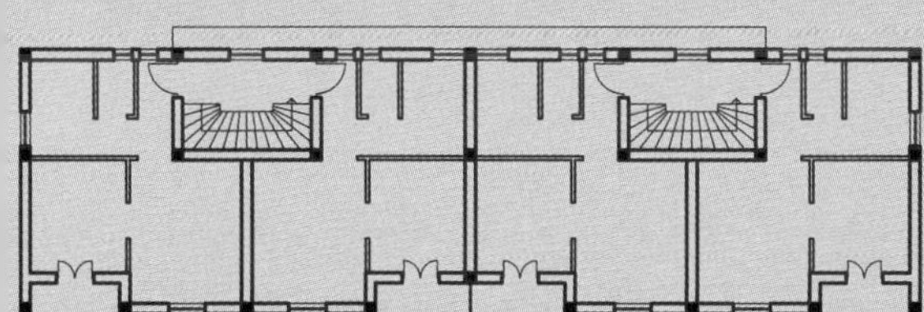

TYPE B1

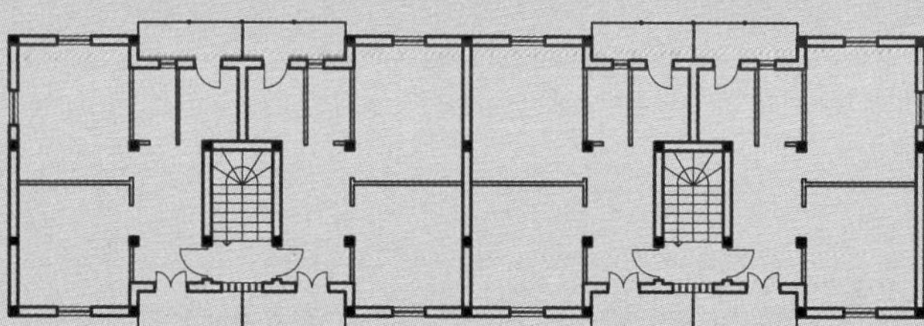

TYPE B2

ROOF TERACE PLAN

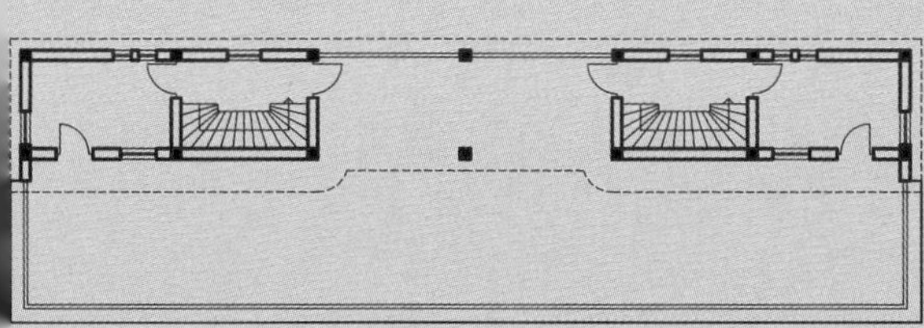

TYPE B1

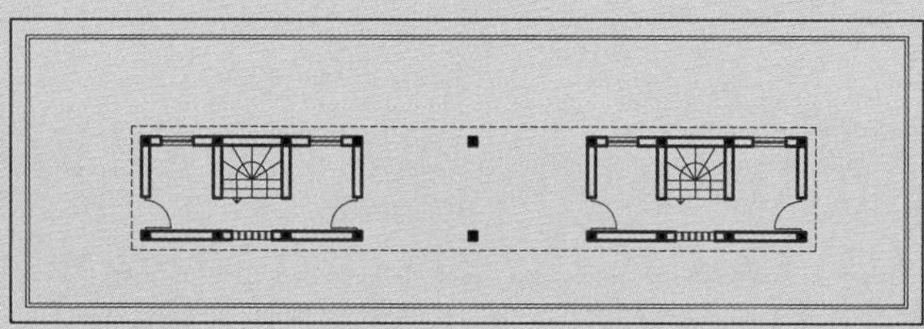

TYPE B2

existing

0 1 2 5

45.1-45.4

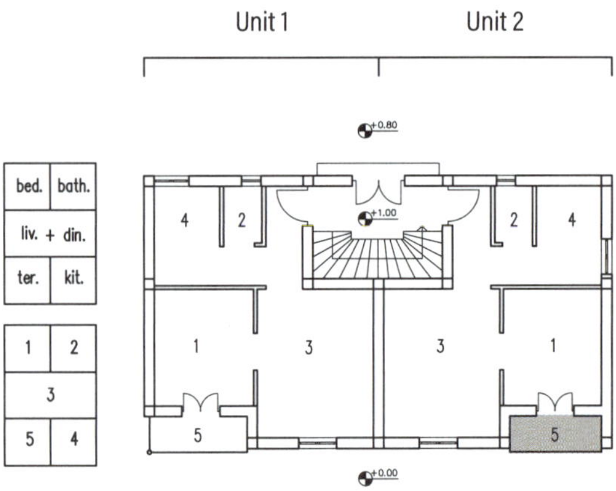

original intention coincides with current use

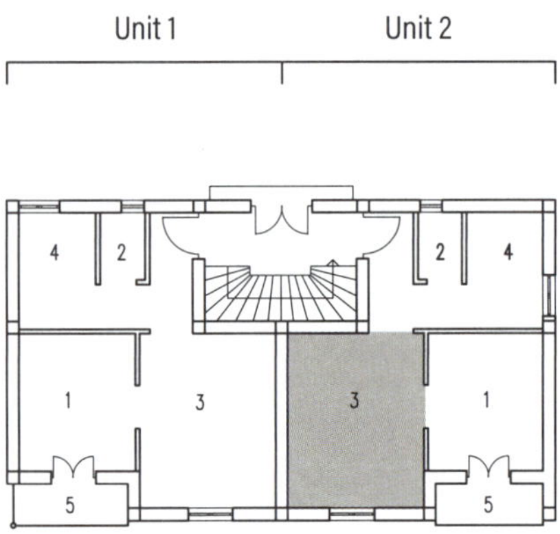

current use

46.1-46.4

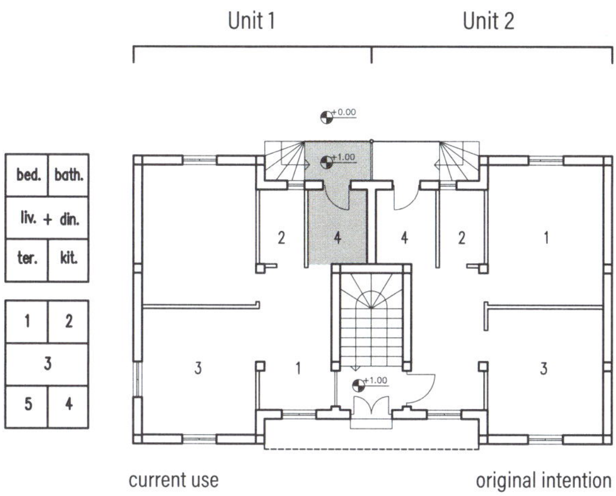
Unit 1
Unit 2
bed.
bath.
liv. + din.
ter.
kit.
1
2
3
5
4
+0.00
+1.00
+1.00
current use
original intention

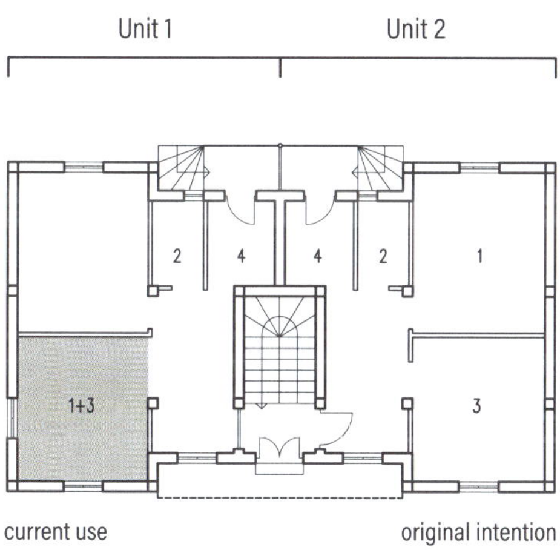
Unit 1
Unit 2
1+3
current use
original intention

47
Roof terrace

48
Inner courtyard

GROUND FLOOR PLAN

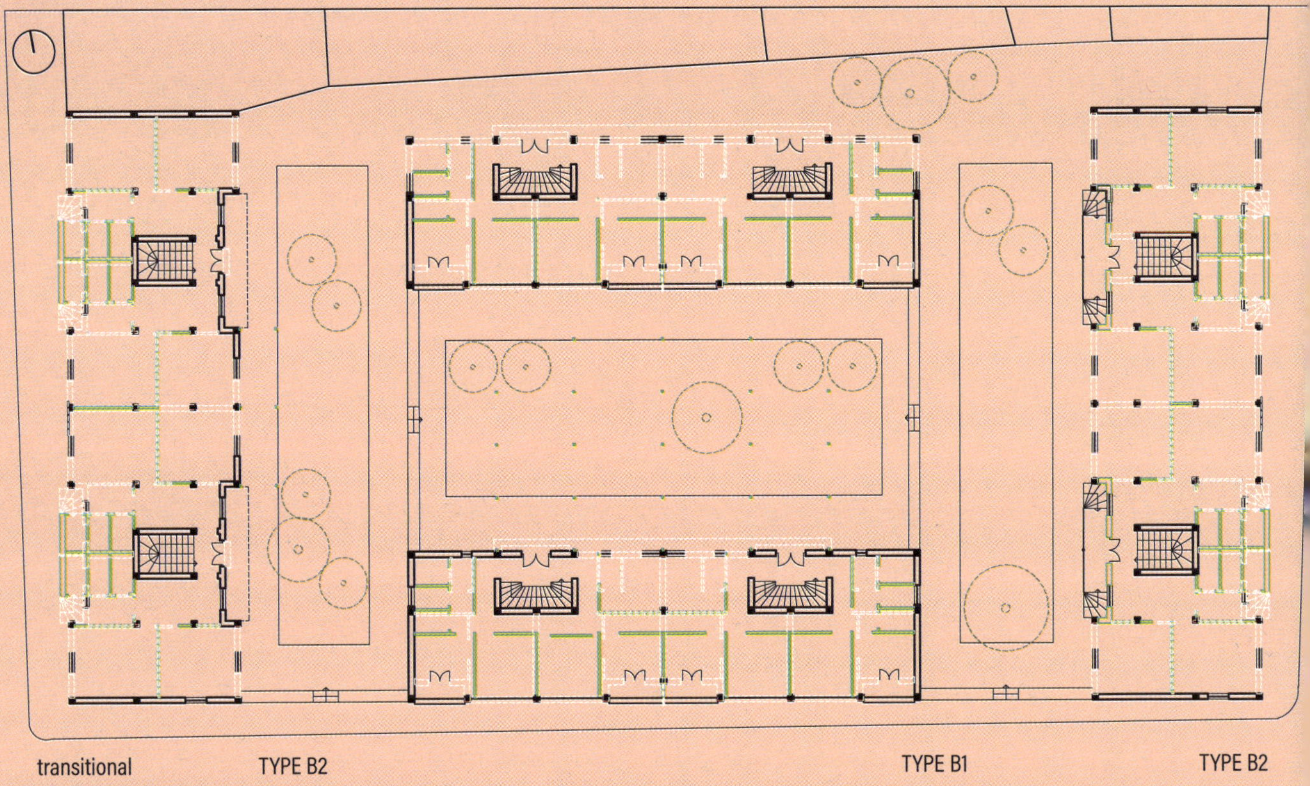

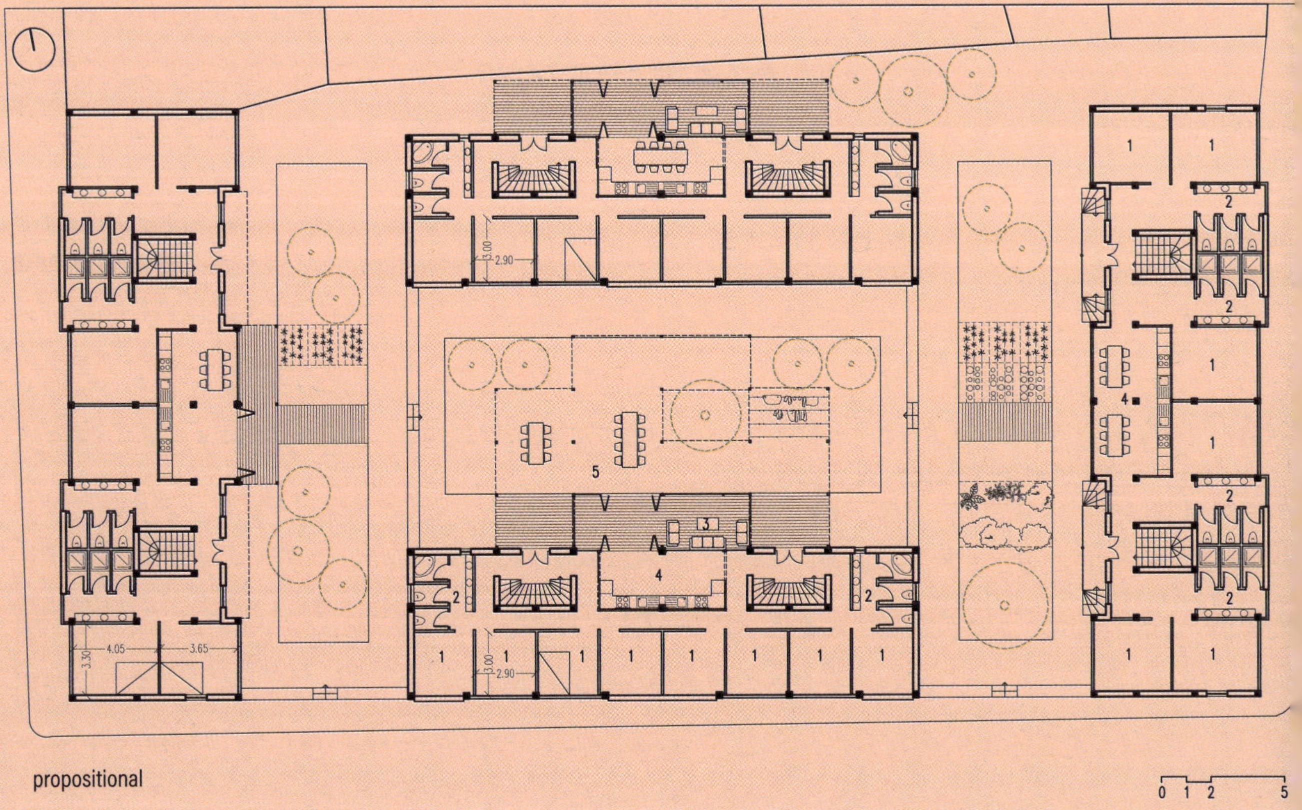

TYPICAL FLOOR PLAN

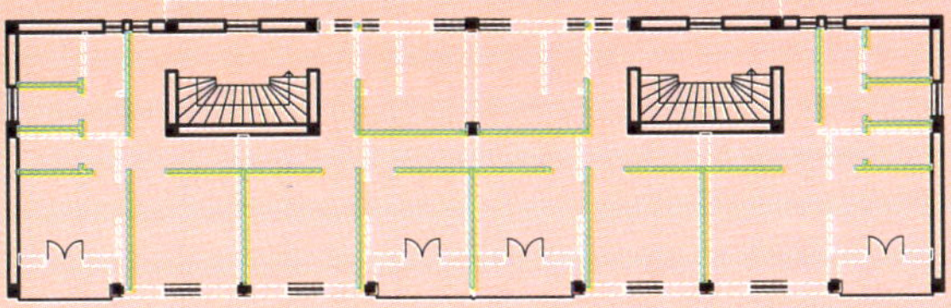

TYPE B1

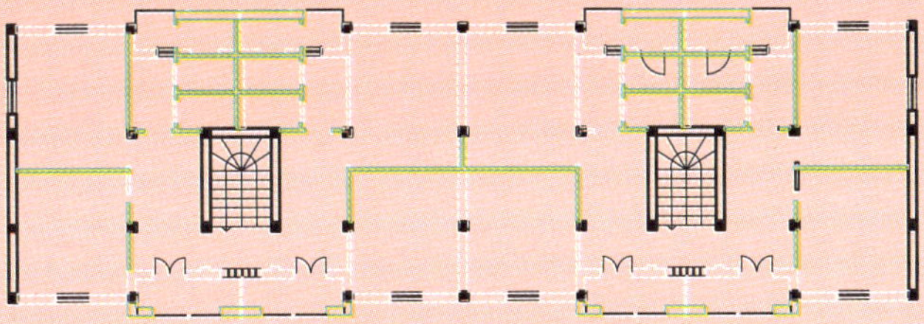

TYPE B2

ROOF TERACE PLAN

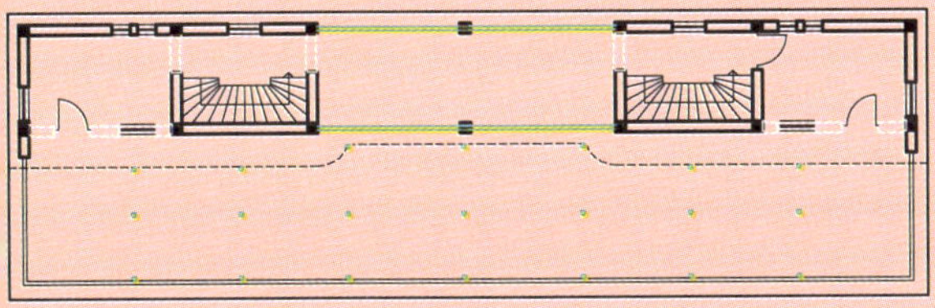

TYPE B1

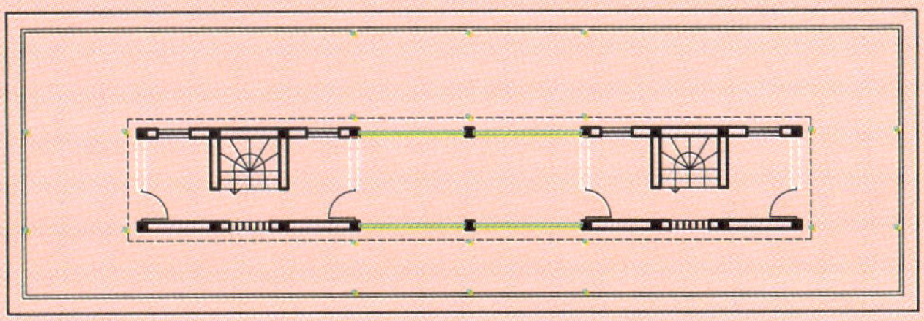

TYPE B2

priv.	bath.
liv.	kit. + din.
ter.	

1	2
3	4
5	

transitional

TYPICAL FLOOR PLAN

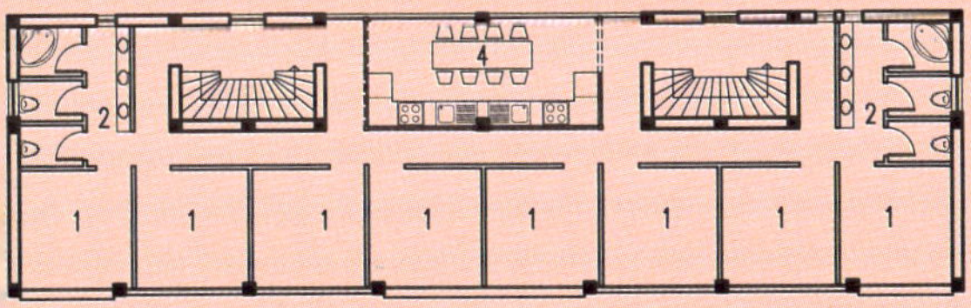

TYPE B1

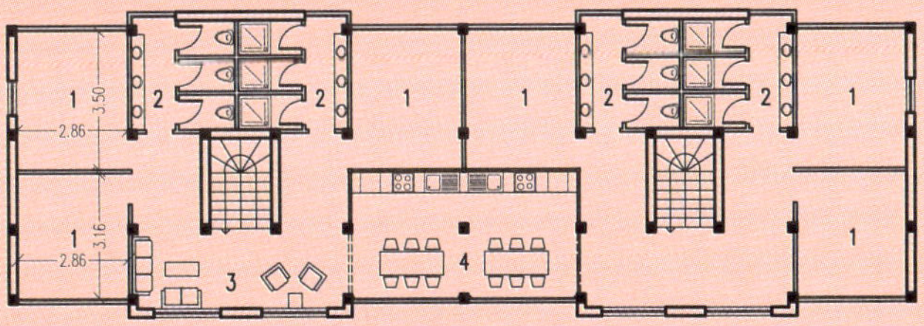

TYPE B2

ROOF TERACE PLAN

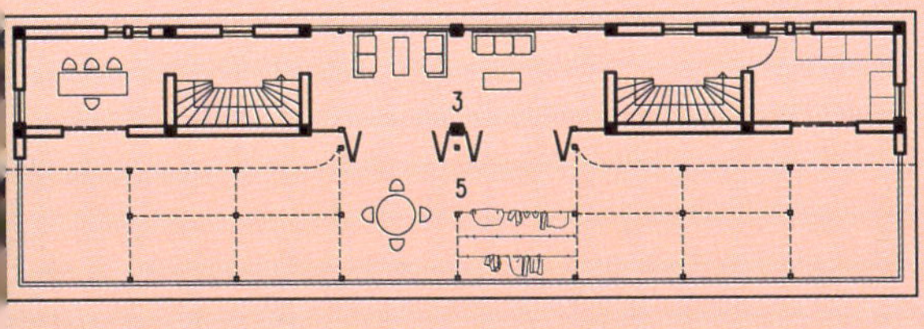

TYPE B1

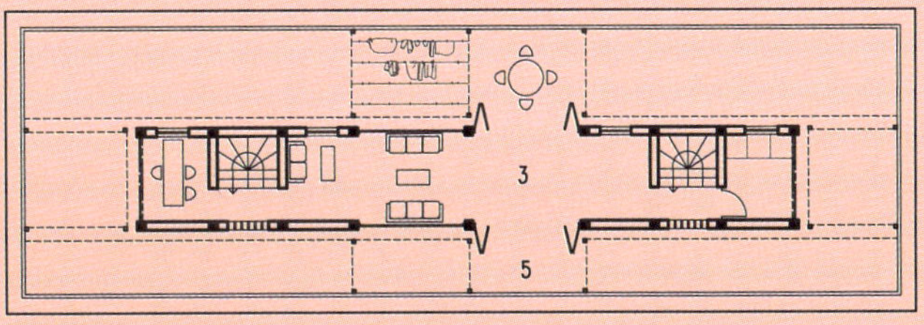

TYPE B2

propositional

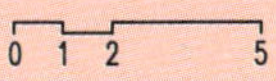

CROSS SECTION / TYPES B1-B2

BIBLIOGRAPHY

- Ackerman, James S. *The Villa: Form and Ideology of Country Houses*. London: Thames and Hudson, 1990.
- Anderson, Kurt."Rebuilding Berlin — Yet Again." *Time*, June 1987, 66.
- Aesopos, Yannis and Yorgos Simeoforidis. *Landscapes of modernisation: Greek architecture 1960s and 1990s*. Athens: Metapolis Press, 1999.
- Aitchison, Mathew ed. *Nikolaus Pevsner: On Visual Planning and the Picturesque*. Santa Monica: Getty Research Institute, 2010.
- Allen, Judith, G. Barlow, Jesus Leal, Thomas Maloutas and Liliana Padovani. *Housing and Welfare in Southern Europe*. London: Blackwell Publishing, 2004.
- Alexatou, Ioanna. "The Power of Collaboration. Interview with Divercity Architects." Casa Viva, July 2014, 38–40.
- Astrapellou, Marilena. "Interview with Nikolas Travasaros." BH-Magazine, 16 June 2013, 24–27.
- Arendt, Hannah. *Crises of the Republic: Lying in Politics, Civil Disobedience on Violence, Thoughts on Politics and Revolution*. New York: Harcourt Brace Jovanovich, 1972.
- Arendt, Hannah. "Introduction into Politics." In *The Promise of Politics*, edited by J. Cohn, 93-200. New York: Schoken Books, 2005.
- Arendt, Hannah. *The Human Condition*. Chicago, IL: University of Chicago Press, 1958.
- Aristotelis. *Ethica Nicomachea* [*Nicomachean Ethics*]. Translated by V. Moskovis. Athens: Law Library, 1993.
- Aristotelis. *Politica* [*Politics*]. Translated by V. Moskovis. Athens: Law Library, 1989.
- Aristotelis. "*Rhetorike* [*Rhetoric*]." In *Anthologia Archaeas Hellenices Grammateias* [*Anthology of Ancient Greek Literature*], Volume II, Part 6, edited by L. Antzoule, G. Kritsele, St. Tsitirides, and Th. K. Stefanopoulos, 137. Athens: Ministry of Education, Research and Theology & Institute of Educational Policy, 2012.
- Aristotle. *Politics*. Translated by Benjamin Jowett. Kitschener: Batoche Books, 1999.
- Aubenque, Pierre. *Le Problème de l'être chez Aristotle* [*The Problem of Being in Aristotle*], fifth edition. Paris: PUF, 2009.
- Aureli, Pier Vittorio. "Appropriation, Subdivision, Abstraction: A Political History of the Urban Grid." Log, no. 44 (2018): 139–67.
- Aureli, Pier Vittorio. *The Possibility of an Absolute Architecture*. Cambridge, MA: MIT Press, 2011.
- Auster, Richard D. and Morris Silver. *The State as a Firm: Economic Forces in Political Development*, Studies in Public Choice, Volume 3. Edited by Randall G. Holcombe. Boston: Martinus Nijhoff Publishing, 1979.
- Balibar, Étienne. *Equaliberty: Political Essays*. Translated by James Ingram. Durham, NC: Duke University Press, 2014.
- Balibar, Étiene. *Identity and Difference: John Locke and the Invention of Consciousness*. London: Verso, 2013.
- Banham, Reyner. "A Walled City: The Barbican in the City of London." *New Society* 30, no. 629 (1974): 222–3.
- Banham, Reyner. "Revenge of the Picturesque: English Architectural Polemics, 1945-1965." In *Concerning Architecture: Essays on Architectural Writers and Writing Presented to Nikolaus Pevsner*, edited by John Summerson, 265–73. London: Penguin, 1968.
- Barbagallo, Camille, Nicholas Beuret, and David Harvie. *Commoning with George Caffentzis and Silvia Federici*. London: Pluto Press, 2019.
- Barraclough, Geoffrey. *The Origins of Modern Germany*. Second edition. Oxford: Basil Black-well Oxford, 1962.
- Bauausstellung Berlin GmbH. *International Building Exhibition Berlin 1987*. Extra Edition. Tokyo: a+u Publishing Co.Ltd., May 1987.
- Bauausstellung Berlin GmbH. *Internationalle Bauausstellung Berlin 1987: Extract from the list of projects*. West Berlin: Bauausstellung Berlin GmbH, 1984.
- Bauausstellung Berlin GmbH ed. *The City as a Place to Live: Efforts in Careful Urban Renewal*. Berlin: Eigenverlag, 1984.
- Behrent, Michael C. and Daniel Zamora. *Foucault and Neoliberalism*. New York: Wiley, 2015.
- Bendix, Reinhard. *Max Weber: An Intellectual Portrait*. Orlando, FL: University of California Press, 1977.
- Benjamin, Walter. *One-Way Street and Other Writings*. Translated by Edmund Jephcott and Kingsley Shorter. London: NLB, 1979.
- Bennett, Tony, Lawrence Grossberg and Meaghan Morris. *New Keywords: A Revised Vocabulary of Culture and Society*. London: Blackwell Publishing, 2005.
- Berlant, Lauren. "The commons: Infrastructures for troubling times." *Environment and Planning D: Society and Space* 34, no. 3 (2016): 393–419.
- Blake, Peter. "Berlin's IBA: A Critical Assessment." *Architectural Record, no.* 8 (1993): 50–52.
- Blake, Peter. *Le Corbusier: Architecture and Form*. London: Penguin Books, 1964.
- Bodenschatz, Harald and Cordelia Polinna. *Learning from IBA-die IBA 1987 in Berlin*. Berlin: Senatsverwaltung für Stadtentwicklung, 2010.
- Borsi, Katharina. "Drawing the region: Hermann Jansen's vision of Greater Berlin in 1910." *The Journal of Architecture* 20, no.1 (2015): 47–72.
- Borsi, Katharina. "Hans Scharoun's 'Dwelling Cells' and the autonomy of architecture." *The Journal of Architecture* 23 no.7–8 (2018): 1104–1142.
- Borsi, Katharina, Nicole Porter and Megan Nottingham. "The Typology of the Berlin Block: History, Continuity and Spatial Performance." *Athens Journal of Architecture* 2, no.1 (January 2016): 45–64.
- Brenner, Neil. "Urban Governance and the Production of New State Spaces in Western Europe, 1960-2000." *Review of International Political Economy* 11, no. 3 (August 2004): 449–462.
- Brenner, Neil and Nik Theodore. "Cities and the Geographies of 'Actually Existing Neoliberalism.'" *Antipode* 34, no. 3 (December 2002): 351–5.
- Brenner, Neil and Nik Theodore. *Spaces of Neoliberalism: Urban Restructuring in North America and Western Europe*. London: Blackwell Publishers Ltd, 2002.

- Burian, Peter. "Logos and Pathos: the Politics of the Suppliant Women." In *Directions in Euripidean criticism: A collection of essays*, 136–142. Durham: Duke University Press, 1985.
- Cacciari, Massimo. *Archipelago*. Translated by Nasos Kyriazopoulos. Athens: P. Travlos, 1999.
- Caffentzis, George. *Clipped Coins, Abused Words, and Civil Government: John Locke's Philosophy of Money*. New York: Autonomedia, 1989.
- Caffentzis, George. *John Locke: Philosopher of Primitive Accumulation*. Bristol: Bristol Radical History Group, 2008.
- Caffentzis, George. "Two Themes of Midnight Notes: Work/Refusal of Work and Enclosure/Commons." In *Towards the Last Jubilee! Midnight Notes at Thirty Years*, edited by Craig Hughes, 24–30. New York: Autonomedia, 2010.
- Cahill, Nicholas. *Household and City Organization at Olynthus*. New Haven: Yale University Press, 2002.
- Castoriadis, Cornelius. "What Revolution is" and "Ecology Against the Merchants." In *Society Adrift: Interviews and Debates, 1974–1994*. Translated by Helen Arnold, edited by Enrique Escobar, Myrto Gondicas and Pascal Vernay, 144-51, 194–6. New York: Fordham University Press, 2010.
- Chamberlin Powell & Bon Architects. *Barbican Redevelopment: Report to the Court of Common Council of the Corporation of the City of London on Residential Redevelopment within the Barbican Area*. Bolton and London: Tillotsons Bolton Ltd, 1959.
- Chadjimichalis, Costis and Giorgos Stathakis. "Athens as a "World" City: From the Anxiety of the Few to the Reality of the Majority." Geographies, no. 7 (2004): 26–47.
- CIAM 8, Hoddesdon. "Summary of Needs at the Core." In *Architecture Culture 1943–1968: A Documentary Anthology*, edited by Joan Ockman, 135–136. New York: Rizzoli International Publications, 1993.
- Cicero, Marcus Tullius. *De Re publica* [*Treatise on the Commonwealth*], Volume I. Translated by Francis Barham. London: Edmund Spettigue, 1841–42.
- Clarke, Jennifer. *The Barbican: Sitting on History*. London: City of London Corporation, Records Office, 1990.
- Colquhoun, Alan. *Modernity and the Classical Tradition: Architectural Essays 1980-1987*. London: The MIT Press, 1989.
- Colquhoun, Alan. "Typology and Design Method." In *Essays in Architectural Criticism: Modern Architecture and Historical Change*, 43–50. Cambridge, MA: Oppositions Books, MIT Press, 1981.
- Conrads, Ulrich ed. *Zeit des Labyrinths: beobachten, nachdenken, feststellen 1956-2006* [*Time of the Labyrinth: Observe, Think, Determine 1956-2006*]. Berlin: Gütersloh, 2007.
- Czempiel, Ernst-Otto and James N. Rosenau. *Governance without Government: Order and Change in World Politics*. Cambridge: Cambridge University Press, 1992.
- Dardot, Pierre and Christian Laval. *Common: On Revolution in the 21st Century*. London: Bloomsbury, 2019.
- Dardot, Pierre and Christian Laval. *The New Way of the World: On Neoliberal Society*. Translated by Gregory Elliott. London: Verso, 2013.
- Davis, John E. *The Community Land Trust Reader*. Cambridge, MA: Lincoln Institute of Land Policy, 2010.
- Davis, John E. and Rick Jacobus. The City-CLT Partnership: Municipal Support for Community Land Trusts. Cambridge, MA: Lincoln Institute of Land Policy, 2008.
- De Angelis, Massimo. *Omnia Sunt Communia: On the Commons and the Transformation to Postcapitalism*. London: Zed Books, 2017.
- De Angelis, Massimo. "Separating the doing and the deed: capital and the continuous character of the enclosures." *Historical Materialism* 12, no. 2 (2004): 57–87.
- De Carolis, Massimo. *Il rovescio della libertà: Tramonto del neoliberalismo e disagio della civiltà* [*The Flipside of Freedom: The decline of neoliberalism and the crisis of civilization*]. Macerata: Quodlibet, 2017.
- De Carolis, Massimo. "The neoliberal (counter) revolution: its parabola and decline." *Phainomena* 26, no. 102/103 (2017): 141–52.
- Deane, Philip. *Constantinos Doxiadis: Master Builder for Free Men*. New York: Oceana Publications, 1965.
- Della Corte, Matteo. *Case ed abitanti a Pompei* [*Houses and inhabitants of Pompeii*], Second edition. Rome: L'Erma di Bretschneider, 1954 [1914].
- Delladetsimas, Pavlos M. "I trechousa dynamike tes anaptyxes tes Athinas: Symvatiko neo pro-typo kai erga ypodomes [The current dynamics of the development of Athens: Conventional new model and infrastructure works]." Geographies, no. 7 (June 2004): 48–64.
- Despotopoulos, Ioannis. "Poleodomike [Town Planning]." Technika Chronika IV, no. 39 (1933): 756–773.
- Ditzen, Lore and Hardt-Waltherr Haemer. "IBA- Alt: 'Ein komplexer Ansatz…:' Hardt-Waltherr Hämer im Gespräch mit Lore Ditzen [IBA – Old building: 'A Complex Proposal…: Hardt-Waltherr Haemer in Conversation with Lore Ditzen]." *ARCH+* no. 57/58 (1982).
- Doxiadis, Constantinos A. "Anthropocosmos: the world of man." DA Review, no. 18 (1966): 2–8.
- Doxiadis, Constantinos A. *Architecture in Transition*. London: Hutchinson & Co, 1963.
- Doxiadis, Constantinos A. *Building Entopia*. Athens: Athens Publishing Centre, 1975.
- Doxiadis, Constantinos A. *Ekistics: An Introduction to the Science of Human Settlements*. London: Hutchinson & Co, 1968.
- Doxiadis, Constantinos A. "Our Greek Headquarters." *DA Review*, (July 1973): 1.
- Doxiadis, Constantinos A. "Peri Chorotaxias [On Land-Planning]." *Technica Chronika* Year I' 20–21, no. 241–244 (January 1942): 1–12.
- Doxiadis, Constantinos A. "Pion ine to periechomenon tes anasigrotiseos tes choras [What is the content of the reconstruction of the country?." *To Vima*, 20 August 1950.
- Doxiadis, Constantinos A. "The Doxiadis Associates Headquarters in Athens." *Architektonike*, no. 13 (1959): 28–32.
- Doxiadis, Constantinos A. "The Formation of Human Room." Ekistics 33, no. 196 (1972): 218–229.

- Emmanuel, Demetres, Thomas Maloutas and Maro Pantelidou-Malouta. *Social structures, practices and concepts: New parameters and changing trends 1 980-2000*. Athens: National Centre for Social Research, 2006.
- Engels, Friedrich. *The Origin of the Family, Private Property and the State*. Translated by Alick West. London: Lawrence and Wishart, 1972 [1884].
- Federici, Silvia. *Revolution at Point Zero: Housework, Reproduction, and Feminist Struggle*. Oakland: PM Press, 2012.
- Fields, Gary. "From land reimagined to landscapes remade: The discourse of improvement and enclosing the common fields." In *Enclosure: Palestinian Landscapes in a Historical Mirror*, 45–91. Oakland, CA: University of California Press, 2017.
- Foucault, Michel. *Security, Territory, Population: Lectures at the College de France, 1977-78*. Translated by Graham Burchell, edited by Arnold I. Davidson. Basingstoke: Palgrave MacMillan UK, 2009.
- Frazer, Alfred. *The Roman Villa*. Philadelphia: University of Pennsylvania Press, 1998.
- Fried, Morton H. *On the Evolution of Social Stratification and the State*. Indianapolis: Bobbs-Merrill, 1960.
- Friedenberg, Jürgen and Ewald Weitz. *Interbau Berlin 1957: Internationale Bauausstellung im Berliner Hansaviertel* [*Interbau Berlin 1957: International Building Exhibition in the Hansa Quarter in Berlin*]. Berlin : Internationale Werbe- und Anzeigen-Gesellschaft, 1957.
- Friedman, Milton. *Capitalism and Freedom*. Chicago, IL: The University of Chicago Press, 2002 [1962].
- Friedman, Milton. "Neo-liberalism and its prospects." *Farmand* (February 1951): 89–90.
- Friend of Zanetti. "Constructing Neoliberal Glasgow: The Privatisation of Space." *Variant* 25 (Spring 2006): 19-22.
- Galland, Olivier and Yannick Lemel. "Tradition vs. Modernity: The Continuing Dichotomy of Values in European Society." *Revue française de sociologie* no. 49 (May 2008): 153–186.
- Gardiner, Stephen. "A Landmark of Distinction." *Observer* 9924, (1981):32.
- Garver, Eugene. Aristotle's Rhetoric: An art of character. Chicago: University of Chicago Press, 1994.
- Giddens, Anthony. *A Contemporary Critique of Historical Materialism*, volume I ("Power, Property and the State"). Berkley, CA: University of California Press, 1981.
- Giudici, Maria S. "Counter-planning from the Kitchen: For a Feminist Critique of Type." *The Journal of Architecture* 23, no. 7–8 (2018): 1203–29.
- Gizele, Vika. *Koinonikoi Metaschimatismoi kai Proeleusi tis Koinonikis Katoikias stin Ellada (1920-1930)* [*Social Transformations and the Origins of Social Housing in Greece (1920-1930)*]. Athens: Epikairotita, 1984.
- Glass, Ruth. *London: Aspects of Change*. London: MacGibbon & Kee Ltd, 1964.
- Global Tools, "Documento 1." *Casabella* 377, no. 5 (1973): 4.
- Gold, John R. *The Practice of Modernism: Modern Architects and Urban Transformation, 1954-1972*. London: Routledge, 2007.
- Gorgas, Carl. "Grossiedlung Siemensstadt." *Die Bauwelt* 21, no. 46 (1930): 1–24.
- Güven, Suna. "Displaying the Res Gestae of Augustus: A Monument of Imperial Image for All." *Journal of the Society of Architectural Historians* 57, no. 1 (1998): 30–45.
- Habermas, Jürgen. *The Philosophical Discourse of Modernity: Twelve Lectures*. Translated by Frederick Lawrence. Cambridge, MA: The MIT Press, 1990.
- Habermas, Jürgen. *The Structural Transformation of the Public Sphere: An Inquiry into a Category of Bourgeois Society*, translated by Thomas Burger and Frederick Lawrence. Cambridge, MA: MIT Press, 1989.
- Haemer, Hardt-Waltherr and Joseph P. Kleihues. *Idee, Prozess, Ergebnis: Die Reparatur und Rekonstruktion der Stadt*, Katalog zur Ausstellung [*Ideas, Process, Result: The Repair and Reconstruction of the City, Exhibition Catalogue*]. Berlin: Senator für Bau- und Wohnungswesen, 1984.
- Hammond, Mason. *City-State and World State in Greek and Roman Political Theory until Augustus*. Cambridge, MA: Harvard University Press, 1951.
- Hall, Peter. *Great Planning Disasters*. Berkeley & Los Angeles: California University Press, 1980.
- Hardt, Michael and Antonio Negri. *Empire*. Cambridge, MA: Harvard University Press, 2000.
- Harvey, David. *Rebel Cities: From the right to the City to Urban Revolution*. London and New York: Verso, 2012.
- Harvey, David. *The Limits to Capital*. Chicago: University of Chicago Press, 198
- Harvey, David. "The 'New Imperialism': Accumulation by Dispossession." *Socialis Register* 40 (January 2004): 63–87.
- Harwood, Elain and James O. Davis. *England's Post-War Listed Buildings*. Newcastle: Batsford Ltd, 2015.
- Hayek, von, Friedrich A. *Law, Legislatio and Liberty*. Chicago, IL: University of Chicago Press, 1973-1979.
- Hayek, von, Friedrich A. *The Road to Serfdom*. London: The Institute of Economic Affairs, 2005 [1944].
- Heathcote, David. *Barbican: Penthouse over the City*. Chichester: Wiley-Blackwell Publishing, 2004.
- Herakleitos [Heraclitus], "Peri Physeos, Apospasmata 1-123 [On Nature, Fragments 1-123]." In *Anthologia Archaeas Hellenices Grammateias* [*Anthology of Ancient Greek Literature*], Volume I, Part 4, edited by L. Antzoule, G. Kritsele, St. Tsitirides, and Th. K. Stefanopoulos, 218–223. Athens: Ministry of Education, Research and Theology & Institute of Educational Policy, 2012.
- Heidegger, Martin. *The Question Concerning Technology and Other Essays*. Translated by W. Lovitt. London, NY: Garland Publishing, 1977.
- Hibbert, Christopher, Ben Weinreb, John Keay and Julia Keay. *The London Encyclopaedia*, third edition. London: Pan Macmillan, 2010.
- Hobbes, Thomas. *Leviathan: Or the Matter, Forme, and Power of a Commonwealth Ecclesiasticall and Civill*. Edited by Ian Shapiro. New Haven: Yale University Press, 2010 [1651].
- Hockenos, Paul. *Berlin Calling: A Story of Anarchy, Music, the Wall and the Birth of the New Berlin*. New York: The New Press, 20

- Homer. *The Odyssey*, volume I, book 1. Translated by A.T. Murray. Cambridge MA: Harvard University Press, 1995.
- Hussey, Edward. "Epistemology and Meaning in Heraclitus." In *Language and Logos*, edited by M. Schofield and M. C. Nussbaum, 33–59. Cambridge: Cambridge University Press, 1982.
- Ince, Onur Ulas. "Enclosing in God's Name, Accumulating for Mankind: Money, Morality, and Accumulation in John Locke's Theory of Property." *The Review of Politics* 73, no. 1 (Winter 2011): 29–54.
- Internationale Bauausstellung ed. *Projektübersicht* [*Project Overview*], third edition. Berlin: Senatsverwaltung für Bau- und Wohnungswesen & STERN GmbH, 1991.
- Jaeger, Werner. *Paideia: The Ideals of Greek Culture*. Translated by Gilbert Highet. Oxford: Oxford University Press, 1945.
- Jappe, Anselme. "Sohn-Rethel and the Origin of 'Real Abstraction': A Critique of Production or a Critique of Circulation?." *Historical Materialism* 21, no.1 (January 2013): 3–14.
- Judt, Tony. *Ill Fares the Land: A Treatise on Our Present Discontents*. New York: Penguin Books, 2010.
- Jung, Carl. *Aspects of the Feminine*. Princeton, NJ: Princeton University Press,1982.
- Kahn, Charles H. *The Art and Thought of Heraclitus*. Cambridge: Cambridge University Press, 1979.
- Kalfa, Konstantina. *Autostegasi, Tora! Atheati Plevra tes Amerikanikes Voitheas stin Ellada* [*Self-help housing now! The invisible side of American help in Greece*]. Athens: Futura, 2019.
- Kalyvas, Stathis, George Pagoulatos and Haridimos Tsoukas. *From Stagnation to Forced Adjustment: Reforms in Greece, 1974-2010*. Oxford: Oxford University Press, 2013.
- Kelsen, Hans. *General Theory of Law and State*. Translated by Anders Wedberg. Cambridge, MA: Harvard University Press, 1945.
- Keynes, John Maynard. The End of Laissez-Faire and the Economic Consequences of the Peace. New York: Prometheus Books, 2003 [1926].Kieran, Stephen and James Timberlake. *Manual: The Architecture of Kieran Timberlake*. New York: Princeton Architectural Press, 2002.
- Kirk, G.S. *Heraclitus: The Cosmic Fragments*. Cambridge: Cambridge University Press, 1954.
- Kleihues, Joseph P. *Berlin-Atlas zu Stadtbild und Stadtraum - Versuchsgebiet Charlottenburg* [*Berlin Atlas on the cityscape and urban space - Case study area Charlottenburg*]. Berlin: Berlin Senate, 1973.
- Kleihues, Josef P. and Wolf J. Siedler. "Modelle für eine Stadt." Article series. *Berliner Morgenpost*, January 1977.
- Kleihues Josef P. and Heinrich Klotz eds. *International Building Exhibition Berlin 1987: Examples of a New Architecture*. Translated by Ian Robson. London: Academy Editions, 1986.
- Koolhaas, Rem and Bruce Mau. *S M L XL*. New York: Monacelli Press, 1995.
- Korda, Martin. *Städtebau* [*Urban Form*]. Stuttgart: B.G. Teubner, 1999.
- Krier, Robert. *Urban Space*. New York: Rizzoli, 1979.
- Kyrtsis, Alexandros-Andreas. *Constantinos A. Doxiadis: Texts, Design Drawings, Settlements*. Athens: Ikaros, 2006.
- Leach, Neil. *Rethinking Architecture*. London and New York: Routledge, 1997
- Krier, Rob. *Stadtraum in Theorie und Praxis* [*Urban Space in Theory and Practice*]. Stuttgart: Karl Kramer Verlag, 1975.
- Latour, Bruno. *We Have Never Been Modern*. Translated by Catherine Porter. Cambridge, MA: Harvard University Press, 1993.
- Lauterpacht, H. "Recognition of States in International Law." The Yale Law Journal 53, no. 3 (1944): 385–458.
- Lefebvre, Henri. *The Production of Space*. Translated by Donald Nicholson-Smith. Oxford, Cambridge, MA : Blackwell, 1991.
- Lefebvre, Henri. *Writings on Cities*. Translated and edited by Eleonore Kofman and Elizabeth Lebas. Oxford: Blackwell Publishers, 1996.
- Leontidou, Lila. *Poleis tes Siopes: Ergatikos epoikismos tis Athinas kai tou Peiraia, 1907-1940* [*Silent Cities: The proletarian colonization of Athens and Piraeus, 1907-1940*]. Athens: Cultural Technological Foundation ETBA, 1989.
- Linebough, Peter. *The Magna Carta Manifesto: Liberties and Commons for All*. Berkeley, CA: University of California Press, 2008.
- Locke, John. *Second Treatise on Government*, edited by Crawford B. McPherson. Indianapolis and Cambridge: Hackett Publishing Company, 1980 [1690].
- "London: Living in the City." *The Architects' Journal* 148, no. 40 (October 1968): 704.
- Lyroudias, Evangelos. "Sygrotima Grafeion Costa Doxiadi' [C.A. Doxiadis Office Building]." Ar-chitektones 77 – B', (Nov-Dec 2009): 15.
- Madden, David and Peter Marcuse. *In Defense of Housing: The Politics of Crisis*. London: Verso Books, 2016.
- Maloutas, Thomas. *I Koinoniki Geographia tis Athinas: Koinonikes Omades kai Domimeno Perivallon se mia Notioeuropaiki Mitropoli* [*The Social Geography of Athens: Social Groups and Built Environment in a South-european Metropolis*]. Athens: Alexandria, 2018.
- Maltby, Richard. *A Lexicon of Ancient Latin Etymologies*. ARCA 25. Oxford: Francis Cairns Publications, 1991.
- Mantouvalou, Maria, Ntina Vaiou and Maria Mavridou. "Athina 2004. Sta monopatia tis pagkosmiopoiisis' [Athens 2004. In the track of globalisation]. *Geographies*, no. 7 (2004): 13– 25.
- Marcuse, Peter and Ronald Van Kempen. *Globalizing Cities: A New Spatial Order?*. London: Wiley Blackwell, 1999.
- Marindin,G. E., William Smith, LLD and William Wayte, *A Dictionary of Greek and Roman Antiquities*. London: John Murray, 1890.
- Marx, Karl. *Capital Volume I*, Pt. VII, 812-829. Translated by Edward Aveling and Samuel Moore. London: Electric Book Co, 2001 [1887].
- Marx, Karl. *Early Writings*. Translated by Rodney Livingstone and Gregor Benton. London: Penguin, 1975 [1843–4].
- Marx, Karl. *Grundrisse: Foundations of the Critique of Political Economy*. Translated by Martin Nicolaus. London: Penguin Books, 1973.

- Massumi, Brian. "In becoming is belonging." In *Parables for the Virtual: Movement, Affect, Sensation*, 68-88. Durham: Duke University Press, 2002.
- Mavrogordatos, George Th. "From Traditional Clientelism to Machine Politics: The Impact of PASOK Populism in Greece." *South European Society and Politics* 2, no. 3 (1997): 1–26.
- McKeon, Michael. *The Secret History of Domesticity: Public, Private and the Division of Knowledge*. Baltimore: Johns Hopkins University Press, 2006.
- Mellor, J.R. *Urban Sociology in an Urbanized Society*. London: Routledge Library Editions - The City, 1977.
- Moschonas, Gerassimos. "The Path of Modernisation: PASOK and European Integration." Journal of Southern Europe and the Balkans 3, no. 1 (2001): 11–24. versity Press, 2006.
- McPherson, Crawford B. *The Political Theory of Possessive Individualism: Hobbes to Locke*. Oxford: Oxford University Press, 2011.
- Mumford, Eric. *The CIAM Discourse on Urbanism, 1928–1960*. Cambridge, MA: MIT Press, 2000.
- Nelson, Anitra and François Schneider. *Housing for Degrowth: Principles, Models, Challenges and Opportunities*. London: Routledge, 2019.
- "New Barbican." *The Architects' Journal*, (14 October 1954): 457–67.
- Nicolin, Pierluigi. "Abitare in città [Living in the City]." *Lotus International*, no. 41, (1984): 5.
- Nietzsche, Friedrich. *The Gay Science: With a Prelude in Rhymes and an Appendix of Songs by Friedrich Nietzsche*. Translated by Walter Kaufmann. London: Penguin Books, 1974 [1882].
- Ostrom, Elinor. *Crafting Institutions for Self-Governing Irrigation Systems*. San Francisco: ICS Press, 1992.
- Ostrom, Elinor and Edella Schlager. "Property-Rights Regimes and Natural Resources: A Conceptual Analysis." *Land Economics* 68, no. 3 (1992): 249–262.
- Papanek, Victor. *Design for the Real World: Human Ecology and Social Change*. London, NY: Bantam Books, 1970.
- Paterculus, Velleius. The Roman History II. Translated by F. W. Shipley. Cambridge, MA: Har-vard University Press, 1924.
- Pedersen, J. Martin. "Properties of Property: A Jurisprudential Analysis." *The Commoner* 14, (Winter 2010): 137–210.
- Pevsner, Nikolaus. "Price on Picturesque Planning." *Architectural Review* 95, (1944): 47-50.
- Philippides, Dimitres. *Constantinos A. Doxiadis: Report to Hippodamus*. Athens: Melissa, 2015.
- Philippides, Dimitres. *Moderna Architectonike stin Ellada* [*Modern Architecture in Greece*]. Athens: Melissa, 2001.
- Pinder, David. "Reconstituting the Possible: Lefebvre, utopia and the urban question." *International Journal of Urban and Regional Research* 39, no. 1 (2013): 28–45.
- Piniara, Ioanna. "Housing policy as a form of urban governance: The Barbican Estate and the enclosure of the urban commons." In *Housing as Commons: Housing Alternatives as Response to the Current Urban Crisis*, edited by Stavros Stavrides and Penny Travlou, 279–94. London: Bloomsbury Academic, 2022.
- Piniara, Ioanna. "(Re)drawing the housing commons: A Typological Reading." *Stoà Journal* no. 2 (2021): 106–19.
- Plato, *Symposion (Peri Erotos)* [*Symposium (On Eros)*]. In *Anthologia Archaeas Hellenices Grammateias* [*Anthology of Ancient Greek Literature*], Volume II, Part 6, edited by L. Antzoule, G. Kritsele, St. Tsitirides, and Th. K. Stefanopoulos, 131-135. Athens: Ministry of Education, Research and Theology & Institute of Educational Policy, 2012.
- Polanyi, Karl. *The Great Transformation: The Political and Economic Origins of Our Time*. Boston: Beacon Press, 1957 [1944].
- Polanyi, Karl. *The Livelihood of Man*, edited by H.W. Pearson. New York: Academic Press, 1977.
- Poulantzas, Nicos. *State, Power, Socialism*. Translated by Patrick Camiller. London: NLB, 1978.
- Price, Barbara J. and William T. Sanders. *Mesoamerica: The Evolution of a Civilization*. New York: Random House, 1968.
- Proudhon, Pierre-Joseph. *The Federative Principle: The Need to Reconstitute the Party of Revolution*. [1863]. (http://theanarchistlibrary.org/library/pierre-joseph-proudhon-the-principle-of-federation.)
- Pugh, Emily. *The Berlin Wall and the Urban Space and Experience of East and West Berlin, 1961-1989*. PhD Thesis, New York: City University of New York, 2008.
- Rice, Charles. *The Emergence of the Interior: Architecture, Modernity, Domesticity*. London: Routledge, 2007.
- Robinson, M. *Excavations at Olynthus: Architecture and sculpture, houses and other buildings*, Part II. Baltimore: Johns Hopkins University Press, 1930.
- Rodriguez, Anton. *Residents: Inside the Iconic Barbican Estate*. London: Barbican Centre, 2016.
- Rossi, Aldo."Aspetti della tipologia residenziale a Berlino [Aspects of Residential Typology in Berlin]." *Casabella Continuità* 288, (July 1964): 11–20.
- Rossi, Aldo. *The Architecture of the City*. New York: Opposition Books, MIT Press, 1988.
- Rowe, Colin. "IBA: Rowe reflects." *The Architectural Review* 1051, (1984): 92–3
- Russel, Frank ed. "Architecture in Progress: Internationalle Bauausstellung Berlin 1984." *Architectural Design and Academy Editions* 53, (1983): 1–128.
- Rybczynski, Witold. *Home: A Short History of an Idea*. London: Penguin Books, 1987.
- Salzman, Philip Carl. "Pastoral Nomads: Some General Observations Based on Research in Iran." *Journal of Anthropological Research* 58, no. 2 (Summer 2002): 245–264.
- Sarigiannes, Georgios and Eliza Papadopoulou. *Synoptike Ekthese gia tis Prosfygikes Perioches tou Lekanopediou Attikes* [*Brief Study on the Refugee Settlement Districts in the Attica Basin*]. Athens: Faculty of Urban and Strategic Planning, National Technical University of Athens, 2006.

Schleiermacher, Friedrich. "Herakleitos ler Dunkle, von Ephesos, dargestellt aus len Trümmern seines Werkes und den Zeugnissen der Alten [Heraclitus the Dark, from Ephesus, depicted from the emnants of his work and the testimonies of the ancient." In *Museum der Alterthums-Wissenschaft* [*Museum of Ancient Science*], volume I, part 3, edited by P. Buttmann and F. A. Wolf, 313–533. Berlin: Deutsche Forschungsgemeinschaft (DFG), 1807.
Schmitt, Carl. *The Nomos of the Earth n the International Law of the Jus Publicum Europaeum*. Translated by G. L. Ulmen. New York: Telos Press Publishing, 2006.
Schoenauer, Norbert. *6,000 Years of Housing*. Third revisited expanded edition. New York: W. W. Norton & Company, 1981.
Sohn-Rethel, Alfred. *Intellectual and Manual Labour: A Critique of Epistemology*. London: Macmillan, 1979.
Spencer, Douglas. *The Architecture of Neoliberalism: How Contemporary Architecture Became an Instrument of Control and Compliance*. London: Bloomsbury Academic, 2016.
Stavrides, Stavros. *Common Space: The City as Commons*. London: Zed Books, 2016.
Stavrides, Stavros, Panagiota Koutrolikou, Ferenike Vatavale, Maria Kopanare, Christina Marathou and Vika Gizele. *Metaschimatismoi tes scheses dimosiou-idiotikou chorou sta sygrotimata koinonikis katoikias ton ellinikon astikon kentron* [*Transformations of the relationship between public and private space in social housing blocks of Greek city centers*]. Athens: National Technical University of Athens, 2009.
Taut, Bruno. "Der Außenwohnraum [The outside living space]." Einfa 2, no. 4 (1931): 2–4.
Theocharopoulou, Ioanna. *Builders, Housewives and the Construction of Modern Athens*. London: Artifice Press, 2018.
Theodoropoulos, Christos. "Pros mia avant-garde istorike prostasia [Towards an avant-garde monument protection]." Architektones, 76 – B', October 2009): 38–40.
Thucydides. *The History of the Peloponnesian War*. Translated by Richard Crawley. New York: DigiReads Publishing, 2009.

- Torgersen, Ulf. "Housing: The Wobbly Pillar under the Welfare State." *Scandinavian Housing and Planning Research* 4, no. 1 (March 2014): 116–126.
- Tournikiotis, Panayiotis. "Ancient and Modern Cities in the Work of Constantinos Doxiadis: The Modern City Facing the Future." Conference Proceedings: *6th International Docomomo Conference, September 20–22, 2000*, 97–112. (Brasilia : Docomomo International, 2004).
- Tranquillus, Suetonius. "The Life of Augustus." In *The Lives of the Twelve Caesars*, Loeb Classical Library. Translated by J. C. Rolfe. London: Heinemann, 1913.
- Ungers, Oswald M. "The Urban Villa: A Prototype for Inner-City Residences." In *The Urban Villa: A multi-family dwelling type*, Cornell Summer Academy 77, edited by O.M. Ungers, H. Kollhoff and A. Ovaska, 1-5. Berlin, Cologne: Studio Press for Architecture, 1977.
- Van Eesteren, Cornelis. "Methodoi organikes poleodomias kai efarmogai auton eis tin polin Amsterdam [Methods of functional town planning and their applications in Amsterdam]." Technika Chronika IV, no. 44-46 (1933): 1027–35.
- Vasileiou, Ioannis. *I Laiki Katoikia: Koinonikes Technikes kai Oikonomikes Apopseis* [*Mass Housing: Social Techniques and Economic Aspects*]. Athens: P.A. Dialisma, 1944.
- Vidler, Anthony. "The Idea of Type: The Transformation of the Academic Ideal, 1750–1830." *Oppositions* no. 8 (Spring 1977): 94–115.
- Von Mises, Ludwig. *Bureaucracy*. New Haven: Yale University Press, 1944.
- Voulgarides, Elias. *I Poiotites kai i chreses tou xulou* [*The Qualities and Uses of Wood*]. Athens: Association of Greek Academic Libraries, 2015.
- Waters, Tony and Dagmar Waters, eds. *Weber's Rationalism and Modern Society: New Translations on Politics, Bureaucracy, and Social Stratification*. Translated by Tony Waters and Dagmar Waters. New York: Palgrave Books, 2015.
- Weber, Max. *Economy and Society: An Interpretive Sociology*, edited by Guenther Roth and Claus Wittich. Berkley: University of California Press, 1978 [1921].
- Williams, Raymond. *Keywords: A Vocabulary of Culture and Society*. London: Croom Helm, 1976.
- Wooditsch, Richard. *The Public Private House: Modern Athens and its Polykatoikia*. Zurich: Park Books, 2019.
- Xenophon. *Apomnemonevmata* [*Memorabilia*]. Translated by E. G. Pantelakes. Athens: Zacharopoulos, 1937.
- Xenophon. *Oikonomikos* [*Oeconomicus*]. Translated by E. Moros. Athens: Zacharopoulos, 1939.

LECTURES:

- Balibar, Étienne. "Towards a New Critique of Political Economy – Session 3." Lecture, the Birkbeck Institute for the Humanities, London, 6 March 2017.
- Belavilas, Nikos, Katerina Christoforaki and Polina Prentou. "Urban Environment Laboratory." Lecture, National Technical University of Athens, Athens, 19 December 2019.
- Meades, Jonathan. "Brutalism: The Savage and the Sublime." Lecture, Barbican Centre, London, 26 February 2015.

DOCUMENTARIES:

- Bêka, Ila and Louise Lemoine, dir. Barbicania. London: Barbican Centre, 2014. DVD.
- Tzirtzilakis, Yorgos, dir. Constantinos A. Doxiadis: A Romantic Pragmatist. Athens: ERT S.A., 2006. TV Broadcast.

CREDITS AND COPYRIGHTS

- p. 35: redrawn and annotated by the author based on a drawing featured in Nicholas Cahill, *Household and City Organization at Olynthus* (New Haven: Yale University Press, 2002).
- p. 37: redrawn and annotated by the author based on a drawing featured in Penelope M. Allison, *Pompeian households: An analysis of material culture* (Los Angeles: The Cotsen Institute of Archaeology, University of California, 2004).
- p. 39: redrawn and annotated by the author based on a drawing featured in Manuel Royo, *Domus imperatoriae: Topographie, formation et imaginaire des palais impériaux du Palatin* (Rome: École française de Rome, 1999).
- p.41 (top): drawn and annotated by the author based on a three-dimensional illustration of the temple featured in Suna Güven,"Displaying the Res Gestae of Augustus: A Monument of Imperial Image for All," *Journal of the Society of Architectural Historians* 57, no. 1 (1998): 30–45.
- (bottom): redrawn and annotated by the author based on a drawing featured in Josephine Shaya, "The Public Life of Monuments: The Summi Viri of the Forum of Augustus," *American Journal of Archaeology* 117, no. 1 (January 2013): 83–110.
- p.47 (top): redrawn and annotated by the author based on a drawing featured in Oliver Heckmann, *Floor Plan Manual Housing*, Fifth, Revised and Expanded Edition (Basel: Birkhäuser Publishers, 2017).
- (center): redrawn and annotated by the author based on a drawing featured at ernst-may-gesellschaft.de.
- (bottom): redrawn and annotated by the author based on a drawing featured in Gernot and Johanne Nalbach (eds.), *Berlin Modern Architecture: exhibition catalogue* (Berlin: Senatsverwaltung fur Bau- und Wohnungswesen, 1989).
- p.59 (top): © Anton Rodriguez
- pp. 59 (bottom), 79: © Sue Barr
- pp. 63,68: © Heirs of Geoffry Powell
- pp. 66, 72, 152-53, 154, 190, 192 (left), 193 (left), 201 (right), 202 (left), 224 (right), 225 (right), 226-27: © Luis Young
- p. 76: redrawn and annotated by the author based on a drawing featured in Chamberlin Powell & Bon Architects, *Barbican Redevelopment: Report to the Court of Common Council of the Corporation of the City of London on Residential Redevelopment within the Barbican Area* (Bolton and London: Tillotsons Bolton Ltd, 1959).
- p. 81: featured in Rainer Nitsche ed., Internationale Bauausstellung Berlin 1987: *Projektübersicht, Offizieller Katalog Berlin*, (West Berlin: Bauausstellung Berlin GmbH, 1987), edited by the author.
- p. 84: featured in Rainer Nitsche ed., Internationale Bauausstellung Berlin 1987: *Projektübersicht, Offizieller Katalog Berlin*, (West Berlin: Bauausstellung Berlin GmbH, 1987), edited and annotated by the author.
- p. 90: © Ungers Archiv für Architekturwissenschaft
- p. 93 (top): featured in Toshio Nakamura, *International Building Exhibition Berlin 1987*, Extra Edition (Tokyo: a+u Publishing, 1987), edited and annotated by the author.
- pp. 93 (bottom), 94 (bottom), 100-01: © OMA
- pp. 94 (top), 97, 98 (top): © Eredi Aldo Rossi / Fondazione Aldo Rossi
- p. 98 (bottom): redrawn and annotated by the author based on a drawing featured in Toshio Nakamura, *International Building Exhibition Berlin 1987*, (Tokyo: a+u Publishing, 1987).
- pp. 104 (top), 115: © Constantinos and Emma Doxiadis Foundation
- pp. 104 (bottom), 121: © One Athens managed by Sodia Properties
- p.107 (top): © Benaki Museum Photographic Archives
- p.107 (bottom): © Yiorgis Yerolympos
- p.110 (top left): © The Bank of Greece
- p.110 (top right): © National Statistical Service of Greece
- p.110 (bottom left): © Yannis Aesopos Architecture
- p.110 (bottom center): © Biris Tsiraki Architects
- p.110 (bottom right): © K-Lab architecture
- pp. 116 (top), 122 (top): redrawn and annotated by the author based on Maps & Drawings 27328, Constantinos A. Doxiadis Archives, © Constantinos and Emma Doxiadis Foundation.
- pp. 116 (bottom), 122 (bottom): redrawn and annotated by the author based on the architects' plans © One Athens managed by Sodia Properties.
- pp.147, 149 (top), 150 (top): © Region of Attica
- p.149 (bottom): © Hellenic Cadastral Service (gis.ktimanet.gr)
- pp. 160-61 (center, bottom): redrawn and annotated by the author based on archive drawings featured in Katharina Borsi, "Hans Scharoun's 'Dwelling Cells' and the autonomy of architecture," *The Journal of Architecture* 23, no.7-8 (2018): 1126.
- Otherwise uncredited drawings, diagrams and photographs were produced by the author.

Ioanna Piniara is an architect and researcher holding a PhD in Architectural Design from the Architectural Association (AA). Her research interests include the study of domesticity as a biopolitical device for the control of bodies and identities, the spatial implications of economy, institutional power and policy in the design of urban housing as well as narratives for the decolonization of housing typologies and urban forms. Ioanna has been a seminar tutor at the AA, a post-doctoral fellow of the 'Architectures of Order' research cluster at the Goethe University Frankfurt and is currently teaching design and theory seminars at the Architecture School of the National Technical University in Athens. She is also the author of "The Housing Question is a Feminist Question: Housing Commons for the New Woman of the German Werkbund" by M Books.

WE HAVE NEVER BEEN PRIVATE
THE HOUSING PROJECT
IN NEOLIBERAL EUROPE

Ioanna Piniara
Based on her Ph.D research undertaken
at the Architectural Association
School of Architecture

PUBLISHED BY
Actar Publishers, New York, Barcelona
www.actar.com

GRAPHIC DESIGN
Olga Pipnik

COPY EDITING AND PROOFREADING
Hunter Doyle

PRINTING AND BINDING
Arlequin & Pierrot

DISTRIBUTION
Actar D, Inc. New York, Barcelona

New York
440 Park Avenue South, 17th Floor
New York, NY 10016, USA
T +1 2129 662 207
salesnewyork@actar-d.com

Barcelona
Roca i Batlle 2-4
08023 Barcelona, Spain
T +34 933 282 183
eurosales@actar-d.com

INDEXING
ISBN 978-1-63840-134-6
LCCN 2024946286

Printed in Europe

Publication date: September 2024

Cover image: © "Private Rooms" by the author

This edition is supported by the Onassis Foundation.

ONASSIS
FOUNDATION